BECOMING A
SUCCESSFUL
STUDENT

BECOMING A
SUCCESSFUL
STUDENT

Laraine E. Flemming
Allegheny Community College

Judith Leet

Scott, Foresman and Company
Glenview, Illinois   Boston   London

Acknowledgments are listed at the back of the book on pages 490–492, which constitutes a legal extension of the copyright page.

Library of Congress Cataloging-in-Publication Data

Flemming, Laraine E.
  Becoming a successful student.

  Includes index.
  1. Study, Method of. 2. Reading (Higher education)
I. Leet, Judith. II. Title.
LB2395.F54 1989   482.4'3   88-29719
ISBN 0-673-18746-2
ISBN 0-673-47049-0 (instructor's manual)

1 2 3 4 5 6-KPF-94 93 92 91 90 89

PREFACE

Becoming a Successful Student is a comprehensive study skills text designed to show students, step by step, how they can achieve college success. In writing it, we had a twofold goal: we wanted to write a book that reflected the most current research in reading, writing, and, critical thinking. Perhaps, more to the point, we wanted to translate theoretical abstractions into practical strategies for learning that students could understand and apply. But, we also wanted to write a book that encouraged students to think about their personal relationship to study and learning. We wanted them to read our book and recognize that their attitude, commitment, and initiative were an essential part of achieving college success.

Thus the opening unit, "Making Yourself a Productive Student," offers a host of practical suggestions for developing motivation, managing time, improving listening, and remembering information, all of them based on current research in cognitive psychology and behavior modification. But, as we explain in our introduction to the *learning journal,* we don't expect our student readers to follow our advice blindly. We expect them to carefully consider and adapt our suggestions to their particular course work and learning style. Our objective in this unit is to make students think about learning, about *why* they do it and how they do it best.

Reflecting current research on the role of reader participation and background knowledge, Unit 2, "Learning From Your Textbooks," opens with a discussion of the many ways in which skillful readers contribute to a writer's message. Although the emphasis here is on the acquisition of specific skills like recognizing organizational patterns, developing inferences, and making predictions, we repeatedly underscore the importance of an active and questioning frame of mind. The focus throughout is on the importance of becoming an active reader, someone who works with the author in order to make sure that communication takes place.

By introducing three kinds of reading—*inspectional, intensive,* and *analytical*—each one appropriate to different purposes and texts, we highlight the importance of mental flexibility and encourage students to match their reading strategies to both material and purpose. Similarly, we introduce six different methods of taking notes. Some like mapping and charts are more appropriate to the kinds of physical description emphasized in the sciences while others like outlining and summarizing are more applicable to history and the social sciences. As always it's the student who must choose the most effective method.

Unit 3, "Preparing for and Taking Exams" is a thorough discussion of test-taking tactics to be used before, during, and after an exam. We show students how to use their textbook and lectures to predict what will be on an exam and how to read and respond to test questions, both short answer and essay. We give them guidelines for creating synthesis sheets, strategies for calming test anxiety, and questions for analyzing previous exams. But here again we do not neglect the role of personal attitude, and we ask students to think long and hard about the way fear of failure can be the underlying reason for poor exam preparation and ultimately poor exam performance.

In *Becoming a Successful Student*, we have addressed critical thinking in every chapter by asking students to evaluate and respond to carefully chosen reading selections designed to stimulate student interest. But it is in Unit 4, "Becoming a Critical Thinker," that we expand upon key concepts and skills like summarizing and synthesizing. At this point, students learn how these skills, previously used to understand the work of others, can now be applied to their own thinking and writing. Explained from this perspective, critical thinking becomes more than a tool for analysis; it becomes a source of personal creativity, and students are encouraged to study the ideas of others in order to develop their own fresh insights and perceptions.

We think it's important, too, that this unit shows students how to apply critical thinking skills not just to completing academic tasks but also to making personal decisions and moral choices. All too often, critical thinking is taught in a vacuum, and students don't really see how it applies to their life. We haven't made this mistake. Instead we show students that critical thinking is an essential part of their personal lives. It affects not just how they manage time and choose courses but how they treat their friends, develop a moral code, and make ethical choices.

Although every chapter of this book gives students a chance to write in response to reading, we use Unit 5, "Writing Papers," to focus exclusively on composing formal essays. Step-by-step, we show students how to do the kind of research, prewriting, and drafting that can transform their initial perceptions into finished, formal papers. Perhaps just as important, this unit allows us to reiterate key concepts previously introduced—only this time from a different perspective, from that of writer rather than reader. In this way, *Becoming a Successful Student* integrates reading and writing and helps students recognize that these are interrelated activities, not separate skills each with its own discrete set of principles and practices.

We recommend this book to you not just because we wrote it but because we believe it fulfills both of our original objectives. It gives students a sound repertoire of learning strategies applicable to a variety of academic tasks. But it also shows them that they themselves are the most significant factor in achieving college success.

Our academic reviewers included Beverly Bozsik, Norwich University; Donna Davidson, College of the Canyons; John A. R. Dick, University of Texas-El Paso Campus; Rina Duron, University of Southern California; Ruth Farrar, Hofstra University; Jill Gidmark, University of Minnesota-General College; Michele Kalina, Sierra College; Paul Kazmierski, Rochester Institute of Technology; James King, Texas Women's University; Susan Misheff, Kent State University-Stark Campus; Paul Panes, Queensborough Community College; Susan Rowland, College of Notre Dame; Michelle Simpson, University of Georgia; Norm Stahl, Georgia State University; Kimberly Tyson, University of Missouri; and Phyllis Weatherly, Southern Technical Institute.

To the Student

In *Becoming a Successful Student* we provide you with a series of step-by-step strategies for improving college study skills. We show you how to understand your textbooks, listen to lectures, take notes, and write papers. We also show you how to manage your time and inspire yourself to study, how to think both critically and creatively. In short, we have tried to tell you everything you need to know in order to achieve success in college. However, it's our hope that you will adapt what we say to your own particular academic tasks, personal goals, and individual learning style. Combine the advice in this book with a strong commitment to learning, and you can't miss becoming a successful student.

Laraine Flemming
Judith Leet

CONTENTS

U N I T   1

MAKING YOURSELF A PRODUCTIVE STUDENT

In this unit, the emphasis is on you—on who you are and what you want from your college experience. Knowing why you are in school will help you maintain a high level of motivation and interest. Once you know what you want to achieve, you will find it easier and more rewarding to study—even in the face of tempting diversions. You will also discover, as we show in Chapter 2, that you can schedule and organize your time more effectively to include both work and fun. You will learn the satisfactions of taking control of your time and making each day a productive step toward your ultimate goals.

In Chapter 3, we banish the notion that a poor memory can defeat your plans for college success. There are no good or bad memories; there are only effective and ineffective methods for remembering. Chapter 3 shows you how to unlock the powerful potential of your memory so that you can improve your ability to learn and remember new information.

In Chapter 4, we discuss the art of listening and show you how to get the most out of classroom lectures and discussions. Upon finishing this chapter, you will realize that the ability to hear is only the first step in good listening.

CHAPTER 1

INSPIRING YOURSELF TO STUDY

HELEN: Let's go to a movie tonight.

DANA: I can't. I have to reread that chapter Professor Hobbs assigned. I don't really understand what *marginal utility* is. Do you?

HELEN: No, I didn't read it. I just wasn't in the mood, and I can't do it tonight because this is the last night they are showing *Back to the Future.* I thought you were dying to see it.

DANA: I am. But I think I'll wait. I want to see if I can do well in economics; I'm probably going to major in it.

OVERVIEW

Helen and Dana illustrate two very different kinds of college students. One is highly motivated and determined to do well; the other is just not in the mood to study and cannot get into the right frame of mind. What explains the difference? How can one student inspire herself to study while the other can't bring herself to do even a minimal amount of work?

The crucial difference is **motivation,** the drive that successful students can master when they work toward some future goal that will make their lives richer. A high level of motivation is what keeps successful students determined to keep working, even when their less motivated friends tell them it's too nice a night to spend with textbooks.

But the objective of this chapter is not simply to *tell* you that motivation is important. We also want to show you how to develop and maintain a *strong sense of purpose*—an essential ingredient of being successful in college. Chapter 1 will help you:

- Define your long-term goals.
- Develop a plan of action for attaining your goals.
- Strengthen your self-image.
- Change unproductive habits.
- Develop specific strategies for maintaining a high level of motivation.
- Keep a journal to heighten self-awareness about how you learn best.

DEFINING YOUR LONG-TERM GOALS

Education is mostly motivation.

—Richard Green, Chancellor,
New York Public Schools

If someone asked you, "Why are you in school?" would you be able to answer? Surprisingly, many students can't, or else they respond with a vague and meaningless statement, such as "I need an education." If asked why, they are once again stumped. It's no wonder that many of these same students are not highly motivated to study. They don't really know *why* they are in school.

Yet for most people, it is the hope of future achievements that keeps them working, day after day, in the present. How many Olympic athletes could tolerate their grueling training without a vision of their long-term goals? Similarly, how many struggling farmers would tend to their crops during a poor season without a strong sense of what the future holds?

To help you identify your long-term goals, we have listed five ways college can enrich a person's life. As you read our list, think about which goals are or should be yours.

1. College can give you a sense of direction and purpose.
Like many freshmen, you may have arrived on campus without a clear vision of what you want to do with your life. You may not even have a solid sense of your own personal talents and gifts. It's important, therefore, that you use your college years to discover what you will do with the rest of your life, both personally and professionally. After taking an American history course given by a particularly stimulating professor, you may discover that you enjoy reading history books. You might even decide that you like history

enough to become a teacher and make the past come alive for other students. Perhaps a biology course will introduce you to the delights of animal behavior, and you will become committed to the animal rights movement. You might even decide to become a veterinarian or a zookeeper.

Or during a journalism course you may discover that you have an unexpected gift for writing, and you then decide to work on your college newspaper or to apply for a summer job as a reporter. Although you may have arrived on campus with little sense of what you can or should do with your life, you don't have to leave that way.

2. College can help you recognize your society's values.

Courses in psychology, anthropology, philosophy, literature, art, and history can give you a better understanding of the many different ways people live their lives. You may learn that in some cultures individuality is not valued the way it is in American society, and that people do not even think in terms of the self, but always in terms of the family or the group. Perhaps you will discover that romantic love, something you may consider a natural part of human experience, did not even exist in the Middle Ages, when people courted more for profit than for passion.

How does the Arab view of women differ from ours? How does the Russian view on personal freedom differ from ours? Through learning how different and varied cultures and people can be, you will be able to think about the values and traditions in your own society. You will gain a perspective for viewing and evaluating them, and for deciding which ones you consciously wish to share and which ones you don't.

3. College can improve your chances of getting an interesting job.

Motivated students know they want a degree because they understand that most employers prefer to hire college graduates. These students have their eyes on the future. They realize that the more college courses and credits they have on their transcript and the more skills they have acquired, the more employable they will be. Motivated students also know that people with degrees usually have the more interesting jobs—jobs where they manage large-scale projects, make challenging decisions, and have the opportunity to travel.

4. College can sharpen your ability to think.

The philosopher and psychologist William James once observed that the goal of education was not so much the transfer of information as the development of mental training. From James's point of view, the ultimate goal of learning was to develop intellectual habits of mind, like the ability to evaluate conflicting opinions or to argue a point convincingly. For James, subject matter was important, but the ability to think hard and well was more important.

A college or university is a unique environment, one in which you will be encouraged to spend time evaluating not just other people's ideas but your own as well. Make the most of this opportunity. Use it to learn and develop in yourself the intellectual habits scholars use in their various disciplines.

5. College can help you discover hidden talents.

Your college years can help you discover gifts and abilities you never knew you had. You could, for example, find yourself in a history class giving an oral report on the causes of the French Revolution. Before you give your report, you might think you can't do it because your legs feel like spaghetti and your voice has become a high falsetto from nervousness. But afterwards, you feel pleased with yourself. You've discovered you have a gift for speaking in front of groups. Once started, you spoke easily and naturally; you even livened things up with a few jokes. It's important that you think of your college years as a time when you can discover gifts and abilities you never knew you had.

Once you can answer the crucial question "Why am I in college?" you will find it easier to make and maintain a commitment to studying. Hard work

Malcolm X knew what his goals were and took steps to achieve them.

will no longer dismay you because your eyes will be set on the future and the promise that it holds.

PRACTICE 1   Think about what you expect to accomplish both personally and professionally. Then make a list of your reasons for being in college.

PRACTICE 2   The following excerpt from *The Autobiography of Malcolm X* describes how Malcolm X undertook and completed a monumental task. In an effort to educate himself, he worked his way, word by word, through every page of the dictionary. When you finish reading this excerpt, write down what you believe were the sources of Malcolm X's motivation. What was it that kept him going?

> I saw that the best thing I could do was get hold of a dictionary— to study, to learn some words. I was lucky enough to reason also that I should try to improve my penmanship. It was sad. I couldn't even write in a straight line. It was both ideas together that moved me to request a dictionary along with some tablets and pencils from the Norfolk Prison Colony school.
>
> I spent two days just riffling* uncertainly through the dictionary's pages. I'd never realized so many words existed! I didn't know *which* words I needed to learn. Finally, just to start some kind of action, I began copying.
>
> In my slow, painstaking, ragged handwriting, I copied into my tablet everything printed on that first page, down to the punctuation marks.
>
> I believe it took me a day. Then, aloud, I read back, to myself, everything I'd written on the tablet. Over and over, aloud, to myself, I read my own handwriting.
>
> I woke up the next morning, thinking about those words— immensely proud to realize that not only had I written so much at one time, but I'd written words that I never knew were in the world. Moreover, with a little effort, I also could remember what many of these words meant. I reviewed the words whose meanings I didn't remember. Funny thing, from the dictionary first page right now, that "aardvark" springs to my mind. The dictionary had a picture of it, a long-tailed, long-eared, burrowing African mammal, which lives off termites caught by sticking out its tongue as an anteater does for ants.

---

* to riffle: to thumb through

I was so fascinated that I went on—I copied the dictionary's next page. And the same experience came when I studied that. With every succeeding page, I also learned of people and places and events from history. Actually the dictionary is like a miniature encyclopedia. Finally the dictionary's A section had filled a whole tablet—and I went on into the B's. That was the way I started copying what eventually became the entire dictionary. It went a lot faster after so much practice helped me to pick up handwriting speed. Between what I wrote in my tablet, and writing letters, during the rest of my time in prison I would guess I wrote a million words.

I suppose that it was inevitable that as my word-base broadened, I could for the first time pick up a book and read and now begin to understand what the book was saying. Anyone who has read a great deal can imagine the new world that opened. Let me tell you something: from then until I left that prison, in every free moment I had, if I was not reading in the library, I was reading on my bunk. You couldn't have gotten me out of books with a wedge. Between Mr. Muhammad's* teachings, my correspondence, my visitors—usually Ella and Reginald—and my reading of books, months passed without my even thinking about being imprisoned. In fact, up to then, I never had been so truly free in my life.

The Norfolk Prison Colony's library was in the school building. A variety of classes was taught there by instructors who came from such places as Harvard and Boston universities. The weekly debates between inmate teams were also held in the school building. You would be astonished to know how worked up convict debaters and audiences would get over subjects like "Should Babies Be Fed Milk?"

As you can imagine, especially in a prison where there was a heavy emphasis on rehabilitation, an inmate was smiled upon if he demonstrated an unusually intense interest in books. There was a sizable number of well-read inmates, especially the popular debaters. Some were said by many to be practically walking encyclopedias. They were almost celebrities. No university would ask any student to devour literature as I did when this new world opened to me, of being able to read and *understand.*

---

* Elijah Muhammad: leader of Black Muslin sect that Malcolm X joined while in prison

DEVELOPING A PLAN OF ACTION

Identifying your long-term goals is the first step toward achieving them. The next step is to **develop a concrete plan of action,** one that identifies the intermediate steps you need to take to achieve what you want. For example, if one of your long-term goals is to improve your chances of doing interesting and varied work like developing computer software, you might decide to take several computer science courses. But maybe your goal is to travel and work overseas. In that case, you might choose to take at least two years of a language. Whatever your particular interests are, you should analyze your goals and determine the specific steps that can turn your dreams into reality.

In mapping out a step-by-step approach to your long-term goals, you should also ask yourself if each step is both realistic and attainable. If you have decided that a knowledge of computers will improve your career choices, plan to become an expert in one or two computer languages. This is an achievable goal. Do not, however, plan to master every computer language ever devised. This is an impossible task that in the end will intimidate rather than encourage you.

Be Prepared for Setbacks

In planning for your goals, you should also prepare yourself for an occasional setback or defeat. By definition, long-term goals take time to achieve, and there is no guarantee that every step you take toward your final objectives will be successful. Perhaps one of your long-term goals is to improve your ability to put thoughts into words. One step in accomplishing that goal may be to take a series of writing courses. But writing is hard work, particularly if you have not had much writing practice in high school. If you do not do as well as you expect in one writing course, should you give up? The answer is absolutely *no.* Instead, seek help from a classmate or your instructor so you can discover the precise areas that need improvement (and take a look at our unit on writing, beginning on p. 380). That way you'll do better in the next course.

Over the course of your college career, you will have to inspire and re-inspire yourself. You will have to be the coach urging the team on, as well as the team who is being revved up. Expect to meet some resistance from within, some failures, some black moods. But if the general trend is one of small, gradual successes, then you are on the right track, and you'll achieve the goals you have set for yourself. Believe that, and you are already halfway there.

Identifying your long-term goals is only the first step in achieving them. The next step is to develop a concrete plan of action, one that identifies the intermediate steps you need to take to reach your goals.

■   **PRACTICE 3**   Write down one of your long-term goals. Then, next to the goal, list some specific intermediate steps you can take to achieve that goal.

EXAMPLE

Long Term Goal

Working overseas as a guide or translator

Intermediate Steps

1. Take Spanish I
2. Schedule time for the language lab — once a week

STRENGTHENING YOUR SELF-IMAGE

There are several kinds of football players. There are those who have it and know it, those who have it and don't know it, those who haven't got it and know it, and those who haven't got it and don't know it. Those who haven't got it and don't know it have won us more games than anybody.
                                                    —Woody Hayes

Research has repeatedly shown that self-image is a crucial ingredient of success or failure. In short, you succeed more often when you think you will do well than when you think you'll fail. For this reason, strengthening your self-image is a central part of inspiring yourself to study. The stronger and surer you feel about yourself, the more energy you will have to reach your goals.

What kind of image do you have of yourself? Do you concentrate on your failings instead of your virtues? If you do, you probably have a distorted image of your character and personality.

If you think you need to strengthen or improve your self-image, the first thing you should do is **identify your positive characteristics** or qualities. Sit down and analyze what you think—not what somebody else thinks—is good about your personality and character. Once you stop and take stock of your strengths, you'll be amazed at how many you really have.

After you have identified your strengths, the next step is to list and analyze what you believe your failings are. Doing this will make you realize that most failings are not fixed character traits that can never be changed. More often, they are habits that can be altered through concentration and discipline. For example, do you consider yourself to be a disorganized or careless worker? Being disorganized or careless is not a genetic trait. If you really want to be more organized, you can develop that personality trait. It just will take a little time and effort on your part. Tell yourself, "In the past, I've been disorganized, but in the future, I'm going to schedule my time so I finish everything I start."

Once you have defined your positive and negative qualities, you must nurture the positive qualities and modify or eliminate the negative ones. You must also come to terms with the fear that plagues 99 percent of the population—the fear of failure. Meet this fear head-on by acknowledging that there will be times when you will not meet the standards you set for yourself. But you don't have to label that failure. Keep in mind that the word *failure* represents an act of interpretation. In other words, it all depends on how you choose to evaluate the situation. The same set of circumstances can be identified either as a failure or as a learning experience for future success. It's up to you to decide which interpretation will help you succeed.

Research has repeatedly shown that self-image is a crucial ingredient of success or failure.

A skater strives to accomplish her goals.

■   PRACTICE 4   Each of the following characteristics is marked with a plus or a minus. Circle each plus or minus that you think you possess. Then look the list over and consider how you can turn those minuses into additional pluses.

1. I'm punctual. +
2. I'm always late. −
3. I finish anything that I start. +
4. I start things but I don't finish them. −
5. I have a sense of humor. +
6. I always look on the bright side. +
7. I tend to be pessimistic. −
8. I'm a very determined person. +
9. I give up too easily. −
10. I can't speak in front of groups. +
11. I like to figure things out, find new solutions to problems. +
12. I tend to prejudge people and ideas. −
13. I have a lot of common sense. +
14. I tend to be disorganized. −
15. I know how to organize my time. +
16. I like to learn new things. +
17. I know how to talk to people. +
18. I'm not serious enough about my work. −
19. I have trouble concentrating. −
20. I don't have enough self-confidence. −
21. I have trouble accepting criticism. −
22. I have a very limited vocabulary. −
23. I like learning new words. +
24. I'm enthusiastic about life. +
25. I believe in myself. +

USING SPECIFIC STRATEGIES FOR SELF-MOTIVATION

Here are ten specific strategies you can use to spark your enthusiasm for studying. Adapt them so they work for you. In general, study yourself as if you are a scientist conducting research, and your objective is to figure out how to make yourself study more efficiently.

1. Write your long-term goals on a piece of paper.
Display the paper in your workplace or else put it in your notebook. Every time you feel your motivation slipping, glance at that slip of paper and think about what you are working toward.

2. Speak to yourself positively about studying.

Develop a list of mottoes or messages related to studying. If you feel your motivation flagging, use them to urge yourself on.

- "I can pass this course, and I'm going to."
- "I can make myself study; a little hard work won't hurt me."
- "I'm close to a breakthrough in precalculus."
- "I will study and prepare and perhaps my chance will come."
  —Abraham Lincoln

3. Take someone you admire as a role model.

Think of someone whose achievements you admire, and find out as much as you can about that person's life. How did this person prepare for his or her career? Were there any setbacks?

Now think of any great athlete you admire and contemplate how he or she prepared for an important game or match. Great athletes *train* for a world-class or an Olympic event. They know that if they are to be mentally and physically prepared for an event, they must leave nothing to chance. Think about your goals and what you must do to attain them. Leave nothing to chance.

4. Be an effective strategist.

Spend five minutes each night reviewing your accomplishments during the day and evaluating your studying strategies. Ask yourself leading questions:

- Did I study for as long as I had intended?
- Did I use my studying time productively?
- Am I keeping up with my assignments?
- Have I fallen behind in one course? If so, what's the best thing to do now?

See Chapter 2 for more on managing your time.

5. Get yourself mentally ready for the next day.

Psych yourself for tomorrow's tasks by asking yourself a series of questions:

- What tasks must I accomplish tomorrow and in what order should I do them?
- What time will I get started tomorrow?
- What is a reasonable amount of time for each task?

By settling firmly in your mind what you plan to do tomorrow, you will prepare yourself to act on those plans.

6. Establish daily work habits and routines.

In an interview, Mary Lou Retton, Olympic gymnast, explained the role of habit in her training program:

> Some days you don't feel like working out. Somewhere inside me, though, is the eye of the tiger. On a down day, it's as if that eye is closed shut. What gets me through, what ultimately opens the tiger's eye, is habit. Habit gets me up at 5 A.M. Habit gets me into the gym. Habit gets me into the routine. Suddenly, the tiger's eye opens again.

Establish for yourself regular hours, a regular place that is comfortable and well-lit, an environment conducive to work—with tempting distractions minimized.

7. Use rewards on yourself.

Psychologists call them "delayed gratification," or "reinforcers," but they provide a short-term reward that you can look forward to. Make a list of those things that you genuinely love to do—listen to music, take a long swim, take a run around the track, have a slice of pizza, whatever—and do one of these things after you have studied productively. Then you'll have the pleasant sensation of being in control, of having earned your rewards.

8. Review your accomplishments to date.

If you feel your motivation flagging, tell yourself how you've been improving.

- "I'm writing my papers a little better than I used to."
- "I'm catching on about how to take notes."
- "I did well on the first quiz—so why not again?"
- "I understand more of what I read."
- "My math skills are really coming along."

9. Attack something you are resisting—but only for ten minutes.

Getting started is often the hardest part, but once you've begun, you'll find it easier to continue. Try also to coordinate your tasks with your energy: do the hardest ones when you are freshest; do the easier ones when you are fading.

10. Find support for yourself.

Look for a friend whose goals are similar to yours and who wants to study. A supportive friend is invaluable. Look for someone who will help you get to the library each evening.

MAKING THE MOST OF EVERY COURSE

Give every course the benefit of the doubt. Try to become enthusiastic about each one. Assume that what you're studying will become more stimulating once you get deeper into it. If you *try* to get interested and caught up in the material, you will have a better chance of becoming truly absorbed in it.

Your teacher, whose lifework is often the subject of the course, far prefers students who respond and raise questions. Your grades may improve with some active classroom participation on your part. But even if your grade is not directly affected by class discussion, the teacher will know who you are when grading your written work.

Often the course that people find most useless while in college turns out to be the one that unexpectedly helps them in some major phase of their career. They find they can write reports well, based on what they considered a dull business writing class, or they can speak persuasively because of what they learned in a speech course. Give each course a chance to help you at some unexpected point in the future.

What Every Successful Student Knows

1. Attend the first class. Instructors usually use the first class to provide an overview of the course, its objectives, and its organization. That overview is important. Don't miss it. You will also need the handouts and course syllabus.

2. Get to know a classmate. It helps to have a friend in class, someone with whom you can discuss assignments or clarify questions. You also can borrow or lend notes when either of you must miss a class.

3. Go to every class. It's tempting to cut class on a beautiful day, but don't do it. Each class provides new information, and you can't afford to have a gap in your knowledge.

4. Talk to your instructor. If you feel confused, don't be afraid to ask your instructor for help. Most instructors will be happy to provide it.

5. Understand the course requirements. Don't discover at the end of the semester that your final paper is worth half of your grade. Make sure you know the course requirements early in the semester.

INTRODUCING THE LEARNING JOURNAL

Each chapter of this book concludes with a brief section called "Journal Assignments." These assignments reflect our hope that you will start and maintain a learning journal, a kind of diary or notebook in which you explore your individual learning style and learning strategies.

There are many ways in which you can use your journal. After you have followed one of our suggestions, you can evaluate our advice, explaining how it worked for you. Were you able to follow our advice exactly, or did you have to modify it to suit your particular assignments and goals? What changes did you make?

Your journal is the place to discover what made one study session succeed whereas another failed. When you finish a successful session, you should use your journal to find out what made it productive.

> 11/20/89: I went to my usual spot in the library—in the corner I've staked out for myself. I didn't do what I usually do, put off the chemistry problems till last. Because I felt rested and sharp, I did the hardest problem first, spending most of my time on that. Having solved it, I had no problem going straight to the remaining problems.

You can also use your journal to explore why a study session was not successful. The following excerpt shows why things did not turn out exactly as one student had planned:

> 11/22/89: When I got to the library, I didn't know what I wanted to do first and I wasted ten minutes picking books up and putting them down, thinking about all the things I had to do. Because I was obviously not concentrating on anything, Matt came over and started talking to me. Suddenly, I wasn't in the mood for studying anymore, and we left the library together.

You can learn a lot about your personal learning style if you use your journal to reflect on how you do or do not complete your study tasks. As you read what you've written, look for patterns in your study habits and ask yourself questions.

- Why do I find it easier to write papers than to take exams?
- Am I good at working with words but afraid of numbers?

- Do discussion groups bring out the best in me, making me think faster and better than I do when I study alone?

Questions like these will help you probe your learning strengths and weaknesses. They will help you develop the kind of self-awareness you need to be productive, efficient, and successful.

Don't think of your journal as just another writing assignment. Your teacher will not grade your jottings or correct your grammar. The entries you make are for your own personal use. They will help you discover not just what you want from college but how best to achieve it.

WORKING SPACE

READING ASSIGNMENT

The following selection by Peter Rondinone, a newspaper journalist, describes his struggle to make it through college when nobody else thought he could or should do it. Answer the questions that follow.

Open Admissions and the Inward "I"

I hung out on a Bronx street corner with a group of guys who called themselves "The Davidson Boys" and sang songs like "Daddy-lo-lo." Everything we did could be summed up with the word "snap." That's a "snap." She's a "snap." We had a "snap." Friday nights we'd paint ourselves green and run through the streets in the park. It was all very perilous.* Even though I'd seen a friend stabbed for wearing the wrong colors and another blown away with a shotgun for "messin'" with some dude's woman, I was too young to realize that my life too might be headed toward a violent end.

Then one night I swallowed a dozen Tunimols and downed two quarts of beer at a bar in Manhattan. I passed out in the gutter. I puked and rolled under a parked car. Two girlfriends found me and carried me home. My overprotective brother answered the door. When he saw me—eyes rolling toward the back of my skull like rubber—he pushed me down a flight of stairs. My skull hit the edge of a marble step with a thud. The girls screamed. My parents came to

---

* perilous: dangerous

the door and there I was: a high school graduate, a failure, curled in a ball in a pool of blood.

The next day I woke up with dried blood on my face. I had no idea what had happened. My sister told me. I couldn't believe it. Crying, my mother confirmed the story. I had almost died! That scared the hell out of me. I knew I had to do something. I didn't know what. But pills and violence didn't promise much of a future.

I went back to a high school counselor for advice. He suggested I go to college.

I wasn't aware of it, but it seems that in May 1969 a group of dissident* students from the black and Puerto Rican communities took over the south campus of the City College of New York (CCNY). They demanded that the Board of Higher Education and the City of New York adopt an open-admission policy that would make it possible for anybody to go to CCNY without the existing requirements: SATs and a high school average of eighty-five. This demand was justified on the premise† that college had always been for the privileged few and excluded minorities. As it turned out, in the fall of 1970 the City University's eighteen campuses admitted massive numbers of students—fifteen thousand—with high school averages below eighty-five. By 1972, I was one of them.

On the day I received my letter of acceptance, I waited until dinner to tell my folks. I was proud.

"Check out where I'm going," I said. I passed the letter to my father. He looked at it.

"You jerk!" he said. "You wanna sell ties?" My mother grabbed the letter.

"God," she said. "Why don't you go to work already? Like other people."

"Later for that," I said. "You should be proud."

At the time, of course, I didn't understand where my parents were coming from. They were immigrants. They believed college was for rich kids, not the ones who dropped downs and sang songs on street corners.

My mother had emigrated from Russia after World War II. She came to the United States with a bundle of clothes, her mother and father, a few dollars, and a baby from a failed marriage. Her first job was on an assembly line in a pen factory where she met my father, the production manager.

---

* dissident: opposed to present conditions
† premise: assumption

My father, a second-generation Italian, was brought up on the Lower East Side of Manhattan. He never completed high school. And when he wasn't working in a factory, he peddled Christmas lights door to door or sold frankfurters in Times Square.

My family grew up in the south Bronx. There were six children, and we slept in one room on cots. We ate spaghetti three times a week and were on welfare because for a number of years my father was sick, in and out of the hospital.

Anyhow, I wasn't about to listen to my parents and go to work; for a dude like me, this was a big deal. So I left the dinner table and went to tell my friends about my decision.

I spent that summer alone, reading books like *How to Succeed in College* and *30 Days to a More Powerful Vocabulary.* My vocabulary was limited to a few choice phrases like, "Move over, Rover, and let Petey take over." When my friends did call for me I hid behind the curtains. I knew that if I was going to make it, I'd have to push these guys out of my consciousness as if I were doing the breaststroke in a sea of logs. I had work to do, and people were time-consuming. As it happened, all my heavy preparations didn't amount to much.

On the day of the placement exams I went paranoid. Somehow I got the idea that my admission to college was some ugly practical joke that I wasn't prepared for. So I copped some downs and took the test nodding. The words floated on the page like flies on a crock of cream.

That made freshman year difficult. The administration had placed me in all three remedial programs: basic writing, college skills, and math. I was shocked. I had always thought of myself as smart. I was the only one in the neighborhood who read books. So I gave up the pills and pushed aside another log.

The night before the first day of school, my brother walked into my room and threw a briefcase on my desk. "Good luck, Joe College," he said. He smacked me in the back of the head. Surprised, I went to bed early.

I arrived on campus ahead of time with a map in my pocket. I wanted enough time, in case I got lost, to get to my first class. But after wandering around the corridors of one building for what seemed like a long time and hearing the sounds of classes in session, the scrape of chalk and muted discussions, I suddenly wondered if I was in the right place. So I stopped a student and pointed to a dot on my map.

"Look." He pointed to the dot. "Now look." He pointed to an

inscription on the front of the building. I was in the right place. "Can't you read?" he said. Then he joined some friends. As he walked off I heard someone say, "What do you expect from open admissions?"

I had no idea that there were a lot of students who resented people like me, who felt I was jeopardizing standards, destroying their institution. I had no idea. I just wanted to go to class.

In Basic Writing I, the instructor, Regina Sackmary, chalked her name in bold letters on the blackboard. I sat in the front row and reviewed my *How to Succeed* lessons: Sit in front/don't let eyes wander to cracks on ceilings/take notes on legal pad/make note of all unfamiliar words and books/listen for key phrases like "remember this," they are a professor's signals. The other students held pens over pads in anticipation. Like me, they didn't know what to expect. We were public school kids from lousy neighborhoods and we knew that some of us didn't have a chance; but we were ready to work hard.

Before class we had rapped about our reasons for going to college. Some said they wanted to be the first in the history of their families to have a college education—they said their parents never went to college because they couldn't afford it, or because their parents' parents were too poor—and they said open admissions and free tuition (sixty-five dollars per semester) was a chance to change that history. Others said they wanted to be educated so they could return to their neighborhoods to help "the people"; they were the idealists. Some foreigners said they wanted to return to their own countries and start schools. And I said I wanted to escape the boredom and the pain I had known as a kid on the streets. But none of them said they expected a job. Or if they did they were reminded that there were no jobs.

Ms. Sackmary told us that Basic Writing I was part of a three-part program. Part one would instruct us in the fundamentals of composition: sentence structure, grammar, and paragraphing; part two, the outline and essay; and part three, the term paper. She also explained that we weren't in basic writing because there was something wrong with us—we just needed to learn the basics, she said. Somehow I didn't believe her. After class I went to her office. She gave me a quick test. I couldn't write a coherent* sentence or construct a paragraph. So we made an agreement: I'd write an essay a day in addi-

---

* coherent: logically connected

tion to my regular classwork. Also, I'd do a few term papers. She had this idea that learning to write was like learning to play a musical instrument—it takes practice, everyday practice.

I remember the day Ms. Sackmary tossed Sartre's* *No Exit* in my lap and said, "Find the existential† motif." I didn't know what to look for. What was she talking about? I never studied philosophy. I turned to the table of contents, but there was nothing under E. So I went to the library and after much research I discovered the notion of the absurd. I couldn't believe it. I told as many people as I could. I told them they were absurd, their lives were absurd, everything was absurd. I became obsessed with existentialism. I read Kafka, Camus, Dostoyevski, and others in my spare time. Then one day I found a line in a book that I believed summed up my unusual admittance to the college and my determination to work hard. I pasted it to the headboard of my bed. It said, "Everything is possible."

To deal with the heavy workload from all my classes, I needed a study schedule, so I referred to my *How to Succeed* book. I gave myself an hour for lunch and reserved the rest of the time between classes and evenings for homework and research. All this left me very little time for friendships. But I stuck to my schedule and by the middle of that first year I was getting straight A's. Nothing else mattered. Not even my family.

When I entered my second year my family began to ask, "What do you want to do?" And I got one of those cards from the registrar that has to be filled out in a week or you're dropped from classes. It asked me to declare my major. I had to make a quick decision. So I checked off BS degree, dentistry, though I didn't enroll in a single science course.

One course I did take that semester was The Writer and the City. The professor, Ross Alexander, asked the class to keep a daily journal. He said it should be as creative as possible and reflect some aspect of city life. So I wrote about different experiences I had with my friends. For example, I wrote "Miracle on 183rd Street" about the night "Raunchy" Rick jumped a guy in the park and took his portable radio. When the guy tried to fight back Rick slapped him in the face with the radio; then using the batteries that spilled, he pounded this guy in the head until the blood began to puddle on the ground. Those of us on the sidelines dragged Rick away. Ross attached notes to my papers that said things like: "You really have a great hit of

---

* Jean-Paul Sartre: (1905–1980), French writer and philosopher
† existential: dealing with the subject of existence and why people exist

talent and ought to take courses in creative writing and sharpen your craft! Hang on to it all for dear life."

In my junior year I forgot dentistry and registered as a creative writing major. I also joined a college newspaper, *The Campus*. Though I knew nothing about journalism, I was advised that writing news was a good way to learn the business. And as Ross once pointed out to me, "As a writer you will need an audience."

I was given my first assignment. I collected piles of quotes and facts and scattered the mess on a desk. I remember typing the story under deadline pressure with one finger while the editors watched me struggle, probably thinking back to their own first stories. When I finished, they passed the copy around. The editor-in-chief looked at it last and said, "This isn't even English." Yet they turned it over to a rewrite man and the story appeared with my by-line. Seeing my name in print was like seeing it in lights—flashbulbs popped in my head and I walked into the school cafeteria that day expecting to be recognized by everyone. My mother informed the relatives: "My son is a writer!"

God, those early days were painful. Professors would tear up my papers the day they were due and tell me to start over again, with a piece of advice—"Try to say what you really mean." Papers I had spent weeks writing. And I knew I lacked the basic college skills; I was a man reporting to work without his tools. So I smiled when I didn't understand. But sometimes it showed and I paid the price: A professor once told me the only reason I'd pass his course was that I had a nice smile. Yes, those were painful days.

And there were nights I was alone with the piles of notebooks and textbooks. I wanted to throw the whole mess out the window; I wanted to give up. Nights the sounds of my friends singing on the corner drifted into my room like a fog over a graveyard and I was afraid I would be swept away. And nights I was filled with questions but the answers were like moon shadows on my curtains: I could see them but I could not grasp them.

Yet I had learned a vital lesson from these countless hours of work in isolation: My whole experience from the day I received my letter of acceptance enabled me to understand how in high school my sense of self-importance came from being one of the boys, a member of the pack, while in college the opposite was true. In order to survive, I had to curb my herd instinct.

Nobody, nobody could give me what I needed to overcome my sense of inadequacy. That was a struggle I had to work at on my own. It could never be a group project. In the end, though people could point out what I had to learn and where to learn it, I was always the one who did the work; and what I learned I earned. And that made me feel as good as being one of the boys. In short, college taught me to appreciate the importance of being alone. I found it was the only way I could get any serious work done.

But those days of trial and uncertainty are over, and the open-admission policy has been eliminated. Anybody who enters the City University's senior colleges must now have an 80 percent high school average. And I am one of those fortunate individuals who in a unique period of American education was given a chance to attend college. But I wonder what will happen to those people who can learn but whose potential doesn't show in their high school average; who might get into street crime if not given a chance to do something constructive? I wonder, because if it weren't for open admissions, the likelihood is I would still be swinging baseball bats on the streets on Friday nights.

---

1. What inspired the author to keep working despite what he called "painful days"?

2. What did Rondinone mean when he wrote, "In order to survive, I had to curb my herd instinct"?

3. Why do you think Rondinone wrote this article? What did he want his audience to know or understand?

4. How did the author's self-image change during his years in school?

5.   Why do you think the author pasted the line, "Everything is possible," to his bed?

6.   What is Rondinone trying to communicate with the title? What does he mean by the "Inward 'I'"?

WRITING ASSIGNMENT: "The Exhilaration of Learning"

In this chapter you have read works by two different people who unexpectedly discovered the exhilaration or excitement of learning. Write a paper in which you describe a similar learning experience, one where you were excited by your own accomplishments. It does not matter where or when the experience took place. It is more important that you express *what* you learned and how you felt about it.

JOURNAL ASSIGNMENTS

1. In 1986, the Carnegie Commission on Education published a report in which members of the commission lamented what they called "careerism," the tendency of many students to think of college as a stepping stone to a career and nothing else. Use your journal to think about this issue in writing. What is wrong with careerism? What does careerism lead to? Do you think you are one of those students practicing careerism?

2. Write a detailed description of yourself twenty years in the future. What kind of person do you expect to be, both personally and professionally?

3. In the following excerpt, writer and teacher Susan Horton explains that people have argued over what "education" is or should be. Read what she writes. Then answer the following question: What do you think "true" education really is?

There have been centuries of debate about what education—true education—really is. Some writers picture the student as a kind of sponge, soaking up what the teacher provides. For some, education only takes place when the student gradually "opens up" or "blossoms" under the teacher's care, the teacher being a kind of gardener who nurtures these fledgling plants. For some, education is leading people from one point to a higher point. John Dewey once defined education as a process of unsettling minds. For him, then, it is not filling minds or leading minds that constitutes genuine education, but the dismantling of solidly held but faulty visions of things that students hold when they come to the teacher.

CHECKING OUT

Check your understanding of Chapter 1 by writing answers to the following questions. You may work alone or with a classmate, whichever you prefer.

1. Why are long-term goals important?

2. When you analyze your long-term goals, what kinds of questions should you ask yourself?

3. What do we mean when we say that the word *failure* represents an act of interpretation?

4. Name three specific things you can do to develop motivation.

5. What is the role or function of the learning journal?

IN SUMMARY

The key to inspiring yourself to study is motivation, the idea that you are working toward some long-term goal that you hope to achieve over time. Once you know *why* you are in school, everything else will more easily fall into place. That's because your work will have a meaning and a purpose. Studying is often hard work. No one is going to deny that. But once you know why you are studying, you will find that hard work does not dismay you because you have a goal and a sense of direction. Studying is a stepping stone toward your future.

CHAPTER 2

TAKING CHARGE OF YOUR TIME

When you make the clock of life your clock, you discover the truth of the
Spanish saying, "Life is short, but wide."

—Kenneth Atchity

OVERVIEW

People who succeed in life are usually masters of time management. They
know exactly where they are going, and they schedule their time to make
sure they get there.

On his way to superstar status as a basketball player, Bill Bradley—who
went on to become a United States senator—made time for daily practice
sessions to develop and hone his skills. During each session, he would go
through a prescribed set of drills in which he had to hit ten out of thirteen
shots or he wouldn't allow himself to begin the next drill.

As a young girl, Chris Evert went home after school every day, changed
her clothes, and headed for the tennis courts to play for several hours.
Determined to be a champion, she scheduled time for the daily practice
sessions that would later make her the number one female player in the
world for many years.

Yet important as time management is, some students will groan or sigh
when we first introduce it as a topic of discussion. They think we're asking
them to transform themselves into people who use every waking minute to
study, who have no time or interest in anything else. Yet *nothing* could be
further from the truth.

Our objective in teaching time management is to show students how they can use their study time efficiently so that they can still play football, go hiking, or attend concerts. From our perspective, time management does not mean sacrificing all leisure activities in favor of studying. It means taking control of your life. It means finding the time to study *and* play. To make time for both, we recommend the following strategies for managing time. Apply them, and you won't be asking people how they find the time for all their activities. They will be asking you.

- Apply the principle of divide and conquer to all difficult tasks.
- Make a weekly schedule.
- Establish your priorities.
- Identify your high-energy prime time.
- Develop a series of deadlines for long-term assignments.
- Analyze and revise your schedule so it works for you.
- Use a daily "to do" list.
- Create the right setting for study.
- Kick the procrastination habit.

APPLYING THE DIVIDE-AND-CONQUER PRINCIPLE

It is easy enough to look at your course syllabuses in September and grow disheartened. Faced with so many readings, so many papers and quizzes, you feel swamped and intimidated by the amount of work you have to do. But we guarantee that you will help yourself greatly right from the start if you remember and apply only one principle: Whenever possible, **divide your assignments into smaller, more manageable subtasks.**

For example, if today is Monday, and you know that by Friday you have to read a chapter of your American government text, schedule your time so that you read only ten or fifteen pages each night. If you leave the whole chapter for one night, chances are that you will not finish or you won't read it at all.

By dividing your readings as we have suggested, you will avoid feeling pressured. In addition, working several days on the same chapter will give you the reinforcement you need to retain more of what you read.

There is also an added bonus to breaking your assignments into more manageable bites. Each time you finish one of your subtasks, you will feel a sense of accomplishment and control—simply because you did what you set out to do. That sense of accomplishment will make you more willing to tackle and complete the next assignment. It is the reward that will encourage you to maintain the study behavior you need to complete your assignments.

You should also apply the principle of divide and conquer to your long-range assignments. If you have a fifteen-page paper due at the end of the term, assign yourself weekly tasks to help you complete that long-range assignment. Those tasks may be very small, such as jotting down any thoughts you already have on the topic, looking through the card catalog for useful books, or developing a plan for organizing your ideas. Step by step you will whittle away at the assignment until you complete it.

> Each time you finish one of your subtasks, you will feel a sense of accomplishment and control—simply because you did what you set out to do.

PRACTICE 1   Make a list of your assignments for the next two weeks. Beside each assignment, write a subtask that you can easily accomplish in the next twenty-four hours. For example, if you have a paper due by the end of the week, assign yourself the task of jotting down some ideas you might use in the paper.

MAKING A WEEKLY SCHEDULE

While you are learning how to monitor your time, we strongly suggest that you make a detailed written schedule of what you plan to do from the time you get up in the morning until the time you go to bed at night. A schedule will help reveal where you use your time productively and where you waste it. Eventually you may switch to a simpler schedule, such as the daily "to do" list we discuss later in this chapter. Initially, the best way to discover where your time goes is by using an hour-by-hour, day-by-day schedule.

Begin by photocopying or drawing a grid that shows hourly blocks of time for each day of the week. The result should resemble Figure 2–1. Next, take that same schedule and fill in your class times, as shown in Figure 2–2.

After you list your class times on the schedule, make enough photocopies to last throughout the term. Use one of the copies to specify what you intend to do this week when you are not in class. Figure 2–3 is an excerpt from a schedule created by Tina Judson, a student famous for her organizational abilities.

	Monday	Tuesday	Wednesday	Thursday	Friday
7 – 8					
8 – 9					
9 – 10					
10 – 11					
11 – 12					
12 – 1					
1 – 2					
2 – 3					
3 – 4					
4 – 5					
5 – 6					
6 – 7					
7 – 8					
8 – 9					
9 – 10					
10 – 11					
11 – 12					

Figure 2-1: Photocopy or Draw a Grid

	Monday	Tuesday	Wednesday	Thursday	Friday
7 – 8					
8 – 9	American Government	Geometry	American Government	Geometry	American Government
9 – 10		Physical Education		Physical Education	Physical Education
10 – 11	Biology		Biology		Biology
11 – 12					
12 – 1				Biology Lab	
1 – 2	American Literature		American Literature	Lab	American Literature
2 – 3					
3 – 4		Sociology		Sociology	Sociology
4 – 5					
5 – 6					
6 – 7					
7 – 8					
8 – 9					
9 – 10					
10 – 11					
11 – 12					

Figure 2-2: Fill in Your Class Times

	Monday	Tuesday	Wednesday
7 – 8			
8 – 9	American Govt. Class	Geometry Class	American Govt. Class
9 – 10	After class review		Review lecture notes
10 – 11	American Govt. Reading pgs 20-40.	Physical Education	Start bibliography for final Research paper.
11 – 12	Biology Class	Intensive Reading of Amer. Govt. pgs 27-57 ↓	Review Biology notes Biology Class
12 – 1	Review Bio. notes.		Review Bio notes
1 – 2	Jot down topics for American Lit essay. FREE	FREE	FREE
2 – 3	American Lit.		American Lit.
3 – 4	Review notes from American Lit.		Review notes from American Lit.
4 – 5	FREE	Sociology Class	Take notes on Revision of Amer. Lit essay.
5 – 6	FREE	Review Soc. notes	Start Geom problem for Thursday.
6 – 7	Free write on topic for Amer. Lit. essay	FREE	FREE
7 – 8	Go over Geometry Problems for errors.	Read Biology pgs. 45-75	Finish Geometry problem
8 – 9	Review notes from Ch 1 - Amer. Govt. pgs 1-27		Write draft of American Lit. essay
9 – 10	FREE		
10 – 11	↓	↓	

Figure 2–3: A Sample Schedule

In examining Tina's schedule, you may have noticed that she's given herself very specific instructions about how to use each hour. For example, 10:00 to 11:00 on Monday is not spent in "study." Instead, Tina has identified exactly what she wants to do, right down to the number of pages to be covered:

10:00 to 11:00—pages 20–40 American government

There is a reason for such exact instructions. When you sit down to study, you do not want to waste ten or fifteen minutes figuring out what you should do first. This is an easy way to divert yourself from doing anything. If you have your mind clearly settled on the specific tasks at hand, you will find it easier to get started.

Scheduling Review Times

Tina's schedule shows time set aside for reviews *before* and *after* class. Such reviews are important, and you should make time for them.

The purpose of **before-class reviews** is to prime yourself for the instructor's lecture by rereading your lecture notes from the last class. As you listen to the new material, you should try to relate it to the previous lecture, linking the unfamiliar to the familiar. But if you are not clear on the content of the previous lecture, then you will have trouble making the necessary connections.

After-class reviews are equally important. Simply put, most of the material you're going to forget disappears from memory immediately after you hear or read it. But research shows that **immediate review can slow down the rate of forgetting** and decrease the amount of information forgotten. If there are times when you cannot sit down for a review right after a lecture, try to review your notes sometime during the same day.

You should also use after-class reviews to clarify your notes. This is the time to make illegible words legible, to fill in or elaborate on key points from lectures.

> While you are learning how to monitor your time, make a detailed written schedule of what you will do from the time you get up in the morning until the time you go to bed at night.

■   PRACTICE 2   Make a photocopy of the grid shown in Figure 2–1 on page 30. Fill in your class schedule. Then fill in the blank boxes with specific instructions to yourself, stating exactly what you will do during your waking hours.

ALLOWING THE RIGHT AMOUNT OF TIME FOR EACH TASK

You may notice that Tina's schedule allots a different amount of time for each subject. Biology, for example, regularly receives two full hours of her attention. But sociology receives only one hour. Tina allots her time in this way because biology is crucial to her goal of becoming a medical technician, and she finds her biology text more difficult to read than her sociology book. In short her schedule reflects her personal priorities and her learning style.

When you make your weekly schedule, you too must decide which courses are more difficult for you to master or more relevant to your long-term goals. Then you can schedule your time accordingly.

People who use their time well **assign each task the appropriate amount of time.** Tina, for example, knows that she could spend two hours perfecting her lab reports, rewriting her results, and redrawing the cells, but she also knows that thirty minutes is all she can spare. Since the lab report is a small percentage of her biology grade, Tina prefers to spend more time writing a long paper on Thoreau, which counts for 40 percent of her American literature grade.

When you plan your schedule, rank your tasks in order of importance. Do not automatically give each assignment equal time—a common mistake; instead ask yourself questions that will help you establish your priorities:

- How important is the assigned material for mastering the course? (If it is important, give it extra time.)
- How relevant is this course to my long-term goals?
- How will my grade on each assignment, exam, or paper affect my final grade in the course?
- How much time can I allot to the task without taking time away from my other important assignments?

In sum, keep evaluating how much time you are spending in terms of the benefits you will receive. Keep checking your schedule to establish or revise priorities. Think of your schedule as flexible. **Put your time where it helps you most.**

Do not automatically give each assignment equal time—**a common mistake;** Instead ask yourself questions that will help you establish your priorities.

■ PRACTICE 3   Make a list of your assignments for this week. Then give each assignment a letter grade that indicates its importance. The following example shows Ellen Bernardi's list. Ellen plans to become a parole officer, and she has used that goal to establish her priorities.

Assignments

Biology lab report—C
Criminology paper—A
World literature—C
   read pp. 206–236
Psychology—A
   read pp. 100–120

FINDING YOUR HIGH-ENERGY PRIME TIME

To make your schedule work, you must have some idea of your **prime time** for studying. This is the time when your energy level is high, your mind is clear, and your motivation strong.

Research suggests that each of us has a daily "prime time" or times when we study most efficiently. For you that time may be in the morning; for your friend it may be in the evening. By paying careful attention to how well you work at different hours of the day, you will learn to recognize those times when you feel fresher, sharper, and more energetic. Then you can schedule your most difficult classes or tasks as close to your prime time as possible.

Giving Yourself a Break

Breaks are important, even if you are working during your prime time. After reading for several hours, your eyes will get tired. But you can avoid eye strain by looking up from the page every fifteen minutes or so. If you spend a minute or two thinking about what you have just read, you will rest your eyes *and* improve your comprehension.

Like your eyes, your powers of concentration have their limits. After several hours, you will find that even the best intentions cannot help you absorb difficult material. What you need is a break of at least one half hour every two hours. During that time, you should do something physically active: take a walk or jog around the block. Relaxed and refreshed after your break, you can return to your work and find that, once again, you are able to concentrate fully. Studies of human learning repeatedly show the same results: **it is better to have several short learning sessions spaced out at intervals than to have one long unbroken period of work.**

How Some Students Take a Break

"My breaks are always basketball breaks. Shooting baskets helps me relax, and then I can work better."   —David Horowitz

"I listen to music. I close my eyes, and I just sit there thinking about anything but homework. Within a half hour, I'm ready to work again."
—Dana Kline

"I tape the soaps in the afternoon. Then at night when I need a break I flip them on for a half hour or so. They're just the kind of mindlessness I need when my head is really smoking."   —Ed Rosenthal

"I take Ping-Pong™ breaks when I think I can't do anymore. After an hour of Ping-Pong, I'm refreshed and ready to return to my desk."
—Ellen Dallard

"I take a thirty-minute break every two hours. Most of the time I just jump rope. That seems to do the trick."   —Gene Perillo

MAKING A LONG-TERM SCHEDULE

Up until now, we have concentrated on explaining how a written schedule can help you meet your weekly assignments. However, you also need to think about a long-term schedule, one that will keep you working toward completing midterm or end-of-term assignments.

In planning this kind of schedule, we recommend using a large desk calendar that shows you every day of the month at a glance. Once you have such a calendar, you can **record the due dates** of all of your midterm or end-of-term assignments. That, however, is just the first step.

The next step is to apply the principle of divide and conquer. Give yourself not just a list of smaller subtasks but also deadlines for when they are due.

Let's say, for example, that you have a ten- or fifteen-page research paper due on December 21. Having noted that assignment on your calendar, you should next figure out the dates when you expect to have completed your individual subtasks. Your list would look something like this one:

1. By September 7, jot down ideas about the topic.
2. By September 15, look at library resources and make a tentative bibliography.
3. By September 30, read at least two books and three articles.
4. By October 15, write a tentative main idea.
5. By October 30, prepare a list or outline of ideas.
6. By November 7, write the first rough draft.
7. By November 21, revise the first draft.
8. By December 7, finish a second draft.
9. By December 16, complete bibliography.
10. By December 17, finish editing the paper.
11. By December 19, finish typing and proofreading the paper.
12. By December 20, hand in paper.

Every item on this list should also be recorded on your monthly calendar on the date it's due. That way you can use the monthly calendar to guide your weekly schedule, where you will allot the daily time you need to meet each deadline you have assigned yourself.

Your deadlines should help you to monitor and control your time. If they become a source of frustration and anxiety, you may need to extend them. But if an extension of a few days becomes an extension of a week, you need to evaluate your schedule to find out why you are not meeting your deadlines. You may have underestimated the time you would need for each task, or you may be procrastinating, postponing tasks until some vague time in the future.

PRACTICE 4   Select one of your end-of-term assignments and write a list of subtasks for the assignment. Then schedule a deadline for each subtask. If you do not have a specific paper or report due, list the dates when you plan to review for your midterm or final exams.

ANALYZING AND REVISING YOUR SCHEDULE

At times you will have to deal with the unexpected—a cousin may arrive without warning or you may be stricken with the flu. Such temporary inter-

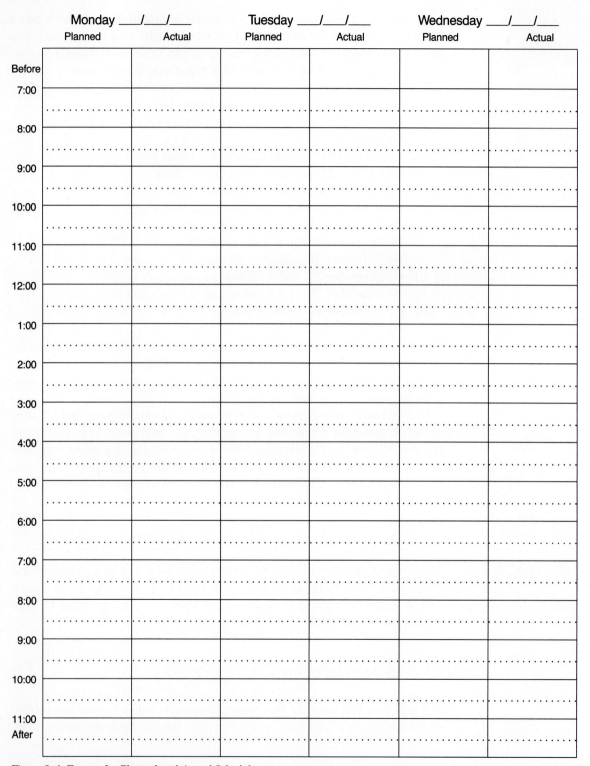

Figure 2–4: Format for Planned and Actual Schedule

ruptions are no reason to revise your basic schedule permanently.

However, you may find that you consistently fail to meet the schedule you have set for yourself. When that is the case, it is your job to discover what is going wrong. One way to do this is to make a schedule like Figure 2–4, where you indicate first what you planned to do and then what you *actually* did.

Analyzing your schedule in this way will help you pinpoint where you may have underestimated the amount of time certain tasks take. You may find, for example, that you cannot read and take notes on thirty pages of biology in one hour and that, realistically, you need two hours to finish thirty pages. To **make your schedule reflect your true pace,** you will assign yourself only fifteen pages for the next day.

You may also discover that you are not following your schedule as closely as you think you are. You may find, for example, that your 9:00 to 11:00 A.M. study period really began at 9:30 because you lingered over a cup of coffee with friends. In addition you left the library early to reserve a basketball court.

It is only by accounting for your time very accurately that you can really find out where it goes. In logging your time every half hour, you may well find that you are wasting not just a few minutes a day but several hours.

> You may find that you consistently fail to meet the schedule you have set for yourself. When that is the case, it is your responsibility to discover what is going wrong.

■   PRACTICE 5   Photocopy Figure 2–4 on page 38 and list what you plan to do with your time for three days this week. Then carry the schedule with you and record how you actually spend your time. When the schedule is complete, compare how you planned to spend your time with how you actually spent it. Is it necessary to revise your schedule?

MAKING A DAILY "TO DO" LIST

Every night I make a list of what I want to do the next day, and I put stars next to the really important things. I do them first. I know some people like to clear the decks and do all the easy things first, but not me.
—Janice Fritz

As the school year progresses, you will become more adept at monitoring your time and may no longer need an hourly schedule. At this point, you may prefer to use a quicker method of scheduling time and establishing priorities. One method to try is a daily **"to do" list,** in which you itemize all of your tasks and highlight the most important ones. The following daily "to do" list was written by Janice Fritz, whom we quoted above. On her list Janice placed asterisks next to any item having a high priority.

<u>To Do Tomorrow</u>

1. Complete at least two math problems.*
2. Review sociology notes.
3. Start review of physics.*
4. Start drafting sociology paper.
5. Go to exhibit of Einstein's papers.
6. Read twenty pages of Einstein's biography.

When you use a daily "to do" list, you can rethink your study plans on an ongoing basis and devise up-to-the-minute strategies for using your time well.

Every night go over your list and cross out completed tasks. If you were not able to complete a few of them, add those tasks to the next day's list, giving them top priority.

Chris Evert scheduled her tasks to achieve her goals. Now she is one of the leading figures in women's tennis.

■ **PRACTICE 6**   Make a "to do" list for the tasks you should complete tomorrow. Remember to asterisk all your high-priority tasks.

MAKING MORE TIME FOR YOURSELF

Finding time begins with an act of will. You also have to look for time in the right places.
—Kenneth Atchity

Are you a person who mistakenly believes that you need a large block of time—two hours or more—to accomplish your tasks? If you are, then you may be wasting stray half hours that could be more fruitful if you plan for them.

If, for example, you travel thirty minutes by bus to a part-time job, you can use that time to read twenty pages of a literature assignment. In case you have to wait to see the dentist, don't waste twenty minutes flipping through old magazines. Instead be prepared: bring along your notebook to review for tomorrow's quiz. Even when you're in the shower or walking to class, see if you can recall the key civil rights cases mentioned in class the day before. Jogging your memory in this way helps reinforce what you have learned. **Always carry some work along with you** that needs to be done, just in case time opens up unexpectedly.

CREATING A FAVORABLE SETTING

If you are serious about managing your time, you need to create a place that will improve your chances of getting work done. Make the scene of your work comfortable. Have enough light, room to spread out, and quiet so that you can become absorbed in the task at hand. According to psychologists who have worked on behavior modification, you **improve your chances for success** if you **remove as many distractions as possible.**

Try to work in one particular place on a regular basis, making your work-place your own special spot. If you like to study in the library, find a carrel and use it every day. If you study at home or in a dormitory, set aside a space that is devoted strictly to work. Your goal is to become a creature of habit who automatically heads toward the designated place for study.

Be sure to have everything you need before you start to study. You don't want to waste twenty minutes looking for your favorite pen. Each evening, when you make up your daily schedule, collect any books, papers, calculators, and pens you think you'll need, and organize them in your backpack or book bag. Don't give yourself a chance to become distracted.

BREAKING THE PROCRASTINATION HABIT

If you want to make an easy job seem mighty hard just keep putting off doing it.
—Michael LeBoeuf

People who procrastinate usually have long-term goals they want to achieve. The problem is they are always putting off the daily work necessary to fulfill or reach those goals. Yes, they do plan to learn Spanish so that they can travel to Spain someday, and, of course, they are going to learn how to use a word processor because it will make writing so much easier for them. The problem is they are always going to do these things tomorrow, not today. But somehow tomorrow never comes because procrastinators keep postponing— and feeling guilty about—what they intend to do.

If procrastinating produces nothing but guilt, why are there so many procrastinators? Some people procrastinate because the tasks they face seem so difficult and demanding that they do not know where to begin. Other people procrastinate because the goal that needs to be achieved is someone else's goal, not their own. These people find it difficult to mobilize their energy and initiative.

But there is a more serious and probably more widespread reason for procrastination—to protect a weak self-image. Unsure of their abilities and fearing failure, many people use procrastination as a way of avoiding being judged or tested. By not putting themselves to the test of achievement, they can always say that they *would* accomplish great things if they *could* only find the time. But unfortunately they can't find the time just now and will have to put those great things off until some future date. In this way they save face and avoid the risk of failure. What's sad about this is that procrastinators may save their pride, but at a terrible cost to themselves. They never work up to their potential, and they let their lives go by without experiencing the thrill that real accomplishment brings.

Battling procrastination is tough, but it can be done, particularly if you follow these guidelines.

1. Know what you want to accomplish.
Target one specific project that you want to accomplish within a specific period of time. The project does not have to apply to a course assignment. While this project may be a paper that you need to write for one of your

A "to do" list will help you use your time wisely.

classes, it may also be a short story that you want to contribute to the college magazine.

2. Let other people know what your project is and when you plan to finish it.
Tell several people you respect what you intend to accomplish. In particular try to find the kind of people who will ask how your work is coming along. Don't pick other procrastinators like yourself. They will avoid asking you about your progress because they don't want you asking them about theirs.

3. Divide and conquer.
Divide your project into a series of subtasks and give yourself deadlines for each and every one. Make sure that the first task on your list takes no more than fifteen minutes to accomplish. Complete that task within twenty-four hours of making your list. After completing that first brief task, cross it off your list and congratulate yourself. Make it a point to tell somebody about your success, openly patting yourself on the back: "I just started a paper that's due three months from now; I really think I'm getting better at not putting things off."

4. Maintain your momentum.
Go on to the next task immediately after completing the first one. Each time you complete a task by its deadline, congratulate yourself or give yourself

some unexpected reward. When you do not finish a task by its deadline, penalize yourself *not by feeling guilty* but by doing something you hate like cleaning your room or doing your laundry. Procrastinators need fixed schedules, and they need to reward themselves for sticking to them. They also need to penalize themselves for failing to follow their time plan.

5. Analyze the causes for postponing your work.

If you find yourself slacking off and falling into your old predictable ways, you need to discover *why* this is happening. You may have taken on a task that is too difficult to accomplish during the time you allotted. If so, rework your schedule to make it more realistic and doable.

Perhaps you fear the assignment will be too hard or too dull. If it looks hard, see if you can figure it out; take it as a personal challenge. Fit the information together piece by piece. You will feel a great sense of achievement if you can conquer and finish it. If you think it might be too dull, give it a chance. It might be more lively than you thought, and even if it turns out to be deadly dull, you still have the invigorating reward of finishing.

If you can't figure out why you are postponing your work, try writing in your journal. Ask yourself questions like these: Fear of failure may lie at the heart of procrastination, but what is so terrible about failing? When I fail, does it mean that I cannot do better the next time? Do I really believe that failure is forever?

6. Do not become discouraged by relapses into old habits.

It is quite natural to fall back into your old habits when you are trying to create new ones. Don't be surprised or angry if you can't stop procrastinating overnight. No one can. However, when you find yourself reverting to old forms of behavior, recite one of your positive motivation statements and tell yourself that you can kick the habit of procrastination; it's just going to take a little time.

Anytime you feel yourself starting to procrastinate, sit down and list for yourself some of the consequences of this seemingly harmless habit; a constant sense of guilt, a mediocre career, unfulfilled potential, and a life of indecision. Is it really worth it?

Procrastinators may save their pride, but at a terrible cost to themselves. They never work up to their potential; they let their lives go by without experiencing the thrill that real accomplishment brings.

WORKING SPACE

READING ASSIGNMENT

Fear of failure is one key reason why many people procrastinate and do not use their time efficiently. In the following article, Michael LeBoeuf, the author of *Working Smart,* offers some suggestions for combating a fear that haunts us all at one time or another.

Fear of Failure

Stop for a moment and think of all the wonderful things in this world that never happened because someone feared failure and hadn't the courage to act. Think of all the books, songs and plays that were never written. Think of all those singers, musicians, painters and sculptors who never developed their talent because they were afraid someone would laugh. Think of all the great labor-saving inventions and cures for presently incurable diseases that were missed because someone was afraid to pursue his far-out theory. And finally, think of all the beautiful relationships that never blossomed because one or both parties feared rejection. This is only a fraction of the price we pay for indulging ourselves in the fear of failure.

The startling fact is that there is no such thing as failure. "Failure" is merely an opinion that a given act wasn't done satisfactorily. As a natural phenomenon* it doesn't exist. Imagine, if you will, one honeybee saying to another, "They put me to work in the hive because I got a 'D' in pollination." Better yet; can you imagine one squirrel telling another, "Max, you're a first-class climber, but your nutcracking is inadequate"? How ludicrous can you get? The fact is animals don't know what failure is. They simply do and enjoy. Failure doesn't stop them because it's totally off their map. If Max can't open a nut, he simply tries another. He doesn't wallow in self-pity or swear to subsist on tree bark for the rest of his life.

Like the other immobilizing emotions, choosing to be governed by the fear of failure has definite payoffs. Being ruled by fear of failure lets you take the easy way out. Rather than accepting the challenge of pursuing a meaningful goal, you can scratch it off your list and tell yourself that success is impossible or not worthwhile.

From *Working Smart,* Michael LeBoeuf, McGraw-Hill Book Company, 1979. Reprinted by permission.
*phenomenon: something that can be identified

Reacting to a fear of failure also provides a false sense of safety and security. You can't lose a race you don't enter. Thus by not doing, you are spared the seemingly needless humiliation of failure. You'll never be a winner but you'll never be a failure either.

If you've ever met with less than success in the past (and who hasn't?), the fear of failure gives you a perfect excuse for not trying in the present or future. After all, what's the point in going to all that trouble for nothing?

Finally, by not trying you give yourself the luxury of becoming a critic. You can put your time and effort into being a spectator and ridiculing all those fools who are out there trying to succeed. The most vociferous* critics are generally frustrated doers who are ruled by their own fear of failure.

Those who give in to their fears and choose the psychological pay-offs overlook one major point. Failure is not a measure of success. In fact, as we already pointed out, failure isn't anything. In life, it isn't what you lose that counts, it's what you gain and what you have left.

If you find yourself immobilized due to fear of failure, here are some ideas to help you overcome it:

1. Set your own standards of success. Remember that failure is arbitrary. Don't allow your life to be ruled by standards other than your own. You don't have to be president of the company because your father was or your wife wants you to be. It's your choice, not theirs.

2. Don't fall into the trap of success-failure thinking. If you set a goal and pursue it, evaluate your own performance in terms of degrees of success.

3. Don't feel you have to succeed or achieve excellence in every-thing you do. There's nothing wrong with a mediocre round of golf (at least that's what I keep telling myself) or a poor set of tennis, as long as you're having fun.

4. Meet your fear of failure head-on. Find something you would like to do but fear failure in, and do it. Even if you don't suc-ceed to the degree you hope to, you won't have any regrets. After all, you will be doing what you want to do. It's better to feel sorry for the things you've done than to regret missed opportunities. All ventures involve risk, but not to venture is to waste your life.

---

* vociferous: noisy

5. If you do feel you have failed, recognize it as a learning experience that will make you wiser and contribute to later successes. Astute young politicians practice this. They join a political race fully realizing they have no chance of winning. However, by throwing their hat in the ring, they get public exposure and learn the ropes of campaigning. All of the exposure and learning can someday contribute to a victorious campaign. We can learn a great deal more from our failures than our successes, provided we avail ourselves of the opportunity.

6. Realize that meaningful success is rarely easy and is usually preceded by a struggle. However, it's those who have the will to see it through that make it. Most of us throw in the towel too soon, when hanging in there a little longer would do the job.

---

1. According to the author, what are some of the benefits of the fear of failure?

2. What did LeBoeuf mean when he wrote, "There is no such thing as failure"? Explain why you agree or disagree with this statement.

3. Does what LeBoeuf wrote apply to you? What would you like to achieve but may not because of your fear of failure?

4. What can you add to LeBoeuf's suggestions for combating the fear of failure?

WRITING ASSIGNMENT: "Carpe Diem"

The Latin phrase *carpe diem* means to seize the day or to grasp the opportunity while it is available. Describe a time when you did not seize the day and lost out on some opportunity or experience you now regret having missed.

JOURNAL ASSIGNMENTS

1. Reread the quotation at the beginning of Chapter 2. How would you interpret the proverb "Life is short, but wide"? What does it mean to you? Even more important, how can you apply it to your own life?

2. Make a list of ways in which you waste time, such as talking on the telephone for hours or taking unnecessary breaks. Then make a second list, describing specific methods you can use to stop wasting time in these ways.

CHECKING OUT

Check your understanding of Chapter 2 by writing answers to the following questions. You may work alone or with a classmate, whichever you prefer.

1. How can you apply the principle of divide and conquer to time management?

2. What is the purpose of making a detailed, written schedule?

3. What is a "to do" list?

4. Why should you regularly study in one particular place?

5. What are some reasons why so many people procrastinate?

IN SUMMARY

Taking charge of your time means paying attention to how and where you spend it. It means giving up the notion that time manages itself without any help from you. You must take charge of your time and your life. Start by scheduling your daily, weekly, and monthly tasks so that you may eventually achieve your long-term goals. Step by step, hour by hour, you are responsible for planning your days and building your future. No one is going to do it for you.

CHAPTER 3

LEARNING AND REMEMBERING

Our ability to retrieve information from our memories is a function of how well it was learned in the first place.

—Josh R. Gerow

OVERVIEW

When people talk about their ability or inability to remember, they usually refer to their memory: "I have a memory like an elephant." "My memory is a sieve." "I don't know what's the matter with my memory." Yet it would actually be more accurate to speak of "memories," since human beings appear to possess at least two different kinds—long-term and short-term.

When you dial the telephone number you've just located in the phone book, you're using **short-term memory,** which stores information for only a few seconds without leaving any permanent trace behind. If someone asked you, even an hour later, to repeat the digits in that number, you would probably draw a blank. Because there was no reason for you to retain the number, your short-term memory discarded it.

But when you respond in class to questions about a chapter you had studied a few weeks ago, you're using your **long-term memory,** which retains information over an extended period of time, maybe even for your lifetime.

The point of all this is that **the transfer of information from short-term to long-term memory is a crucial step in any kind of learning.** It's one you should know more about.

Sometimes the transfer of information takes place spontaneously with no conscious effort on your part—particularly in situations involving great novelty or powerful emotion. Most people, for example, remember every detail of their first kiss, even forty or fifty years later. The emotion and novelty of the event have etched it into their long-term memory; they couldn't forget it if they wanted to.

But few experiences possess the power and novelty of your first kiss. Thus the transfer of information from short-term to long-term memory usually demands thought and effort. You have to make it happen. In this chapter we will show you how.

- Understand the difference between *in-depth remembering* and *verbatim memorization.*
- Distinguish between relevant and irrelevant information.
- Learn how to organize information into chunks.
- Make paraphrasing a habit.
- Personalize new information, linking what you hope to learn to what you already know.
- Take a multilevel approach to remembering: recite, write, and visualize.
- Apply the three principles of effective memorization: overlearning, anticipation, mnemonic devices.

DISTINGUISH BETWEEN IN-DEPTH REMEMBERING AND VERBATIM MEMORIZATION

I'm afraid I won't do well in school because I have a hard time remembering things. In grade school we had to memorize and then recite poems. I could never do it.

—Marla Smithers, student

Marla's complaint is not an unusual one. Many students feel anxious about their ability to remember. Yet in our experience, much of their anxiety stems from the fact that they, like Marla, equate in-depth remembering with verbatim memorization. The two, however, are very different learning activities.

Verbatim memorization relies on your ability to learn and recall the author's or speaker's original words with few substitutions, deletions, or deviations. Verbatim memorization is how you learn a list of names, dates, or definitions. It's the kind of memory work you did in grammar school, where you, like Marla, probably had to learn plays or poems "by heart."

In our experience, when students complain about their inability to remember, many of them mean that they haven't been able to look at a page of notes or listen to a lecture and recall the material **verbatim**—or word for word. They haven't been able to memorize it. But, in fact, there's no reason why they should. Except for those very few people with miraculous memories, verbatim memorization of a whole page or lecture is impossible. More to the point, it is only appropriate for specific kinds of material.

In a language course, for example, it's essential to memorize lists of nouns and verbs while a physiology course will require you to memorize the names of the bones in the human body. On the whole, this kind of word-for-word memorization is necessary when you are studying lists of unrelated facts and random figures that have no internal logic or organization of their own. They just have to be learned exactly as they appear in the original text or lecture.

While memorization certainly plays a role in college study, most of your courses will stress the kind of **in-depth remembering** that makes the author's or speaker's original words less important than the *concept, principle,* or *generalization* they express. For most of what you need to learn in college, understanding the concept will be more important than remembering the exact wording.

Imagine, for example, that your art history book contained the following sentences:

> In Egyptian art, size and placement of people or objects depended on their importance in the society rather than on natural perspective. This is illustrated in Figure 14, where the image of the Pharaoh is represented as twice the size of his servants.

Would memorizing that passage word for word help you respond to this question on an essay exam?

> In Egyptian art, people and objects were represented to show their importance or power; natural perspective did not play a significant role in composition. Pick one of the following paintings and explain, in detail, how the perspective used represents power relationships within Egyptian society.

This question does not require you to recall the author's words. It requires you to understand and apply the concept or generalization communicated by those words. It calls, in short, for in-depth remembering, *not* verbatim memorization.

In-depth remembering takes place when you really dig into a subject by tearing it apart and putting it back together again so that you thoroughly understand it. It's the product of intensive thought and study, as described in Figure 3–1.

Studying to Achieve In-Depth Remembering

Janice Fritz is a good student, well organized and efficient. Here is her approach to studying in order to remember an important passage. She does *not* try to memorize but instead she studies the material so thoroughly that she knows it and can explain it clearly to her classmates.

1. Read the passage carefully to get a sense of the author's message.
2. Then read it again carefully, looking for connections between ideas, that is, how one idea relates to another.
3. Jot down the key terms and ideas in a notebook.
4. Write a label or title beside each paragraph in the text, saying what it covers.
5. Jot down a personal connection to material: "Birds have temperatures in limited range. So do I: my temp ranges between 96 and 102."
6. Identify any spot where meaning is murky; mark for rereading.
7. Recite silently key ideas and how they connect; ask yourself:
   - Can I identify key points and the connections between them?
   - Can I explain this passage clearly to a classmate?

When she has gone through this process, Janice has learned the meaning of the passage thoroughly. She has slowly fitted together the pieces of the text so that they make sense to her. All the pieces add up to a consistent whole, and therefore she is confident she has grasped the author's message. The information is hers to use, to apply in another context, and to know for the exam.

Figure 3–1

When reading textbooks or taking lecture notes, try to distinquish between material that needs to be memorized and the material that needs to be remembered in-depth. Then adapt your methods of study accordingly. Lists of names, dates, and definitions can be studied on the run while you sit on the bus or wait in the doctor's office. Because simple repetition is one of the keys to memorization, you can easily make flash cards or lists to carry with you and look at in your spare moments.

Reserve your more intensive and prolonged study sessions for material that you must learn in-depth rather than memorize. During these sessions, you'll employ much more than simple repetition. In the rest of this chapter, we show you how to select, paraphrase, and personalize new information so that you will be able to remember and apply the concept behind the words.

■ PRACTICE 1   Here are some examples of exam questions. Next to each one, put an I to indicate that in-depth remembering is required or a V to indicate that verbatim memorization is called for.

1. **List the three principal parts for each of the following German verbs:** *hoopen, sprechen,* **and** *ziehen.*
2. **Explain how World War I influenced writers like Ernest Hemingway, F. Scott Fitzgerald, and Gertrude Stein.**
3. **What five elements make up more than 90 percent of the earth's crust by weight?**
4. **Describe the various economic changes that contributed to the Civil War.**
5. **What elements do all proteins contain?**
6. **During the semester we have discussed three different theories of language development. After describing each one in detail, select the one you consider the most accurate and explain why.**
7. **Write down the correct formulas for each of the following metals.**
8. **As you know from your reading, historians differ about the effectiveness of John F. Kennedy's presidency. Some call him a great president. Others claim he had more style than substance. Identify your own position and explain why you think he was an effective or ineffective president.**
9. **After looking carefully at the following diagram, label the bones in the inner ear.**
10. **List the key dates and events that led up to the Seneca Falls Convention in 1848.**

THE KEY: INTEND TO REMEMBER

If you don't make a conscious effort to remember new information, you probably will forget it. For example, if you park your car in a huge, multi-level garage and *don't* make a mental note of where it is, you shouldn't be surprised if you forget its location. When there is no intention to remember, most of us do forget. Therefore, anytime you want to remember something you read or hear, make a mental note of it, saying to yourself, "I must remember this."

In applying this principle, however, you have to **be selective.** Not everything you hear in a lecture or read in a chapter is equally important, so there

Just as bees piece together one large hive out of smaller parts, your short-term memory can work more efficiently if you "chunk" smaller pieces of information into topics.

is no useful reason for remembering every point or detail. In fact, if you try to remember everything, you will do yourself more harm than good. The human memory has an enormous capacity for retaining information. But it has its *limits*. When bombarded with more information than it can handle, the mind responds with confusion.

To deal with the limitations of memory, you have to **evaluate all incoming information, deciding what is essential and what is not,** what to pay attention to and what to ignore. After you have made these decisions, the next step is to make a conscious effort to remember, telling yourself, "I have to remember this; it's important."

GET INTO THE HABIT OF CHUNKING INFORMATION

According to current research on how the memory works, our short-term memories have a limited capacity. It appears that we can attend to and remember only about nine pieces or chunks of information at a time. Initially, that may seem a disheartening piece of news. It sounds as if we can remember very little of what we read or hear. After all, nine isn't a very big number. Or is it?

Actually, it all depends on how you define the word *chunks*. For example, if you try to remember the following series of single digits: 3-1-2-4-8-5-6-4-1-

4-2-3, you will have problems. That's more than nine separate pieces or units of information.

But now try to remember this series: 312-413-514-615. Like most people, you probably found it easier to remember the second set of numbers. That's because it is organized into a pattern containing only four chunks of information. True, each chunk consists of several numbers, but no one said that a chunk of information had to be a single number or word. Chunks can be large or small. Their size depends on the amount of information and how you choose to organize it.

Our point is simply this: Make your short-term and long-term memories work together efficiently by learning how to **chunk information.** This will be easier to do once you have read the following pages and have a clear understanding of how academic readers and writers structure classroom lectures and textbook readings.

THE ESSENTIAL PATTERN: MAIN POINT AND SUPPORTING DETAILS

Academic writers and speakers usually organize their lectures and writings around a **main point** or generalization. A **generalization** groups together, summarizes, or interprets a wide variety of individual experiences or events. Therefore, when you listen to a lecture or read a textbook, be alert for general statements like these:

Generalization 1: Other thinkers prior to Charles Darwin helped pave the way for the theory of evolution, which undermined the Victorian belief that species were not subject to change.

Generalization 2: Recent evidence indicates that scientists may have found a way to control symptoms of the common cold.

Generalization 3: In a terrible cycle of violence, abused children often grow up to be abusive parents.

General statements like these usually raise questions in a alert reader. Skillful readers ask themselves: Who were these other thinkers who preceded Darwin? What evidence is there that scientists can help a cold? How do we know that abused children grow up to be abusive parents? To answer these questions, academic speakers and writers provide a series of more specific statements designed to convince and clarify. These are the **supporting details.**

Although supporting details can take many forms—illustrations, statistics, exceptions, studies, and reasons—their function is always the same: they explain and elaborate the writer's or speaker's main point. Look, for example, at the way supporting details clarify each of the three generalizations introduced above:

Generalization 1: Other thinkers prior to Charles Darwin helped pave the way for the theory of evolution, which undermined the Victorian belief that species were not subject to change.

Supporting Details: In 1753 George de Buffon proposed that some animals had apparently evolved over time.

Jean-Baptiste Lamarck, a protégé of Buffon, suggested that human beings had developed from other species.

A decade later, Erasmus Darwin, the grandfather of Charles, stressed the importance of competition in the formation of species.

Generalization 2: Recent evidence indicates that scientists may have found a way to control symptoms of the common cold.

Supporting Details: Several studies indicate that cold symptoms are caused by *kinins*, normal proteins that cold viruses stimulate in the body.

Scientists hope to use a kinin-blocking drug that would inhibit or eliminate the cold.

Scientists feel it is more useful to treat the symptoms of a cold rather than to wait for the development of a cure, such as a vaccine.

Generalization 3: In a terrible cycle of violence, abused children often grow up to be abusive parents.

Supporting Details: They grow up feeling that physical violence is a natural response to stress.

Because abusive parents have a poor self-image, they often abuse the child who is most like themselves.

Filled with self-hatred, abusive parents are, nevertheless, unable to control their behavior.

Understanding how academic speakers and writers organize their material is the first step toward learning how to chunk and remember new information effectively. The next step is to know the kinds of questions that will help you reduce your lectures and readings to a manageable number of chunks.

1. What is the main point? What generalization, principle, or concept does the author or speaker want to explain?
2. What supporting details explain the main point?
3. Which supporting details are important to my personal understanding of the main point?

We'll use the following excerpt to illustrate how questions like the above can help you chunk information.

Sex Drives and Sexual Behavior

As a physiologically based drive, the sex drive is unique in a number of ways. First, the survival of the individual does not depend on its satisfaction. If we don't drink, we die; if we don't regulate our temperature, we die; it we don't eat, we die. If we don't have sex—well, we don't die. The survival of the *species* requires that an adequate number of its members respond successfully to a sex drive, but an individual member can get along without doing so.

Second, most physiologically based drives, including hunger, thirst, and temperature regulation, provide a mechanism to replenish and maintain the body's energy. When satisfied, the sex drive depletes bodily energy. In fact, the sex drive motivates the organism to seek tension, as opposed to those drives that seek to reduce tension to return to homeostasis.*

Third, to the extent that the sex drive is physiologically based, it is based in the activity of the autonomic nervous system and the hormones produced there. Although hormones may play a role in other physiologically based drives, their influence is thought to be minimal; in relation to sex drive, hormones are often of prime importance. The hypothalamus does play a role in the sex drive, but hormones are most immediately involved in activating sexual responsiveness.

Fourth, a related point about the sex drive that makes it different from the rest is that it is not present at birth, but requires a level of maturation (puberty) before it is apparent. The other drives are present, and even most critical, early in life.

—Josh R. Gerow, *Psychology: An Introduction*

---

homeostasis: tendency of living things to maintain a constant internal environment

Typically writers of textbooks introduce their main point within the first three paragraphs, and this excerpt is no exception. The key generalization appears in the first sentence: The sex drive is unique.

Aware that readers might not know exactly how the sex drive is unique, the author itemizes the four essential differences between this drive and other drives. Although the author uses four paragraphs to describe these differences, we can reduce these paragraphs to four brief chunks of information: (1) failure to satisfy the sex drive does not result in death; (2) the sex drive depletes the body's energy while other drives replenish that energy; (3) hormones play a prime role; (4) unlike other drives, this one is not present at birth.

At this point, it is up to the individual reader to decide how many chunks of information he or she should *intend* to remember. Most readers, for example, are fully aware that people who do not have sex don't die. Therefore we can further reduce the amount of information to be integrated into long-term memory.

Generalization: The sex drive is unique.

Supporting Details: 1. Instead of replenishing bodily energy, the sex drive depletes it.
2. Hormones are more important than they are to other drives.
3. Sex drive is not present at birth.

But then again, chunking is a very individual process, and readers with a background in physiology, already familiar with the study of life processes, might need to remember only one or two ways in which the sex drive differs from other drives. Because how you chunk depends on the type of material and your familiarity with it, chunking is a creative skill you can use to improve your ability to remember.

> Understanding how academic speakers and writers organize their material is the first step toward learning how to chunk and remember new information effectively.

PRACTICE 2   In each of the following sets of sentences, one sentence is more general than the others. It could serve as the main point of a lecture or reading. Put a check next to the more general sentence.

1. a. Visual communication is particularly important among certain fish, birds, and insects.
   b. Female grackles solicit the attention of males by fluttering their wings.
   c. Fireflies use flashes of light to attract one another's attention.

2. a. Although it's commonly assumed that lie detectors can, without error, separate the innocent from the guilty, nothing is further from the truth.
   b. In one case, a criminal easily outwitted the lie detector by using meditation techniques that kept his pulse and heartbeat calm and under control, even when he was lying.
   c. Lie detectors are subject to a variety of errors.

3. a. Throughout his life, George Orwell, the author of *1984* and *Animal Farm,* pursued a variety of occupations.
   b. In his youth, Orwell was a policeman in the Burmese army.
   c. Although his term of service lasted a little more than five years, Orwell hated being a policeman.

4. a. Titian, the sixteenth-century painter, was inspired by the story of Susannah and the elders.
   b. In Titian's painting, Susannah is bathing while one of the elders hides in the background.
   c. The Bible has frequently been a source of artistic inspiration.

5. a. Greenpeace is a non-violent organization devoted to the preservation of the sea and its inhabitants.
   b. In their ship, the *Rainbow Warrior,* Greenpeace volunteers track ships they believe might be harmful to the ocean environment.
   c. In 1985, the *Rainbow Warrior* was severely damaged by saboteurs who wanted to stop Greenpeace's anti-nuclear demonstrations.

■ PRACTICE 3   Read the following selections. Then in the blanks that follow, list the chunks of information you would store in long-term memory if you were to be tested on this material.

Research on Meditation

There is no doubt that many people can enter meditative states of consciousness. The doubts that have arisen about meditation cen-

ter on the claims for the psychological experiences and benefits '
that can be derived from meditating.

One of the major claims for meditation is that it is a reasonably
simple and very effective way to enter a state of relaxation.
Indeed, the reduction of arousal is taken to be the main advantage
of meditation. The claim is that by meditating, one can slow bodily
processes and enter a state of physical as well as psychological
calm.

Recently, David Holmes (1984) reviewed the experimental evidence for somatic (bodily) relaxation through meditation. On a
number of different measures of arousal/relaxation, including
heart rate, respiration rate, muscle tension, and oxygen consumption, Holmes found *no differences* between meditating subjects
and subjects who were simply resting or relaxing. After reviewing
the data of dozens of experiments, Holmes concluded, ". . . there
is not a measure of arousal on which the meditating subjects were
consistently found to have reliably lower arousal than resting subjects. Indeed, the most consistent finding was that there were not
reliable differences between meditating and resting subjects. Furthermore, there appear to be about as many instances in which
the meditating subjects showed reliably higher arousal as there
are instances in which they showed reliably lower arousal than
their resting counterparts."

Another claim that is often made about meditation is that people
who practice meditation are better able to cope with stress, or
pressure, or threatening situations than are people who do not
practice meditation. Once again, Holmes (1984) reports that he
could find *no* evidence to support this claim. In fact, in four of the
studies he reviewed, Holmes found that under mild threat, meditating subjects showed *greater* arousal than did nonmeditating
subjects.

—Josh R. Gerow, *Psychology: An Introduction*

_____

_____

_____

_____

Mindbenders

For some reason, a lot of people don't seem to like the minds they were born with. A great deal of our energy, it seems, is spent in finding ways to "bend" our minds and change our moods. And (in spite of popular beliefs) the search is not a new one. With all the universal problems facing our ancestors, they immediately set about learning to make booze. Also, we find hallucinogens were important in many of our earliest known cultures. The search for mindbenders continues today, however, in ways our ancestors could only imagine. (The ancient Greeks, for example, were not big on sniffing transmission fluid.) So some of the things we will mention here have been with us for ages, while others are so new that we really don't know how they act or what their long-term effects are.

We can begin by noting that "drugs" are psychoactive agents. That is, they can alter mood, memory, attention, control, judgment, time-and-space sense, emotion, and sensation. Fortunately, probably none do all of these at once. Most can be placed along a continuum between stimulation (an excitatory state) and depression (a state of reduced mental activity). Here, we will review a few general principles about a few of the major groups. Not unexpectedly, we will find that all have potential for abuse.

Abuse may arise because of our tendencies to overdo the drug or to overly rely on the drugs. Overuse can cause dependence or addiction. There are two major forms of drug dependence. Physical dependence occurs when the drug is necessary simply to maintain bodily comfort. It's disuse causes sometimes agonizing discomfort (called withdrawal symptoms). Psychological dependence exists where a drug is necessary for mental or emotional comfort. Withdrawal symptoms here can be as severe as they are for physical dependence.

—Robert A. Wallace, *Biology:*
The World of Life

_____

_____

_____

_____

_____

THE POWER OF PARAPHRASING

Try to remember material you have not truly understood, and you won't be able to integrate the new information into your existing store of knowledge. That's what makes paraphrasing so important. When you can **paraphrase by translating an author's or speaker's words into your own,** you can rightly say that you have understood those words. And make no mistake: Understanding is the first prerequisite of in-depth remembering.

The point of paraphrasing is to substitute your words for someone else's— without altering the original meaning of those words. You can add or delete words. You can change the length and order of sentences. But you cannot change the original point or insight. We'll use the following passages to illustrate.

> **Original Text:** Speech and sex are linked in obvious ways. Let the reader, if he doubts this, start talking like a member of the opposite sex for a while and see how long people let him get away with it.
> —Edward Hall, *The Silent Language*

> **Paraphrased Version:** Your gender noticeably affects how you speak. Men and women who do not agree with this should try speaking like a member of the opposite sex for a time. Nobody would let them continue with it for very long without making some comment.

Now compare the original text with the paraphrased version. The language differs and so does the length, but the meaning is approximately the same. This is an example of successful paraphrasing. The same is not true, however, of the statement that follows:

> **Inaccurate Paraphrase:** The way you speak affects people's attitude toward you. People distrust men who talk like women or women who talk like men.

This paraphrase distorts the meaning of the original, which says nothing about any kind of value judgment placed on people who don't follow the speech patterns of their gender. In this case, more than the words have been changed. The meaning has been altered as well.

■ PRACTICE 4   Each of the following sentences describes an aspect of human creativity. Paraphrase each one, being sure to retain the meaning while altering the language.

1. Reading is to the mind what exercise is to the body.
   —Augustus Hare

   _____

   _____

2. Employ your time in improving yourself by other men's writing
   so that you shall come easily by what others have labored for.
   —Socrates

   _____

   _____

3. The foolishest book is a kind of leaky boat on a sea of wisdom;
   some of the wisdom will get in anyway. —Oliver Wendell Holmes

   _____

   _____

4. Creativity is so delicate a flower that praise tends to make it
   bloom while discouragement often nips it in the bud.
   —Alex F. Osborn

   _____

   _____

5. The preschool years are often described as some golden age of
   creativity, a time when every child sparkles with artistry. As
   those years pass, however, it seems that a kind of corruption
   takes over, so that ultimately most of us mature into artistically
   stunted adults. —Howard Gardner

   _____

   _____

CONNECTING THE UNFAMILIAR TO THE FAMILIAR

The extent to which we remember a new experience has more to do with how it relates to existing memories than with how many times or how recently we have experienced it.
—Morton Hunt

Research suggests that we remember more readily when we can link the unfamiliar to the familiar. To put this theory into practice, we suggest you make every attempt to **personalize new information,** linking it any way you can to your own individual experience, background, and knowledge. These personal associations not only will improve your understanding of the material but also will help you remember it. They will give you a way of retrieving new and unfamiliar information.

Having learned, for example, that an extra twenty-first chromosome causes Down's syndrome, you may connect that information to your neighbor's child, a lovable little girl born with this condition. Later on, when trying to remember the cause of Down's syndrome, you will think first of the little girl and then of the genetic abnormality that caused her illness.

For another illustration, take the example of student Paul Keys, who wanted to be sure that he learned the term *biogenesis,* which is important in the study of biology. When the definition was given in a lecture, he carefully recorded it: "The concept that life comes only from life under conditions that now prevail on earth." But in order to remember it, Paul did more than record the definition; he made a conscious effort to personalize it by linking his own personal experience to the original definition.

> biogenesis: "The concept that life comes only from life under conditions that now prevail on earth." You can't make live things out of dead ones, at least not given earth's present conditions. In the movie, *The Bride of Frankenstein,* both the monster and his bride defy the theory of biogenesis by being created out of dead people.

When you study, try to create links between what you are learning and what you already know. Look for ways in which the new material is similar to or different from your individual knowledge and experience. Those associations may mean nothing to someone else. After all, for those who have never seen *The Bride of Frankenstein,* Paul's notes might not be very useful. But that's not important. What's important is that you **forge a link between yourself and the material you are studying.**

Elsa Lancaster as the bride of Frankenstein. Personalize what you know and what you are learning.

TAKE A MULTILEVEL APPROACH TO REMEMBERING

All too often, when we try to remember something, we rely on one method of recording that information. We use just our ears or just our eyes. We use words but not pictures. We write but don't recite. Yet studies show that people understand and retain new information more effectively if they use what we call a multilevel approach, one that combines words with pictures, seeing with hearing, and writing with reciting.

For example, if you are reading a detailed description of how an organism looks, functions, or develops, don't just rely on words. Use your imagination to create a mental picture of the thing described, and visualize it in as much detail as possible. When you are finished creating your mental picture, get a blank sheet of paper and make a **drawing** or a diagram based on your visual image.

And don't forget recitation. Studies show that people who recite key points to themselves while they read remember material more readily than those who don't use recitation. Much like paraphrasing, **recitation** helps the short-term memory retain new information longer, thereby giving long-term memory a chance to respond, organize, and record. If, like some students, you feel awkward reciting aloud because you don't want to be seen talking to yourself, try to study with a friend. Then you can take turns reciting to each other. However you do it, silently or aloud, you'll find that the extra time spent reciting works to your advantage.

Although many studies show that the ability to visualize is a crucial element in creative thinking, our culture does not encourage **visualization.** If you, like most of us, have difficulty using visualization as a learning technique, take some time to work on the directed visualization exercise that follows.

> To understand and retain new information more effectively, take a multilevel approach, one that combines pictures with words, seeing with hearing, and writing with reciting.

■ PRACTICE 5   Read this passage. Then follow our directions for visualizing what you have read.

> **Nimbostratus clouds are thick grayish or white clouds that appear in the form of a patchy series of sheetlike masses in the sky. They are usually composed of water droplets, occasionally of ice crystals. When you see nimbostratus clouds, rain—or some other form of precipitation—is likely.**
>
> **—Joseph S. Weisberg, *Meteorology***

Now create your mental image step by step. Begin by imagining one thick gray or white cloud. Then imagine several that form "sheetlike masses." Next make your mind's eye zoom in on one cloud in particular and see its composition of "water droplets." Once you can visualize the clouds, get a pencil and some paper and write your own description of nimbostratus clouds.

THREE PRINCIPALS OF VERBATIM MEMORIZATION

Because you will take courses in which verbatim remembering is required, you should know and apply three principles of effective memorization: (1) combine anticipation with repetition, (2) overlearn to make relearning easier, and (3) use mnemonic devices whenever possible.

Combine Anticipation with Repetition

Most students know that memorization requires some form of repetition. If given a list of names or dates to learn, they dutifully look at it over and over again. But there is a better way to memorize, a more active method that combines anticipation with repetition and decreases the time needed for learning isolated facts, figures, or names. The trick is to arrange the dates, definitions, or terms you want to learn so that you can **first anticipate** the correct answer and **then check** to see if you were correct.

gene	the unit of heredity
allele	one or two alternative forms of a gene
gene frequency	the proportion of an allele in a population relative to the proportions of other alleles
chromosomes	the cellular structure that contains the genes
DNA	deoxyribonucleic acid, the chemical of the gene
gene pool	the entire genetic makeup of a population
cytosine	a pyrimidine base, important to the structure of DNA

With a list like this one, you can first anticipate what each term means and then look to see if you were correct. This kind of **self-testing** is a more active method of memorization because it forces you to search your memory for the right answer *before* you confirm or contradict it by looking at your list. Although this method will probably increase the time you spend on individual memorizing sessions, it will decrease the overall number of sessions. Above all, you'll discover that combining anticipation with repetition anchors the information more firmly in your memory so that you retain it longer.

Overlearn to Make Reviewing and Exams Easier

Overlearning during the early stages of studying will make relearning during exam reviews considerably easier. So don't stop your memorization sessions the first time you correctly anticipate every answer. Instead, **overlearn the material** by giving yourself at least two more study sessions to review the memorized material. You'll find that the material you learned in November for midterms will come back to you more readily in December when finals roll around. Because your long-term memory has so thoroughly recorded the memorized information, relearning will be easier than it would have been if you had stopped after your first successful session of memorizing.

Most important, overlearning is the best way to reduce test anxiety. You *know* that you know the material.

Use Mnemonic Devices

Mnemonic devices are nothing more than jingles, rhymes, sayings, or names designed to help you recall information you have committed to memory. Although you may not realize it, you have probably been using mnemonic devices for years in order to remember isolated pieces of information that are otherwise difficult to retain in memory. In the spring or fall, for example, many people use the mnemonic device "Spring forward, fall backward" as a way of remembering how they should set their clocks. Likewise many young music students memorize the notes of a musical staff by using two different mnemonic devices, one for lines, "Every good boy deserves favors"; the other for spaces, "Face."

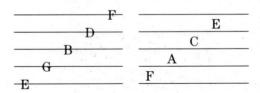

For years zoology students have used the sentence "King Philip came over from Greece singing" in order to remember the categories into which all living things are divided: kingdom, phylum, class, order, family, genus, and species.

Although many mnemonic devices are passed on from generation to generation, you can certainly create your own. One ingenious student invented the sentence "Sam Marlowe hated Ernest Owen" in order to remember the names and order of the Great Lakes: Superior, Michigan, Huron, Erie and Ontario.

While mnemonic devices can take many forms—words, rhymes, or songs—their function is always the same: they help you memorize separate bits of information that cannot be associated or linked in any meaningful way.

Some Useful Strategies for Learning and Remembering

1. Translate the author's or speaker's words into your own language.

2. Create a mental image of what you read or hear. If possible, turn that image into a moving picture.

3. Draw your own diagrams, charts, or time lines.

4. Even if you agree with what you read or hear, think of possible objections that someone with a different perspective might raise.

5. Create your own concrete examples of important generalizations. Think of how these generalizations might apply to your own life.

6. Think of exceptions to the generalization being discussed.

7. Develop analogies in which you liken one process to another.

8. Mentally, or on paper, reduce arguments to their most skeletal structure, identifying the author's or speaker's claim as well as the reasons used to support that claim.

9. Use the margins of your textbook or notes to keep a running dialogue with the speaker or author.

10. Tape a passage of your textbook. Then play the tape and write what you think of while you hear it.

11. After finishing a section, see if you can recite the key points.

12. Start a discussion group in which you informally discuss what you are learning.

Figure 3–2

■   PRACTICE 6   For each column, invent a mnemonic device that will help you memorize the names of the planets and the elements of the periodic table.

Planets
Mercury
Venus
Earth
Mars
Jupiter
Saturn
Uranus
Neptune
Pluto

Elements
Hydrogen
Helium
Lithium
Beryllium
Boron
Carbon
Nitrogen
Oxygen
Fluorine
Neon

WORKING SPACE

READING ASSIGNMENT

The following article by Morton Hunt describes some of the powers of memory. Read the article and answer the accompanying questions.

The Strengths (and Occasional Failings) of Human Memory

—The human memory spontaneously compresses information into what researchers call "chunks." A chunk is any coherent* group of items of information that we can remember as if it were a single item: a word is a chunk of letters, remembered as easily as a single letter (but carrying much more information; a well-known date—say, 1776—is remembered as if it were one digit; and even a sentence, if familiar ("A stitch in time saves nine"), is remembered almost as effortlessly as a much smaller unit of information. . . . A chess master has roughly 50,000 patterns of pieces (board situations) stored in memory; by means of these chunks, he can rapidly recognize what is

———————
*coherent: related, unified

happening in a game and make his moves without deep analysis, whereas the novice must laboriously work out the outcome of each possible move. In the same way, the person with a good deal of experience in business and social life has chunked all sorts of interpersonal information, and can therefore recognize at a glance what is happening in many a situation and act appropriately; the novice flounders and makes gaffes.*

—The ability of actors and opera singers to commit long roles to memory through study and repetition impresses most of us. But equally impressive is what we all do every day with material we see or hear only once: We remember not the precise form but the meaning. Within a handful of seconds (by actual laboratory measurement) we forget the verbatim details of a heard or read sentence, yet remember its content. Chances are that right now you can accurately restate the substance of the first sentence of this paragraph—dealing with actors and opera singers—but are unable to recall its exact wording. We do this all the time, with virtually everything we experience; the system in our heads files away a great deal of meaning without any need for repetition or memorization.

—Dr. Stephen M. Kosslyn, a young psychologist I met at Harvard (he is now at Brandeis), has for several years been exploring the ways we use visual images stored in memory; he has come up with some striking discoveries, one of which he demonstrated to me with great simplicity. "Imagine a tiny bee, off in the distance," he said, and I did so. "Now," he said, "tell me: does the bee have a dark head or a light head?" My eyes went blank as I did what he knew I would do—zoomed in mentally to take a closer look. (The bee, I saw, had a dark head.) Kosslyn had made his point: we use stored images as if they were film or tape that we project in the mind, and then inspect them as if they had become actual pictures. A lot of thinking takes place in this way: we use stored images to answer questions such as how to get from where we are to some other place, whether the trunk of the car will hold all our luggage, and so on. Some psychologists even maintain that much of our most important and creative thinking takes place in images rather than in words.

We rarely notice any of these powers of memory: what we notice are its limitations or defects. We are often aware, for instance, that we cannot recall things we think we know like the back of our own hands—which, in fact, we don't know all that well; try, without look-

---

*gaffes: mistakes

ing, to visualize the back of your own hand in detail, and then look and see how much you've missed. Try to draw a telephone dial that you have used a thousand times this past half year; you'll be surprised. Or try to draw a common penny: including the features on both sides, there are eight things to be remembered, but in one recent study most people could recall and correctly locate only three. . . .

Here are a few other limitations of memory of which we are often, and uncomfortably, aware:

—Under stress we may forget things that we know well. Junior executives, at a company dinner, may fumble the name of the superior they are introducing to their mate. Performers about to go onstage to make a debut may forget the words or music they have rehearsed so long and thoroughly; desperate efforts to remember are of no avail. Cognitive science has an explanation: the stressful input takes up most of the mind's conscious equipment and so impedes* the retrieval of information from long-term memory. . . .

—At times we are unable to think of some word or name we know but use only occasionally. We may feel we almost have it—for instance, we feel sure it starts with *b*, or has three syllables, or has the sound "on" in it (and research shows that such intimations† are correct more often than not)—yet the word "bubonic" remains tantalizingly on the tip of the tongue. The suggested explanation: we file words and names in memory in several ways—by their meaning, by their initial sound, and so on—but with infrequently used words or names, these cues may not supply enough information to lead us to the word or name; we need still more. . . .

—Events we witness do not always, or even usually, remain unchanged in memory; we fill in missing details by inference, or alter them in accordance with questions we are asked or suggestions made to us, and have no way of retrieving the original—and are not even aware that anything has happened to it. Elizabeth Loftus of the University of Washington, who . . . specializes in memory research, has shown brief films of auto accidents to students and then asked them loaded questions about what they saw. When she asked, "Did you see the broken headlight?" one out of every seven said yes, although no broken headlight had appeared. She also showed students a videotape of a disruption of a class by eight demonstrators; then she asked half the students, "Was the leader of the four demonstrators who

---

*impedes: hinders, blocks
†intimations: hints

entered the room a male?" but, with the other half, replaced the word "four" by the word "twelve." A week later she asked both groups how many demonstrators there had been; the answers of the "four" group averaged 6.4, while those of the "twelve" group averaged nearly 9.

Similarly, as other studies have shown, all of us continually revise our memories of our lives to harmonize with the events that have happened or are happening to us; we are unable to distinguish between what really happened and what we now think happened, since the original memory no longer exists. In one study, a majority of people interviewed in 1964 and again in 1974 recalled, at the second interview, earning a considerably higher income and having far greater work drive in 1964 than had been the case.

---

1.   What makes one person better than another at chunking?

2.   How does stress affect memory?

3.   According to Hunt, is eyewitness testimony absolutely reliable? Cite the portions of the article that support your response.

4.   Given what Hunt says about how we remember the past, do you think he would consider an autobiography to be fiction or nonfiction? Explain your answer by referring to statements in the article.

WRITING ASSIGNMENT: "Remembrance of Things Past"

Describe a childhood experience that you did not consciously try to remember but which, nevertheless, has stayed with you all of your life. Begin by describing the experience in as much detail as possible. In the final paragraphs, explain what it was about the experience that etched it so deeply in your memory. Was it the novelty, the intensity of emotion, or the insight the experience offered that made it stay with you while other experiences faded and disappeared?

JOURNAL ASSIGNMENTS

1. Ask yourself if you have been making progress in the management of your time. If you answer yes, write a paragraph explaining how you know that you have made progress. If your answer is no, write a paragraph defining the specific problems that are keeping you from efficiently managing your time.

2. Review the list of motivation techniques offered on pages 12–14 in Chapter 1. Check off the techniques you have used. If you haven't used any, select at least two and put them into practice, not tomorrow but today.

3. How would you paraphrase the following quotation by the writer Hart Crane: "One must be drenched in words, literally soaked in them, to have the right ones form themselves into the proper pattern at the right moment."

CHECKING OUT

Check your understanding of Chapter 3 by writing answers to the following questions. You may work alone or with a friend, whichever you prefer.

1. What is the difference between in-depth remembering and verbatim memorization?

2. Why is paraphrasing important?

3. What does it mean to personalize new information?

4. What do you do when you chunk information?

5. What is the essential pattern of presentation used in academic textbooks and lectures? Describe it.

6. What does it mean to take a multilevel approach to remembering?

7. What are the three principles of memorization?

IN SUMMARY

Students who worry about remembering what they read or hear in school usually worry for the wrong reasons. They assume that remembering requires them to retain the author's or speaker's exact words. Yet, for the most part, the author's or speaker's language is less important than the point or meaning he or she hopes to convey.

In the majority of cases, you will be better off if you paraphrase what you hear or read, changing the words while retaining the meaning. *And don't stop there.* If you really want to remember a key concept or principle, find a way to personalize it by linking it to your own personal experience or knowledge. In addition, use as many senses as possible to anchor that new information firmly in memory. Write. Recite. Visualize.

For those times when you do need to remember verbatim, or word for word, you can make that task much less difficult by applying the three basic principles introduced in this chapter: (1) combine anticipation with repetition, (2) overlearn to make relearning easier, and (3) use mnemonic devices whenever possible.

CHAPTER 4

THE ART OF LISTENING AND NOTETAKING

The best listeners listen alertly, expecting to learn something and to help create new ideas.
—Stuart Chase

OVERVIEW

Some people have a knack for listening. While you are talking, they watch your face with an attentive expression. When you finish, they respond with a question or comment that shows they have understood exactly what you were trying to say.

But you must have noticed that some people are not such good listeners. As you speak, they look everywhere but at you. When you finish, they respond with a question or comment that seems to belong to another conversation. They may even ask you the very same question you thought you had answered five minutes before.

Listening is an art. But it's one that not all of us have mastered. As a matter of fact, research suggests that the ability to listen often begins to decline at an early age, somewhere around the time we leave elementary school. It's as if the more chances we have to speak, the less time we take to listen.

The lack of good listening skills is a problem—not just because it may cause you to lose friends. It can also seriously limit your chances of succeeding in school. Since lectures are a primary source of how information is dispensed in college, good listeners have an advantage. They understand and remember more; they take better notes; and they respond more quickly to questions.

We therefore suggest that you make a commitment to improving your listening skills. To help you fulfill that commitment, the following chapter offers some specific suggestions for becoming a more skillful and more attentive listener:

- Think of listening as a process that demands your full and alert participation.
- Take specific steps to become a better listener.
- Maintain your concentration, no matter how early the hour or how poor the speaker.
- Recognize the various ways instructors tell their listeners to pay attention.
- Adapt your method of taking notes to the material being discussed.
- Use a notetaking format that gives you room to write.
- Get into the habit of reading and revising your lecture notes during after-class reviews.
- Ask questions in class.

DEVELOPING A LISTENING FRAME OF MIND

On the surface, listening to lectures might seem a passive activity that requires little more than an acute sense of hearing. However, that's like saying that anyone with good vision is a good reader. And you know that's not true. You can have twenty-twenty vision but still have difficulty understanding what you read. By the same token, you might be able to hear a pin drop from ten feet away yet leave a lecture hall without having understood the speaker's message. It all depends on your frame of mind, on your willingness to **take responsibility for learning from lectures.** If you sit through a class without following the lecture closely, there's a good chance the speaker's voice will become just so much background noise.

Although the ability to hear is an obvious prerequisite to good listening, it is the power of your mind—not your ears—that allows you to absorb and remember what you hear. While outwardly quiet and still, good listeners are mentally in motion. As soon as the lecture begins, they **listen for some statement of purpose** that will define the speaker's general objective or goal. Is it to outline the steps of the scientific method or to describe some of the controversies surrounding mandatory drug testing? Good listeners know that identifying the speaker's purpose will help them during the lecture to decide what is crucial information and what is not.

Skillful listening, like skillful reading, demands your full participation. You have to work with a speaker much like you have to work with an author; your tasks are to discover the overall purpose or goal of the lecture, identify the essential information, and infer the appropriate connections between ideas.

With all this to do, you cannot walk into a classroom or lecture hall and assume it is the speaker's job to make everything clear to you while you sit back and relax. After all, if you don't get anything out of the lecture, you're the one who has the most to lose. It's your grade that will suffer.

Above all, remember that listening is not some natural ability like breathing, which needs no training. Good listening is an art. Like any other art or skill, it can be improved through conscious study and practice. Start today to discover your strengths and weaknesses as a listener, making a determined commitment to develop the former and eliminate the latter.

> Skillful listening, like skillful reading, demands your full participation.

■ PRACTICE 1   Schedule a few minutes a day just to practice listening. The following are a few of the things you can do.

1. **Go for a walk and listen for five different sounds.**
2. **Take turns with a friend, reading brief passages of prose. After each reading, see how well you can translate the passages into your own words.**
3. **Listen to news programs on the radio. After each news item, mentally paraphrase key points.**
4. **Listen to the noises in your house or room. How many different noises do you hear?**

FIVE STRATEGIES FOR BETTER LISTENING

In the previous pages, we encouraged you to think about listening as an active process that demands your full participation and concentration. Now we want to identify five specific things you can do to improve the way you listen to lectures.

1. Prepare for a lecture before you hear it.

Research in reading shows that the more background knowledge you have about a subject, the more easily you will understand the author's message. Research on listening supports a similar conclusion: the more you know about a lecture *before* you hear it, the more easily you will follow the speaker's train of thought.

In practical terms, this means you should attempt to deepen and enrich your knowledge of the topic or subject being lectured upon. Let's say, for example, that your syllabus announces the title of every lecture. Before each one, look through your textbook to find out what chapters cover the same or related topics. A quick scanning of those chapters the day before the lecture will markedly improve your ability to understand and remember the speaker's key points when you do finally hear them.

If you don't know the title or subject of the next lecture, you should, in any case, review your notes from the previous lectures. Usually each new lecture builds upon or refers to points made in earlier ones. It's to your benefit, therefore, to have a clear understanding of any material previously introduced. Ideally, you should both review earlier lectures and get a jump on the new material by reading ahead in your text.

2. Keep an open mind.

Yes, it helps to have advance knowledge about the subject of a lecture. But you have to be careful not to let prior knowledge prejudice your reaction to the lecture. Imagine that you had prepared for a lecture on Nathaniel Hawthorne's *The Scarlet Letter* by doing some "suggested reading"—in this case a critical work on Hawthorne. You had read and liked an essay claiming that Hawthorne's heroine, Hester Prynne, reflected his feminist sympathies because she lived life on her own terms. But when you went to the lecture on the novel, your instructor took an opposite approach, arguing that Hawthorne was an anti-feminist, who used Hester to illustrate the intolerable loneliness and isolation awaiting an independent woman who defied authority.

Having decided beforehand that you agreed with the interpretation offered in the essay, you might be tempted to close your mind to the rest of the lecture. *Don't do it.* Instead keep an open mind and listen to the lecture closely. Then, when you have more time, compare both viewpoints and decide which one makes the more sense.

3. Maintain a positive mental attitude.

It is possible to dislike thoroughly the subject of a lecture as well as the lecturer. But giving in to those negative feelings can only interfere with your resolution to become an alert listener. If you enter a classroom thinking,

"This is going to be a real bore," you have given yourself a harmful message. No matter what you feel toward the instructor or the subject, listen with a positive mental attitude, replacing negative feelings with constructive statements like the following: "I'm going to find a way into this subject and discover a perspective that interests me." "If I listen closely, maybe I can anticipate some of the questions on next Friday's exam or get an idea for the paper due in two weeks."

4. Always take notes.

Notetaking should always be part of your listening behavior. Taking notes forces you to select, condense, and organize the contents of a lecture. As you know from previous chapters, these kinds of vigorous mental activities encourage in-depth understanding and remembering.

See pages 85–88 for further information on notetaking.

5. Respond to what you hear.

Imagine that your American literature instructor opens a lecture by claiming Herman Melville's *Moby-Dick* is an undisputed American classic that has stood the test of time. In response to that statement, you jot down some marginal questions like "What makes a classic?" "Who decides that a book has passed the test of time?" "Will Stephen King's *Pet Sematary* be a classic someday?"

Skillful listening, much like skillful reading, relies heavily on your willingness to develop your own individual response to what is said. When you listen to lectures, you should do more than record the speaker's ideas. You should also challenge, confirm, or question what is being said, bringing to bear your own experience and knowledge.

■   PRACTICE 2   To evaluate your listening behavior, fill out the following questionnaire. See if you can honestly answer *yes* to each question.

1. **Do you make an effort to identify the goal or purpose of the lecture?**
2. **Do you take notes while you listen?**
3. **Do you vary your notetaking method with the material, changing as you move from a chemistry lecture to one on American literature?**
4. **Do you leave space for your personal responses when you take notes?**
5. **Do you read and revise your notes within twenty-four hours of the lecture?**

6. Do you prepare for a lecture *before* you hear it by consciously considering what you already know about the subject to be discussed and reviewing your notes or reading other materials related to the lecture?
7. Do you listen for verbal cues that indicate important points?
8. Do you make a conscious effort to sift information as you listen, deciding what is crucial and what is not?
9. Do you make it a point to sit in the front of the class where you cannot possibly daydream or doodle without attracting the professor's attention?
10. Do you try to keep an open mind, even when the lecturer's ideas differ from what you already know or believe?

TAKE STEPS TO STOP DAYDREAMING

KATHY: I just can't keep my mind on Professor Hartkopf's lectures.

PAUL: I know what you mean. The material is not that interesting, and he's not a good speaker. I had the same problem last semester. But I trained myself to pay attention no matter what. I just don't let myself daydream.

Some lectures and lecturers will just naturally stimulate your best listening behavior. Imagine, for example, that you are planning to be married at the end of the month, and your sociology instructor, a lively and witty speaker, is discussing problems commonly encountered by newlyweds. Your natural interest in the topic plus the speaker's own native gifts all but guarantee your best listening behavior.

Now imagine a different set of circumstances. It is eight o'clock in the morning; you have been up for about forty-five minutes and are still sleepy. The topic of the lecture is the properties of metal, and your instructor speaks in a dull monotone, fails to make eye contact, and shows little visible enthusiasm for her subject. This is a deadly combination. You are not personally inspired by the subject, and your instructor does not know how to present it in a way that could stimulate your interest. What do you do now?

What you *don't* do is assume that it's the instructor's responsibility to make the material interesting. Nor should you become annoyed if you feel your attention lagging. This kind of annoyance will distract you and open the door to daydreaming. You could leave the class without remembering a word that was said. If you are faced with a lecturer who doesn't immediately arouse your interest or enthusiasm, don't drift into daydreams. Instead **double your efforts to concentrate by anticipating questions, evoking personal associations, and drawing diagrams** of main points and supporting details.

In order to generate the energy you'll need to change your listening habits, think consciously about the advantages good listeners have over poor ones. In one analysis of a history course, for example, tape recordings revealed that 80 percent of the material covered during exams had been presented through lectures. This is not an unusual figure because in many courses, lectures are a pivotal source of information. It stands to reason, therefore, that better listeners make better students. Remember this every time you think that improving your listening habits demands more energy than you care to muster.

PRACTICE 3   Before each lecture, make yourself a daydreaming tally sheet. Each time you find yourself drifting from the lecture, make a check and tell yourself "I have to concentrate." At the end of each lecture, look at your tally sheet and compare it with the one from the previous day. If the number of checks has diminished even by one, give yourself some small reward.

Monday	Tuesday	Wednesday	Thursday	Friday
✓	✓	✓	✓	✓
✓	✓	✓	✓	
✓	✓	✓	✓	
✓	✓	✓		
✓	✓			

NOTETAKING: WHAT'S IMPORTANT?

Good lecture notes require that you mentally sort and sift information, deciding what to record and what to omit. Yet many students believe there isn't enough time to evaluate what they hear. But in fact, listeners have time on their side; they can think four times faster than a speaker can talk. They can hear what is said, evaluate its importance, and decide whether or not to write *before* the speaker moves on to another point.

Once we have convinced our students that they have enough time to think before they write, someone usually raises this question: "How do you know what's important and what's not?" That's a good question, one that has no simple answer—particularly since what is important varies with the subject matter. Facts and figures, for example, may be extremely important to the study of any science, but they become much less important when the subject is American literature. Although it would make learning much easier—and probably less interesting—if there were one or two simple rules for deciding what is crucial and what is not, there just aren't any rules that consistently apply to every lecture or lecturer.

However, while there are no hard and fast rules about what you should record, there are certain guidelines you can follow to make sure you get the most out of every lecture.

1. Use the purpose of the lecture to decide what's relevant.

Knowing the purpose of the lecture will help you decide what to record and what to leave out. Let's say that at the beginning of class, the instructor announces the purpose of her lecture: she will outline the stages or steps involved in the development of a hurricane. You would respond to that statement by listening for and recording the individual stages or steps.

Now imagine that during the same lecture your instructor digresses and talks about the extensive damage done by a particular hurricane in 1944. Yes, you would still listen attentively. But you would probably reduce your notetaking considerably because the information is not essential to the instructor's stated purpose.

You may interpret Nathaniel Hawthorne's *The Scarlet Letter* differently, depending on your prior knowledge. It's important to keep and open mind; don't let your prior knowledge prejudice your reaction to a lecture.

2. Listen for verbal cues.

Always listen for verbal cues. Sentences and phrases like "This is a central point," "Remember, too," "Significantly," and "Keep in mind" are the speaker's way of saying: *Pay attention.* Much like the authors of textbooks, good lecturers make every effort to tell their listeners what is essential and what is not. Good listeners, in turn, recognize and respond to the verbal cues speakers provide.

3. Record everything written on the blackboard.

Some instructors actually outline their lectures on the board and point to key statements as they talk. Others emphasize an important point by jotting down a key word or phrase as they come to it. Although instructors vary in the way they use the blackboard, you can generally assume that anything they choose to write on the board is important and should not be ignored.

4. Be attuned to repetition.

Most speakers return to key concepts they want to emphasize, repeating them to make sure you remember them. Phrases like "As I mentioned previously," "This you will remember from the previous lecture," and "Here, in another context" are all clues to key points.

5. Listen for all the points in a list.

When instructors take the time to enumerate causes of some event ("There were four reasons for Hitler's rise to power") or steps in a process ("There are five separate stages in the development of coal") chances are good the information is important.

6. Get a sense of proportion.

Say the title of the day's lecture is "The Computer Revolution." If your instructor spends forty minutes illustrating the effects computers will have on the American work force and ten minutes describing the way computers have affected education, you can reasonably assume that the instructor feels the former topic is more important than the latter. The more time a lecturer spends on a subject, the more important it probably is.

7. Pay attention to body language.

Imagine that you ask your best friend how he's feeling and he responds with a simple "Fine." But at the same time, he looks at the floor, shuffles his feet back and forth, and avoids your eyes. After interpreting his body language, you determine that he is not fine at all. Something is wrong. You can tell from the way he behaves.

Body language, so crucial to assessing the feelings or attitudes of your friends, also plays a role in lectures. Some lecturers point a finger at the class every time they make a key statement, others pause and wipe off their glasses, while others pace around the room. The kinds of gestures or movements that signal a significant point vary from instructor to instructor. But, consciously or unconsciously, most do speak with their bodies as well as their voices. Your job is to figure out what kinds of nonverbal cues your instructor favors.

Learn to "see" a sound. Nonverbal cues may signal significant points.

ADAPTING YOUR NOTETAKING TO THE MATERIAL

Just as there is not one way to take notes from a text, there is no simple method appropriate to all types of lectures and lecture styles. Good listeners are flexible; they adapt their notes to the subject and the style of the lecture.

For an illustration, let's say you are taking notes on a lecture that explains in chronological order the different theories of thinking that emerged in the late nineteenth and early twentieth centuries. Given the purpose of the lecture, you might decide that **informal outlining** is your best method of recording in sequence several different main points and supporting details. (For more on informal outlining, see Chapter 8.)

1. Middle of 19th century, associationism dominant theory

    a. belief that mental life had 2 components, (1) ideas or elements and (2) associations or links

    b. goes back to Aristotle

    c. reformulated by Locke and Hobbes in 17th and 18th centuries to include 4 points:

        1. Atomism: all mental life can be atomized into specific ideas and associations

        2. Mechanization: process of thinking based solely on strength of association

        3. Empiricism: all knowledge comes from sensory experience
        4. Imagery: all thinking involves some form of imagery

2. Late 19th century, psychology becomes more of a science, subject to empirical methods

    a. Wundt often identified as father of psychology

        1. divided study of psych. into 2 classes (1) simple psychical processes like reflexes, sensation, and perception (2) more complex psychical processes like thinking and learning.

        2. thought more complex ones could not be studied

3. Early 20th century, Wurzburg group tried to refine old associationist theories and study them through controlled experiments

The ideas here are more abstract than concrete; they are more concerned with theoretical explanation than physical description. In addition the sequence, or order in which they are introduced, is important. Informal outlining is the ideal method for taking notes on this kind of material.

But many times, order is not an important element of the speaker's subject or style. He or she may wish to offer several different generalizations about one topic, without placing any emphasis on sequence. When this is the case, you may find **mapping** more appropriate than informal outlining. Figure 4–1 shows a map that records the factors influencing the rate of death in microscopic forms of life.

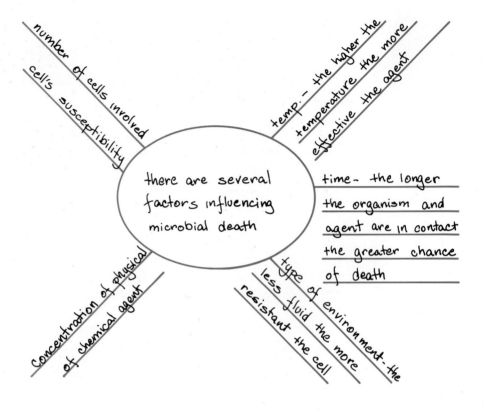

In courses that emphasize concrete physical description, you might choose to draw a **diagram** of what you hear to emphasize the visual nature of the material. The diagram in Figure 4–2 illustrates the kind of notes you might take on a lecture describing the layers of the earth.

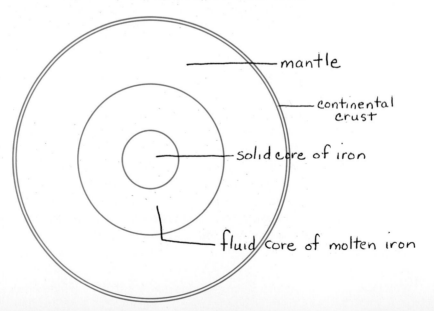

GIVE YOURSELF ROOM TO THINK

If you want to respond to what you hear by jotting questions and comments in the margins of your lecture notes, you have to consider the physical format of your notes and **give yourself room to think in writing.** From our point of view, the best notetaking format is one that divides each page into two parts of unequal proportions. Figure 4–3 shows a page that has been divided into unequal parts, one-third on the left and two-thirds on the right.

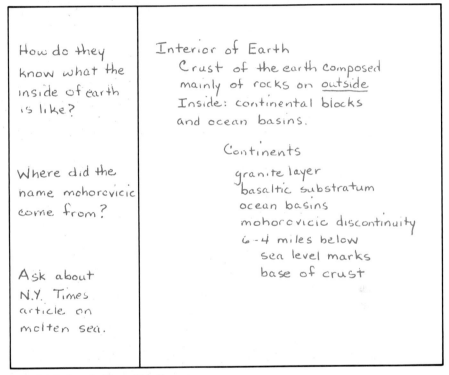

How do they
know what the
inside of earth
is like?

Where did the
name mohorovicic
come from?

Ask about
N.Y. Times
article on
molten sea.

Interior of Earth
Crust of the earth composed
mainly of rocks on <u>outside</u>
Inside: continental blocks
and ocean basins.

Continents
granite layer
basaltic substratum
ocean basins
mohorovicic discontinuity
6-4 miles below
sea level marks
base of crust

Figure 4–3: Sample Notetaking Format

This format gives you space to record key points from the lecture on the right; it also gives you space to record your own questions or comments on the left.

You should also consider how much space to leave between the individual points you record. When you review your notes, you may need to add information, and the additional empty space will come in handy. You will be able to elaborate on what you wrote down initially without turning the page into a crowded and unreadable jumble of notes.

READING AND REVISING YOUR NOTES

You learned in Chapter 3 that forgetting is most rapid right after learning. If, however, you take time to review and revise your notes within twenty-four hours of the lecture, *you can slow down the rate of forgetting.*

Your goal at this point is to read your notes and look for places where what you've written doesn't seem to make sense. If you can't sort out your short-hand by yourself, borrow a classmate's notes. If that doesn't clarify matters, ask your instructor for help. Also check over any new or specialized vocabulary to make sure the definitions are correct. Again, you might want to compare your notes with a friend's. Generally, it's a good idea to review your notes with a classmate so that you can fill in the gaps for each other.

During your review, you should continue jotting down responses to what's been said. Are there any questions you need to ask? Is there some point with which you disagree? Is there an idea that you might want to explore for a paper? Remember, the more you personally respond to and think about what you've heard in the lecture, the better your understanding will be.

ASK QUESTIONS

Some students are afraid to ask questions during a lecture even if their professor specifically asks for them. For these students, questions are a sign of personal failure or inadequacy. They believe that truly bright students don't need to ask questions. Bright students understand everything the first time around.

In fact, nothing could be further from the truth. Just think about it. Classroom lectures are designed to pack a maximum amount of information into a short amount of time. It would be a rare student, indeed, who could grasp all that information without posing a question or two.

When you listen to lectures, don't be surprised if some points confuse or puzzle you. Even more important, don't be ashamed to admit your confusion. **Think of your questions as a sign of interest and commitment.** Most instructors will be pleased you asked them. They know that some portions of their lecture probably need further discussion because their students are not experts in the field. But since instructors *are* experts, they are not always sure which points need elaboration. Instructors must rely on students' questions to tell them what needs clarification.

Any time you feel nervous about asking a question, think of the times you have wanted to ask one but were afraid to do so. Then somebody else asked the same question, and your instructor responded with "I'm glad you brought that up.'' If *you* have a question about a lecture, there's a very good chance somebody else in your class has the same one. So don't be afraid to ask it. You're not alone, no matter how alone you may feel.

Having told you that asking questions is a strength, not a weakness, we should point out that there are effective and ineffective ways to pose questions. But if you apply the following guidelines, yours will be effective.

1. Write out your question before you ask it.
Have you ever had a question in mind, but then you became so nervous when called upon that it flew out of your head? When you are first learning to speak up in class, this is not uncommon. The problem, however, can be avoided: just write down your question *before* you ask it. Then if you get nervous while talking, you can look at what you've written. As you grow more comfortable speaking in class, you may not have to write out your questions. But initially this is a good way to prevent the sudden amnesia that sometimes comes with nervousness.

2. Phrase your question precisely.
In your question, identify, as precisely as possible, the point or detail you didn't grasp. A question like "Can you please go over once more the way environment makes cells more or less resistant to disease?" will get you the information you want. An unspecific question like the following will not help you: "What was that last thing you said before you talked about pasteurization?"

3. Listen carefully to the questions of your classmates.
Do not get so caught up in your own need to ask a question that you don't listen to what others say. The result can be embarrassing: your instructor might tell you that she has already answered the question you're asking.

4. Look for a mentor.
One or two students in every class usually know how to ask questions without becoming flustered or nervous. Study their behavior. See if they do anything you might want to imitate. Do they speak slowly, taking their time to make questions clear and precise? Do they jot down the instructor's answer and respond to it? Do they pause and start over if they feel they're not framing their question clearly enough? If they don't understand the instructor's answer, do they say "Could you go over that again; I'm still not sure I understand." These are all characteristics worth imitating.

5. Be polite about the way you pose a challenging question.
Sometimes your questions may directly challenge or oppose your instructor's

point of view. There's nothing wrong with that as long as you are polite about how you ask your questions. You can expect a tart reply if you phrase them like this: "Do you seriously believe that there are stages or passages in personality development even though current research doesn't support that theory?" Opposing someone's point of view doesn't mean you have to insult his or her intelligence.

The following question would get much better results: "What do you think of the current research on personality development? Doesn't new research suggesting that major character traits remain stable throughout a person's lifetime undermine theories of predictable stages or passages in a person's life?"

If you think that asking questions is an admission of failure, you need to develop a new perspective. A willingness to ask questions is a sign of a bright, curious mind. It's also a sign of confidence. People who are really sure of themselves aren't afraid to say "I don't understand." Keep that thought in mind the next time you are afraid to raise your hand and ask a question.

WORKING SPACE

READING ASSIGNMENT

The following article by Walter W. Stevens identifies two ways in which speakers can manipulate listeners. As you read, ask yourself if anything said in the article applies to you.

Listening in Groups

Polarization, an old technique, is unfamiliar to many people, although it is a perfectly ethical but powerful psychological device used to advantage by both the principled orator* and the dema-gogue.† Every citizen should recognize and understand its implications. The speaker who wishes to polarize an audience will maneuver it into taking joint action. He may use humor to get his listeners to laugh together; he may ask for a show of hands; he may get them to sing or chant together; he may ask them to stand together, kneel

*orator: public speaker
†demagogue: rabble rouser

together, pray together, rise together, sit together, or read together. These procedures are repeated again and again for it takes time to polarize a group; but, as most skillful orators know, it is well worth the effort.

What happens to a listener when he becomes polarized? He tends to relinquish his own set of values and to adopt the values of the audience. Instead of many diverse, individual reflective* responses to a speech, we observe a unified group response. As the group reacts, so does each person conform. Independent critical appraisal of what is being said is reduced to a minimum because nonconformity in a polarized group is socially unacceptable, even if it is only silent mental disagreement. The auditor† is reduced to a private in a military drill platoon. When the speaker says, "Right face," he does so along with everybody else without asking himself, "Why should I do a right face?" He has become a victim of a type of group hypnosis. The critical listener resists polarization. He identifies polarizing devices for what they are—emotional and psychological straitjackets that rob him of his individualism. He is aware that his critical judgment is impaired when he is under their spell. . . .

A phenomenon similar to polarization is *social facilitation*, the effect of the members of a group upon each other because of their physical proximity.†† Obviously, stimuli move from speaker to auditor and from auditor to speaker; but in addition, each listener tends to be stimulated more than he realizes by the reactions of other persons near him. As a member of an audience, one has heard at some time a very poor speech or has attended a poor play or recital. Perhaps the only reason that one did not get up and walk out of the hall was that such an action would have been embarrassing. At the conclusion of the performance one felt as if he wanted to throw a tomato, but instead he applauded. Why? It was clapping time; everybody was clapping. To take another example, we have all laughed heartily with a group as we turned to the person next to us and asked, "What did he say?" Why were we laughing? It was social facilitation. Allport defined social facilitation as "an increase of response merely from the sight or sound of others making the same movements." It is radiation of social influence which can be obvious but more often occurs subliminally.§ The larger the group and the more emotional the stimulation presented by the speaker the greater the effect of social facil-

---

*reflective: thoughtful
†auditor: listener
††proximity: nearness
§subliminal: below the threshold of conscious perception

itation.

The critical listener tries to maintain his intellectual free will. No matter what the audience thinks of the speaker, no matter how it reacts to his skill and charm, the reflective auditor attempts to make an individual judgment independent of others in terms of his own criteria, to make his response truly his and not one subliminally forced upon him by the group. But so often the reaction of the audience in part determines the individual listener's reaction to the speaker; that is, his response tends to be a compromise between his impressions and those of the group. And social facilitation operates most irresistibly when the audience is polarized.

We like to think that we possess a high degree of rationality, but the psychological consequences of polarization and social facilitation are so subtle that usually we are unable to recognize and oppose them when they occur. After the occasion, we may still be at a loss to explain why we responded as we did.

—————

From *Western Speech*, Summer 1961, pp. 168–170.

———————————————————————

1. In your own words, define *polarization* and *social facilitation*.

2. In what kinds of speaking or listening situations do you think these two concepts would be important?

3. Does the author believe that a person can remain above this kind of manipulation? Cite portions of the essay that support your answer.

4. Do you think you have ever been manipulated in this way? Explain your answer.

WRITING ASSIGNMENT: "Is Anybody Listening?"

With a group of three or four classmates, develop some material for an informal *listening clinic.* For one of the following social problems, write a paper that (1) offers one possible solution to the problem, and (2) explains why you think your solution would improve matters. Then, give each person time to read his or her paper aloud while other members of the group take notes. When the speaker is finished, let each member verbally summarize what he or she heard in order to compare notes with one another and with the original paper.

1. drug abuse among athletes
2. the lack of shelters for the homeless
3. child abuse
4. the abuse of elderly people in nursing homes
5. the high rate of suicide among adolescents
6. mistreatment of experimental animals in medical laboratories
7. prison parolees who repeat their original crimes
8. the threat of an AIDS epidemic
9. random drug testing for those who pose a risk to public safety
10. If you feel you can't write about any of these social problems, develop a topic of your own choosing. Just be sure that your topic is a current social problem familiar to your classmates from newspapers or television.

JOURNAL ASSIGNMENTS

1. Imagine that you have a problem you want to discuss with someone. Write a description of the person you ideally would want to talk to about it. What is your personal image of the ideal listener?

2. In his book *College: The Undergraduate Experience in America* (Harper and Row, 1988), Ernest L. Boyer suggests that colleges, to avoid emphasizing careers to the exclusion of all else, introduce what he calls the "enriched major."

   Therefore, what we propose, as a centerpiece of the undergraduate experience, is the *enriched major.* By an *enriched major* we mean encouraging students not only to explore a field in depth, but also to help them put their field of special study in perspective. The major, as it is enriched, will respond to three essential questions: What is the history and tradition of the field to be examined? What are the social and economic implications to be understood? What are the ethical and moral issues to be confronted?

In your journal, explore how this concept might be applied to your own major, actual or potential.

CHECKING OUT

Check your understanding of Chapter 4 by writing answers to the following questions. You may work alone or with a friend, whichever you prefer.

1.   What is a listening frame of mind?

2.   What are four ways to improve your listening behavior?

3.   What are four ways in which lecturers signal significance?

4.   Describe a one-third/two-thirds format. What is its value?

5.   What are three things you can do to make sure you pose effective questions?

6.   What is the purpose of reviewing your notes right after a lecture?

IN SUMMARY

The ability to hear is only the first and most basic prerequisite for good listening. To be a good listener, you have to be mentally active and alert. You have to listen for key points, anticipate shifts in thought, respond to what you hear, and adapt your notetaking to the material. This kind of listening is hard work, but it's work that pays off in better learning and higher grades.

U N I T   2

LEARNING FROM YOUR TEXTBOOKS

This unit will teach you how to learn from your college textbooks. Chapter 5 will show you what skillful readers do to make sure that they grasp the author's intended message, and Chapter 6 will explain how you can become more adept with words. Chapter 7 will identify three different reading strategies—inspectional, intensive, and analytical—and you will learn how and when to use them. In Chapter 8, you'll discover that there are many different ways to take notes. It's up to you to choose which method to use, depending on your course material and purpose. In Chapter 9, you will learn how to adapt your reading strategies to the kind of compressed scientific writing that may have confused you in the past. By the time you finish this unit, you will know everything you need to know in order to become a truly skillful reader.

CHAPTER 5

DEFINING THE SKILLFUL READER

I don't understand it. My roommate and I read the same textbooks, but we don't get the same results. When he's finished, he understands what he's read, and I'm just more confused than ever.

—Paul Yashenko, student

OVERVIEW

Like Paul, you may have noticed that there are real differences in the way college students read their textbooks. It's true. Two students can spend the same amount of time reading a chapter, but when they finish, one will have a clear understanding of the material while the other will have only a vague notion of the author's intended meaning. The question is why? Why is there such a difference in the way students read their texts? What makes one reader more skillful than another? In Chapter 5, we provide not one but several different answers.

- Skillful readers are mentally active; they help create the author's intended message.
- Aware of the differences between college textbooks and popular novels or magazines, skillful readers *adapt their reading strategies to the material.*
- Reading between the lines, skillful readers use their knowledge of the world and of language to draw appropriate *inferences.*

- Attuned to the *cues* language provides, skillful readers use those cues to *anticipate* or predict how a writer's thought will develop.
- Skillful readers know the value of background information, and they constantly try to enlarge the store of personal knowledge they can bring to their reading.

SKILLFUL READERS WORK WITH THE AUTHOR

Books must be read as deliberately as they are written.
—Henry David Thoreau

Skillful readers have the right mind-set about reading. They see it as an **active quest for meaning,** one that requires them to work with the author by asking questions about the text and by mobilizing what they know about language and the world in order to understand the author's message. Less skillful readers, however, have a different attitude. They see reading as a passive activity that does not require them to do anything but open a book, read the page, and wait for the author's message to sink in.

To get a clear image of how this difference in attitude reflects itself in reading behavior, go to the library for an hour or so and observe the different ways people read books. Skillful readers will be hunched over their text, scribbling in the margins, and reciting key points. Although they'll look up now and then to rest their eyes, they won't let themselves respond to every noise they hear or every person who walks by.

Less skillful readers will be there too. But they will usually be slumping in their chairs, resting their heads on their hands, or propping themselves up with their elbows. There probably won't be any sign of a pencil, pen, or felt marker in their hands. Nor will they be reciting. Instead, they will be looking at the clock, watching the entrance for new visitors, and occasionally staring out the window with dreamy expressions on their faces. They feel they have done their part by going to the library and opening a book. Everything else is the author's responsibility. What they don't realize is that **skillful reading depends upon a constant interaction between the reader's mind and the author's words.**

To illustrate exactly what we mean by an "interaction between the reader's mind and the author's words," we'll take you through the following excerpt paragraph by paragraph. We'll show you how skillful readers work with an author to help create the text they read:

Endotherms

Birds and mammals comprise the **endotherms** (*endo,* inside), the so-called warm-blooded creatures. They have evolved physiological methods of keeping their body temperatures within very narrow limits. Their bodies can carry out biochemical activities more efficiently by having specialized to within a range of temperatures that is conducive to biochemical reactions.

The first thing skillful readers would do is respond to the heading "Endotherms." They would raise questions like What are endotherms? Do I know anything about them? What does the author intend to say about them? In an effort to answer that last question, skillful readers would then read the first paragraph looking for sentences needing clarification or explanation.

As you can see, the first sentence of the paragraph does not fall into either category. Sentences 2 and 3, however, are more promising. They explain that endotherms have evolved in such a way that their range of body temperatures is very restricted; therefore they can carry out biochemical activities more efficiently. Because these sentences raise questions that need to be answered—questions like How did they evolve? and What are those physiological methods?—it's very possible that they express the main point of the selection. But we cannot be sure until we read the second paragraph:

Interestingly, both birds and mammals are descended from the reptiles. Mammals appeared at about the time the dinosaurs made their entrance, about 150 million years ago (the birds evolved a little later). While the great dinosaurs were thundering around the earth terrorizing everything in sight, the mammals were existing as tiny mouselike forms that probably terrorized only insects.

Because it explains how endotherms evolved, the second paragraph tells us we are indeed on the right track.

The third paragraph continues to describe the evolution of endotherms, but it also answers the second question we raised: What are those physiological methods that keep their bodies within a restricted range of temperatures? The paragraph provides two answers: (1) the insulation provided by fur and feathers, and (2) the efficient four-chambered heart.

After the disappearance of the dinosaurs, the number of birds and mammals burgeoned.* As they radiated out over the earth, invading

---

* burgeoned: increased

newly vacated niches,* the endotherms began to change and specialize in innumerable ways. Nonetheless, both birds and mammals, having sprung from the same distant stock, had certain critical traits in
common—traits related to temperature control. First, they were well-
insulated creatures, with their fur and feathers. Second, they had a
more efficient four-chambered heart. Theirs was a powerful organ
able to pump enough fuel and oxygen throughout the body to stoke
the cells' metabolic† furnaces. Remember, the cost of struggling
against the environment to maintain a constant internal temperature
would have been metabolically expensive and would have required
increasingly efficient physiological mechanisms.

—Robert A. Wallace, *Biology: The World of Life,* *4th Ed.*

Now the author's main point is clear. Over an extended period of time,
endotherms evolved physiological methods for keeping their body temperatures within a very restricted range, and that limited range of temperatures
allows them to perform biochemical activities more efficiently.

But what's important here is *not* the evolution and specialization of endotherms. What's important is that you recognize how we arrived at our
understanding of the author's main point. We used the author's opening
statements to make predictions about how his thoughts would develop.
Then we used the remaining paragraphs to confirm those predictions. This is
what skillful readers do to help recreate an author's message.

If you want to be a skillful reader, you cannot sit back and wait for the
author's message to penetrate. While you read, your mind should be constantly raising and answering questions like the following:

Questions That Skillful Readers Raise and Answer

1. Does the heading give me any clues about how the passage will
   develop?

2. Do I myself have any background knowledge about this subject?

3. Which sentences in the opening paragraphs seem to need more
   clarification or explanation? Which ones are likely to be developed
   in the remaining paragraphs?

4. What one train of thought seems to continue from paragraph to
   paragraph?

---

* niches: corners

† metabolic: chemical changes in living cells by which energy is provided

5. Are there any words or phrases like *however, unfortunately, on the contrary,* or *on the other hand* that signal a change of direction in the author's thought?

6. How would I paraphrase the main point of each paragraph?

7. What is the main point of the entire selection? What does the author want me to know?

8. What kinds of supporting details does the author use—studies, statistics, examples, reasons?

9. Which ones are more important? Which ones less? Which ones should I remember? Which ones can I ignore?

10. Is my understanding of this passage consistent with the author's words? Is there any way in which my interpretation and the text do not match?

If you want to be a skillful reader, those are the kinds of questions you need to raise and answer while you read. Questions like these will help you re-create in *your own mind* the author's intended meaning.

> Skillful reading depends upon a constant interaction between the reader's mind and the author's words.

SKILLFUL READERS ARE FLEXIBLE READERS

Some students are puzzled by the fact that they can read popular novels or magazines without much difficulty, yet they still have trouble reading their college texts. After all, reading is reading, isn't it?

The answer is both yes and no. Although all reading requires you to decode and interpret words on a page, different kinds of writing make different demands on readers. To give you an illustration, imagine that you have decided to read—purely for the pleasure of it—the following excerpt from Stephen King's best-selling novel *Pet Sematary:*

> Louis hushed, looking around uneasily. Here the ground mist was thinner, but he still couldn't see his own shoes. Then he heard crackling underbrush and breaking branches. Something was moving out there—something big.

He opened his mouth to ask Jud if it was a moose (*bear* was the thought that actually crossed his mind), and then he closed it again. *The sound carries,* Jud had said.

He cocked his head to one side in unconscious imitation of Jud, unaware that he was doing it, and listened. The sound seemed at first distant, then very close; moving away and then moving ominously* toward them. Louis felt the sweat on his forehead begin to trickle down his chapped cheeks. He shifted the Hefty Bag with Church's body in it from one hand to the other. His palm had dampened, and the green plastic seemed greasy, wanting to slide through his fist. Now the thing out there seemed to be so close that Louis expected to see its shape at any moment, rising up on two legs, perhaps, blotting out the stars with some unthought-of, immense and shaggy body.

Bear was no longer what he was thinking of.

Now he didn't know just *what* he was thinking of.

Then it moved away and disappeared.

Louis opened his mouth again, the words *What was that?* already on his tongue. Then a shrill, maniacal laugh came out of the darkness, rising and falling in hysterical cycles, loud, piercing, chilling. To Louis it seemed that every joint in his body had frozen solid and that he had somehow gained weight, so much weight that if he turned to run he would plunge down and out of sight in the swampy ground.

The laughter rose, split into dry cackles like some rottenly friable† chunk of rock along many fault lines; it reached the pitch of a scream, then sank into a guttural chuckling that might have become sobs before it faded out altogether.

Somewhere there was a drip of water and above them, like a steady river in a bed of sky, the monotonous whine of the wind. Otherwise Little God Swamp was silent.

Louis began to shudder all over. His flesh—particularly that of his lower belly—began to creep. *Yes, creep* was the right word; his flesh actually seemed to be moving on his body. His mouth was totally dry. There seemed to be no spit at all left in it. Yet that feeling of exhilaration persisted, an unshakable lunacy.

In responding to this excerpt, you probably didn't analyze each sentence. You probably recognized immediately that King's purpose in writing was *not* to develop one main point. King is a storyteller who invites his readers to

---

*ominous: menacing
†friable: easily crumbled

enter imaginatively the horrific world of his novels. When you are reading his work, the best response is to let yourself visualize and experience the atmosphere he creates, as King makes you hear crackling underbrush and cackling laughter. In this case, reading is akin to daydreaming.

That response, so appropriate for King's novel, would be totally inappropriate for the following textbook excerpt, in which the author explains one main point: no one could have predicted the enormous growth of radio in the 1930s and 1940s.

> No one could have foreseen the massive growth of radio that took place during the 1930s and 1940s. Radio became a major entertainment medium with its own star system. It broadcast music and made big bands and individual musicians famous. It presented plays, comics, operas, sports, and hundreds of other types of programs. In particular, it brought rapid and dramatic news coverage by commentators and announcers with their own special styles. Radio not only expanded the consciousness of its listeners concerning events in the world but also placed before them personalities that were larger than life—such as Franklin D. Roosevelt, patent medicine man Dr. Brinkley, and the political priest Father Charles E. Coughlin. It was through their radio broadcasts that these men gained a following and a place in history.
>
> Even the Great Depression of the 1930s did not slow the growth of radio. If anything, the hard times helped the industry. Advertisers were looking for ways to stimulate sales, and they turned to radio because the listening audience continued to grow. People who were out of work or out of money hung on to their radios despite their troubles. Radio was free, and it brought music, comedy, and plays into their homes to provide a bright spot in the face of hardship. The furniture could be repossessed and the car remain unrepaired, but the radio would be kept.
>
> —M. DeFleur and E. Dennis,
> *Understanding Mass Communication*

To respond appropriately to this excerpt, you do have to read every sentence, mentally sifting and sorting the message of each one until you decode the author's message and discover (1) what point the author is making, (2) what supporting details the author uses to explain it, and (3) what supporting details you need to remember, given your own personal knowledge and the purpose of your reading.

Skillful readers know that different kinds of texts demand different strategies; thus, they do not approach their textbooks as if they were novels or newspapers. Instead, they work to develop a clear sense of how textbook authors generally organize and present information, making use of that knowledge whenever they approach a reading assignment.

MAKING INFERENCES

In your everyday life, you make **inferences** all the time. You use what people say or do to draw conclusions about thoughts and feelings they have never directly expressed or stated. Imagine, for example, that you are standing in line to see the latest comedy from Hollywood, and you watch the audience from the previous show leaving. If most people have smiles on their faces and are still laughing, you *infer* that they liked what they saw, even though no one directly tells you so. But if they leave muttering and looking dejected, you infer the opposite: they hated the movie.

The making of inferences, so essential to everyday life, is no less crucial to reading. Skillful readers know that authors often leave out information they think their readers can and will supply. The following passage is an example:

Many people get nervous in the presence of fog, and with good reason. If you're driving a car, a fog can be lethal. You can't see, and you may even find ice forming on your car. If you are walking through a fog, the dense cloud gives you a feeling of isolation, of "What's out there. . .?" What, exactly, *is* fog?

Fog is a ground-based stratus cloud composed of microscopic water droplets or ice crystals. If the air happens to be below freezing, this water vapor may form ice on cars unfortunate enough to be passing through it.

Fog comes about when (1) moisture is added to a warm air mass or when (2) a moist air mass is cooled to its dew point. In the second case, a mass of air cools either because it comes into contact with cooler ground or water, or because it expands rapidly, or because it receives an invasion of cooled air. The moisture condenses out of the air mass and a thick cloud forms on the ground. So you see, the blankets of fog that we see so often along coastlines or along the shores of lakes are really stratus cloud formations that are sitting on the ground. These dense coverings of condensing water vapor are the result of air cooling to saturation, although the air may sometimes be supercooled before condensation takes place. If so, the fog forms quite rapidly.

—Joseph Weisberg, *Meteorology*

In the first paragraph of the above passage, the author raises a question: "What, exactly, *is* fog?" The remaining paragraphs serve as an answer, even though the author never explicitly says to his readers: "Here now is the answer to the question I posed in paragraph 1." He expects you to infer the appropriate connection and recognize that paragraph 2 begins to answer the question posed in paragraph 1.

In this next example, the author doesn't expect you to make the connection between paragraphs. She expects you to infer the main point of the entire passage.

> As little as twenty or thirty years ago, pregnancy was considered "women's work," and an expectant father didn't have much to do until the day of birth. Then his job was to get his wife to the hospital on time and wait, while nervously smoking cigarettes and pacing the hospital corridors. It was a rare thing for the father to be present during the birth of his child, and the practice was not encouraged. It was assumed that the nervous father would get in the way and be a nuisance. Even after mother and child were at home, fathers weren't expected to play a major role in child care; their job was to be the family provider, not the baby's nurse and caretaker. That was mother's role.
>
> Today, however, it is not uncommon to see fathers-to-be wearing tee shirts that say anything from "We're having a baby" to "We're expecting." In addition, hospitals report that increasing numbers of men are attending pregnancy classes with their wives—in order to better assist them at the birth of their child. And today's fathers expect to do more than be present while their wives give birth. They also want to play a major role in caring for the newborn baby, and recent studies show that a good percentage of fathers no longer think it is their wife's job to get up during the night when the baby cries. From their point of view, they want to share both the joy *and* the drudgery of having a child.

If you asked a reader to explain the main point of this passage, you would probably get an answer like the following: "The father's role in child care has changed dramatically in a very short time." However, there is no explicit statement of that generalization anywhere in the passage. Given the specific details supplied by the author, **the reader is expected to read between the lines** and infer it.

It is not unusual for the reader to be called upon to make such inferences.

Skillful readers know that no text contains every piece of information needed to communicate its message. They are therefore alert to those places where an author expects the reader to contribute to the text by supplying some suggested point, detail, or connection.

> The making of inferences, so essential to everyday life, is no less crucial to reading. Skillful readers know that authors leave out information they think their readers can and will supply.

■   PRACTICE 1   In this selection, the renowned writer Isaac Asimov raises an interesting question, "What is intelligence, anyway?" Read the selection and answer the questions that follow.

> **What is intelligence, anyway? When I was in the army, I received a kind of aptitude test that all soldiers took and, against a normal of 100, scored 160. No one at the base had ever seen a figure like that, and for two hours they made a big fuss over me. (It didn't mean anything. The next day I was still a buck private with KP— kitchen police—as my highest duty.)**
>
> **All my life I've been registering scores like that, so I have the complacent feeling that I'm highly intelligent, and I expect other people to think so, too. Actually, though, don't such scores simply mean that I am very good at answering the type of academic questions that are considered worthy of answers by the people who make up the intelligence tests—people with intellectual bents similar to mine?**
>
> **For instance, I had an auto-repair man once, who, on these intelligence tests, could not possibly have scored more than 80, by my estimate. I always took it for granted that I was far more intelligent than he was. Yet, when anything went wrong with my car, I hastened to him with it, watched him anxiously as he explored its vitals, and listened to his pronouncements as though they were divine oracles—and he always fixed my car.**
>
> **Well, then, suppose my auto-repair man devised questions for an intelligence test. Or suppose a carpenter did, or a farmer, or, indeed, almost anyone but an academician. By every one of those tests, I'd prove myself a moron. And I'd be a moron, too. In a**

world where I could not use my academic training and my verbal talents but had to do something intricate or hard, working with my hands, I would do poorly.

1. What do you think is the correct answer to the question, "What is intelligence, anyway?"

_____

2. Was the answer stated in the passage or did you have to infer it?

_____

MAKING PREDICTIONS

Skillful readers know it is easier to follow a writer's train of thought when they can anticipate or predict what he or she is going to say next. They are therefore always alert to the ways in which the language of one sentence or passage provides clues about what is to come.

Take, for example, the following paragraph:

> In the first years of chimpanzee research, these seemingly gentle and benign animals were found to live in loosely coordinated communities. Within these communities groups of chimps came and went apparently without incident. To observers, the animals appeared to be living in a peaceful Garden of Eden where aggression and violence never reared their ugly heads. It was assumed that the chimps' vegetarian diet was one reason for their lack of aggression. With vegetation plentiful, they never had to fight over prey.

In some detail, this paragraph tells us what researchers once thought about the chimpanzee's eating habits, behavior, and temperament. But it also suggests that the next paragraph will not agree with or confirm those original beliefs. We can make this prediction based on words like "seemingly," "appeared," "apparently," and "assumed." All of these words suggest that things are not necessarily what they seemed to be at first.

After reading the above paragraph, skillful readers would have definite expectations about what was to come next. They would assume that the author is about to present a new and more up-to-date version of the chim-

Defining skills is a matter of attitude and practice, whether it's reading or painting.

panzee's world, one where life is not so peaceful and harmonious. As you can see, their prediction would be quite correct.

> We now know chimpanzees hunt actively for prey and are quite carnivorous. Although chimpanzees do share what they hunt, rivalry over food can develop. When this happens, brutal battles take place in which the animals fight viciously using their teeth and fists. At times they even resort to cannibalism and eat the bodies of their rivals.

Clearly this paragraph affirms the prediction that chimpanzees are not at all the gentle creatures once imagined by a generation of researchers.

However, don't assume that your predictions will always be confirmed by the text. Sometimes you will have to modify or even completely contradict your original prediction because authors often open with a position or point completely opposite to the one they actually develop as the selection unfolds.

Look, for example, at how one author opens a discussion of age and creativity:

> "Experience takes away more than it adds," wrote Plato. "Young people are nearer ideas than old people."

After reading that opening quotation, you might think that the author, Alex Osborn, is going to discuss the way age diminishes creativity. But would you think that after reading the next sentence?

> With due respect to Plato, how could he say that while listening to the sixty-year-old Socrates as he presented one new idea after another?

Contrary to that opening quotation, the author is actually intent on discussing the way in which age need *not* influence creativity, and it's therefore crucial for you to revise your first prediction based on the opening sentence.

Skillful readers know it is easier to follow a writer's train of thought when they can anticipate or predict what he or she is going to say next. They are therefore always alert to the way in which the language of one sentence or passage provides clues about what is to come.

■ PRACTICE 2   Here are the opening sentences to five paragraphs. Read them and in the blanks that follow, write down your expectations of how the paragraph will continue.

1. **In colonial America, bundling was a fairly common practice. It involved two people, a man and a woman, sleeping together in their clothes. Ostensibly* at least, the purpose of bundling was the conservation of firewood.**

_____

2. **We all like to believe that we are incapable of self-deception. Although we openly admit that one or two misguided individuals will lie to themselves, we counter that admission by insisting that such people are the exception, never the rule.**

_____

_____

*ostensibly: apparently, on the surface

3. **There was a time when it was assumed that children of divorced parents would always be better off it they remained with the mother. The assumption was that only a mother was capable of such solitary child care.**

---

4. **In the early days of their relationship, Sigmund Freud and Carl Jung were in agreement about the origins of psychic disturbance, but eventually they disagreed violently and broke off all contact with each other.**

---

5. **In 1985 Mary Beth Whitehead agreed to be a surrogate mother for would-be parents William and Elizabeth Stearn. What she could not know when she signed the surrogate contract was the way she would feel when the time came to give up the baby she had carried for nine months.**

SKILLFUL READERS KNOW THE VALUE OF BACKGROUND KNOWLEDGE

The explicit meanings of a piece of writing are the tip of an iceberg of meaning; the larger part lies below the surface of the text and is composed of the reader's own relevant knowledge.

—E. D. Hirsch

In a recent study of reading comprehension, a group of students were asked to read and answer questions on two passages. The first passage was about an American wedding; the second about an Indian one. Although both passages were very similar in their level of difficulty, the students had more trouble reading the passage describing the Indian wedding than they had reading the passage about the American wedding. The reason for the difficulty was not that the words or the sentences in one passage were more difficult than in the other. The problem was that American students, for the most part, lacked any background knowledge about Indian weddings. As a result, they had trouble making sense of the passage. They couldn't make a connection between the words on the page and the cultural behavior that was being described.

This study and others like it show just how much a reader's own store of personal knowledge affects his or her understanding of what is written. The principle here is a simple one: **the more background knowledge you bring to a text, the easier it will be for you to read it.**

At this point you may be saying to yourself, "I don't think it's simple at all. If I'm having a tough time with my American government text because I don't have any background knowledge, just how am I supposed to get that knowledge?"

Well, it's true you can't get it overnight. But you can apply the principle of divide and conquer: you can spend some time each day exploring sources— other than your textbook—that might introduce the same material in simpler form. Faced with a difficult chapter on the making of the Constitution, for example, you should write down some key names and terms you can use to guide your search for relevant background. Here as an illustration is a sample list drawn from a chapter titled "Making a Constitution":

> Federalism
> Alexander Hamilton
> Thomas Jefferson
> Amendments
> Benjamin Franklin
> Articles of Confederation
> Continental Congress
> Bill of Rights

Once you have a list like this one, schedule time for any one or all of the following activities:

1. Find and read encyclopedia articles dealing with the people, the events, or the terms on your list. If general encyclopedias like the *Encyclopedia Americana* or *Encyclopaedia Britannica* don't have enough information, try more specialized ones like the *International Encyclopedia of Social Sciences* or the *Encyclopedia of American History.*

2. Check the reference section of your library for specialized dictionaries like the *Encyclopedic Dictionary of American History* or the *Penguin Dictionary of Biology.* They are specially designed to give brief and simple definitions and descriptions of the names, terms, and events essential to an understanding of their subject matter.

3. Look in your local newspaper for announcements of exhibits or lectures that might be related to your list. And don't overlook the possibility of learning from art exhibits. Often the artwork displayed makes reference to the people and events that were important at the time of its creation. Thus an exhibition of eighteenth-century painting, called "Colonial America," might give you insights into the events leading up to the Constitution.

4. Read biographies of people mentioned in your textbook. Biographers often provide useful summaries of the key issues that concerned their subject. Even more important, by concentrating on the personal side of political or scientific issues, biographers often make them more lively and more readily accessible to your understanding.

5. Talk to other students who have taken the course you are struggling with; discuss with them some key points or issues mentioned in your textbook.

6. Even if you are dealing with events that happened a long time ago, like the making of the Constitution, see what you can find out about your topic in the *Readers' Guide to Periodical Literature,* which indexes popular magazines. Events, like the framing of the Constitution, and people, like Thomas Jefferson, are not confined to the pages of history books; they frequently appear as the subject of articles in magazines like *Time*

Draw inferences and supply connections. What can you infer about this photo?

and *Smithsonian*. Once again, the treatment in these magazines will probably be simpler and more accessible than that of your textbook.

If you make a commitment to expanding and enriching your personal knowledge of the subjects discussed in your textbooks, you will be astounded at how much better you both understand and remember what you read. Instead of reading words and wondering what they mean, you will be able to recreate mentally the world and times those words represent.

WORKING SPACE

READING ASSIGNMENT

Read this poem by Philip Larkin very carefully. Then answer the questions that follow.

A Study of Reading Habits

When getting my nose in a book
Cured most things short of school,
It was worth ruining my eyes
To know I could still keep cool,
5   And deal out the old right hook
To dirty dogs twice my size.

Later, with inch-thick specs,
Evil was just my lark:
Me and my cloak and fangs
10 Had ripping times in the the dark.
The women I clubbed with sex!
I broke them up like meringues.

Don't read much now: the dude
Who lets the girl down before
15 The hero arrives, the chap
Who's yellow and keeps the store,
Seem far too familiar. Get stewed:
Books are a load of crap.

1. What does the author mean in the first stanza when he says "getting my nose in a book/Cured most things short of school"?

2. What kinds of books is the author describing in the first stanza? in the second?

3. How would you describe the author's response to those books?

4. In the poem, what is the author's reason for claiming, "Don't read much now"?

5. In line 17 of the poem, the author tells his readers to get drunk instead of reading a book. How could drinking be a substitute for reading? What are some similarities between the two?

WRITING ASSIGNMENT: "The Power of Books"

The French philosopher Montaigne said, "Books relieve me from idleness, rescue me from company, blunt the edge of my grief." Write a few paragraphs in which you first explain what Montaigne meant by this statement. Then in your final paragraph, indicate if any of it applies to you or not.

JOURNAL ASSIGNMENTS

1. In 1988, the *New York Times* reported that only 39 percent of all freshmen who were surveyed thought of college as a place to develop their philosophy of life. Is college helping you formulate your philosophy of life? Describe your present philosophy in a few paragraphs.

2. Use your journal to think in writing about some person or experience early in your life that positively or negatively influenced your attitude toward education and learning.

3. According to the writer Virginia Woolf, "The backbone of writing is the fierce attachment to some idea." What does she mean by the "backbone" of writing? Does your writing have such a backbone? What does she mean by "the fierce attachment to some idea"?

CHECKING OUT

Check your understanding of Chapter 5 by writing answers to the following questions. You may work alone or with a friend, whichever you prefer.

1. What is the difference between active and passive reading?

2. If you are a skillful reader of novels, does it automatically follow that you will be a skillful reader of textbooks?

3. What do you do when you make an inference?

4.   What role do inferences play in reading?

5.   How can background knowledge affect your reading ability?

IN SUMMARY

Reading may look like a passive activity that requires you to do little more than sit back and let the author's message sink in. But as usual, appearances are deceiving. Truly skillful readers know that reading is a collaborative art in which they have to work with the author in order to create meaning. They have to make predictions, draw inferences, supply connections, and in general use their knowledge of the world to fill in gaps in the text left by the author.

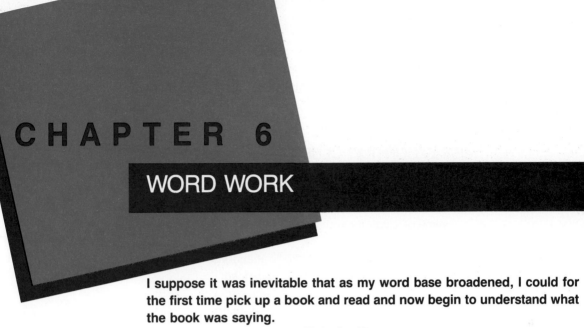

CHAPTER 6

WORD WORK

I suppose it was inevitable that as my word base broadened, I could for the first time pick up a book and read and now begin to understand what the book was saying.

—Malcolm X

OVERVIEW

At times it might seem as if your textbooks were written in a foreign language. That's not surprising. It's not unusual for writers, particularly writers of textbooks, to use words that aren't part of everyday speech and conversation, yours or anyone else's.

Because many of the words in your texts are new and unfamiliar, they may confuse or intimidate you when you first encounter them. That feeling of confusion does not have to last if you make a commitment to the kind of word work outlined in this chapter.

- Use clues from the *context* or passage in which a word appears.
- Learn some essential *Greek and Latin prefixes and roots* to help you define new words by breaking them into meaningful parts.
- Use a vocabulary notebook to collect and study new words.
- Know the kinds of information your dictionary contains.

Start scheduling time for regular word work, and you'll see immediate results. The language of your textbooks will no longer be a source of frustration and confusion. Like Malcolm X's, your "word base" will be adequate to the task at hand.

USING CONTEXT CLUES

When the following words are presented in a list, without the benefit of a **context** or surrounding passage, it's quite possible you might not know what some of them mean:

> remuneration
> phenotype
> vitriolic
> eclectic
> irritability

But when we put these same words into a context, there's a good chance you can **develop an approximate definition** for each one. Although those definitions might not be the exact ones that appear in a dictionary, they will be close enough for you to grasp the message or main point of each passage:

> There was no *remuneration* for the acting job, but he didn't care. Payment wasn't as important as the opportunity.

In this case, context defines the word *remuneration,* making it a **synonym** for the word *payment.* Were you to infer that remuneration means payment or reward, you would be correct.

In the next passage, you don't have to infer the meaning of the word *phenotype;* the author supplies it in parentheses.

> In nature, it's hard to determine how much the *phenotype* of an organism is determined by heredity and how much by environment. (The term *phenotype* refers to the physically manifested or observable characteristics of an organism.)

This explicit defining of a word or term is typical of science texts. Aware that much of their vocabulary is *specialized,* or not widely known by the general reader, authors of science texts make it a practice to define words they assume will be unfamiliar, providing a definition the *first time* the word appears in the text. Often, science authors doubly highlight the definition by using (parentheses), *italics,* **boldface,** or asterisks***—typographical devices that signal "pay attention."

In the next example, you again have to infer the definition of an unfamiliar word, in this case *vitriolic*. Notice, however, that the context clue is an **antonym,** rather than a synonym. Because you learn what vitriolic does *not* mean—"sweet and kind"—you can deduce what it does mean—"cruel and harsh."

> In public interviews, the president's tone was gentle and kind, and no one, outside of his staff, knew about his *vitriolic* tongue, which had reduced more than one employee to tears.

Initially, "irritability" may have been the only word on our opening list that you were sure you knew. You probably defined it as "a feeling of annoyance or irritation." But, here again, context is crucial, in this case because it acts to correct your original definition. When used within the field of biology, the word *irritability* takes on a specialized meaning. Aware that readers might substitute a general definition where it does not apply, the author pointedly supplies the appropriate *specialized* definition.

> Basic to an understanding of the evolution and operation of nervous systems is an understanding of *irritability.* Defined as a capacity to respond to a stimulus, irritability is basically a chemical phenomenon.

In the following passage, there is no antonym or synonym. Nor is there an explicit definition of the word *eclectic.* The author does, however, supply several examples of eclectic behavior, examples that help the alert reader develop an approximate definition—"wide-ranging or various."

> I am always surprised at how *eclectic* his interests are. He reads everything from Shakespeare to Stephen King, and appreciates all kinds of music. You can find both Bach and Bruce Springsteen on his shelves.

The point of all our examples is this: before you reach for a dictionary to define a word, try first to determine its meaning through context. If you cannot develop a meaning that fits the passage, then check the **glossary** of your textbook. Many academic authors reserve a section near the end of their book to define all key terms, making the glossary the first and best place to look up words. If that fails, turn to a dictionary and see what you can find there. This is the sequence skillful readers follow. Less skillful ones—who unfortunately don't always trust their own judgment enough—think they have to turn to the dictionary first; they don't even attempt to determine word meaning through context. Such overreliance on the dictionary is not an efficient strategy, particularly if you are reading a book in which every page contains several unfamiliar words. You can lose the thread of an author's discussion by spending too much time looking in the dictionary.

■ PRACTICE 1   After reading each sentence or passage, write out an approximate definition for each underlined word.

1. In 1933 the prohibition against drinking was *abrogated* by the Twenty-first Amendment.

_____

2. Through the use of a *seismograph,* geologists were able to determine the force of the earthquake.

_____

3. One-celled plants reproduce by a process called *fission:* the cell divides or splits into two parts.

_____

4. David was the opposite of his withdrawn and silent sister; he had been a *loquacious* child, and he was an even more loquacious adult.

_____

5. The success of the revolution is *contingent* upon the army's support.

_____

6. The mind of a cat is an *inscrutable* mystery. You can never guess what a cat is thinking.

_____

7. Gorillas are anything but the *malevolent* creatures they are portrayed to be in horror stories. On the contrary, they are gentle and peace-loving beings.

_____

8. When titles are too long to be repeated in a speech or a report, *acronyms* are extremely useful devices. For example, instead of referring repeatedly to the Women's Army Corps, we say WACs, and we say NATO in place of the North Atlantic Treaty Organization.

_____

9. My in-laws always talk in *clichés*. Tell them you're in trouble, and they tell you, "Don't worry, every cloud has a silver lining." Ask them for money, and they say, "Neither a borrower nor a lender be." Just once I'd like them to say something that hasn't been said so many times before.

_____

10. Understandably, the American colonists took *umbrage* at England's refusal to acknowledge their political rights. They showed their anger in a variety of ways, from refusing to buy English imports to tarring and feathering English sympathizers.

_____

BREAKING WORDS INTO PARTS

Context is not your only clue to word meaning. Often you can define a word by breaking it down into its Greek or Latin parts. At first glance, for example, you might be puzzled by the italicized word in the following sentence:

After the injection is administered, the patient may begin to feel *euphoric.*

Here the context of the italicized word is ambiguous and suggests opposing meanings. The injection might make the patient feel good *or* bad. It's not clear which. But what if we tell you that the Greek prefix *eu* means good? Combine this information with context, and it becomes clear that the injection will make the patient feel good rather than bad. The initial ambiguity has disappeared.

Whenever you can combine context clues with your knowledge of Greek and Latin prefixes and roots, your chances of correctly defining a word are greatly improved. We suggest, therefore, that part of your word work be devoted to learning some of the Greek and Latin prefixes and roots that commonly appear in English words. You can start by learning the lists on the following pages.

For this kind of verbatim memorization, flash cards are perfect. Put the prefix or root on one side, the definition on the other, and carry the cards with you so that you can study them during your spare moments.

A prison cell. Unless you know the context of the word, you don't know which *cell* a writer means.

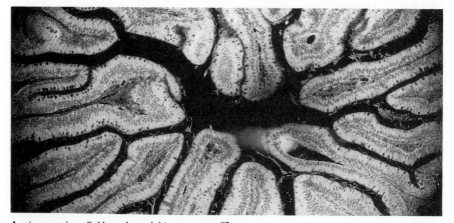

A microscopic cell. How else might you use *cell*?

Whenever you can combine context clues with a knowledge of Greek and Latin prefixes and roots, your chances of correctly defining a word are greatly improved.

List 1: *Greek and Latin Prefixes and Roots*

fid L	faith
mal G	bad, evil
circum L	around
auto G	self
fort L	strength
ver L	true
lumen L	light, shine
mon L	warn
locut, loqu L	talk, speech
simil L	like

■ PRACTICE 2   Using context *and* your knowledge of the prefixes and roots in List 1, write out an approximate definition for each underlined word.

1. **Although his speech was clear and direct, his writing was impossibly *circuitous*. It took him forever to get to the point.**

_____

2. **In the Middle Ages, *malefactors* were punished according to their crimes. Pickpockets, for example, were likely to have their hands cut off.**

_____

3. **For a painting to be termed realistic, there has to be a high degree of *verisimilitude* between the actual object and the artist's representation.**

_____

4. From this distance, the planet appears to be surrounded by a
   luminous ring of light.

   _____

5. It is not unusual for people who have been highly criticized in
   life to be *eulogized* after their death.

   _____

6. The Algerians had grown tired of their French leaders and
   were determined to fight for the *autonomy* of their country.

   _____

7. His title was "assistant administrator of human resources,"
   but it was a *euphemism* for file clerk.

   _____

8. The American public was astonished by the degree of internal
   fortitude Jackie Kennedy showed after the shocking assassi-
   nation of her husband.

   _____

9. The general's rule was first to *admonish* a soldier verbally. But
   if the soldier made the same mistake again, he would be
   harshly punished.

   _____

10. In meetings, even those people who are normally straightfor-
    ward and direct start to engage in the most time-consuming
    circumlocutions. The assumption seems to be that if it takes a
    long time to make a point, it must be important.

    _____

List 2: *Greek and Latin Roots*

gam G	marriage
ambi L	both
poly G	many
spec L	see
reg, rec L	straighten, rule
ven L	come
sent L	feel
pre L	before
hetero G	different
micro G	small

■ PRACTICE 3   Using context *and* your knowledge of the prefixes and roots in List 2, write out an approximate definition for each underlined word.

1. In that religion, *polygamy* is encouraged, and one woman can have many husbands.

_____

2. It's not clear that the situation can be *rectified;* it may be beyond repair.

_____

3. His feelings toward his brother were *ambivalent.* There were times when he admired him deeply and times when he despised him.

_____

4. All along she felt a terrible *presentiment* about the trip; she was not surprised when things started to go wrong.

_____

5. Not surprisingly, people from very different backgrounds do not always share the same *perspective.*

_____

6. The members *convened* at the appropriate site, but once there they couldn't agree on anything.

_____

7. Mensa, a society for people with high scores on intelligence tests, is an interesting group. Except for all being bright, the members are unusually *heterogeneous* and consist of people of very different ages, occupations, and backgrounds.

_____

8. In that country, the family is a *microcosm* of society at large. Understand how the family functions and you will understand the entire system of complex social relations.

_____

9. As a *prelude* to her lecture on African wildlife, she showed a number of colored slides.

_____

10. Do you have any idea what her real *sentiments* are? She's not a person who shows her feelings, and I never know what she's thinking.

_____

List 3: *Greek and Latin Prefixes and Roots*

gen G	birth, begetting
chron G	time
voc L	call
clam L	cry out
ten L	hold
string L	draw, bind tightly
path G	feeling, suffering
pan G	all
syn G	together
theo G	god

■   PRACTICE 4   Using context *and* your knowledge of the prefixes and roots in List 3, write out an approximate definition for each underlined word.

1. They usually tell the story in *chronological* order, but occasionally they use flashbacks to vary the expected order and make a dramatic point.

   _____

2. This disease has a *genetic* basis. Parents know at birth what their child's chances are for developing normally.

   _____

3. From childhood, he knew his *vocation* was for the priesthood.

   _____

4. Pit bull terriers are very *tenacious*. Once they attack they don't give up.

   _____

5. The rules for membership were *stringent*. Dress, behavior, even speech, were very carefully controlled.

   _____

6. The sudden *exclamation* from the crowd told her that her words had struck a powerful note.

_____

7. Born into a wealthy family, he didn't have much *empathy* for people on welfare. He didn't understand the real hardship of their lives; he himself had never lacked for anything.

_____

8. That drug may seem to be a *panacea,* but in time it will hurt rather than heal you.

_____

9. The dancers could not seem to *synchronize* their movements. Everyone was doing something different, and the result was hilarious.

_____

10. *Monotheism* in ancient Egypt was introduced by the Pharaoh Akhenaton. Before him, the Egyptians believed in many different gods.

_____

List 4: *Greek and Latin Prefixes and Roots*

uni L	one
bi L, **di** G	two
tri L, G	three
quadri L, **tetra** G	four
quinque L, **penta** G	five
sex L, **hex** G	six
septem L, **hepta** G	seven
oct L, G	eight
nona L	nine
dec L, G	ten

■ PRACTICE 5   Using context *and* your knowledge of the prefixes and roots in List 4, write out an approximate definition for each underlined word.

1. It wasn't a *bilateral* agreement by any means. He made the decision without consulting his business partner.

    _____

2. When the children knocked over the photographer's *tripod*, the camera went crashing to the ground.

    _____

3. She liked making *unilateral* decisions and frequently angered other members of the group.

    _____

4. Because their voices blended so beautifully, they decided to form a *sextet*.

    _____

5. With this investment, you can *quadruple* your interest if you're lucky, and lose your shirt if you're not.

    _____

6. Lawrence Durrell wrote a *tetralogy* called the *Alexandria Quartet*.

    _____

7. He constructed a *nonagon* out of colored paper.

    _____

8. They thought the old man was a *septuagenarian* but they could not be completely sure of his age.

    _____

9. The formula calls for a _decigram_.

_____

10. The architect designed a library in the shape of a _hexagon_.

_____

List 5: _Greek and Latin Prefixes and Roots_

The following list provides a good introduction to the prefixes and roots commonly used to create the specialized vocabularies of the sciences.

phot G	light
astro, aster G	star
vor L	eat, devour
hemo G	blood
cyto G	cell
derm G	skin
proto G	the earliest form, or first in time
dors L	back
hydro G	water
thermo G	heat

■   PRACTICE 6   Using context _and_ your knowledge of the prefixes and roots in List 5, write out an approximate definition for each underlined word.

1. On the table was a strange-looking specimen. Pure white all over, the _dorsal_ side of the creature showed a pronounced speckling, almost like a tattoo.

_____

2. They have detected a great deal of _photoactivity_ around the mysterious object in space.

_____

3. The earliest symptoms of the disease are fairly mild. The patient will exhibit a rapid breathing and may show evidence of a slight *dermatitis.*

_____

4. As *carnivores,* wild dogs relied heavily on their abilities as hunters to catch the prey they needed for food.

_____

5. The majority of *asteroids* are located between Jupiter and Mars.

_____

6. *Cytochemistry* was her special area of interest.

_____

7. They needed a *thermograph* to take more precise measurements.

_____

8. Because he suffered from a rare disease, he had to spend two days a week sitting in front of a *hemodialysis* machine; it was the only way to rid his blood of poisonous toxins.

_____

9. They needed a *hydroscope* to find the wreckage.

_____

10. At the archaeological site, they found the jaw bone of a *proto-human.*

_____

Visual images and symbols can help you learn new words.

KEEPING A VOCABULARY NOTEBOOK

I actually like learning new words. Knowing them makes me feel more sure of myself, more confident about how well I read and understand. I don't have the feeling that people are writing in some language I don't speak.

—Ron Krause, student

Using the context or structure of words as an aid to meaning is important. It does not, however, free you from the responsibility of learning new words. There will always be words that you cannot define through analysis of context or structure. If you want to avoid turning to the dictionary every few minutes, you should enlarge the number of vocabulary words you know *on sight*, without reference to any outside source.

One good way to accomplish this is to start and maintain a **vocabulary notebook.** Use one section for recording and learning general vocabulary words; use another for specialized words.

General vocabulary words are those that could appear anywhere—in the pages of a textbook or in an article in *Time* magazine. Anyone might use them, not just those individuals involved in some special field of study.

Specialized vocabulary words are much more restricted in use and rarely appear outside of academic or scholarly works. Two examples are words like *polynomial* in mathematics and *biogenesis* in biology. In addition to words that sound strange and unfamiliar, most specialized vocabularies contain a number of words that lead two lives. They have one meaning in general conversation but quite another when used in the context of a particular discipline. Examples would be words like *root* in math or *cell* in science.

Having suggested that you keep a notebook in order to enlarge both kinds of vocabularies, we realize this raises an important question: How do you know what words to record? We answer that question in the next section.

Enlarging Your Specialized Vocabulary

Textbook authors don't try to keep the specialized vocabulary of their discipline a secret. Introducing you to key words and phrases is one of their main purposes in writing, and they do everything possible to highlight the specialized vocabulary essential to their subject matter. You, in turn, have to be attuned to the devices authors use to emphasize key terms.

1. Look for word lists with headings like "Key Terms," "Words for Study" or "Basic Terminology."

Such headings are the author's way of highlighting the specialized vocabulary you need to learn. In addition to listing these terms on the opening (or closing) pages of chapters, the author usually defines them the *first time* they appear within the chapter. Look for such a list in any chapter you're assigned to read; jot down the words *before* you begin reading; and fill in the definitions as they appear. If, by the end of the chapter, you don't have a definition for every word, check the glossary, or ask your instructor for help.

2. Pay attention to any words or phrases set off from the text.

Here, for example, the author has doubly highlighted the phrase *greenhouse effect*—first in the margin, then in the text itself.

The Greenhouse Effect   We mentioned earlier that, as re-radiated energy enters the atmosphere, carbon dioxide and water vapor selectively absorb energy of certain wavelengths. This absorption traps and retains heat. The atmosphere thus plays a crucial role as a blanket to moderate the temperatures of the Earth. This is called the **greenhouse effect.** People coined this phrase because they thought that the atmosphere traps the Earth's heat in the same way that the glass in a greenhouse traps heat. This is not accurate. However, the expression is still used.

—Joseph Weisberg,
Meteorology

With such devices, the author tells you that "greenhouse effect" is an important term, one you should learn.

In similar fashion, textbook authors often introduce definitions of key terms within the text. Then, for emphasis, they repeat both the term and the definition in the margin.

A Definition of Language

language
A collection of arbitrary symbols that have significance for a language-using community and that follow certain rules of combination

How shall we characterize this "momentous and mysterious product of the human mind" called language? The following definition is somewhat complex, but it makes a number of psychologically important points about language. It is a paraphrase of a definition offered by Charles Morris (1946). **Language** is a large collection of arbitrary symbols that have significance for a language-using community and that follow certain combinatorial rules.

—Josh Gerow, *Psychology:*
An Introduction

Such repetition is a sure sign of importance, a strong signal that you should record both term and definition.

3. Pay special attention to familiar words that are carefully redefined in the text. If an author takes the time to define a word that is already part of your general vocabulary, don't ignore the definition, confidently assuming you already know what the word means. The word *ego,* for example, when used in everyday conversation, usually means "the capacity for self-love," as it does in statements like "He doesn't have much of an ego" or "She has a big ego." That definition, however, clearly does not apply in the following sentence:

According to psychoanalytic theory, the ego is that part of the mind which has the most contact with the external world.

When used in this context of psychology, the word *ego* takes on a new meaning, far different from the one used in ordinary conversation.

If you want extra help with the specialized vocabulary used in a particular discipline, look in the reference section of your local or college bookstore for paperback dictionaries bearing titles like *A Dictionary of Music* or *A Dictionary of Astronomy.* You can use such references to supplement the definitions in your textbook.

If an author takes the time to define a word that is already part of your general vocabulary, don't ignore the definition, confidently assuming you already know what the word means.

■ PRACTICE 7   After reading the following excerpt, list, with their definitions, the specialized vocabulary words you think the author of this selection wanted you to understand and remember.

Homeostasis and the Delicate Balance of Life

Homeostasis refers to the tendency of living things to maintain a constant internal environment (from the Greek *homios,* same, and *stasis,* standing). The term is a bit misleading, however, because no living thing strictly maintains a constant internal environment. One reason is that maintaining such rigid constancy would place a great demand on the organism's metabolic machinery. Another reason is that some change must occur in order for things to stay the same. That is, as the environment changes, the body's internal processes must also shift in order to counteract the outside changes and keep the internal conditions stable. So cells do change as they constantly monitor, metabolize, and adapt. The result is a certain internal constancy, and that is what homeostasis is all about.

Feedback Systems.   Often, the steady state is maintained by *feedback* mechanisms. Feedback occurs when the product of an action influences that action. Biologically, the most important kind of feedback action is called *negative feedback.* Negative feedback occurs when an increase in a system's product causes a slow-down of that system, or when a reduction of the product stimulates the system to increase its activity. One kind of "cruise control" on an automobile engine (a device that keeps the car moving at a certain speed) works because as the motor runs faster, valves are closed, causing the car to slow down. As it slows, the valves are reopened, and the car accelerates, keeping its speed within certain limits. Because of negative feedback mechanisms, you don't have to constantly nibble and fast to keep your blood sugars at the proper level. When blood sugars are low, the liver simply breaks down some of its stores of glycogen and releases glucose into the blood. As blood sugars rise, the liver releases less glucose.

Positive feedback works on the opposite principle: the product of a system increases the activity of that system. Using the example of an automobile, with positive feedback, accelerating the motor would tend to open the carburetor and cause the engine to run even faster. Such an engine might be revved to such limits that it would explode. Obviously, homeostasis would operate primarily through the more delicate mechanisms of negative feedback, but this is not to say that living things are not sometimes subjected to positive feedback.

—Robert A. Wallace, *Biology*

_____

_____

_____

_____

_____

Enlarging Your General Vocabulary

Deciding what specialized vocabulary words to learn is not a difficult task. Usually the authors of your texts will indicate what words you need to know, and your instructors will supplement the list. But deciding what general vocabulary words you want to learn is a bit trickier. Of course, you could follow the example of Malcolm X and learn every word on every page of the dictionary. But that would be too time-consuming and impractical. After all, many of the words in the dictionary have no bearing on anything you will ever think about or learn. Do you need to know, for example, that *aba* is a woven fabric made of goat hair or that *cess* was what the Irish once called a tax on land? You might consider learning such exotic words as these in order to become a whiz at playing *Scrabble,* but they probably won't help you read your textbooks.

Instead of going through the dictionary page by page and word for word, we suggest three more efficient ways for deciding which words to add to your general vocabulary:

1. Browse through dictionaries.

Get into the habit of leafing through the pages of a dictionary, looking for words that seem familiar or useful. The word *ubiquitous* might suddenly leap out at you as one that you had often seen or heard without knowing that it means "seeming to be everywhere at the same time." Or you might discover that the word *petulant* perfectly describes the behavior of your cousin who, since childhood, has always been cranky and irritable for no particular reason. By browsing through the dictionary looking for words that are familiar to you or that can help you describe your experience, you avoid the pitfall of learning words that have little relevance to your experience or interests.

2. Buy or borrow a book dealing with words, their history and use.

There are a number of books—many of them paperback—written expressly for vocabulary improvement and most do contain words that would make useful additions to your vocabulary notebook. Some of these books, however, do little more than list the words and their definitions. Because lists of words apart from any meaningful context are difficult to learn, these books should be avoided. Look instead for books that go beyond simple definitions to provide specific information about word use or history, as well as specific examples of the word in context. An example from one such book, *1000 Most Important Words* by Norman Schur, follows:

> **endemic** (en dem´ ik) *adj.* Anything *endemic* is characteristic, peculiar to a particular place, race, nation, sect. This word is used, for example, of diseases that flourish regularly in certain parts of the world: Dysentery is *endemic* to India, Egypt, and to much of the rest of the Third World. Not only illnesses, but also customs and folkways can be said to be *endemic* to a particular place or sect: Community singing is *endemic* to Wales. Vendettas are *endemic* to Sicily. From New Latin *endemicus,* based on Greek *endemos;* note the *demos* (people), from which we get *democracy.*

3. Spend fifteen minutes each day reading either a daily newspaper or a weekly news magazine.

As you read, circle two or three words that you don't know. After you finish the article, go back to the circled words to see if you can define them through context. Then look them up, comparing your approximate definition with the dictionary's. Once you have a clear sense of what the words mean, add them to your notebook.

■   **PRACTICE 8**   On your weekly schedule or daily "to do" list, schedule several fifteen-minute sessions devoted to browsing through the dictionary or reading the newspaper. For each session, record at least one new word that in some way interests or intrigues you.

TEN STRATEGIES FOR LEARNING NEW WORDS

Although you will certainly develop your own individual style of learning new words, we offer ten suggestions that have proven effective.

1. Write words and their definitions in separate columns.
Arrange your vocabulary notebook so that the word you want to learn appears next to the left margin while all definitions appear to the far right, as shown:

Topography	the surface features of the earth

Arranging words and definitions in this way will help you take a more active role during reviews. Instead of looking at the words and definitions without thinking about them, you can test yourself by covering each definition and then trying to recall the definition *before* you actually look at it for confirmation.

2. Record your own personal definition as well as the formal dictionary definitions.
In addition to recording the formal definitions you find in the dictionary or glossary, make up your own definitions, using more familiar and more informal language. To learn *peremptory,* for example, you should certainly record the dictionary definition, "dictatorial." But you should also jot down a more familiar definition like "bossy."

3. Give new words a context as well as a definition.
Whenever possible record the sentence (or sentences) in which new words appear, as we have done in the following example:

General Vocabulary

sanguine   bloodstained
                Professor Von Helsing pulled his sanguine sword
                from the vampire's heaving chest.

Specialized Vocabulary

endogamy   marriage restricted to members of the same group.
                            Although the three major religions do stress the
                            importance of endogamy, the practice is declining.

4. **Collect various examples of the word in context; be alert to the way in which context can change meaning.**

At this point you know that *sanguine* means bloodstained, but what if you started to collect sentences like the following?

> His sanguine personality made him a delight to be with.

> As I child I was more sanguine in nature, not so dark and moody as I am now.

Obviously you would realize that *sanguine* can also mean "optimistic" or "cheery," and you would add that second meaning to your original definition.

5. **Look for antonyms and synonyms that can help you learn new words.**

To learn the word *imperious*, for example, compare and contrast it with words like *arrogant* and *humble*. When learning the word *dorsal*, meaning "back," learn the word *ventral*, meaning "front."

6. **Create your own analogies.**

To learn the word *osmosis*, an essential term in biology, create an analogy like the following:

> In the process of *osmosis*, the cell membrane functions like a gatekeeper. It lets in the appropriate visitors and keeps out the inappropriate ones.

7. **Associate the word you want to learn with someone you know.**

To remember that *laconic* means "using a minimum of words," imagine the characters that Clint Eastwood plays in his movies. *Laconic* is the perfect word to describe them.

8. **Use diagrams to express relationships among words.**

To remember the word *incensed*, which means "furious," you could represent it on a scale, or continuum, reflecting increasing degrees of anger:

distressed $\rightarrow$ irritated $\rightarrow$ angry $\rightarrow$ irate $\rightarrow$ incensed

9. Create a visual image of the word in action.

If you want to learn the word *surreptitiously,* which means "in a secret or underhanded fashion," visualize a burglar tiptoeing up carpeted stairs or a child passing a note in class.

10. Periodically review your notebook for words you can group together.

Over time, you will probably collect a number of words with similar meanings. For example, the words *petulant, sulky, sullen, morose,* and *baleful* all refer to unhappy and irritable feelings. Grouping them together will help you remember them; it will also make you think about the different shades of meaning they suggest.

Similarly, consider grouping together words that stem from the same root. The words *vita, vitality,* and *vitiate* are examples of words called **cognates,** which means they have a common origin. Grouping them together will help you remember what they mean.

■   **PRACTICE 9**   How many different contexts, and therefore different meanings, can you create for the following words?

1. cell	**4. center**
2. form	**5. drive**
3. eye	

■   **PRACTICE 10**   In the left column are five words used to describe people, their personalities and temperaments. For each one, write down some of the associations or images you would use to remember what the words mean.

WORD   **DEFINITION**

diffident   **shy**

_____

_____

gregarious   **sociable**

_____

_____

loquacious   **talkative**

_____

_____

vivacious   **lively**

_____

_____

avaricious   **greedy**

_____

_____

DECIPHERING THE DICTIONARY

Browsing through the dictionary to collect useful new words would be an easy matter were all of the entries like this one:

> **der•ry** (dè´ rē) n. pl. **-ries.** A meaningless word used as a refrain or chorus in old songs.

This is a neat and compact entry, with one brief definition and no confusion. But not all entries are so concise. Consider this second one, taken from the _Random House Dictionary of the English Language:_

> **ex•ten•u•ate** (ik sten´ yōō āt´), v.t., -at•ed, -at•ing. **1.** to represent (a fault, offense, etc.) as less serious: _to extenuate a crime._ **2.** to serve to make (a fault, offense, etc.) seem less serious. **3.** to underestimate, underrate or make light of: _Do not extenuate the difficulties we are in._ **4.** _Archaic._ a. to make thin, lean, or emaciated   b. to reduce the consistency or density of. [1375 - 1425; late ME (adj.) L _extenuātus,_ ptp. of _extenuāre,_ equiv. to _ex-_ EX-¹ + _tenuāre to make thin or small; see -ATE¹_] —**ex•ten´u•at´ing,** adj. —**ex•ten´u•at´ing•ly.** adv. — **ex•ten´ u•at´ ive,** adj. —**ex•ten´ u•at´ or,** n.

a hat	i it	oi oil	ch child		a in about
ā age	ī ice	ou out	ng long		e in taken
ä far	o hot	u cup	sh she	ə =	i in pencil
e let	ō open	ù put	th thin		o in lemon
ē equal	ô order	ü rule	ŦH then		u in circus
ėr term			zh measure	< = derived from

in at ten tion (in'ə ten'shən), *n.* lack of attention; carelessness; negligence.

in at ten tive (in'ə ten'tiv), *adj.* not attentive; careless; negligent. **—in'at ten'tive ly,** *adv.* **—in'at ten'tive ness,** *n.*

in au di bil i ty (in ô'də bil'ə tē), *n.* a being inaudible.

in au di ble (in ô'də bəl), *adj.* that cannot be heard. **—in au'- di bly,** *adv.*

in au gu ral (in ô'gyər əl), *adj.* 1 of, for, or having to do with an inauguration: *an inaugural address.* 2 beginning; first. *—n.* the address or speech made by a person when formally admitted to office.

in au gu rate (in ô'gyə rāt'), *v.t.,* **-rat ed, -rat ing.** 1 install in office with formal ceremonies: *A President of the United States is inaugurated every four years.* 2 make a formal beginning of; begin: *The invention of the airplane inaugurated a new era in transportation.* 3 open for public use with a formal ceremony or celebration. [< Latin *inauguratum* consecrated by augury < *in-* for + *augurare* act as an augur, predict < *augur* taker of omens, augur] **—in au'gu ra'tor,** *n.*

in au gu ra tion (in ô'gyə rā'shən), *n.* 1 act or ceremony of installing a person in office. 2 a formal beginning; beginning. 3 an opening for public use with a formal ceremony or celebration.

in aus pi cious (in'ô spish'əs), *adj.* with signs of failure; unfavorable; unlucky. **—in'aus pi'cious ly,** *adv.* **—in'aus pi'- cious ness,** *n.*

in-be tween (in'bi twēn'), *adj.* 1 being or coming between. 2 of neither one kind nor the other. *—adv.* between. **—in'- be tween'ness,** *n.*

in board (in'bôrd', in'bōrd'), *adv., adj.* 1 inside the hull of a ship or boat: *an inboard motor.* 2 in or toward the middle of a ship or boat. 3 in or toward the central axis of an aircraft or spacecraft.

in born (in'bôrn'), *adj.* born in a person; instinctive; natural.

in bound (in'bound'), *adj.* inward bound: *an inbound flight.*

in bred (in'bred'), *adj.* 1 inborn; natural: *an inbred courtesy.* 2 produced by breeding between closely related ancestors: *an inbred strain of horses.* *—v.* pt. and pp. of **inbreed.**

in breed (in'brēd', in brēd'), *v.t.,* **-bred, -breed ing.** 1 breed from closely related organisms. 2 produce or develop within.

in breed ing (in'brē'ding), *n.* breeding from closely related organisms so as to preserve desired or eliminate undesired characteristics.

in-built (in'bilt'), *adj.* built-in: *in-built safeguards.*

inc., 1 including. 2 incorporated.

In ca (ing'kə), *n.,* pl. **-ca** or **-cas.** 1 member of an ancient people of South America who had a highly developed culture and ruled a large empire in Peru and other parts of South America before it fell to the Spaniards in the 1500's. 2 ruler or member of the royal family of this people. **—In'can,** *adj.*

in cal cu la bil i ty (in kal'kyə lə bil'ə tē), *n.* a being incalculable.

in cal cu la ble (in kal'kyə lə bəl), *adj.* 1 too great in number to be counted; innumerable. 2 impossible to foretell or reckon beforehand. 3 that cannot be relied on; uncertain. **—in cal'- cu la bly,** *adv.*

in can desce (in'kən des'), *v.i., v.t.,* **-desced, -desc ing.** glow or cause to glow with heat. [< Latin *incandescere* begin to glow < *in-* (intensive) + *candescere* become white-hot]

in can des cence (in'kən des'ns), *n.* a being incandescent.

in can des cent (in'kən des'nt), *adj.* 1 heated to such a high temperature that it gives out light; glowing with heat; red-hot or white-hot. 2 shining brightly; brilliant. 3 having to do with or containing a material that gives light by incandescence. **—in'- can des'cent ly,** *adv.*

incandescent lamp, an electric lamp with a filament of very fine wire that becomes white-hot and gives off light when current flows through it; light bulb.

in can ta tion (in'kan tā'shən), *n.* 1 set of words spoken as a magic charm or to cast a magic spell. 2 the use of such words. [< Latin *incantationem < incaniare* enchant < *in-* against + *caniare* to chant]

in can ta tion al (in'kan tā'shə nəl), *adj.* incantatory.

in can ta to ry (in kan'tə tôr'ē, in kan'tə tōr'ē), *adj.* of or like an incantation.

in ca pa bil i ty (in'kā pə bil'ə tē), *n.* a being incapable; incapacity.

in ca pa ble (in kā'pə bəl), *adj.* 1 without ordinary ability; not efficient; not competent: *An employer cannot afford to hire incapa-* ble workers. 2 **incapable of,** a without the ability, power, or fitness for: *I felt incapable of playing such difficult piano music.* b not legally qualified for: *A foreigner is incapable of becoming President of the United States.* c not susceptible to; not open or ready for: *incapable of exact measurement.* **—in ca'pa ble ness,** *n.* **—in ca'pa bly,** *adv.*

in ca pac i tant (in'kə pas'ə tənt), *n.* chemical or drug which affects the body or mind so as to temporarily paralyze or disable the recipient. Incapacitants have been developed for use in warfare.

in ca pac i tate (in'kə pas'ə tāt), *v.t.,* **-tat ed, -tat ing.** 1 deprive of ability, power, or fitness; disable: *Her injury incapacitated her for working.* 2 legally disqualify. **—in'ca pac'i ta'- tion,** *n.*

in ca pac i ty (in'kə pas'ə tē), *n., pl.* **-ties.** 1 lack of ability, power, or fitness; disability. 2 legal disqualification.

in car ce rate (in kär'sə rāt'), *v.t.,* **-rat ed, -rat ing.** imprison. [< Late Latin *incarceratum* imprisoned < Latin *in-* + *carcer* prison] **—in car'ce ra'tion,** *n.* **—in car'ce ra'tor,** *n.*

in car na dine (in kär'nə dən, in kär'nə dīn, in kär'nə dēn'), *adj., v.,* **-dined, -din ing.** *—adj.* 1 blood-red. 2 flesh-colored. *—v.t.* make blood-red or flesh-colored. [ultimately < Latin *in- + carnem* flesh]

in car nate (*adj.* in kär'nit, in kär'nāt; *v.* in kär'nāt), *adj., v.,* **-nat ed, -nat ing.** *—adj.* embodied in flesh, especially in human form; personified; typified: *the Devil incarnate, evil incarnate.* *—v.t.* 1 make incarnate; embody: *Lancelot incarnated the spirit of chivalry.* 2 put into or represent in concrete form; realize: *The sculptor incarnated her vision in a beautiful statue.* [< Latin *incarnatum, < in- + carnem* flesh]

in car na tion (in'kär nā'shən), *n.* 1 a taking on of human form by a divine being. 2 **the Incarnation,** (in Christian theology) the union of divine nature and human nature in the person of Jesus; assumption of human form by the son of God. 3 embodiment.

in case (in kās'), *v.t.,* **-cased, -cas ing.** encase. **—in case'- ment,** *n.*

in cau tious (in kô'shəs), *adj.* not cautious; reckless; rash. **—in cau'tious ly,** *adv.* **—in cau'tious ness,** *n.*

in cen di a rism (in sen'dē ə riz'əm), *n.* 1 crime of setting property on fire intentionally. 2 the deliberate stirring up of strife, violence, or rebellion.

in cen di ar y (in sen'dē er'ē), *adj., n., pl.* **-ar ies.** *—adj.* 1 having to do with the crime of setting property on fire intentionally. 2 causing fires; used to start a fire: *an incendiary bomb.* 3 deliberately stirring up strife, violence, or rebellion: *incendiary speeches.* *—n.* 1 person who intentionally sets fire to property. 2 person who deliberately stirs up strife, violence, or rebellion. 3 shell or bomb containing chemical agents that cause fire. [< Latin *incendiarius* causing fire < *incendium* fire < *incendere* to set on fire]

in cense¹ (in'sens), *n.* 1 substance giving off a sweet smell when burned. 2 the perfume or smoke from it. 3 something sweet like incense: *the incense of flowers, the incense of flattery.* [< Old French *encens* < Late Latin *incensum* < Latin *incendere* to set on fire, burn]

in cense² (in sens'), *v.t.,* **-censed, -cens ing.** make very angry; fill with rage. [< Latin *incensum* inflamed, enraged, set on fire < *in-* (intensive) + *candere* glow white] **—in cense'ment,** *n.*

in cen ter (in'sen'tər), *n.* (in mathematics) the center of the inscribed circle of a triangle.

in cen tive (in sen'tiv), *n.* thing that urges a person on; cause of action or effort; motive; stimulus. *—adj.* inciting; encouraging. [< Latin *incentivum < incinere* cause to sound < *in-* on + *canere* sing]

incenter—Point P is the incenter.

in cep tion (in sep'shən), *n.* a beginning or originating; commencement: *the inception of a plan.* [< Latin *inceptionem < in-* on + *capere* take]

in cep tive (in sep'tiv), *adj.* 1 beginning; initial. 2 (in grammar) expressing the beginning of an action. *—n.* an inceptive verb.

The second entry opens like the first. It offers a phonetic explanation of how to pronounce the word (ik sten´ yoo̅ āt´), identifies the part of speech *(v.t.)*, as a verb (a transitive verb, meaning it takes an object), and lists possible endings (-ated, -ating). But here the resemblance ends. The second entry contains not one but three definitions currently in use:

1. to represent (a fault, offense, etc.) as less serious
2. to serve to make (a fault, offense, etc.) seem less serious
3. to underestimate, underrate or make light of

Definition 3 is followed by a sample sentence—"Do not extenuate the difficulties we are in." Definition 4 is labeled *Archaic*, which identifies two meanings of extenuate that are no longer in use: "a. to make thin, lean or emaciated; b. to reduce the consistency or density of."

There is also a bracketed explanation of **etymology** or word origin, telling you that the word entered the English language between 1375 and 1425 as an adjective *(adj.)*. Finally, the entry explains that the word *extenuate* is derived from the Latin word *extenuatus,* a form of the Latin verb *extenuare,* meaning to make thin or small.

Because dictionary entries can be quite detailed, it helps to know what kinds of information you can expect to find. To help you browse with ease, we have compiled a list of frequently used entry terms, symbols, and labels.

Some Common Terms, Symbols, and Labels

- **Numbers** (1, 2, 3, 4) are usually used to identify and separate definitions. Keep in mind, however, that not all dictionaries list their definitions of a word in the same order. Some give the most *common* meaning first while others give the *oldest* known definition first and conclude with the most current one. Check the introductory pages of your dictionary to discover which method has been used.

- **Brackets** [ ] frequently set off explanations of word origin. The most common abbreviations found within these brackets are L. for Latin, G. or Gr. for Greek, OE. for Old English, ME. for Middle English and Fr. for French.

- The label **Vulgar** in an entry warns that the word is socially unacceptable.

- The label **obs** or **Obsolete** announces that a particular word or word meaning is no longer in use. The word *consort,* for example, used to mean escort or accompany when Middle English was spoken. But today that meaning is obsolete.

- Labels like **Informal** or **Slang** indicate that the word is appropriate in a friendly conversation but not in a formal report or speech. The word *thingamajig,* for example, would be considered appropriate in everyday conversation but inappropriate in a formal lecture or paper.

- *n., v., adj., adv., pron., prep., conj.,* and *interj.* are labels for **parts of speech.** They tell you if the word can be used as a noun, verb, adjective, adverb, pronoun, preposition, conjunction, or interjection.

- Labels like **syn.** or **Synonyms** introduce words similar in meaning to the entry word, as you can see from the following entry:

> **con•sid•er** (ken•sid′ ər) *v.* **-ered, -ering, -ers.** —*tr.* **1.** To deliberate upon; examine; study. **2.** To regard as; think or deem to be: *considered him a fool.* **3.** To believe, especially after deliberation; judge: *considers waste criminal.* **4.** To take into account; make allowance for: *Consider that he's just a beginner.* **5.** To have regard for; pay attention to: *Consider her feelings.* **5.** To regard highly, esteem. **7.** To think about as possible or acceptable: *refused to consider the other possibilities.* —*intr.* To think carefully; reflect. [Middle English *consideren,* from Old French *considerer,* from Latin *considerâ,* to observe (originally a term of augury, meaning "to observe the stars carefully").] —**con•sid•er•er** *n.*
> **Synonyms:** *account, deem, reckon, regard.*

- After the label **Usage,** you will find an explanation of how to use the defined word correctly. Look, for example, at the usage notes that accompany the word *conscious* in the *American Heritage Illustrated Dictionary:*

> **con•scious** (kōn′ shəs) *adj.* **1. a.** Having an awareness of one's own existence, sensations, and thoughts and of one's environment. **b.** Having a particular preception; aware: *conscious of having offended her.* **2.** Not asleep or stuporous; awake: *conscious after surgery.* **3.** Subjectively known and felt: *She spoke with conscious pride.* **4.** Intentionally conceived or done; deliberate: *a conscious insult.* **5.** Having or showing self-consciousness: *conscious of her lump.* **6.** Concerned about or interested in something. Often used in combination: *fashion-conscious.*
> —*n.* The component of waking awareness perceptible by an individual at any given instant. Preceded by *the* [Latin *conscius,* knowing with others, participating in knowledge, aware of: *com-* with + *scire,* to know.] —**con•scious•ly** *adv.*
> Usage: *Conscious, subconscious, preconscious* and *unconscious.* These are psychological terms referring to aspects of the workings of the mind. *Conscious* refers to mental processes, such as thoughts or

emotional reactions, of which a person is aware. *Subconscious* pertains to thoughts or feelings outside the immediate awareness either wholly or partly. *Preconscious* refers to mental processes that are outside the consciousness, but are easily brought into the conscious mind. *Unconscious* alludes to all mental processes that a person is not aware of, including thoughts or feelings that have been forgotten or repressed, and also images, instincts, desires, and the like. It is often used interchangeably with *subconscious.*

- The symbol < means "from," and it shows descent from one language to another. To indicate that the word *corroborate* meaning to confirm came from Latin, the entry would read < *corroboratus.*

- The label **Rare** tells you that a word is not often found in contemporary English. The word *nocent,* for example, meaning "harmful" or "injurious," is seldom used and is usually followed by the label **Rare.**

- **Idioms** are brief and familiar expressions that are unique to a particular language. Although speakers of that language understand idioms, their meanings are not predictable from the words used in the expression. Idioms usually appear at the end of an entry and are printed in boldface as in the following entry for *blood:*

> **17. have someone's blood on one's head or hands,** to be to blame for someone's affliction or death: *Though a criminal, he had no blood on his hands.* **18. In cold blood,** deliberately; ruthlessly: *The dictator, in cold blood, ordered the execution of all his political enemies.* **19. Make one's blood boil,** to inspire resentment, anger, or indignation: *Such carelessness makes my blood boil.* **20. Make one's blood run cold,** to fill with terror; frighten: *The dark, deserted street in that unfamiliar neighborhood made her blood run cold.*

Although the above list will help you understand the entries in most dictionaries, it's no substitute for reading the introduction to your own dictionary. To know exactly what kinds of information your dictionary offers, you have to spend some time reading its opening pages.

■ PRACTICE 11   Using a desk or college dictionary, answer the following questions. (Pocket dictionaries, useful for carrying to class, won't have the kind of detailed entries you will need.)

   1. Which of the common dictionary terms, symbols, and labels do you find when you look up the word *infer*?

2. **What are some synonyms for the word** *bicker?*
3. **How many definitions can you find for the word** *bring?*
4. **What part of speech is the word** *brindled?*
5. **What does the word** *sesquipedalian* **mean? From what language did it originate?**
6. **What is the etymology of the word** *quisling?*
7. **Does the first syllable in the word** *heinous* **rhyme with the word** *pain* **or with the word** *high?*
8. **What does the word** *constant* **mean when it is used by mathematicians?**
9. **List two different meanings of the word** *console.*
10. **If you wanted to find synonyms for the word** *consternation,* **meaning** *sudden confusion,* **under what entry word would you look?**

WORKING SPACE

READING ASSIGNMENT

In the following newspaper article, Sheila Klass tells the story of a man who couldn't resist using big words to explain the simplest thoughts. After you finish reading the article, think about what Klass wants you to understand about language—its use and its abuse.

For Mr. Johnson, the Elements of Style

Leonia, N.J.—He was a chunky man in his early forties. I noticed him because he took notes. Copious notes. In freshman composition, there is not a lot of lecture material worth taking down, but he—I will call him Kenneth Johnson—copied assiduously.* That was one of his words: assiduously. Others were: corroborate, temerity, altercation, depredation, contumacy, tergiversation, crepitant. He had hundreds

---

* assiduosly: diligently, persistently
 corroborate: to strengthen or support
 temerity: recklessness, boldness
 altercation: argument or fight

depredation: robbing or plundering
contumacy: stubborn resistance to authority
tergiversation: evasion or desertion
crepitant: rattling, cackling

of them, perhaps thousands, that he had hoarded for years and was now squandering recklessly in my class.

Witness the opening paragraphs in his autobiographical essay: "My appellation is Kenneth Johnson. I am employed at the General Post Office as a clerk and I hope to surpass that job very soon. I consider myself a voracious worker with interminable amounts of energy. . . . I have taken innumerable and costly courses in Building Your Vocabulary and Personal Confidence Development. These scholastic endeavors have emboldened me to attend college and pursue a baccalaureate degree. . . . To be or not to be someone; that is the question. I want to be someone more than a postal clerk."

He went on that way for four pages. He could spell and he understood grammar better than most of his classmates, but his skills were buried under the thick camouflage of vocabulary. Kenneth Johnson was in love with words. Monumental words.

I'd been teaching freshman English courses long enough to know that the worst thing that can happen to a shaky freshman is a slash attack on his writing, red bleeding all over his pages. I couldn't see any brief way of helping Mr. Johnson, so I underlined "appellation" and "prognosticate,"* and wrote "Diction" in the margin along with a note asking him to see me in my office.

He was there waiting when my last class let out. "I fail to perceive what is wrong with my essay," he said, his voice unsteady. "I cannot fathom why you wrote 'Diction' and drew red lines all over my paper."

"Not all over it. Just in two places," I said. "Diction means your choice of words and the way you use them."

"I comprehend that. But why did you write it on my paper?"

"Mr. Johnson," I began softly, "good writing is straightforward and simple. The writer says what he has to say as clearly as he can."

He shook his head emphatically. "Why do you want to denigrate† me?"

"I don't, Mr. Johnson. Not at all."

He just went right on. "I travail all day in the post office. I come here after a long day's work to pursue my education, and then you go and scribble red marks on my paper."

"Let's go over the writing," I said. "Look at the very first line. 'My appellation is Kenneth Johnson.' "

"Well, it is."

---

* prognosticate: predict
† denigrate: reduce in stature or importance

"It's too fancy. Why not say, 'My name is Kenneth Johnson'?"

"Is 'appellation' wrong there?"

"It's wrong stylistically. It's too formal. You wouldn't say that to anyone, so why write it?"

"But I do say it," he said. "Whenever I'm introduced to someone, I say, 'My appellation is Kenneth Johnson.' "

I believed him. "Look, Mr. Johnson, there's formal English for official use, for documents and critical writing. Then there's informal English, which is the language used to carry on everyday business. That's what I'm asking for. Informal English."

He wasn't listening. "I was the stellar* student in each of the vocabulary courses I took at the Metropolitan Evening Academy. I became something of a personage† there. I am not vainglorious,†† but I may say that my virtuosity with language confounded my instructors."

He leaned forward, elbow on the desk, his hand supporting his forehead, his eyes closed. For years and years, he had subjected himself to pitiless self-improvement courses and I was now destroying what he had so carefully constructed.

"Let me lend you a book," I offered, searching about in my desk drawer, "a very famous book, *The Elements of Style*. These two writers, Strunk and White, explain the way the language works much better than I can."

"That little paperback?" He stared at it disdainfully. "I already own two hardcover rhetorics."

"If you memorized this book," I said, "you would know most of what you need to know about writing."

He took up the book and riffled through the pages. I could see that he was bucked up. Kenneth Johnson was no weakling, no quitter.

"Take it and look it over before you decide about the class," I suggested.

"This book is easy," he said, getting up. "I'll know it by heart in a couple of weeks." Suddenly, he inclined his head. "My name is Kenneth Johnson," he practiced, and put forth his hand, which I took gratefully. "I still think 'appellation' sounds better."

About a half hour after that, I was arrested. I had boarded the "A train" and was glancing at advertisements and graffiti, when I saw the bright placard, red letters on a blue background:

---

* stellar: star

† personage: important person

†† vainglorious: boastful

Improve Your
Vocabulary and Change
Your Life
Words Make the Man

There were lots of little tickets attached to the bottom with the
name, address, and phone number of the school. I went over and
pulled off one ticket, and then a few, and then all. Next, I went for
the placard. The few passengers in the car edged away nervously.
The cop came along just as I was gloriously finishing the shredding.

I'll do what he said. Tell it to the judge. It was the first real blow I
had struck for English in years.

---

1.   What is the main point of this article?

2.   Is that point stated somewhere in the article, or did you have to
     infer it?

3.   What does the author mean when she says "his skills were buried
     under the thick camouflage of vocabulary"?

4.   What kind of *tone* or voice did you read in the article? Do you
     think the author is being humorous or serious about her subject?

5.   Why does the author equate pulling down the placard with "striking a blow for English"?

6.   According to this article, when would you use formal English? When would you use informal English?

7.   Given this article, do you think the author would discourage students from learning new words? What exactly would her advice be?

WRITING ASSIGNMENT: "Personifying Words"

One way to learn new words is to *personify* them, treating them as if they were human beings. This is what student Maria Sofranski has done to clarify her understanding of the words *compassion* and *empathy.*

> Compassion can often be seen with her big sister Empathy. Now that I think of it, they are really apart. They have been around the block and back, so they know better than to make snap judgments. They always put themselves in the other person's shoes, always remember to walk a mile in his moccasins, and they never forget their own mistakes and how they longed for understanding when they made them. They are great to have around when the chips are down.

Now try your hand at personifying one of the words introduced in Practice 10: diffident, gregarious, loquacious, vivacious, avaricious.

JOURNAL ASSIGNMENTS

1. Describe your personal relationship to your language. Do you think you use words with ease, or do you find it difficult to find the words to express your thoughts? Would you say that new words delight or intimidate you? Do you think you need to improve your knowledge of words?

2. What do you think the poet Emily Dickinson is saying about words and their use?

> A word is dead
> When it is said,
> Some say.
> I say it just
> Begins to live
> That day.

CHECKING OUT

Check your understanding of Chapter 6 by writing out answers to the following questions. You can work alone or with a friend, whichever you prefer.

1. What is the difference between a general and a specialized vocabulary?

2. When should you turn to a dictionary to define an unfamiliar word?

3. Name three ways to learn new words.

4. How can a basic knowledge of Greek and Latin help you in your reading?

5. What does the label *Archaic* mean?

6. What are three examples of English idioms?

IN SUMMARY

Use your vocabulary notebook to expand and enrich both your general and specialized vocabularies. In addition, sharpen your ability to decipher context clues, and spend a few minutes each day mastering Greek and Latin prefixes and roots. When you can use context clues *and* your knowledge of word parts to define new words, you will greatly reduce your reliance on the dictionary.

This kind of consistent word work will improve your ability to understand your textbooks. But it will also increase your self-confidence by making you feel more comfortable with your own language. The language of your teachers will also be yours, and you will know that you truly belong in college.

CHAPTER 7

THREE STRATEGIES
FOR READING TEXTBOOKS

The art of reading is among other things the art of adopting the pace the author has set. Some books are fast and some are slow, but no book can be understood if it is taken at the wrong speed.

—Mark Van Doren

OVERVIEW

In Chapter 5, you learned that *flexibility* is an essential characteristic of skillful readers. In this chapter, we will take that explanation a step further and describe three different strategies for reading college textbooks. Which strategy you choose for a specific assignment depends on your purpose in reading and the difficulty of the material.

- A rapid *inspectional* reading will give you the chapter's overall purpose or objective and help you anticipate what is to come.

- An *intensive* reading at your normal speed will give you the message of the chapter and show you how each individual section contributes to the chapter as a whole.

- Used only for particularly demanding texts, an *analytical* reading will help you decipher difficult and detailed textbook passages.

Some chapters will benefit from all three kinds of reading. Others will become clear with only two—a brief inspectional reading followed by a more intensive one. Occasionally, if you think the material is easy to understand, you might even omit the inspectional reading and rely solely on a careful intensive reading to discover the author's message. It's up to you to determine exactly which strategies will best suit your assignment.

INSPECTIONAL READING

Reading researchers differ a great deal in their attempts to describe reading—what it is and what it entails. But on one point they all agree: the more often readers can anticipate what a text will be about, the easier it is for them to understand its message. Readers who know what to expect find it easier to discover an author's key points and to distinguish between relevant and irrelevant information—the two major tasks of any reading assignment.

Translating theory into practice, skillful readers usually try to predict what a chapter will say *before* they actually read it. To this end, they focus on *selected portions* of the chapter in order to get a general sense of its length, content, and structure.

The key phrase here is "selected portions." An inspectional reading of a chapter should take no more than ten or fifteen minutes. That should be enough time for you to complete these basic steps:

1. Read the chapter title and any opening questions or objectives.
The chapter title is a crucial clue to understanding the author's topic and purpose. In addition to the title, textbook authors frequently open a chapter with a list of questions the chapter will answer or objectives it will meet. This kind of introductory material is enormously helpful because it can tell you, in a few words, what to look for as you read. Never ignore such opening lists. Read them carefully. Use them to focus your attention during another more careful reading of the chapter—what we call an intensive reading, described later in this chapter.

2. Read the introduction.
Speakers don't just walk on stage and plunge into a speech. They are introduced by someone who provides background information about both the speaker and the speech and thus lays the groundwork for what is to come. This is not just a polite formality. It's a way of making sure that the audience understands the underlying purpose or point.

Because they know that introductions can aid readers, many textbook authors open their chapters with a section titled **Introduction** or **Overview** in order to announce the **chapter's purpose** or **objective.** Aware of this practice, skillful readers actively search for sentences that offer an explicit statement of purpose like the following.

Having explored the characteristics of an economic boom in the previous chapter, we will now extend that discussion by showing how such inflationary spending almost invariably leads to an economic downturn or depression.

If skillful readers fail to find such sentences, they use introductory anecdotes, questions, or quotations to infer the chapter's purpose. Such advance knowledge makes it easier for them to understand and relate the chapter's individual parts.

3. Read the chapter headings and turn them into questions.

By reading just the **Major** and *Minor* headings of a chapter, you can learn what topics the chapter will cover and how thoroughly the author will explain them. But you should also **use the headings to raise questions about the chapter,** questions that will help you focus your reading and maintain your concentration. Should you see, for example, headings like "Learning While Asleep," or "Learning on the Right Side of the Brain," turn those headings into questions like "Can we learn while asleep?" and "What kind of learning is done with the right side of the brain?" **Then read to discover the answers.**

Age, race, religion, social class, and propinquity are factors that you must consider when choosing a mate. The sample chapter, "Mate Selection," on pages 173–181 covers such issues.

4. Look at all the visual aids.

There is still truth in the old saying: one picture is worth a thousand words. It is to your benefit to look at all the visual aids—everything from photographs to boxes to tables—that an author uses. Whatever form they take, those visual aids serve the same purpose: they highlight and clarify key points. They can therefore suggest a great deal about the chapter *before* you actually launch in and read it.

5. Turn to the end of the chapter and read any review questions, summaries, or conclusions.

As a reader, it's your task to sort out what is essential in a chapter and what is not. However, authors, particularly textbook authors, who almost always teach the subjects they write about, know that their readers need help with this task, and they provide that help in the form of final sections bearing headings like **Summary, Review, Questions,** or **Conclusions.** The purpose of these sections is to sum up the essential points in a chapter; they are the author's way of saying, "This is what you should know after reading what I have written."

6. Prepare yourself for a more thorough reading by mobilizing your own personal knowledge of the subject.

As we pointed out in Chapter 5, writers expect their readers to help create the text they read. This will be easier to do if you get in the habit of calling up what you already know about the topic at hand before you actually start to read. Imagine, for example, that you are going to read a chapter on how the media shape public opinion. Now is the time to think about how television, radio, film, and newspapers have affected you personally. Has your opinion of a political candidate ever been changed by a newspaper editorial? Do you know anyone who stopped smoking because of the warnings about smoking that are broadcast on television?

To be sure, there will be some topics about which you will have little or no personal knowledge. But this will happen less often than you think, once you make a concentrated effort to forge links between what you are about to read and what you already know.

Reading researchers differ a great deal in their attempts to describe reading—what it is and what it entails. On one point they all agree: the more readers can anticipate what a text will be about, the easier it is for them to understand its message.

■ PRACTICE 1   Take a few minutes to do an inspectional reading of the sample chapter ''Mate Selection,'' on choosing a mate, on pages 173–181 of this text. When you are finished, underline the sentence or sentences that you think define the purpose of the chapter. Then, on the basis of your inspectional reading, list some points that you expect the author to make about mate selection.

The author's main points about mate selection are

1. _____

2. _____

3. _____

4. _____

5. _____

■ PRACTICE 2   Use the major or minor headings in the sample chapter (on pages 173–181) to develop three or four questions about mate selection. Then, using your personal knowledge about why people do or do not marry, write a short answer to each question.

1. _____

   _____

2. _____

   _____

3. _____

   _____

4. _____

   _____

INTENSIVE READING

I would advise you to read with a pen in your hand, and enter in a little book short hints of what you find that is curious, or that might be useful; for this will be the best method of imprinting such particulars in your memory, where they will be ready.
—Benjamin Franklin

A brisk inspectional reading will give you the key point or purpose of a chapter. Sometimes it can even tell you what generalizations or topics are explained in each major division or section of the chapter. But to understand those generalizations or topics thoroughly, you have to do an intensive reading in which you read, at your normal speed, the entire chapter, not just selected portions.

To be productive, **an intensive reading must be purposeful.** It must have an aim, and you should know what you're looking for. That's why questions like the following are important. They will help you focus your attention and keep you alert to key points and relationships.

1. Based on the headings, what predictions can I make about each chapter section?

The headings or titles that introduce each section of a chapter can tell you something about the author's purpose in writing. The heading "Three Types of Blood Vessels," for example, tells you that the author is going to describe in detail the three types of blood vessels in the human body. A heading like the following, however, suggests that the author is going to concentrate on one main point: "Einstein's Theory of Relativity: A Revolution in Both Science and Philosophy."

Along the same lines, headings that pose questions like "Does the mind really influence the body?" implicitly tell you that the author's intention is to provide an answer. Finding that answer should be your goal in reading. As you know from Chapter 5, readers who can correctly predict how an author's train of thought will develop have the advantage. It's important, therefore, that you pay careful attention to headings throughout the chapter. Use them not just to raise questions about the chapter but also to predict the contents of the chapter.

2. What does each chapter section contribute to the overall message of the chapter?

Keep in mind that each chapter section is part of a larger whole. That means you can't read each section as if it appeared in isolation. When you finish each section of a chapter, you should mentally **synthesize** or combine what you have just read with what you already know. In more specific terms, that means you have to ask yourself questions like the following: "What does the point made in this section contribute to the chapter's overall purpose or objective?" "How does this section further develop the author's train of thought?" True, the author will provide some guidance through the use of *transitional sentences* like the following: "Having explored Martin Luther King, Jr.'s role in the civil rights movement, we now turn to a discussion of Malcolm X." (For more on transitions, see pp. 206–207.) Still, it's primarily your job to *infer* how each section relates to the overall purpose or message of the chapter.

3. What specialized vocabulary do I need to master this material?
During an intensive reading, look for any specialized vocabulary. More to the point, you have to be alert for those places where the author provides the appropriate definitions. Mark or record these for further study.

4. What portions of this text are particularly important? What should I intend to remember?
Your instructor's lectures and course requirements will help you decide what you have to learn from a text and what you do not. You also have to be alert to the different ways authors highlight important points. While some rely on typographical cues like **boldface** and *italics*, others prefer more direct statements like "It is important to point out here . . ." and "Of specific significance is . . ." Good writers, valuing clarity, make every attempt to emphasize key points in the text while good readers look for the visual and verbal cues that signal importance.

5. What passages should I mark for further reading?
To be understood, some chapters may require nothing more than a thorough intensive reading. This is particularly true if the material is familiar and the author's style is clear and direct. There is, however, only one way to be sure that a passage does not require an additional analytical reading: **do regular comprehension checks.** After you finish each section of the chapter, look up from your text and see if you can paraphrase what you've just read. If you have no difficulty paraphrasing what the author said, you can congratulate yourself and go on to the next section. But if you do have difficulty, and if the passage is important, mark it for a detailed analytical reading.

6. What is my personal response to what the author says?
Your goal as a reader should go beyond simply understanding an author's message. To really learn from your textbooks, you need to respond to what you read, mulling over an author's ideas and thinking about how they affirm, contradict, or expand what you already know and believe.

To develop the kind of **responsive understanding** we describe, follow in the footsteps of Benjamin Franklin by recording your comments and responses in the margins of your textbook. The margins are a good place to paraphrase key points in preparation for review. (For more on marking a text, see Chapter 8, pp. 190–194.) They are also the place to *apply* what you're reading to your own store of knowledge and experiences. After reading, for example, how Sigmund Freud thought human beings tried to repress or forget what displeased or frightened them, you might note in the margins that your Aunt Mabel never wants to talk about her hard experiences as a child of alcoholic parents.

You might also *compare* what you are reading to what you already know, mentioning in the margins that current research on how people think suggests Freud was right: we tend to remove from consciousness those things that challenge our established system of values. The kind of comment you make is not important. You can agree or disagree with the author's claims; you can cite evidence that affirms or denies them. What is important is that you think about and respond to what you are learning from the printed page. The act of reading should be a meeting of minds—yours and the author's.

■   PRACTICE 3   Do an intensive reading of our sample chapter "Mate Selection" on pp. 173–181. When you are finished, see how well you can answer the following questions:

1. **What are some of the specialized vocabulary words used in this chapter?**

_____

_____

_____

2. **What generalizations does the author offer about age and the selection of a mate?**

_____

_____

_____

3. According to the chapter, how many factors enter into the selection of a mate?

_____

_____

_____

4. What role does propinquity play in selecting a mate?

_____

_____

_____

5. According to the chapter, what role does sexual attraction play in the selection of a mate?

_____

_____

_____

6. How does the author support his generalization that class plays a crucial role in the selection of a mate?

_____

_____

_____

■ PRACTICE 4   For Practice 2, you relied solely on your personal experience and knowledge to pose and answer questions about the sample chapter. Now go back and reread those questions, but this time, answer them on the basis of what you learned from the chapter. When you are finished, compare your first set of answers with your second, looking for places in the chapter where your reading changed your original perspective or outlook.

ANALYTICAL READING

Webster's defines *analysis* as "the separating or breaking up of any whole so as to find out its nature, function, relationship." This definition is crucial to understanding what we mean by the term **analytical reading**—a slow, step-by-step process in which you tear sentences apart in order to recombine and re-create them in words you understand.

The amount of analytical reading you do will vary from textbook to textbook, depending on the subject matter, the author's style, and your own familiarity with the material. In reading your introductory psychology text, you may find that only one or two passages require this kind of detailed analysis. But don't be surprised if every page in your chemistry text demands this slow, phrase-by-phrase, passage-by-passage approach to reading. For however much analytical reading you do, the basic steps are as follows:

1. Use context to shape your expectations.

Always begin an analytical reading by looking carefully at the text preceding the passage you don't understand. Ask yourself a question like "At this point, what would the author be likely to say next?" Look as well at the text that follows the passage giving you difficulty. Authors frequently develop a complicated theoretical discussion through specific examples or illustrations, and it often helps to study the illustrations *before* you do an analytical reading of the more theoretical material.

2. Divide each sentence into meaningful parts.

Go through the passage sentence by sentence and divide each one into groups of words that, in isolation at least, make sense to you. For an illustration, see how we have divided the following sentence:

> The thesis is/ that value consensus/ fosters mutually rewarding interaction/ and leads to interpersonal attraction./ It is reasoned/ that the sharing of similar values,/ in effect,/ is a validation of one's self/ which promotes/ emotional satisfaction/ and enhances communication.

If, as here, these groups of words are abstract, follow step 3.

3. Paraphrase the author's words, making abstract terms more concrete wherever possible.

The most difficult language to understand is the kind filled with *abstract* words that make little or no reference to *concrete* experience. But you will be able to decipher even the most difficult passages if you substitute concrete words or phrases that refer to specific people, events, and experiences. Here, as an example, is our paraphrased version of the passage in step 2. Notice how hard-to-picture abstractions like "interpersonal attraction" and "value consensus" have been translated into more concrete and specific language.

> Sociologists think that when people agree on the same values they are more likely to fall in love. They also believe that sharing the same values makes people feel happier and more content. It's also easier to talk to someone who shares your outlook on life.

To clarify the meaning of a passage, replace an abstract phrase with your own concrete paraphrase:

Abstract Phrase	Concrete Paraphrase
Achievement in sports	Winning a gold medal in the Olympics
Capacity for personal affiliation	The ability to make and keep friends
Scholastic attainment	Getting good grades
It is reasoned that	People think
Contemporary conjugal life-style problems	The difficulties married people face in their everyday life together
The ambiguity of language	Words are hard to pin down. They can have several meanings.
The scientific method	Developing a hypothesis or theory and testing it to prove its accuracy
Social problems	Homelessness in America, unwed mothers, abused kids
Residential propinquity	Living close by in the neighborhood
Weak familial ties	No family feeling

Figure 7–1: Dealing With Abstractions

4. Look up any key words that are stumbling blocks to comprehension.

If, when you paraphrase, you can't figure out the meaning of a word that seems central to the passage, first check the glossary. If that fails, try the dictionary. Sometimes knowing the meaning of just one key word can eliminate all your confusion, and everything will fall into place.

5. Check to see if your paraphrase fits the larger context.

Even if the passage you have been working on begins to make sense by itself, you should still do a comprehension check to see if your understanding of the passage fits within the larger context. Once again, look at the material that comes before and after. Does your paraphrase follow from and lead up to those portions of the text?

Having introduced those five steps for analytical reading, we think a word of caution is in order here: if you do a careful analytical reading of a passage and still don't grasp the author's message, it's time to get some help. Ask your instructor how he or she would interpret the material. You might be having trouble because your definition of a key term is not appropriate to the context. Or it might even be that this portion of the text is not written clearly enough for student readers and requires the expertise of your instructor. Don't browbeat yourself if you can't make sense out of a complicated passage. Give it your best effort, and if that doesn't work, ask for help. This is nothing to be ashamed of. After all, you're the student, not the teacher. (For more on analytical reading, see the appendix, pp. 491–492.)

> You will be able to decipher even the most difficult passages if, for all abstract words, you substitute concrete words or phrases that refer to specific people, events, and experiences.

■ PRACTICE 5   Read the following excerpt from "Mate Selection" (part of which we cited earlier as an example of a highly abstract passage). Then write a paraphrased version in the blanks that follow, substituting concrete language for abstract words or phrases.

The thesis is that value consensus fosters mutually rewarding interaction and leads to interpersonal attraction. It is reasoned that the sharing of similar values, in effect, is a validation of one's self

which promotes emotional satisfaction and enhances communication.

This is not to deny the possibility that a binding relationship may develop between dissimilar persons, but to suggest that such a relationship is less likely to occur as spontaneously or persist as permanently. Although dissimilar persons can provide new information, be unpredictable and therefore exciting, and at times give a more objective and accurate appraisal of the self, they also create more uncertainty about one's status and esteem, and anxiety over acceptable conduct and speech.

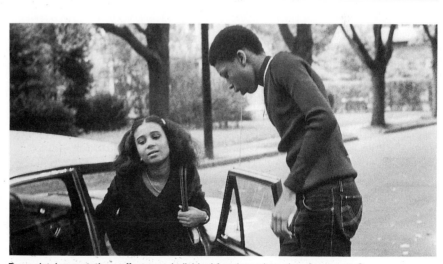

Do societal expectations affect your individual freedom when choosing a mate?

Three Strategies for Reading Textbooks

Inspectional Reading	How To Do It	Purpose
	• force yourself to turn pages quickly • read introduction • read all headings, lists, tables, boxes	• to get a sense of a chapter's overall point or purpose before readings • to help you raise questions about chapter • to help you anticipate what is to come
Intensive Reading	How to Do It	Purpose
	• read at a comfortable rate • read to answer questions about headings • do regular comprehension checks	• to figure out what each individual section contributes to chapter as a whole • To identify difficult or confusing passages that need analysis • to re-create author's message
Analytical Reading	How to Do It	Purpose
	• read slowly, word for word • break sentences down into meaningful phrases or chunks • paraphrase • check to see if your paraphrase fits the rest of the passage	• to decipher dense texts like chemistry or philosophy • to understand passages that were confusing the first time around • to analyze exam questions accurately • to understand poetry

Sample Chapter

MATE SELECTION

Introduction

Several hundred years ago, the son of the president of the French parliament asked his father whether it was true that he intended to marry him off to a certain young lady. "Son," replied the father, "mind your own business."[1] To modern American youth, accustomed as they are to freedom of marital choice, such a statement seems humorous indeed. Yet in times past, arranged marriages—particularly at the upper class levels—were more or less expected.

In view of the fact that marriages are no longer arranged, however, the next logical question becomes, "On what basis *do* we choose mates?" Surely for young adults there can be no more pertinent question. After all, it is logical to assume that marital discord is caused not so much by issues arising *after* marriage as by the *imperfect choice of a partner.*

While for most young people there seems to be an adequate supply of potential mates, the supply is not limitless. On the contrary, mate selection in all societies operates within formal or informal circumscriptions. An American youth, for instance, is expected to marry someone in the same age category. It is presumed, further, that he or she will marry within the same race and, to a lesser extent, within the same religion and socio-economic class. Young Americans are thus faced with a neat interplay between societal expectations and individual freedom of choice. . . .

The Age Factor

Age is an obvious circumscribing factor in the selection of a marriage partner. To begin with, most people in our society marry within their own age range. There are exceptions, to be sure, but it is more or less expected that first marriages will involve two individuals whose ages are relatively close.

Another consideration is the fact that women customarily neither date nor marry men who are younger than themselves; in fact, government figures reveal that in only 15 percent of American marriages are wives older than their husbands. On the average, husbands are two or three years older than their wives.

The implications here are greater than is generally realized, for in point of fact the expected age differential greatly reduces the number of eligible partners for both sexes. To illustrate, if the customary marital age range were three years in either direction, a 22-year-old person could choose a mate in the 19–25 age bracket, *provided it made no difference which sex was older.* But since it is expected that a man will at least be no younger than his bride, the hypothetical 19–25 age range is almost halved, with the actual span shrinking to 19–22 for the man and 22–25 for the woman.

In the college situation, age differentials have a significance that is all too clear to students. On an age basis, the freshman girl can date virtually any boy in college. By the time she is a senior, this marriage market has shrunk to one-quarter of its original size. In the case of the boy, the situation is reversed, for on an age basis a college senior has four times as much dating opportunity as he had when he was a freshman.

A final age-limiting factor is the American custom of early matrimony. The age at marriage in the United States has fallen since the turn of the century. In 1900, the average (median) age at first marriage for men was 26, and for women, 22. Corresponding figures at the present time are roughly 23 for men and 21 for women: The downward trend seems to have leveled off, however, and today's figures are slightly higher than they were two decades ago. (The average age at marriage for college graduates—both men and women—is a year or two higher than that of the general population.)

On a cross-cultural basis, Americans seem to marry young compared with most other industrial societies. Our median age at first marriage, for example, is lower than that of England, France, Norway, Switzerland, Austria, and Japan. The highest medians have traditionally been those of Ireland—31.4 for males and 26.5 for females.

It should be added, parenthetically,* that the age factor seems to be much more important to the young than to the middle-aged and the old. A 5-year age difference between mates at age 20 may loom large. This same difference at age 40 or 50 may seem quite small. Also, as one gets older the age factor becomes more flexible (by definition!), since the majority of one's age group are already married. Thus in the Dean-Gurak study, the investigators found that "once-wed women have husbands closer to their own age (average difference, 3.2 years) than do twice-wed women in their second marriage (average difference, 5.1 years)."[2]

Race

It seems to be sad but true, apropos of marriage and divorce statistics, that the things people are most interested in are those about which we have the least information. This is certainly true in the area of interracial and interreligious marriage. In the case of interracial marriage, for example, we do not have—and never have had—satisfactory figures on the subject. We do have data based on U.S. Census samples, and also some information gleaned from the vital statistics of a certain number of states. Both types of data involve some well-known methodological limitations, and in view of this fact we are fortunate in

being able to make at least some generalizations.

To begin with, the interracial marriage rate—no matter how it is computed—has been increasing. Virtually all the studies are in agreement on this point: for example, surveys by Aldridge and Monahan based on state vital statistics, and a data-analysis by Heer, based on decennial census samples.

Despite the increase, however, the ratio of interracial marriages to total marriages remains quite low, a conclusion borne out, again, by all of the above studies. Indeed, one of the reasons for the increase is the fact that the black-white marriage rate started a generation or so ago from a base of near zero. An earlier study showed that in 1939 interracial marriages accounted for 0.08 percent of all U.S. marriages. (Up to 1967, interracial marriages were illegal in some 20 states. In that year, the Supreme Court ruled that such prohibitions were unconstitutional.) The writer would estimate that, even at the present time, well under 1 percent of U.S. marriages are between blacks and whites.

Since blacks comprise around 12 percent of the population, it is apparent that the practice of racial endogamy serves to delimit mate selection for both races. As Eshleman puts it: "Despite scientific findings and the removal of legal barriers, the restrictions concerning interracial marriages still remain the most inflexible of all the mate-selection boundaries."[3]

What of the future? Will the interracial marriage barriers ultimately break down? The point can be argued either way. On the one hand, people are reportedly taking a more tolerant view toward such marriages, a view that seems especially pronounced on the part of younger people and those with a college education. In answer to the question, "Do you approve of marriage between whites and non-whites?" Gallup Poll figures covering a 10-year period were as follows:"

---

*parenthetically: as an aside, in passing

	Approve (%)	Disapprove (%)	No Opinion (%)
1968	20	72	8
1972	29	60	11
1978	36	54	10

The same survey showed that nonwhites were more than twice as likely as whites to express approval of interracial marriage (66 percent versus 32 percent). Also, respondents with higher education were more likely to have high approval rates:

	Approve (%)	Disapprove (%)	No Opinion (%)
Grade School	19	70	11
High School	32	57	11
College	53	40	7

On the other hand, opinion polls to the contrary, there does not appear to be any concerted effort to boost the interracial marriage rate. From a mate-selection view, blacks and whites seem almost compartmented into two groups. Times may change, however, and no one can say just what the future will bring.

Why do certain people marry across racial lines? A number of theories have been proposed. Some writers feel that those who intermarry are somehow "different" from the bulk of the population. They may, perhaps, feel rejected by their own group; or they may be rebelling against parental authority. Other writers contend that those who intermarry do so simply as a "protest against bigotry." Still others feel that interracial marriage represents a "lure of the exotic."

"The inherent problem with most of these notions as motives for outmarriage," writes Porterfield, "is that they are too unsystematic, fragmentary, and often speculative. In many instances they are derived on the basis of individual cases or small samples." In Porterfield's own study of black-white intermarriage the following conclusions were drawn:

The results of this survey strongly suggest that a majority of interracial dating and marriage is not related to some pathological abnormality or to any crusade against prejudice. Grounds for interracial marriages are usually the same as those for marriage between persons of the same race. . . .

Most of these couples cited love and compatibility as their primary motives for getting married. . . . Most of them reported that their initial relationships were based on shared interests, ideas, and values.[4]

For reasons that are by no means fully understood, interracial marriages much more often involve a black male and a white female rather than the other way around. Also, on the basis of one or more studies, there is a suggestion that interracial marriages (1) show a relatively high rate of prior divorce on the part of one or both partners; (2) involve couples who marry at a comparatively late age; (3) involve a white female who is foreign-born or of foreign parentage; and (4) produce fewer children than other marriages.

Religion

The extent of religious intermarriage in the United States depends in good part on the particular religion or denomination being considered. Among the Old Order Amish, mate selection outside the group is virtually nonexistent. On the other hand, intermarriage among the various Protestant denominations—Episcopalians, Baptists, Lutherans, Presbyterians, Methodists, and others—seems to be quite common. If, in Protestant households, husband and wife are usually of the same denomination, it may not be because of endogamous mate selection but because one party often "converts" after marriage.

When questions are raised concerning religious intermarriage, however, what is usually meant is the pattern involving Protestants, Catholics, and Jews, and we are fortunate in having some excellent studies available. Special mention should be made, in this connection, of the late Dr. Thomas Monahan, who—more than any other sociologist—fought for the inclusion of both race and religion on vital-statistics registration forms. Without such information, our knowledge of the intermarriage process would be severely limited.

It is common knowledge that all three major religious groups encourage their members to marry within the fold, although there is some variation among the three. The most flexible are the Protestants, the most rigid are the Jews, with the Catholics falling in between. A Catholic priest will marry a Catholic and a non-Catholic, provided certain stipulations are met, but most rabbis will not marry a Jew and a non-Jew. Wise men know, however, that the marriage market sometimes makes its own rules.

It should not be forgotten that Jews and Catholics represent minority religions in the United States, so that young people of both faiths are overexposed, statistically speaking, to the larger Protestant group. In certain areas the proportion of Catholics or Jews is so small that the forces of religious exogamy (marrying outside the group) have been almost irresistible.

The Jews have a special problem apropos of numbers. While they are traditionally an endogamous people, they comprise a bare 3 percent of the U.S. population. If they adhered to strict religious endogamy, the Jews would be excluding themselves from 97 percent of the larger market. In practice, they have been increasingly active in the larger market, although their intermarriage level varies from place to place—from less than 5 percent in Providence, Rhode Island, to more than 50 percent in Indiana. Overall, however, a number of studies have been undertaken in various parts of the United States, as well as in Canada, and the increase in the Jewish intermarriage rate is unmistakable.

On the basis of the available evidence, the writer would estimate that somewhere in the area of 30 percent of current Jewish marriages are mixed. While religious endogamy is still a significant force in Jewish mate selection, it is not so pervasive as it once was.

Numerically, the most significant interreligious marriage pattern is that involving Protestants and Catholics. There are in excess of 50 million Catholics in the United States; hence, if religious endogamy prevailed, both groups—Catholics and Protestants—would face sizable restrictions in terms of mate selection. However, as in the case of the Jews, a wide array of studies indicates that Catholic intermarriage has been heading upward.

Overall, research findings indicate that a third or more of present-day Catholic marriages in this country are mixed. It should be added, however, that while both Jewish and Catholic intermarriage rates have been increasing, substantial numbers of both groups remain opposed to the idea.

Sociologists have also been interested in studying the *characteristics of the intermarried.* Jewish males, for instance, are much more likely to be involved in mixed marriages than are Jewish females. In the case of Protestant-Catholic marriages, no parallel tendency has been ascertained. The following will give some idea of the findings that have been reported in one or more studies.

As compared with those who marry within their own faith, persons who intermarry are likely to have:

1. Weak religious and familial ties.
2. A high rate of prior divorce.
3. A civil rather than a religious ceremony.
4. Parents who were involved in a mixed marriage.
5. A high rate of premarital pregnancy.
6. An urban background.

There seems to be little doubt that (1) interreligious marriage has been increasing in the United States, and (2) persons who intermarry have certain social characteristics that differentiate them from those who marry within their own faith. Of equal significance is the fact that public opinion on the subject is also softening, as evidenced by public opinion surveys. Gallup Poll figures, for example, indicate that less than 15 percent of the respondents are opposed to marriages between Jews and non-Jews, or between Protestants and Catholics.

Social Class

It seems to be a common observation that persons with similar intelligence levels tend to marry one another, an observation that has been borne out by numerous studies. As based on I.Q. tests, the correlation between spouses ranges from roughly .32 to .55, which approaches the same relationship as that found between siblings. The fact that husband and wife are fairly similar in I.Q. seems to have been established beyond a reasonable doubt, and social scientists have turned to other facets of mate-similarity.

Sociologists, for example, have zeroed in on the so-called class structure in the United States. Although concepts and definitions vary somewhat, one commonly used set of criteria refers to factors such as occupation, income, and education. On this basis, do young people tend to choose mates within their own social stratum, or is class exogamy the rule? Again, studies over many decades indicate a marked tendency toward social-class endogamy.

In his classic study of Elmtown, a small Midwestern city, Hollingshead found that in the 1940's social-class endogamy was clearly the rule:

Elmtowners will tell you that "love alone" is the thing; "it brings young people together." They will argue that people marry when "Miss or Mr. Right comes along," and not before. But in a very large number of cases Miss and Mr. Right belong to families who are members of the same class grouping in the community. If we include the immediately adjacent classes, then almost all cases are included. In short, the romantic complex operates, in large part, within the confines of the class system.[5]

Another well-known study, by Centers in the late 1940's, involved a national cross section of the population. Dividing occupations into broad groupings of (1) business executive, (2) professional, (3) small business, (4) white collar, (5) skilled manual, (6) semiskilled, and (7) unskilled, Centers found that both men and women were more likely to marry partners of their own occupational stratum than of any other single stratum. It was found that while there was a substantial amount of occupational exogamy, cross-class marriages for the most part involved adjacent occupational groupings.

Throughout the 1960's and 1970's a wide variety of investigations reaffirmed the principle of social-class endogamy. Surveys by Rockwell, and by Dean and Gurak—when taken in conjunction with the earlier studies—make it clear that for several decades young Americans have had a pronounced tendency to marry within their general socio-economic or educational level. Eckland estimates that between 50 and 80 percent of the marriages in the United States are endogamous for social class, "the exact figures depending on the nature of the index used and the methods employed to calculate the rate."[6]

Propinquity

Propinquity refers to nearness in place, or proximity, and for almost 50 years one of the truisms in sociology has been that young people tend to marry those who live near by. The original propinquity study was done by Bossard in 1932. Transcribing street addresses from 5,000 consecutive marriage licenses issued in Philadelphia, he discovered that one-sixth of the applicant-pairs lived within a block of each other, one-third lived within five blocks, and more than half lived within twenty blocks of each other. As the author aptly concluded: "Cupid may have wings, but apparently they are not adapted for long flights."[7]

In the ensuing decades, dozens of replication studies* have been undertaken in such diverse cities as Columbus, Ohio; New Haven, Connecticut; Nashville, Tennessee; Seattle, Washington; and others. Rural as well as urban areas have been investigated, as have such distant places as Ontario, Canada; Oslo, Norway; and Karachi, Pakistan. And while research design has been amplified and sharpened, Bossard's original findings have been basically substantiated. Cherished notions about romantic love aside, it appears that, when all is said and done, the "one and only" may have a better than 50-50 chance of living within walking distance!

Interestingly enough, in the most recent study—a small survey reported by Peters in the late 1970's—the investigator found residential propinquity to be operative in both first and second marriages, with the figure slightly higher for second marriages!

Why, apparently, is residential propinquity such a near-universal phenomenon? Why, indeed, since—it has been argued by Catton and Smircich—the number of potential mates *actually increases with the distance away from one's residence!* The answer is a bit complicated, and has to do with the interplay among such factors as religion, social class, nationality, and propinquity.

Do Italians tend to marry other Italians, for example, because of similar religion and nationality—and perhaps social class? Or do they tend to marry one another simply as a result of living in the same neighborhood? Or

are there elements of truth in both propositions? At the moment, the relative influence of these various endogamous factors has not been determined.

Basic Theories of Mate Selection

Role Theory.   One of the most commonly used terms in sociology, "role" refers to a set of social expectations that are appropriate for a given position or status. These expectations serve as behavioral guidelines, reminding the individual what he or she should and should not do by virtue of being a male, female, employer, college student, and the like. Most people find it more rewarding to fulfill the roles society has set forth than to "buck the trend." In modern society, nevertheless, there is enough disagreement on roles to evoke a fair amount of social conflict.

As applied to mate selection, persons would tend to choose partners on the basis of courtship and marital role agreement. It would be unlikely, according to the theory, for a man who believed that woman's place is in the home to marry a career woman. Nor would it be likely for a woman who thinks men should be active in community affairs to marry a laissez-faire* man.

Note that it is not the roles themselves, but the agreement on role playing that is the important factor. A compatible couple would be one in which both spouses play the expected or agreed-upon roles, almost irrespective of what these roles actually are.

Role theory has been extensively analyzed by sociologists, although its application to mate selection is a relatively new development. As we shall see, however, several investigators have incorporated the concept of role into their own theories of marital selection. What-

---

*replication study: study repeated to reproduce same conditions
*laissez-faire: let whatever happens happen

ever the final answer may turn out to be, it is likely that "role" will prove to be one of the ingredients.

Values.   Values refer to ideals, customs, or behavior patterns about which people have such strong emotional feelings that they think of them as "good," "bad," "right," or "wrong." Coombs, who has written extensively on the subject, believes that values are so important to those who hold them that "they are accepted without question." Indeed, because values are so central to a person's mode of conduct, Coombs feels that mates tend to be chosen on the basis of similarity of values. "For therein," he writes, "lies emotional security."

> The thesis is that value consensus fosters mutually rewarding interaction and leads to interpersonal attraction. It is reasoned that the sharing of similar values, in effect, is a validation of one's self which promotes emotional satisfaction and enhances communication.

> This is not to deny the possibility that a binding relationship may develop between dissimilar persons, but to suggest that such a relationship is less likely to occur as spontaneously or persist as permanently. Although dissimilar persons can provide new information, be unpredictable and therefore exciting, and at times give a more objective and accurate appraisal of the self, they also create more uncertainty about one's status and esteem, and anxiety over acceptable conduct and speech.[8]

Coombs is also of the belief that endogamous factors such as race, religion, and social class operate largely as a function of values. For example, a person may wish to marry someone of the same religion, not only because marrying a member of "the Church" may be an important value in itself, but because individuals with similar backgrounds will probably develop similar value systems—thus setting the stage for mate selection. This theory has the advantage of simplicity and also seems to be borne out by common observation. Also—and most important—is the fact that in addition to Coombs' own corroborative investigation, studies by Rich, by Hutton, and by Murstein all show some support for the value theory. Whether similarity of values is in fact central to the mate-selection process—and if so, precisely which classes of values are involved—will have to be determined by continued research.

Exchange Theory.   Another theory of mate selection conceives of all social behavior as a kind of "exchange." Exchange theory, according to Huston, assumes not only that human actions are goal-oriented, but that "social transactions are regulated by the interactants' desire to derive maximum pleasure and minimum pain from others." Huston adds that "more formally, exchange theory suggests that individuals are most attracted to persons who provide the highest ratio of rewards to costs."[9]

Edwards, who has applied exchange theory to mate selection, points out that a typical situation is where "one party gives a certain portion of his time and labor for which he receives a certain amount of appreciation and esteem. The resources exchanged need not be of the same kind. What is important is the mutually held expectation that reciprocation will occur."

The same author goes on to say that, in terms of marital selectivity, each party tends to maximize his or her gains and minimize his or her costs:

1. Within any collectivity of potential mates, a person will seek out that individual who is perceived as maximizing his rewards.
2. Individuals with equivalent resources are most likely to maximize each other's rewards.
3. Pairs with equivalent resources are most

likely to possess homogamous characteristics.

4. Mate selection, therefore, will be homogamous with respect to a given set of characteristics.[10]

Edwards does not attempt to classify the resources that will be perceived as equivalent, and in this sense exchange theory—as applied to mate selection—can hardly be called definitive. On the other hand, the theory has the advantage not only of explaining why homogamous tendencies "work," but also of serving as a foundation for the development of a more precise theoretical formulation.

Complementary Needs.   Although the idea that mate selection may be a function of personality need-fulfillment is fairly old, it remained for Winch to formulate a definitive theory of the subject and put the theory to empirical test. According to Winch, an individual chooses for a mate someone who provides him or her with maximum need-gratification. However, maximum gratification occurs when the specific need-patterns of the man and woman are *complementary rather than similar.* Among the specific complements that Winch posits are hostility-abasement, dominance-deference, nurturance-succorance, achievement-vicariousness, and others. For purposes of simplification, Winch offers the following hypothetical illustration:

Let us assume that there is a chap by the name of Jonathan, and that Jonathan's most distinguished characteristic is a need to be dominant in interpersonal relationships. We shall assume further that among his acquaintances are two girls, Jean and Jennifer. Jennifer is like Jonathan in being dominant and in being intolerant of differences in viewpoint, whereas Jean does not have strong convictions and is used to being governed by the judgments and wishes of others. If we are informed that Jonathan is

about to marry one of these women, and if on the basis of the information cited above we are asked to guess which one, probably we should agree that Jean would be the more likely choice for Jonathan to make. . . . Thus Jonathan should see Jean as a "truly feminine, tractable, agreeable young lady who knows when and how to help a man," whereas to Jean, Jonathan might well appear as a "vigorous and decisive tower of strength." I should expect further that Jonathan would be repelled by Jennifer and would see her as bossy, unfeminine, and probably shrewish.[11]

Winch does not assume that all aspects of complementarity necessarily register at the conscious level. It may be that in those areas where the couple do not consciously recognize the complementary factors, both parties are more comfortable if they do not have to acknowledge the arrangement. Winch continues: "Let us assume that Jennifer, the bossy woman, marries a passive, compliant chap—say, Herbert. . . . Because the pattern of dominance, although complementary, would run counter to the conventional conceptions of sex roles (she being a 'masculine' woman and he a 'feminine' man), it seems likely that neither party would wish to admit to himself or to anyone else that this pattern of dominance was a bond between them."

Winch's own research confirmed his general theory, but a number of subsequent investigations failed to provide corroboration. And while several corollaries* have been proposed—both by Winch and by others—development of complementary-need theory seems to have come to a dead end. Even so, Winch's efforts—coming when they did—served to revitalize socio-psychological thinking on the subject of mate selection.

---

*corollaries: additional propositions, also unproven

Questions

1. Specifically, how important is the age factor in the American mate selection process? As based on research findings, has it been determined that there is a "best marrying age"? Explain.

2. Interracial marriage in the United States has been increasing. On the basis of your own observation, would you predict that the increase will continue, level off, or reverse itself? Explain.

3. A number of theories have been proposed to explain why some people marry across racial lines. What are these theories, briefly? What conclusions, in this connection, can be drawn from Porterfield's study?

4. The Jews have a special problem in regard to interreligious marriage. What is this problem, according to the text?

5. What are some of the characteristics of those who marry across religious lines? In this regard, can you think of some additional areas of research that might prove to be of interest?

6. Empirical studies have shown rather clearly that, over the past several decades, Americans have tended to marry within their own social class. Why should this be so? Discuss in some detail.

7. What does the text mean by *propinquity*, and what bearing does propinquity have on mate selection?

8. Differentiate among homogamy, heterogamy, and complementary needs.

9. What does the sociologist mean by *role theory*, as applied to mate selection? Give some examples.

10. Of the various theories of mate selection discussed in the preceding pages—homogamy, heterogamy, role theory, values, exchange theory, complementary needs—which one, in your opinion, is the most convincing? Why?

[1] Quoted in Bernard Murstein, *Who Will Marry Whom?* (New York: Springer, 1976), p. 5.

[2] Gillian Dean and Douglas Gurak, "Marital Homogamy the Second Time Around," *Journal of Marriage and the Family*, August, 1978, p. 563.

[3] J. Ross Eshleman, *The Family: An Introduction*, (Boston: Allyn and Bacon, 1978), p. 321.

[4] Ernest Porterfield, *Black and White Mixed Marriages* (Chicago: Nelson-Hall, 1978), pp. 64–65.

[5] August Hollingshead, "Class and Kinship in a Middle Western Community," *American Sociological Review*, August, 1949, p. 475.

[6] Eckland, p. 78.

[7] James Bossard, "Residential Propinquity as a Factor in Marriage Selection," *American Journal of Sociology*, September, 1932, p. 222.

[8] Robert Coombs, "Value Consensus and Partner Satisfaction Among Dating Couples," *Journal of Marriage and the Family*, May, 1966, pp. 166–173.

[9] Ted L. Huston, *Foundations of Interpersonal Attraction*, (New York: Academic Press, 1974), p. 20.

[10] John Edwards, "Familial Behavior as Social Exchange," *Journal of Marriage and the Family*, August, 1969, pp. 518–526.

[11] Robert Winch, *Mate Selection*, (New York: Harper, 1958), p. 97.

WORKING SPACE

READING ASSIGNMENT

Do an inspectional reading of the following textbook selection. When you are finished, answer the questions that follow.

Birth Order: Introduction

Being the firstborn child in your family is important if you want to increase your odds of becoming an astronaut or president. If you are not quite as ambitious as all that, it is still important to get there before all your other brothers and sisters. Everything you will ever be does not, of course, depend simply on the order of your birth. But it does seem to make a difference in the kind of person you will eventually become.

So You Want to Be President? Psychologist Louis Stewart analyzed presidential elections in periods of social crisis (during or just before wars) and discovered that eight of the nine men elected during these times were firstborn or only sons. In less stressful times, of twenty-one presidents elected only eight were firstborn or only sons. Apparently we're willing to give the kid brother a chance when things are going smoothly, but if there is trouble we tend to lean on the older brother (Goodall, 1972). If you want to be president but weren't the firstborn, the next best is to be third in line. Thirty-two percent of all presidents were third sons. Only one has been a fourthborn, and none has been born later even though families used to be quite large.

Scientific psychology has been interested for some decades in the effects of birth order or ordinal position in the family on intellectual achievement and social adjustment. Data suggest that a great proportion of you taking psychology classes are firstborn children—more than would be expected by chance. Schachter's findings are that more graduate students in psychology and education are firstborn, more medical students are firstborn, and that the firstborn have a higher high-school grade-point average than laterborn children. . . .

Why Should Birth Order Make a Difference?
There are several possible reasons and many theories why birth order

affects the child. The firstborn usually has the smallest birth weight in the family. Yet within a couple of years this child will be heavier and taller than laterborn children at the same stage and age of growing up. By adulthood, no significant differences will remain in height or weight between eldest and laterborn siblings (Clausen, 1966).

Usually, no other children will get the amount of attention, energy, and concern that the firstborn receives before a brother or sister comes along. The firstborn is also more likely to be a planned child and more likely to be breast-fed for a longer period of time (Sears, Maccoby, and Levin, 1957). But he must also suffer inexperienced parents who may be unsure of themselves and therefore less consistent in taking care of him. The parents will spend more time with him, talk to him more, and spank him more often than they will the children who come later.

Parents regularly report they are much more relaxed with laterborn children than with their firstborn (McArthur, 1956; Sears, 1950). They also display greater permissiveness about the behavior of their laterborn children, whereas they tend to be overconcerned with the details of upbringing with their first child. This concern and anxiety are eventually reflected in the child's image of himself and produce the need to win approval, which is never fully satisfied.

One of the most consistent findings relating to birth order is that firstborn children achieve eminence in higher proportion than do their siblings. Many factors account for this success. One of the most important is that achievement in academic pursuits must start very early, and firstborns perform better in the classroom from the beginning. They are not smarter, but they try harder to achieve in the school setting. This striving seems to reflect the aspirations and pressures of the parents (after all, it is their first entry in the race of life). With this background under their belts, firstborns tend to go on to become serious, conscientious adults.

The Need to Affiliate

Our modern concern with birth order was triggered by a study done in 1959 by Stanley Schachter. By accident, really, he found that college-age female students who were firstborn or only children regularly chose to wait with other people when they expected to receive a painful electric shock in an experiment. Interestingly those who were laterborns didn't care as much whether they awaited alone or with others. Schachter thought this difference between "firsts and onlies" and "laterborns" was due to motivation. He argued that firstborns must have a stronger need to affiliate than do laterborns, and that this motivational difference is particularly apparent under conditions of stress.

Schachter's research turned up some interesting findings in a study on the effectiveness of fighter pilots as a function of birth order. Firstborns are inferior to laterborns in this role presumably because of increased anxiety about being on their own during periods of stress. Being with others seems to be comforting to firstborns (Wrightsman, 1960), but laboratory experiments may be too artificial to tell us how firstborns handle their affiliative needs when anxious. Irving Sarnoff and Philip Zimbardo (1961), in fact, maintain that this reaction depends on what emotion the firstborn is feeling. Indeed, the evidence on the association between birth order and affiliative behavior has been confusing (Warren, 1966).

No Cheers for the First Born. Some researchers have suggested that firstborns find physical pain or the prospect of being hurt more frightening than do laterborn individuals. Thus, when told they were to be given severe electric shock, firstborn females reported more fear than did laterborn females, and they asked the experimenter to stop actual electric shock sooner than did laterborn females.

Nisbett (1968) figured that, if this were true, you would expect firstborns to stay away from activities where the risk of physical injury was high. He checked their participation in dangerous sports and found that they are less likely to play sports involving high risk than are laterborn persons.

Sibling Position

Walter Toman (1970) has a fascinating theory that, although parents are important in deciding what kind of person you will become, the order of your birth and the number of brothers and sisters you have is even more important. As families expand, Toman thinks children turn to each other for the psychological support they cannot get from the parents. Thus, brothers and sisters (siblings) have a vital impact on the way you learn to relate to others. The kind of person you choose for a spouse, friend, or working partner may be determined by the kinds of siblings you lived with while growing up. Adult relationships may duplicate the ones you have had with brothers and sisters. According to Toman, the more exact the duplication, the greater the chance that your adult relationships will last and be happy. A boy raised with sisters, for example, gets used to interacting with girls, and females lose the "different" or "strange" quality to him. But a boy raised with brothers may feel uncomfortable around women and prefer the company of men. Sibling position is particularly important in Toman's theory. He believes oldest children will learn to be leaders, just as younger children will get used to being followers. Thus, firstborns will grow up looking for relationships they can dominate, whereas the opposite will be true if you are a younger child in the family.

Toman uses his theory to predict how marriages will work:

Suppose that the older brother of a sister *marries the* younger sister of a brother. *They are getting in marriage precisely the peer relation that they had at home. He is used to a girl his junior, and she to a boy her senior. Hence there should be no conflict over their dominance rights. And both of them are used to the other sex, so they should have no great sex conflicts either. If this fellow had married an oldest sister of sisters, however, he could have expected some problems. Both partners would expect to have seniority rights and each one would try to rule the other. In addition, the wife would have had little experience in getting along with men. [Toman, 1970, p. 45]*

If you are an only child, however, you have a serious disadvantage as far as marriage goes. The only child has only parents to learn from and may have a hard time getting along with peers. You may be looking for a father or mother rather than a peer when you marry, and you may not want to have children of your own since you want to remain a child yourself. You can be an only child even if you have brothers and sisters, if you differ more than six years in age from them. The age gap lets you grow up like an only child. . . .

The Only Child. Despite statistics that show only children very often grow up to be outstanding, there has been a longstanding prejudice against the one-child family. The usual notion is that an only child will be "spoiled"—that he's overindulged, maladjusted, egocentric, and never learns the give and take of life (Kramer, 1972). Some parents, in fact, feel they must have a second child just to salvage the first. Most only children actually enjoy striking advantages both as children and adults. A disproportionately high number of only children appear as National Merit Scholars, science prize winners, astronauts, doctors, and persons listed in *Who's Who in America.*

Toman's is an interesting approach to the problem of birth order, but it is difficult to tell how accurate these broad descriptions are.

Like all theories that put people into neat categories, it fits everyone a little, some a lot, and others not at all. Since most of us are subject to a thousand and one influences in our lives, sibling position is just one of many ways we learn about people. It depends on the particulars of your own family structure whether this one influence becomes significant. It is apparent we have not yet properly assessed the meaning and impact of birth order in human life.

Summary

1. Most of the research done on birth order indicates that more firstborn than laterborn children achieve eminence. One reason this may be so is that firstborns do better in school. This performance is in turn based on the fact that firstborns try harder to achieve because of the aspirations and pressures of their parents.

2. Because parents tend to handle their firstborns with great anxiety and a lack of confidence, many firstborn children probably grow up feeling a need to win approval to bolster their belief in themselves.

3. Walter Toman has suggested that the number of brothers and sisters you grew up with is more important than birth order. Brothers and sisters influence the way you learn to relate to others more than do parents. Further, you will tend to replicate your family situation through your choice of spouse and in the way you treat your children.

---

1. The title of the chapter is "Birth Order." What does that title mean to you? What do you already know about it?

2. From your inspectional reading, what do you think is the purpose of this chapter?

3. List several questions you will try to answer when you do an intensive reading.

4. Now do an *intensive* reading of the chapter, marking it to reflect your own responses, to highlight key points, and to note difficult passages. When you are finished, write an answer to this question: What is the main point or message of this selection and how does it *add* to your understanding of why and how people choose a mate?

WRITING ASSIGNMENT: "Choosing a Mate"

At this point, you know a great deal about what other people say is important in selecting a mate. But what do *you* think is important in mate selection? Write a paper in which you generally define at least three different factors that did or will influence your choice of a mate. For each one, use a specific example that will clarify what you have in mind.

JOURNAL ASSIGNMENTS

1. Now that you are aware of the three strategies for reading textbooks, how do you think you can adapt them to help yourself most? Which of your textbooks will require an analytical reading? Which ones will not?

2. What do you think the American philosopher Ralph Waldo Emerson meant when he said, "One must be an inventor to read well"?

CHECKING OUT

Check your understanding of Chapter 7 by writing answers to the following questions. You may work alone or with another student, whichever you prefer.

1. What is the goal of an inspectional reading?

2. What do skillful readers look for when they read the introduction to a chapter?

3. What is the purpose of an intensive reading?

4. What are "comprehension checks," and when should you use them?

5. What does the phrase "responsive understanding" mean in concrete terms?

6. Does every textbook chapter require an analytical reading?

7. Define the terms *abstract* and *concrete*.

IN SUMMARY

There is no one correct way to read a textbook. The reading of textbooks, like reading in general, requires you to be intellectually flexible. You have to consider your familiarity with the subject matter, look at the author's style, and adjust your reading strategies accordingly. While some textbooks, like those in philosophy or chemistry, may demand all three kinds of reading—inspectional, intensive, and analytical—others will require no more than one intensive reading. No one but you can make that decision.

Beyond choosing the right strategy (or strategies), keep in mind that the reading of textbooks demands a dialogue between reader and writer. To make that dialogue take place, you must react and respond to what you read, mentally searching your own experience and knowledge to discover which statements you affirm and which you question—or even outright contradict.

C H A P T E R 8

ORGANIZING INFORMATION FOR REVIEW

I don't use any one method to prepare for reviews. If a textbook seems easy to me, I just underline key points and jot notes in the margin. But if I think it's hard, I do more: I mark pages to highlight key points, and I also make my own outline. What method I use depends on the kind of book I'm reading and the type of test I have to take.

—Jennifer McClaine, student

OVERVIEW

When you review for exams, the last thing you want to do is reread the very same material you read the first time around. Think about it. During your reading, you undoubtedly discovered that some portions of the chapter were more important or more difficult than others. The pages or notes you study when reviewing should reflect those discoveries. If they don't, you're wasting time and energy—two things you need a large supply of when preparing for exams.

To use your time and energy efficiently, you have to organize the information covered in your text, highlighting what you need to learn and remember, while disregarding anything of lesser importance. With this objective in mind, Chapter 8 offers four possible methods of organizing information for review:

- Efficient *marking of a text* will highlight key points and relationships while considerably reducing the amount of text you need to reread during reviews.

- *Informal outlining* produces a skeletal blueprint of the author's ideas, the order in which they were presented, and their relationship to one another.

- *Mapping* focuses less on the order of ideas and concentrates more on giving visual form to the underlying pattern or structure of the text.

- *Summarizing* reduces each major section of a chapter to one-quarter of its original length by eliminating all but the most essential supporting details.

For purposes of explanation, we introduce and explain each method individually, but, in fact, there's no reason why you should rely exclusively on just one method. Instead, try varying or combining methods according to the difficulty of the material and your particular needs. Here again, flexibility is the key—the choice is yours.

MARKING A TEXT

Some students don't like to take notes on a separate sheet of paper. They prepare for reviews by underlining or highlighting key points in the text and jotting notes in the margins. Then they review only the material they have underlined or marked in some way.

This method can certainly be effective, but a word of caution is in order. Your objective in marking a text for review is to highlight content and relationships selectively while reducing the amount of text you need to reread. To meet this objective, you have to analyze and evaluate the material you're reading. Otherwise you could end up with pages that look like this:

media agents of socialization

The means of mass communication in America—especially newspapers, magazines, radio, and television—are ever-present agents of socialization. They affect our attitudes and beliefs in several ways. We rely on them heavily, of course, for information. But information does not come to us on every subject. It comes to us in respect to selected subject areas only—subject areas selected by the media as "news," for example. The media cannot tell us what to think, but they can certainly influence what we think about. As political scientists put it, they help put things on our thinking agenda. We will discuss the *agenda-setting* role of the media further when we turn our

agenda setting role

attention to the formation of public opinion on issues, later on in this chapter. But it is clear that this role of the media is a part of the socialization process—is involved in the development of our general attitudes and beliefs—as well as part of the development of opinion on particular political issues. And the two are somewhat intertwined. If we have a generally good feeling toward business, for example, we would be less likely to oppose special tax breaks for business.

—Fred Harris, *America's Democracy*

Pages marked like our sample will not save you time. On the contrary, during reviews you'll waste time trying to figure out which among all those carefully marked sentences are truly important or significant.

Because careless marking can do more harm than good, it's worth your while to learn and apply the following guidelines for marking the pages of your textbook:

1. Mark selectively.

Not every sentence in a chapter is equally important. You should, for example, search the chapter introduction for a statement of purpose and mark it when you find it. If there is no explicit statement of purpose, infer one and write it in the margin. Don't assume, however, that you have to mark every sentence thereafter. Remember: your objective is to sort information and to highlight only the *essential* elements.

2. Mark pages only after you have read them.

Authors don't always open with their main point. Sometimes they begin with introductory material and delay making their real point until the second or third paragraph. Occasionally, they will even begin with the supporting details and wait until the last paragraph to introduce the generalization they want to explain. You can't be sure which method an author is using until you have read the entire section. For this reason, **don't make decisions about what to mark or underline until you have finished your reading.** What you think is important at the beginning may be quite different from what you think is important at the end.

3. Identify topics in the margin.

As you read, jot down the topics of key paragraphs, using a word or phrase to indicate the subject under discussion. Is the author comparing three kinds of property acquisition or describing the events leading up to the American

Revolution? These marginal notes will prove invaluable later on when you prepare for exams. They will be your **stimulus cues:** key words that will help you remember—without looking at the text—the main points of the passage. (For more on stimulus cues, see Chapter 10.)

4. Paraphrase main points and supporting details.

Use paraphrasing to check your comprehension. If you cannot paraphrase what you have read, there is a good chance you haven't really understood it. Mark it for rereading.

5. Develop your own personal symbols for marking and use them consistently.

Although you may not realize it, marking a page for review does not necessarily mean underlining. There are other symbols you can use, like stars * * * to suggest importance, exclamation points !!! to indicate surprise, circles to highlight specialized vocabulary, and boxes to call attention to transitional words like *first, second,* and *third.* Figure 8–1 shows the variety of symbols at your disposal. When combined with underlining, they will give you a precise system for evaluating the author's message as well as for noting your own personal responses. As an added bonus, deciding on the appropriate symbol for the information you want to emphasize will help you avoid the mindless underlining we have warned against.

An outline is similar to a pyramid—both start out broad and then narrow to a specific point.

Developing Your Own Code of Symbols

≡≡≡	Use **double underlining** (sparingly) to highlight a key generalization or principle.
✱ ✱ ✱ ✱	Use **asterisks** to indicate possible test questions.
1, 2, 3, 4	Use **numbers** to identify a series of supporting details or to itemize a list of characteristics.
ex., ill., res., f, stdy., stat., exc.	Use **abbreviations** to identify the kinds of supporting details used by the author: examples, illustrations, reasons, facts, studies, statistics, exceptions.
◯	Use **circles** to highlight specialized vocabulary, key terms, and statistics.
?	Use **question marks** to indicate unclear points.
!	Use **exclamation points** to register your surprise at the author's statements.
∿∿∿	Use a **wiggly line** under troublesome words to indicate confusion.
See also or compare p.27	Use **cross-references** to encourage the habit of comparing closely-related statements in text.
☐	Draw **boxes** around transitional words and phrases (like *first, second, third, next, similarly, likewise, for example, for illustration*) to help you recognize supporting details.
⟶	Use **arrows** to identify passages needing an analytical reading.
‖	Use **vertical lines** to emphasize a key passage.

Figure 8–1: Common Symbols for Marking Texts

6. When you underline, turn each sentence into a telegram and mark the fewest words possible.

Because each word in a telegram costs money, people who send telegrams are highly selective. They use only those words that are absolutely necessary to convey their message: Arrive Sunday, 9 P.M. Penn Station, Love Mike. The senders of such abbreviated messages know that their readers have enough experience with the language to fill in the gaps.

Oddly enough, many students, who would willingly send the most abbreviated of telegrams, are nervous about not underlining every word on every page. Yet *not every word or phrase* in a sentence is *equally important,* even when that sentence appears in a textbook. You should **underline only those words essential to the author's message.** This practice will do more than reduce the amount of material you have to reread. It will also *force* you to pay complete attention to the text and help you avoid thoughtless underlining.

7. Periodically check your underlining.

Every now and then check your marked pages to see if your underlining makes sense. Can you read the underlined words and phrases and make quick connections between them? When you read over your underlined words and phrases, do they add up to comprehensible ideas? Are you highlighting only the essential elements and eliminating irrelevant or minor details? If the answer to those questions is yes, you are underlining with maximum efficiency.

The following is an excerpt from our sample chapter on mate selection. Note how we have marked the text to highlight essential elements and indicate relationships.

age restricts our choice of partners

(1) Age is an obvious circumscribing factor in the selection of a marriage partner. To begin with, most people in our society marry within their own age range. There are exceptions, to be sure, but it is more or less expected that first marriages will involve two individuals whose ages are relatively close.

(2) Another consideration is the fact that women customarily neither date nor marry men who are younger than themselves; in fact, government figures reveal that in only 15 percent of American marriages are wives older than their husbands. On the average, husbands are two or three years older than their wives.

The implications here are greater than is generally realized, for in point of fact the expected age differential greatly reduces the number of eligible partners for both sexes. To illustrate: if the customary

Ex.

marital age range were three years in either direction, a 22-year-old person could choose a mate in the 19–25 age bracket, *provided it made no difference which sex was older.* But since it is expected that a man will at least be no younger than his bride, the hypothetical 19–25 age range is almost halved, with the actual span shrinking to 19–22 for the man and 22–25 for the woman.

Ex.

In the college situation, age differentials have a significance that is all too clear to students. On an age basis, the freshman girl can date virtually any boy in college. By the time she is a senior, this marriage market has shrunk to one-quarter of its original size. In the case of the boy, the situation is reversed, for on an age basis a college senior has four times as much dating opportunity as he had when he was a freshman.

③ A final age-limiting factor is the American custom of early matrimony. The age at marriage in the United States has fallen since the turn of the century. In 1900, the average (median) age at first marriage for men was 26, and for women, 22. Corresponding figures at the present time are roughly 23 for men and 21 for women. The downward trend seems to have leveled off, however, and today's figures are slightly higher than they were two decades ago. (The average age at marriage for college graduates—both men and women—is a year or two higher than that of the general population.)

On a cross-cultural basis, Americans seem to marry young compared with most other industrial societies. Our median age at first marriage, for example, is lower than that of England, France, Norway, Switzerland, Austria, and Japan. The highest medians have traditionally been those of Ireland—31.4 for males and 26.5 for females.

It should be added, parenthetically, that the age factor seems to be

*The older you get
The less age
matters to
marriage*

much <u>more important</u> to the <u>young than</u> to the <u>middle-aged</u> and the old. A five-year age difference between mates at age twenty may loom large. This same difference at age 40 or 50 may seem quite small. Also, as one gets older the age factor becomes more flexible (by definition!), since the majority of one's age group are already married. Thus in the Dean-Gurak study, the investigators found that "once-wed women have husbands closer to their own age (average difference, 3.2 years) than do twice-wed women in their second marriage (average difference, 5.1 years.)"

> Your objective in marking a text for review is to highlight key points and relationships selectively while at the same time reducing the amount of text you need to reread.

PRACTICE 1   Choose the passage you think has been efficiently marked. In the blanks that follow, explain what was wrong with the passages you did not choose.

1   **Darwin's theory of <u>natural selection</u> is occasionally criticized as being <u>"only a theory."</u> However, <u>many critics</u> seem to forget that** *theory* **in science is a <u>relatively lofty position.</u> What, then, does the term mean?**

  Perhaps we can best describe a theory by showing how one can be developed. Suppose someone comes up with <u>an idea—one</u> <u>**that explains certain observed phenomena in nature.** At first, **it is**</u> <u>**regarded as just that, an idea.**</u> **But after it has been carefully described and its premises precisely defined, it may then become a** *hypothesis*—**an idea that can be tested. In a sense, the hypothesis is the <u>first part of an "if . . . then" statement.</u> The "then" predicts the result of the hypothesis, so one can know by testing if**

the hypothesis is sound. A hypothesis can also stand as a provisional statement for which more data are needed. If rigorous, carefully controlled testing supports the hypothesis, more confidence will be placed in it, until it finally gains the status of a theory. The theory itself, however, may remain unproven and unprovable. A hypothesis, then, is a possible explanation to be tested, whereas a *theory* is a more-or-less verified explanation that accounts for observed phenomena in nature.

2   Darwin's theory of natural selection is occasionally criticized as being "only a theory." However, many critics seem to forget that *theory* in science is a relatively lofty position. What, then, does the term mean?

Compare definitions

Perhaps we can best describe a theory by showing how one can be developed. Suppose someone comes up with an idea—one that explains certain observed phenomena in nature. At first, it is regarded as just that, an idea. But after it has been carefully described and its premises precisely defined, it may then become a *hypothesis*—an idea that can be tested. In a sense, the hypothesis is the first part of an "if . . . then" statement. The "then" predicts the result of the hypothesis, so one can know by testing if the hypothesis is sound. A hypothesis can also stand as a provisional statement for which more data are needed. If rigorous, carefully controlled testing supports the hypothesis, more confidence will be placed in it, until it finally gains the status of a theory. The theory itself, however, may remain unproven and unprovable. A hypothesis, then, is a possible explanation to be tested, whereas a *theory* is a more-or-less verified explanation that accounts for observed phenomena in nature.

Hypothesis = explanation to be tested

Theory = more or less verified explanation

3

Key question

Darwin's theory of natural selection is occasionally criticized as being "only a theory." However, many critics seem to forget that *theory* in science is a relatively lofty position. What, then, does the term mean?

Hypothesis = an idea that can be tested

Perhaps we can best describe a theory by showing how one can be developed. Suppose someone comes up with an idea—one that explains certain observed phenomena in nature. At first, it is regarded as just that, an idea. But after it has been carefully described and its premises precisely defined, it may then become a *hypothesis*—an idea that can be tested. In a sense, the hypothesis is the first part of an "if . . . then" statement. The "then" predicts the result of the hypothesis, so one can know by testing if the hypothesis is sound. A hypothesis can also stand as a provisional statement for which more data are needed. If rigorous, carefully controlled testing supports the hypothesis, more confidence will be placed in it, until it finally gains the status of a theory. The theory itself, however, may remain unproven and unprovable. A hypothesis, then, is a possible explanation to be tested, whereas a *theory* is a more-or-less verified explanation that accounts for observed phenomena in nature.

—Robert Wallace,
Biology

_____

_____

_____

_____

■ PRACTICE 2   Make up a list of symbols that you think will be useful for marking pages. You can use some of the symbols we suggest in Figure 8–1, or create some of your own.

■ PRACTICE 3   Using the code you have created, mark the following extract.

Chemical Effluents*

Perhaps the most dangerous water pollutants are from inorganic sources, because many of them are so new that we know almost nothing of their long-term effects. However, we do know of the existence of over five million chemicals, about 45,000 of which are used commercially, with literally hundreds more being added to the list each year. We also know that well over 250 synthetic chemicals were isolated from the drinking water of only eighty American cities.

The dangers of releasing chemicals we know nothing about is underscored by evidence that some familiar compounds can be more dangerous than we thought. For example, we learned only around 1950 that nitrates, a common constituent of agricultural fertilizers and water supplies, could alter hemoglobin so as to impair its oxygen-carrying capacity. Even later, it was found that certain bacteria in the digestive tract can convert nitrates to highly dangerous and carcinogenic nitrites. Nitrate water pollution is especially dangerous in certain areas of California, Illinois, Wisconsin, and Missouri.

Heat Pollution

A rather subtle and often ignored form of water pollution is *heat*. Water absorbs heat, for example, when the water is used as a coolant or lubricant in manufacturing or energy production

---

*effluent: something that flows out

(including nuclear energy). The problem is that when water is returned to its source at this higher temperature, it may alter the forms of life in the water. Furthermore, a temperature rise of only a few degrees is sufficient to cause such changes. Some species may perish, while others begin to thrive under these new conditions, and the organisms affected may range from the producers to the highest level of consumers. Thus, delicate balances, which have been established as the result of long periods of evolution, can be seriously disrupted.

But why is the addition of only a little heat so critical? How does it exert its effect? Basically, heat pollution works in two ways: (1) by increasing the rate at which aquatic organisms consume oxygen, while, at the same time, lowering the oxygen-carrying capacity of the water (reducing the ability of the biological system to decompose waste), and (2) by increasing the rate of evaporation of the water, thus raising the concentration of pollutants left behind.

INFORMAL OUTLINING

Mike: I like to outline a book that's complicated. It helps me understand how the information fits together.

Sharon: Outline! You mean where every A has to have a B or it's all wrong? I can't outline to save my life. I'd rather not take notes.

Like Sharon, many students are intimidated by the thought of outlining. They worry about whether or not to use capital or lowercase letters, Roman or Arabic numerals, sentences or phrases. And they're not sure where to indent. But, in fact, those kinds of questions apply only to the formal outlines some instructors assign as part of a paper or a speech.

They do *not* apply to the kind of **informal outlining** we suggest here. When you outline for purposes of review, your goal is to develop a clear blueprint of the author's ideas, one that shows *you* the order in which they were presented and their relationship to one another. Exactly how you do this—with numbers, letters, or any other kind of symbol—is up to you.

If you want to create a useful outline, one that concisely and completely records the essential information of a chapter, stop worrying about proper outline format, about whether or not to use capital or lowercase letters. Concentrate, instead, on using these five suggestions for outlining success:

1. Begin your outline with the chapter's statement of purpose.

Make the chapter's statement of purpose the first item on your outline. Place it flush against the left margin of your paper. This kind of placement makes it clear that everything else in the outline is **subordinate** to or dependent upon that statement.

2. Use indentation to reflect relationships.

Sentences or phrases representing the key points in each major section of the chapter should be aligned one underneath the other. This is your way of showing that they are **coordinate** or equal in importance. In turn, **indent** all examples, reasons, studies, or statistics used as supporting details beneath the general point they explain. In this way, you make clear their subordinate status, as shown in Figure 8–2.

Chapter Statement of Purpose

   Major Heading

      Main Point

         Supporting Detail

         Supporting Detail

   Major Heading

      First Main Point

         Suppporting Detail

         Supporting Detail

      Second Main Point

         Supporting Detail

         Supporting Detail

   Major Heading

      Main Point

         Supporting Detail

         Supporting Detail

Figure 8–2: Indent to Show Relationships

3. Use the text's major headings to divide your outline into sections and to indicate how the author's thought develops.

Major headings announce that the author is moving on to something new and different—unlike subordinate **minor headings,** which identify different parts of the same discussion. Including major headings in your outline is a good way of being sure that you are accurately tracking the twists and turns in a writer's train of thought. (See Figure 8–2.)

4. Be selective about supporting details.

If, for example, an author provides four different *illustrations* to explain one key generalization, ask yourself if you really need to record all four in order to understand the author's point. Chances are you don't. If the author also gives an anecdote to clarify this same point, write "Linda Brown story" if it will jog your memory; otherwise omit it.

5. Use your words rather than the author's.

You might need to copy definitions of specialized vocabulary words or a few direct quotations exactly as they appear. But for the most part, *paraphrase the author's original language* to insure that you have truly understood what you have read and aren't just copying down meaningless words. If possible, *condense* whole sentences into brief phrases. Remember: not every word or every phrase in a sentence is equally important.

To illustrate informal outlining, we show on page 203 a partial outline of our sample chapter on choosing a mate. As you can see, our outline contains no Roman numerals, and we have mixed phrases with sentences. But our informal style does not mean the outline is not useful. On the contrary, it still meets the three basic criteria of a good informal outline that you will want to use:

1. Record the essential elements of the chapter
2. Show how the writer's train of thought develops
3. Indicate coordinate and subordinate relationships

Outlining is an excellent method of organizing information for reviews, particularly when you are studying complicated and detailed material presented in a chronological order that makes sequence important. By forcing you to sort ideas and uncover connections, outlining will improve your comprehension and help you remember the essentials of what you've read.

Title: Mate Selection

Purpose of chapter: To answer the question:
How do we choose a mate?

Age

1. Age limits mate choice.
   a. Most ~~people~~ marry someone close in age.
   b. Women don't date younger men,
      greatly reducing number of eligible partners.
      ex. Freshman girl can date any boy in
          college; senior girl's marriage market
          shrinks to ¼ of its original size

Race

1. Practice of racial endogamy affects choice
   of mates.
   a. Most inflexible of all restrictions on
      choice of mate
2. Not clear if barriers will break down in
   the future.
   a. Opinion polls suggest increasing tolerance
   b. No real effort being made to increase
      interracial marriage rates.
3. Common characterestics of interracial marriage
   a. Relatively high rate of prior divorce.
   b. Involve couples who marry at a late age
   c. Involve a white female who is foreign-
      born or of foreign parentage.
   d. Tend to produce fewer children.

When you outline informally for purposes of review, your goal is to develop a clear blueprint of the author's ideas, one that shows you the order in which they were presented and their relationship to one another.

■   PRACTICE 4   Read and informally outline the following excerpt from a chapter that explores the individual contributions of several American presidents.

THE PRESIDENCY: EVOLUTION AND PERFORMANCE

The evolution of the presidency is the story of a cumulative increase in the role—or, better, the roles—that the president is expected to play in the American political system, and, more recently, in the world. Every great president has left the office somewhat changed. The presidency is like a family dwelling that each new generation alters and enlarges. Confronted by some new need, a president adds on a new room, a new wing; what began as a modest dwelling has become a mansion; every president may not use every room, but the rooms are available in case of need.

The Contributions of the Presidents

Symbolic Head of the Nation: Washington Washington's greatest legacy to future presidents was, perhaps, in creating and acting out superbly the symbolic roles that presidents have generally played ever since. He served as head of the country for official, semiofficial, and popular functions, as a key spokesman for national unity, and as a symbol of the obligation imposed on all officials and all Americans to obey the Constitution and to behave according to the spirit of constitutionalism. In playing the role of constitutional monarch to a republic,* Washington was assisted both by his

beliefs and by his practices. For he appears to have believed that the president could and should be free of partisan† attachments. Yet he himself was a staunch Federalist†† who was prone to see "the spirit of party" in others, but not in his own administration. "He is to be blamed," a modern critic has written, "not for allying himself with a party, but for not knowing that he had done so, and for denouncing those opposed to his party as opposed to the government. He was most in the grip of party feeling at the time when he was being represented as being above it."[1]

Washington's deeds helped to preserve his own image of himself as above partisanship.§ For in Alexander Hamilton, his secretary of the treasury, Washington had a lieutenant who came as close as any American cabinet member ever has to being a prime minister to the president. It was Hamilton who discharged many of the political duties that later presidents discharged themselves, and it was therefore Hamilton, not Washington, who became the prime target of the emerging opposition. It was Hamilton who developed the administra-

---

*republic: a constitutional form of government, often a democracy
†partisan: party
††Federalist: in Washington's time, a person who believed in a strong national government as opposed to Jefferson who wanted a less centralized government
§partisanship: party interests

tion's major policies, struggled to build a durable presidential coalition, and mobilized the Congress on behalf of presidential policies.

Party Leader: Jefferson   Under Jefferson, these two roles—constitutional monarch and prime minister, chief magistrate and party leader, president of the country and head of a faction within the country—were fused.

No president since Jefferson has played the role of party leader with more consummate skill. Before he became president, and as an important instrument in gaining the office, Jefferson and his staunch ally Madison had forged the political party, which in due time was to be called the Democratic-Republican, and finally the Democratic party, as a nationwide organization with many of the features of modern parties. As president, Jefferson perfected the instrument he had helped to construct. He was perhaps as professional a party leader as has ever occupied the White House.

Yet if Jefferson saw himself as a spokesman both for the nation as a whole and for the majority (and the party) that elected him, he accepted the fact that he must work in and through the Congress, the only legitimate representative of the popular will. In this respect, Jefferson reflected the traditional republican doctrine expressed by the delegates to the Constitutional Convention. This view. . . holds that the true representative of the people is the legislature: the task of the executive is to "execute" the commands of the legislative body. In persisting as long as it did in its original decision to have the chief executive elected by Congress, the Convention was to some extent reflecting this deeply ingrained respect for the representatives of the legislative body. . . . Not even Jefferson claimed that the president might be as representative of the popular will or of a national majority as the Congress.

Spokesman for National Majorities: Jackson   It was Jackson who proclaimed this role for the president and thereby justified his use of the veto against congressional majorities. Jackson and his followers formulated a revolutionary new concept of the democratic executive: Because in the American system, the national leader elected by and responsible to the people was the only official elected by votes cast over the whole nation, he was therefore the most legitimate representative and could speak, as no other official could, for the majority of the nation.

As a result of a gradual change in the method of electing the president, Jackson had, in fact, rather better grounds for claiming to be the elected spokesman of the nation than Jefferson had. You will recall that the Constitution directs that "each state shall appoint, *in such manner as the legislature thereof may direct,* a number of electors" who, in turn, choose the president (Article II, italics added). At first, in most states the legislatures themselves chose the presidential electors; when Jefferson was named president in 1800, the electors were chosen by the state legislatures in ten of the sixteen states. By 1828, however, only two states out of twenty-four (Delaware and South Carolina) still followed the old practice. When Jackson was re-elected in 1832 the only state in which electors were chosen by the legislature was South Carolina—which, incidentally, stubbornly persisted in this outdated practice until 1860. Thus by Jackson's time the electoral college was already becoming a quaint but for the most part reliable way of designating the choice for president. Consequently, in Jackson's view, if there were a clash between president and Congress, the president had as much—if not more—right to speak for the people of the country, or a majority of them, as the Congress.

---

[1] Joseph Charles, *The Origins of the American Party System* (New York: Harper Torchbooks, 1961), p. 44.

SUMMARIZING A CHAPTER, SECTION BY SECTION

When summarizing a chapter, your goal is to **reduce each major section to about one-quarter of its original length.** To accomplish this, you need to be *very selective,* including in your summary the main point (or points) while eliminating all but the most essential supporting details.

For sociology and psychology texts, which place less emphasis on facts and figures and more emphasis on concepts and generalizations, chapter summaries that reduce each major section of the chapter to a paragraph or two can be the ideal vehicle for taking notes. But they are obviously less appropriate for chemistry or biology textbooks in which specific facts and figures play a more significant role. This kind of scientific writing does not readily lend itself to the drastic reduction of material that summarizing demands. (For more on scientific writing, see the next chapter.)

If you decide that chapter summaries are appropriate for some of your textbooks, the following pointers will help you write summaries that are concise without being incomplete.

1. Mark the text before you summarize it.

First read and then mark the major section you're summarizing. Highlight or underline the main point and identify the supporting details you think should be included in your summary.

2. Use the first sentence to identify the main point of the section.

The last thing you want is a summary that precisely records supporting details while neglecting the generalization they serve to explain. Thus it's a good idea to make each summary of a major section open with a statement of the main point or controlling idea of that section.

3. Select only the most useful supporting details.

Since summaries are condensed versions of the original material, you need to be selective about recording supporting details. Yes, do include the names of those experts or researchers who have made unique contributions in the field, but be wary of including the name of every man or woman cited. They won't all be equally important. Similarly, record the results of crucial studies but avoid detailed explanations of how they were conducted.

4. Use transitions to make connections between ideas.

In writing your summary, you will often bring together ideas that originally appeared paragraphs apart. To avoid producing a choppy and confusing version of the original material, think about where you need to include the appropriate **transitions** in order to indicate relationships between ideas. (See Figure 8–3 for some specific examples.)

Some Common Transitional Words and Phrases

Use transitions to:

indicate a new point of view.	**indicate continuation of the same or similar point of view.**
In contrast	By the same token
However	Similarly
But	Along the same lines
On the contrary	Moreover
On the other hand	As well as
Just the opposite	Likewise
Despite the fact	Furthermore
	Also
	In addition

indicate a cause and effect relationship.	**introduce specific illustrations.**
Thus	In the following case
Therefore	For example
For this reason	For an illustration
As a result	Such as
Consequently	A specific instance
In response	For instance
Because of	

Figure 8–3: Include Transitions When Writing Summaries

5. Rely on your own words.

Although you will want to retain the specialized vocabulary from the chapter, you should paraphrase most of the author's words. Here again, paraphrasing serves as a *comprehension check* as well as a reinforcement for remembering. As a sample of how our suggestions should be applied, here is a summary based on one section of our sample chapter "Mate Selection" (pp. 175–177). After you read the summary, compare it to the original selection in order to see what we retained and what we left out.

Religion clearly places some restriction on our choice of mates, and all three major religious groups, Protestants, Jews, and Catholics, encourage members to marry someone of the same religion. But studies show that religious intermarriage has increased, as public opinion against it has decreased. The most flexible about intermarriage are the Protestants, the most inflexible are the Jews, with Catholics falling somewhere in between. But in a real way, *exogamy* (or marriage outside the given group) is being forced upon Jews and Catholics because they represent religious minorities. Not surprisingly, the practice of *endogamy* (or marriage only with other members of the same group) is not as common as it once was.

■   PRACTICE 5   Read and summarize the following selection.

An Indian History

The confusion started when Columbus thought he had reached India and mistakenly called the natives of America *Indians* (Forbes, 1964). Estimates of the number of Indians in what is now the United States in 1492 range from 700,000 to 1,000,000. By the time Indians became official wards of our government in 1871, their population had been reduced to less than half a million (Marden and Meyer, 1968).

In the years from 1607 to 1778, English and Dutch settlers engaged in friendly barter and trade with the Indians, until the white men decided they needed Indian land. In 1754 the British Crown formulated a policy of protecting Indian land and when America became independent the policy was continued on paper; in actuality, however, the Indians were slowly forced off the land and pushed west.

On June 30, 1834, Congress passed *An Act to Regulate Trade and Intercourse with the Indian Tribes and to Preserve Peace on the Frontiers.* Indian country supposedly included all land west of the Mississippi but not within the states of Missouri and Louisiana or the territory of Arkansas. No white persons were permitted to trade in Indian country without a license, and none would be permitted to settle in Indian country (Brown, 1970). The act was to be enforced by the military, but before these laws could be put into

Robert Lindneux's "Trail of Tears" depicts the forced relocation of American Indians during the 1800s.

effect, a new wave of white settlers swept westward to form the territories of Wisconsin and Iowa. The "permanent Indian frontier" had to be shifted further west.

The great Cherokee nation was one of the victims of this act. It had survived more than one hundred years of the white man's wars, diseases, and whiskey, but now the Cherokees were to be moved west. When gold was discovered in their territory, it was decided that the Cherokees must be moved quickly. So, during the fall of 1838, General Winfield Scott's soldiers rounded them up and started them on the long winter trek westward. One of every four Cherokees died from cold, hunger, or disease on this march. A nearly similar fate awaited the Choctaws, Chickasaws, Creeks, and Seminoles forced to give up their homelands in the South. In the North, what few members were left from the Shawnees, Miamis, Ottawas, Hurons, Delawares, and other tribes were sent west beyond the Mississippi.

The independent and undisciplined pioneer pushed farther into the Indian country. Reflecting the white man's aggressive society, he soon demolished the native culture (Sheehan, 1972). In 1871, Congress declared that all Indians were wards of the federal government, and from 1887 to 1914 their lands were reduced from 138 million acres to 47 million acres. Then, as a permanent solution to the "Indian problem," the children were sent to boarding schools to forget their language and Indian ways.

MAPPING

If you are one of those students who can visualize where words appear on a page, you will probably discover that **mapping** is your favored method of taking notes. Because it uses geometric shapes and pictures to record information and show relationships, mapping is also favored by students who like to make and use diagrams when they read. Mapping is not, however, only for those with a strong visual memory: anyone can use maps to organize information. It's just that some students may use them more regularly than others.

Some textbook selections will lend themselves to mapping more readily than others. For example, reading selections that *compare and contrast* two events, objects, or people by pointing out similarities and differences readily lend themselves to mapping because the map can reflect the underlying structure, as in Figure 8–4.

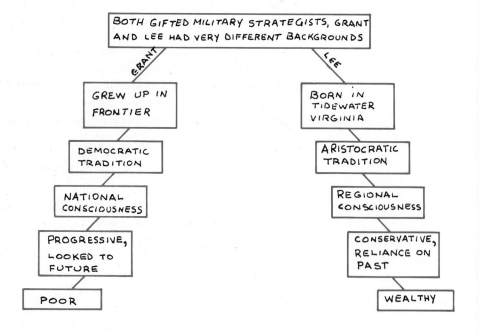

Figure 8–4: Mapping

To be effective as a study aid, your map should give you, practically at a glance, a clear and concise image of the chapter's organization and content. In general, your map should fit on a single page, and the page should not be so cluttered that you can't figure out how one piece of information relates to another.

Because maps are very individualized creations, you can use a variety of shapes and symbols, from circles with spokes to trees with branches, to create your own individual map of the material covered. But whatever symbols you decide to use, follow three basic steps:

1. Use some form like a circle, square, or triangle to highlight the chapter's explicit or implied statement of purpose.

Whatever you do, don't lose sight of the point your map was created to explain or illustrate. So make sure the chapter's purpose or objective stands out by putting it in the middle or top of the page:

Many factors affect our choice of a mate.

2. Attach a series of spokes to the chapter's statement of purpose.

On each of these lines, set down the generalization or concept explained in each major section of the chapter.

Age
Race
Religion

Many factors affect our choice of a mate.

3. Add the supporting details necessary to explain each main point.
Here as an illustration is the completed map of our sample chapter on mate selection:

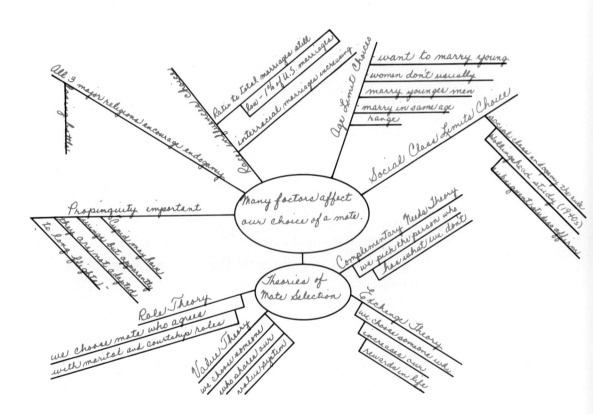

■   PRACTICE 6   Read and map the following selection.

PHYSICAL PROPERTIES OF MINERALS

Minerals are solids formed by inorganic processes. Each mineral has an orderly arrangement of atoms (crystalline structure) and a definite chemical composition which give it a unique set of physical properties. Since the internal structure and chemical composition of a mineral are difficult to determine without the aid of sophisticated tests and apparatus, the more easily recognized physical properties are frequently used in identification. A discussion of some diagnostic physical properties follows.

Luster

Luster is the appearance or quality of light reflected from the surface of a mineral. Minerals that have the appearance of metals, regardless of color, are said to have a *metallic luster.* Minerals with a *nonmetallic luster* are described by various adjectives, including vitreous (glassy), pearly, silky, resinous, and earthy (dull). Some minerals appear partially metallic in luster and are said to be *submetallic.*

Color

Although **color** is the most obvious feature of a mineral, it is often an unreliable diagnostic property. Slight impurities in the common mineral quartz, for example, give it a variety of colors, including pink, purple (amethyst), white, and even black. When a mineral, such as quartz, exhibits a variety of colors, it is said to possess *exotic coloration.* Other minerals, for example, sulfur, which is generally yellow, and malachite, which is bright green, are said to have *inherent coloration* because their color does not vary significantly.

Streak

Streak is the color of a mineral in its powdered form and is obtained by rubbing the mineral across a piece of unglazed porcelain termed a *streak plate.* Although the color of a mineral may vary from sample to sample, the streak usually does not, and is therefore the more reliable property. Streak can also be an aid in distinguishing minerals with metallic lusters from those having nonmetallic lusters. Metallic minerals generally have a dense, dark streak, whereas minerals with nonmetallic lusters do not.

Hardness

One of the more useful diagnostic properties is **hardness,** the resistance of a mineral to abrasion or scratching. This is a relative property that is determined by rubbing a mineral of unknown hardness against one of known hardness, or vice versa. A numerical value can be obtained by using **Mohs scale** of hardness, which consists of ten minerals arranged in order from 1 (softest) to 10 (hardest) as follows:

Hardness	Mineral
1	Talc
2	Gypsum
3	Calcite
4	Fluorite
5	Apatite
6	Orthoclase
7	Quartz
8	Topaz
9	Corundum
10	Diamond

Any mineral of unknown hardness can be compared to these or to other objects of known hardness. For example, a fingernail has a hardness of 2.5, a copper penny 3, and a piece of glass 5.5. The mineral gypsum, which has a hardness of 2, can be easily scratched with your fingernail. On the other hand, the mineral calcite, which has a hardness of 3, will scratch your fingernail but will not scratch glass. Quartz, the hardest of the common minerals, will scratch a glass plate with ease.

Cleavage

Cleavage is the tendency of a mineral to break along planes of weak bonding. Minerals that possess cleavage are identified by the smooth surfaces which are produced when the mineral is broken. The simplest type of cleavage is exhibited by the micas. Because micas have excellent cleavage in one direction, they break to form thin, flat sheets. Some minerals have several cleavage planes which produce smooth surfaces when broken, while others exhibit poor cleavage, and still others have no cleavage at all. When minerals break evenly in more than one direction, cleavage is described by the number of planes exhibited and the angles at which they meet when broken.

From *Essentials of Geology* by Frederick K. Lutgens and Edward J. Tarbuck, Merrill, 1986. Reprinted by permission of the publisher.

WORKING SPACE

READING ASSIGNMENT

The following chapter focuses on self-esteem. Read it and then organize the information it contains, using any one of the four methods described in Chapter 8. Then answer the questions that follow.

SELF-ESTEEM

Awareness of self and self-esteem are particularly relevant parts of the human personality. Coopersmith (1968) has noted the relationship between self-esteem and psychological health and asserted it is important that we devote more attention to building up the positive aspects of human personality. For Coopersmith, the most important factor for effective behavior is self-esteem.

Research on Self-Esteem

In their research Coopersmith (1968) and his co-workers found that youngsters with a high degree of self-esteem are active, expressive individuals who tend to be successful both academically and socially. They lead rather than merely listen in discussions. They are eager to express opinions, do not avoid disagreement, and are not particularly sensitive to criticism. In addition, they are highly interested in public affairs, show little destructiveness in early childhood, and are little troubled by feelings of anxiety. They appear to trust their own perceptions and reactions and have confidence that their efforts will be successful. They approach other persons with the expectation that they will be well received. Their general optimism stems not from fantasies but rather from a well-founded assessment of their abilities, social skills, and personal qualities. They are not self-conscious or preoccupied with personal difficulties. They are much less frequently afflicted with psychosomatic troubles such as insomnia, fatigue, headaches, or intestinal upset than are persons of low self-esteem.

Boys with low self-esteem present a picture of discouragement and depression. They feel isolated, unlovable, incapable of expressing or defending themselves, and too weak to confront or overcome their deficiencies. They are fearful of angering others and shrink from exposing themselves to notice in any way. In the presence of a social group, they remain in the shadows, listening rather than participating. They are sensitive to criticism, self-conscious, and preoccupied with inner problems. This dwelling on their own difficulties not only intensifies their feelings of defeat but also isolates them from opportunities for friendly, supporting relationships. In the words of Epstein and Komorita (1971): "It is likely that the low self-esteem person will 'externalize' responsibility for his actions and attribute the consequences of his behavior to factors beyond his control. On the other hand, the high self-esteem individual presumably views himself as determining the outcome of his behavior" (p. 2). Thus, one's confidence that life can be gratifying may rest squarely on the self-concept, which may decide whether one succeeds or fails in life.

When Coopersmith looked into the backgrounds of boys who possessed high self-esteem, he found that close relationships existed between the boys and their parents. The mothers and fathers showed interest in the boys' welfare, were available for discussion of problems, and encouraged mutual activities. They clearly indicated that they regarded the boy as a significant person worthy of their deep interest. The boys came to

regard themselves in a similar, favorable light.

The parents of the high-self-esteem children also proved to be less permissive than the parents of children with low-self-esteem. Though the less permissive parents demanded high standards of behavior and were strict and consistent in enforcing rules, their discipline was not harsh or punitive. By comparison, the parents of the low-self-esteem boys tended to be exceptionally permissive, yet used harsh punishment when their children gave them trouble.

Buss on Self-Esteem

In the words of Buss (1973):

There are two kinds of self-judgments, one temporary and the other enduring. Temporary self-evaluation refers to specific behaviors [in] particular situations: "That was stupid of me," "I played very well today," or "I really out-maneuvered them this time." These transient reactions, limited in time and place, are of less interest to the student of personality than are the more generalized and enduring evaluations each person makes of himself. The latter evaluations are more central to the self and represent the residuals of some of the most fundamental life experiences: affection from others and one's own achievements. [p. 495]

Buss has designed a *model of self-esteem* to account for the ups-and-downs we all experience in our feelings about ourselves.

The core of self-esteem is formed by the unconditional love of the parents. They love the child simply because he is theirs. They make no demands and place no conditions on their affection. Thus, the infant learns that the most important figures in his life think he is valuable merely because he exists. Love without limits or conditions forms a major part of the core of self-esteem. It creates a permanent feeling of self-love and the expectation that others will offer affection. There is also a peripheral self-esteem that consists of (1) the continued affection of the parents (now with conditions laid down—more love when the child is good, less when he is bad) and (2) the affection of other members of the family and a wider circle of friends. This second part of peripheral self-esteem depends on accomplishments. At first the child performs to please his parents, but gradually his goals are based more and more on group norms.

According to Buss, by middle childhood the core of self-esteem has been established. If the core is sufficient, the person will always be able to fall back on a reserve of self-love. If the core is insufficient, the person will always be driven to seek affection or to demand respect for achievement. "The person who seems *driven* to appeal for love or *driven* to accomplish requires inordinate esteem from others to compensate for his lack of self-esteem. Without a sufficient core of self-esteem, he needs continual assurance of his own worth" (Buss, 1973, p. 497).

Together, the work of Coopersmith and the theorizing of Buss underscore the importance of self-esteem as a core facet of the personality. We may each have personalities composed of differing traits in differing degrees, but these combinations are not very significant, compared to the degree to which we are able to esteem ourselves and behave accordingly.

---

1. The title of this selection is "Self-Esteem." What main point does the author make about self-esteem?

2. What connection can you make between this article and the discussion of self-image in Chapter 1, pages 10–11?

3. What two kinds of self-judgment are described in the article?

4. Self-esteem can vary with the context or the setting. How would you evaluate your self-esteem in each of the following roles: as a student, as a son or daughter, as a wage earner, and as a social success?

WRITING ASSIGNMENT: "The Role of the Past on the Present"

Write a paper in which you first describe an incident in childhood that powerfully affected your self-esteem. Then explore the way in which that incident has affected your present behavior or performance.

JOURNAL ASSIGNMENTS

1. Experiment with the four methods of organizing information for review and evaluate each one. Is there one that you think will work especially well for you? If so, why?

2. Think about how you are doing with time management. Are you making a regular "to do" list by now? Is it helping you organize your time? If not, why not? What method of time management are you using instead?

3. The writer Henry Miller claimed, "We should read to give our souls a chance to luxuriate." What did he mean by that? Is it important to let your soul "luxuriate"?

4. What specific steps have you taken to meet your long-term goals?

CHECKING OUT

Check your understanding of Chapter 8 by writing answers to the following questions. You may work alone or with another student, whichever you prefer.

1.   Why is there no *one* correct method of taking notes?

2.   All four methods require you to do *what* with the material you are organizing for review?

3. What kind of material lends itself to informal outlining? to mapping? to chapter summaries?

4. When you take notes, should you try to record every piece of information in the original text? Why or why not?

5. What do the terms *coordinate* and *subordinate* mean?

6. What is the difference between major and minor headings?

IN SUMMARY

In Chapter 8, we have introduced four separate methods of organizing information for review. Which one you choose depends on your personal needs and the subject matter you are studying. But whichever method or combination of methods you decide to use, the same basic principles apply. First, you must **be selective,** making conscious decisions about what to learn and what to ignore. You must also **choose a method appropriate to the subject matter** you're studying. Chapter summaries, for example, are good for taking notes on sociology textbooks but are less helpful when you want to record scientific information. Remember, too, to **paraphrase wherever possible.** Paraphrasing is a first-rate way of checking your comprehension. If you can't explain the author's ideas in your own language, you probably don't have a good grasp of those ideas. Finally, keep in mind that **connections are almost as crucial as content.** Yes, do highlight and record the essential elements of each page, but don't forget to show how one point relates to another, indicating all coordinate and subordinate relationships.

CHAPTER 9

READING SCIENCE

Science is based on what has gone before. We begin with what is already known in the field and then ask, What is *not* known.

—Alice S. Huang, Ph.D

Many students say they like science and are excited by it. Nevertheless they have trouble reading scientific writing. This is understandable. Science textbooks *are* among the most difficult books to read for several reasons. Definitions of key terms and explanations of important concepts are introduced once and seldom repeated. Unlike other textbooks, those in the sciences do not rely on repetition to ensure comprehension. In addition, science texts contain more specialized vocabulary words than those in the humanities or social sciences, and they are saturated with information not normally found in the everyday conversation of nonscientists. When was the last time you had a casual conversation about atomic weight or the stages in cell division?

Few of us possess the type of background knowledge that encourages understanding of science textbooks, a fact that makes them difficult to read. To compensate for the density of unfamiliar information, skillful readers process the material very slowly, fitting it together piece by piece until the author's message makes sense.

It's also true that illustrations in science textbooks play a more prominent role than they do in social science or humanities texts. That means you have to study the accompanying illustrations as carefully as you do the textual explanation. This is something some of us are not used to doing, but it's something we have to learn if we want to understand scientific writing.

Saying, however, that science textbooks are difficult to read is not to say that you can't improve your ability to read them. You most certainly can. You just have to supplement your usual strategies for reading textbooks with a few that are specifically adapted to the study of science. In Chapter 9, we suggest the following reading strategies for mastering science texts:

- Understand the goals and methods of scientific inquiry; use that knowledge to focus your reading.

- Learn what to look for in passages that explain systems of classification.

- Study the accompanying illustrations as carefully as you do the textual explanations.

- Be prepared for the use of scientific symbols in the text.

THE GOALS AND METHODS OF SCIENCE: INQUIRING MINDS WANT ANSWERS

One way to view science is as an intellectual approach, a style of thinking and a set of methods all designed with one goal—to exclude or at least minimize the chance of being misled by an observation. This is really what the scientific method is all about. It is a set of rules for not getting fooled.

—Boyce Rensberger

In the opinion of Boyce Rensberger, a noted science writer, "Children are born scientists." Explorers from infancy, children do not take the world for granted. For them it's an intriguing puzzle, one that arouses their curiosity. It is this curiosity that fuels their seemingly endless questions about how the world operates.

Unlike the rest of us, scientists do not abandon this deep interest in the world when they grow up. For them it remains a puzzle, and they continue to pose questions on large issues: "Why do our cells age?" "What are black holes?" and "What causes cancer?" In the simplest, yet perhaps truest, terms, the goals of a scientist are to understand how the world works and what materials it's composed of.

But scientists obviously do more than pose intriguing questions. They also try to answer them. To find correct answers to hard questions, they apply the **scientific method.** Although many scientists begin with wild guesses or clever hunches to explain some natural phenomenon, they know that if they want to be taken seriously they must subject their ideas to rigorous investigation. To begin their study of any scientific question, they try to develop a sound **hypothesis** or tentative explanation, which can be tested by a series of experiments or observations. Ideally, scientists try to make their hypotheses assume the form of predictions. Then they either wait for natural events or create in their laboratory the conditions that will confirm or deny their initial hypothesis. In either case, this study or experimentation can be a demanding and time-consuming process.

In the seventeenth century, for example, people believed that every appearance of a comet was a unique event. But then the British astronomer Edmund Halley detected a pattern or regularity in the appearances of certain comets and predicted that the same comet that had appeared in 1680 would reappear in 1758. Halley's hypothesis was eventually confirmed by observation, but he died long before he could see his prediction fulfilled.

Similarly, it often takes time and great effort to create the kind of laboratory conditions or instruments that will allow for the *controlled testing* and observation necessary to turn a good hunch or guess into scientific knowledge. The father of bacteriology, Robert Koch, had to search long and hard for the right pure culture or medium in which isolated bacteria would grow. Only then was he able to confirm what many people had guessed but could not prove scientifically—that there is a cause-and-effect relationship between bacteria and disease.

In the world of science, one experiment in which a prediction proves

Scientists try to develop theories that describe natural phenomena.

correct is never enough—and rightly so. Scientists must *replicate* or repeat their experiments in order to be positive that *coincidence* or *chance* has not played a role. In addition, the findings of an experiment are seldom universally accepted until scientists from other laboratories have replicated similar experimental conditions and produced the same results. It is only at this point that a hypothesis becomes an established theory and enters the pages of your textbooks.

SCIENCE AND THE ANALYTICAL READER

Science builds cumulatively; that is, you have to know first principles before you can understand what follows. Therefore you have to learn basic steps very carefully before you can move on to the more advanced steps.

Knowing something about the goals and methods of scientists should affect the way you read your science textbooks. Aware, for example, that scientists are always trying to develop theories that explain or describe natural phenomena or what happens in nature, you need to be alert for those places in your textbooks where authors offer theoretical explanations of how some phenomenon works. When you find such passages, read them analytically using questions like the following to guide and focus your thinking:

1. What object, event, or process is the author trying to explain or describe?

2. Does the theory or hypothesis (a) explain a cause-and-effect relationship; (b) describe the *physical composition* of some object, structure, or being; or (c) outline a process?

3. What kinds of proof or research have been offered in support of this theory? Did any particular conditions or instruments have to be produced or did any events have to take place before the theory could be universally accepted?

4. Is the theory associated with any particular person or group of people like Watson and Crick who discovered DNA? What did each person or group contribute to the theory's development? How did the theory advance existing knowledge?

5. Does the theory have any known flaws or discrepancies?

Let's now apply those questions to the following passage.

William Harvey's discovery, published in 1628, straightened out the confused explanation of how arteries, veins, blood, and the heart were related. Through a series of experimental demonstrations, Harvey showed that there was one coordinated circulatory system with the heart at the center as pump. This was a twofold advance. First, it signaled the beginning of the end of hidebound* faith in Galen's† unscientific teachings, and launched the modern era of scientific medicine. Second, it revealed an important physiological mechanism linking many other systems of the body. For example, once it was clear that blood circulated through the lungs, a means was established for understanding how oxygen was carried throughout the body. Harvey also drew in the digestive system, showing how circulating blood carried nutrients to all other tissues.

There was, however, one embarrassing gap in Harvey's story of circulation. He had the blood flowing out through the arteries and back through the veins, but he could not produce any evidence of how the blood got from the end of an artery into a vein for the return trip. All the other points of Harvey's new theory were backed up by experimental data, gathered mostly through dissections of animals, some living long enough for Harvey to examine their beating hearts. Lacking anything better than a magnifying glass, Harvey could not see the microscopic blood vessels called capillaries that link arteries to veins. He calculated, however, that if there were no connection, the heart would quickly drain the veins of all blood and burst the arteries. Since this plainly doesn't happen, he asserted that even though they couldn't be seen, there had to be tiny blood vessels that linked arteries with veins.

—Boyce Rensberger,
How the World Works

In this passage, the author describes a process—how blood circulates through the body—and explains that William Harvey was the first person to understand the human circulatory system. He also tells his readers exactly how Harvey's discoveries affected existing scientific thought: (1) it undermined faith in the unscientific theories of the Greek philosopher Galen, paving the way for modern medical research, and (2) it provided information about a physiological mechanism that influenced other systems of the body.

Scientists spend their lives trying to explain the world's mysteries. In our time many questions have been solved, but many remain to be solved—perhaps by your generation. Your job as a reader of science is to analyze passages that describe both what scientists already know and what they are still puzzled by and cannot explain.

---

*hidebound: firm, unquestioned
†Galen: ancient Greek philosopher

UNDERSTANDING CLASSIFICATION

When you read history or psychology textbooks, you'll occasionally run across a paragraph that explains a system of classification where the author describes how some large group can be broken down into smaller subgroups or categories.

However, even a brief inspectional reading of your science textbooks should tell you that passages explaining systems of classification play a more significant role than they do in nonscientific texts. In science books, passages dealing with classification are not just more frequent but also much longer. They often extend far beyond a single paragraph to encompass several pages. When this is the case, the author will usually open with a general statement telling you what the larger group is and how many subgroups comprise it. Then in subsequent paragraphs the author describes each subgroup in greater detail.

This selection is a good example:

Sea-floor sediments can be classified according to their origin into three broad categories: (1) lithogenous ("derived from rocks") sediment; (2) biogenous ("derived from organisms") sediment; and (3) hydrogenous ("derived from water") sediment. Although each category is discussed separately, it should be remembered that all sea-floor sediments are mixtures. No body of sediment comes from a single source.

Lithogenous sediment consists primarily of mineral grains which were weathered from continental rocks and transported to the ocean. The sand-sized particles settle near shore. However, since the very smallest particles take years to settle to the ocean floor, they may be carried for thousands of kilometers by ocean currents. As a consequence, virtually every area of the ocean receives some lithogenous sediment. However, the rate at which this sediment accumulates on the deep-ocean floor is indeed very slow. From 5000 to 50,000 years are necessary for a 1-centimeter layer to form. Conversely, on the continental margins near the mouths of large rivers, lithogenous sediment accumulates rapidly. In the Gulf of Mexico, for example, the sediment has reached a depth of many kilometers.

Since fine particles remain suspended in the water for a very long time, there is ample opportunity for chemical reactions to occur. Because of this, the colors of the deep-sea sediments are often red or brown. This results when iron on the particle or in the water reacts with dissolved oxygen in the water and produces a coating of iron oxide (rust).

Biogenous sediment consists of shells and skeletons of marine animals and plants. This debris is produced mostly by microscopic organisms living in the sunlit waters near the ocean surface. The remains continually "rain" down upon the sea floor.

The most common biogenous sediments are known as *calcareous* ($CaCO_3$) *oozes*, and as their name implies, they have the consistency of thick mud. These sediments are produced by organisms that inhabit warm surface waters. When calcareous hard parts slowly sink through a cool layer of water, they begin to dissolve. This results because cold seawater contains more carbon dioxide and is thus more acidic than warm water. In seawater deeper than about 4500 meters (15,000 feet), calcareous shells will completely dissolve before they reach bottom. Consequently, calcareous ooze does not accumulate where depths are great.

Other examples of biogenous sediments are *siliceous* (SiO_2) *oozes* and phosphate-rich materials. The former is composed primarily of opaline skeletons of diatoms (single-celled algae) and radiolaria (single-celled animals), while the latter is derived from the bones, teeth, and scales of fish and other marine organisms.

Hydrogenous sediment consists of minerals that crystallize directly from seawater through various chemical reactions. For example, some limestones are formed when calcium carbonate precipitates directly from the water; however, most limestone is composed of biogenous sediment.

One of the principal examples of hydrogenous sediment, and one of the most important sediments on the ocean floor in terms of economic potential, is **manganese nodules.** These rounded blackish lumps are composed of a complex mixture of minerals that form very slowly on the floor of the ocean basins. In fact, their formation rate represents one of the slowest chemical reactions known.

To read such passages skillfully, keep in mind questions like the following:

1. What is the larger group that is being divided?

2. How many subgroups are formed through this division? What is the name of each group?

3. What are the characteristics of each one?

4. Does the author offer any representative examples of the subgroups?

From *Essentials of Geology*, Frederick K. Lutgens and Edward J. Tarbuck, Merrill, 1986. Reprinted by permission of the publisher.

5. What are the crucial differences cited? Do the subgroups share any important similarities?

When you can answer these questions, you understand the passage well and can begin taking notes. For your notes, consider making a chart to represent the system of classification described, similar to the chart in Figure 9–1.

Lithogenous	**Biogenous**	**Hydrogenous**
1. Consists of mineral grains weathered from continental rocks	1. Consists of shells and skeletons of marine animals; most common are known as calcareous oozes ($CaCO_3$)	1. Consists of minerals that crystallize directly from sea water
2. found in every area of ocean	2. Does not accumulate when depths are great because shells completely dissolve before hitting bottom	2. Principal example manganese nodules, blackish lumps that form very slowly on floor of ocean basins
3. 5,000 to 50,000 years for 1 centimeter layer to form but on continental margins more rapid. Ex: Gulf of Mexico	3. Other examples are siliceous oozes (SiO_2)	
4. red or brown color due to water reacting with dissolved oxygen and forming a coat of iron		

Figure 9–1: Chart to Represent a System of Classification

If you are taking several science courses, consider including charts in your repertoire of notetaking strategies. Like maps, charts give visual form to the underlying structure of the passage, making them useful for taking notes on long passages that explain a complicated classification. Such passages have a clear-cut underlying structure carefully built in by the author. The more you can mimic that structure in your notes, the more readily you will remember what you have read.

■   PRACTICE 1   After reading the following selection, make a chart that visually represents the structure of the author's explanation.

Once streams acquire their load of sediment, they transport it in three ways: (1) in solution *(dissolved load);* (2) in suspension *(suspended load);* and (3) along the bottom *(bed load).*

The dissolved load is brought to the stream by groundwater and to a lesser degree is acquired directly from soluble rock along the stream's course. The quantity of material carried in solution is highly variable and depends upon such factors as climate and the geologic setting. Usually the dissolved load is expressed as parts of dissolved material per million parts of water (parts per million, or ppm). Although some rivers may have a dissolved load of 1000 ppm or more, the average figure for the world's rivers is estimated to be between 115 and 120 ppm. Almost 4 billion metric tons of dissolved mineral matter are supplied to the oceans each year by streams.

Most streams, but not all, carry the bulk of their load as suspended load. Usually only fine sand-, silt-, and clay-sized particles can be carried this way, but during floodstage larger particles are carried as well. Also during floodstage, the total quantity of material carried in suspension increases dramatically, as can be verified by persons whose homes have been sites for the deposition of this material. During floodstage the Hwang Ho (Yellow River) of China is reported to carry an amount of sediment equal in weight to the water that carries it. Rivers like this are often appropriately described as "too thick to drink, but too thin to cultivate."

A portion of a stream's load of solid material consists of sediment that is too large to be carried in suspension. These coarser particles move along the bottom of the stream and constitute the bed load. In terms of the erosional work accomplished by a down-cutting stream, the grinding action of the bed load is of great importance.

The particles composing the bed load move along the bottom by rolling, sliding, and saltation. Sediment moving by *saltation* appears to jump or skip along the stream bed. This occurs as particles are propelled upward by collisions or sucked upward by the current and then carried downstream a short distance until gravity pulls them back to the bed of the stream. Particles that are too large or heavy to move by saltation either roll or slide along the bottom, depending upon their shape.

Unlike the suspended and dissolved loads, which are constantly in motion, the bed load is in motion only intermittently, when the force of the water is sufficient to move the larger particles. Although the bed load may constitute up to 50 percent of the total load of a few streams, it usually does not exceed 10 percent of a stream's total load. For example, consider the distribution of the 750 million tons of material carried to the Gulf of Mexico by the Mississippi River each year. Of this total, it is estimated that approximately 500 million tons are carried in suspension, 200 million tons in solution, and the remaining 50 million tons as bed load. Estimates of a stream's bed load, however, should be viewed cautiously because this fraction of the load is very difficult to measure accurately. Not only is the bed load more inaccessible than the suspended and dissolved loads, but it moves primarily during periods of flooding when the bottom of a stream channel is most difficult to study.

ANALYZING AND INTERPRETING ILLUSTRATIONS

Illustrations in social science texts highlight and emphasize key points and can be a clue to what is important in an author's explanation.

Within scientific textbooks, however, illustrations play a more fundamental role: they are an essential part of the explanations science writers provide for their readers. As you will see in the following excerpt, the author consistently refers the reader to the individual line drawings accompanying the text explanation. It is largely through the drawings that the authors hope to make specialized terms like *internal force, deformation,* and *vertical displacement* meaningful.

Internal Forces and Deformation

Anything that carries load develops internal forces that cause it to deform. When lifting barbells, weightlifters experience internal forces within their bodies: their muscles elongate and contract. When a heavy truck goes over a bridge, internal forces develop in the structure that cause the roadway to *deflect,* that is, to bend. Because bridges are constructed of stiff materials such as concrete and steel, these deformations are small, too small to see with the naked eye. When a boy, however, crosses a thin plank, supported on two sides of a small river bank, you can easily see the thin board bend or deflect,

From *Essentials of Geology,* Frederick K. Lutgens and Edward J. Tarbuck, Merrill, 1986. Reprinted by permission of the publisher.

as in Figure 9–2a.

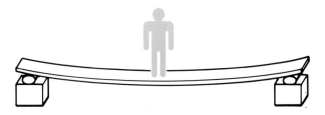

Figure 9–2a

In the study of *statics,* which covers the behavior of loaded bodies at rest, computations are based on Newton's Second Law, which states that force equals mass times acceleration:

$$R = Ma \qquad\qquad \text{(Eq. 1)}$$

where R = resultant force acting on the body

                   M = mass [related to weight]

                   a = acceleration

In Figure 9–2b, we see a workbench loaded by a piece of heavy

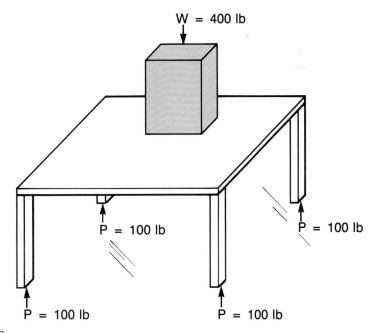

Figure 9–2b

equipment, a machine that weighs 400 lbs. The force exerted by the machine on the top of the table is represented by an arrow labeled W. The arrow indicates that the force of 400 pounds is pushing down on the workbench. Upward forces or reactions exerted by the floor on the table legs are represented by the letter P.

Since the table is obviously at rest, its acceleration equals zero: When a equals zero, the right side of Equation 1 equals zero, and we can write:

$$R = 0 \qquad\qquad\qquad \text{(Eq. 2)}$$

Expressing R in terms of the forces acting on the table, we express Eq. 2 as

$$4P - 400 = 0$$

and solving for P, we find

$$P = 100 \text{ lbs.}$$

where a force acting up is considered positive and a force acting down is considered negative.

Physically, you can see there is as much force acting upward as acting downward. Equation 2 is called an equation of static equilibrium.

Vertical displacement or *deflection* occurs as the plank in Figure 9–2a develops curvature when the boy stands in the center. Curvature is produced when the upper surface of the plank shortens and goes into a state of compression, and the lower surface of the plank is put into tension as the fibers of the wood at that location stretch. If the boy weighs 200 lbs, the reaction at each support is 100 lbs.

When the plank bends (see Figure 9–2c), the distance from A to B shortens, and the upper surface is placed in *compression*. The distance from C to D elongates, and the lower surface is put into *tension*. The vertical displacement is labeled △ (delta). This same kind of deformation and vertical displacement occurs in a bridge, but the small displacements produced by loads can only be measured by instruments—not perceived by eye.

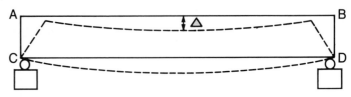

Figure 9–2c

In responding to this passage, skillful readers would automatically study the illustration *each time* the author refers to it. They would mentally match up the labels and arrows in the drawings with the descriptions in the text in order to see, for example, how Figure 9–2a represents the *deflection* or bending explained in the text. In this way, the reader could fully grasp the basic first steps of statics the author wants to explain.

In matching text and drawing, note that most authors try to place their figures *after* the first reference to it in the text. Also figures and tables are usually numbered by chapter number and then by sequence: Figure 9–3, for example, would be located in Chapter 9, after two earlier figures.

Process Diagrams

Process diagrams outlining the steps or stages in some event or happening are among the most common types of scientific illustrations and deserve particularly close and careful scrutiny. Figure 9–3 is a block diagram that outlines the process of "negative feedback."

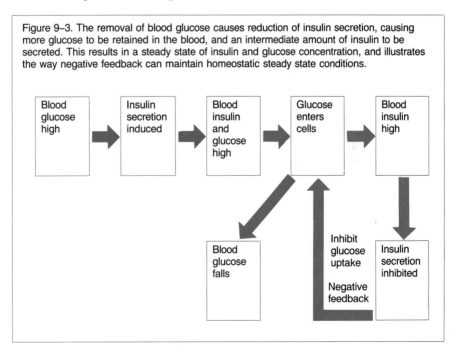

Figure 9–3. The removal of blood glucose causes reduction of insulin secretion, causing more glucose to be retained in the blood, and an intermediate amount of insulin to be secreted. This results in a steady state of insulin and glucose concentration, and illustrates the way negative feedback can maintain homeostatic steady state conditions.

Figure 9–3: The Removal of Blood Glucose

To understand this process diagram, look carefully at the individual steps or stages represented by the blocks. Study not just what happens in each one but the order they follow as well. Remember, too, that diagrams of a process usually use arrows to indicate both the order of the steps and the relationship between them. If you want to understand the process described, you have to study the arrows, noting how one step stems from, leads to, or affects another step.

Tables

In scientific writing, authors frequently use tables to illustrate graphically similarities and differences among members of the same class or group. In Table 9-1, for example, the author uses a table to explain how chemotherapy—the treatment of disease with chemicals—actually works on the body. While the middle column identifies each chemotherapeutic agent, the "mode of action" column indicates *how* those agents work, and the "preferential use against" column indicates *what* bacteria they destroy most effectively.

When confronted with a table, study the left-hand column and the column headings to identify the kind of information listed in each column. Be prepared as well to compare and contrast the information provided in the individual columns, particularly if the author directs you to do so within the text. Follow the author's directions precisely and move your eyes from the author's words to the item cited on the table. This is the only way to fully understand the author's intended explanation.

Whatever type of scientific illustration you encounter in your reading—line drawing, process diagram, or table—study it carefully, keeping in mind these three pointers:

1. Each time an illustration is mentioned, look at it before you continue to read the text.

2. Read the captions. They explain the purpose or point of the illustration.

3. Note the direction of any arrows used. Study all labels that identify or separate parts of the illustration.

> Within scientific textbooks, illustrations play a fundamental role: they are an essential part of the explanations science writers provide for their readers.

Mode of Action	Chemotherapeutic Agent	Preferential Use Against
I. Antimetabolites	Para-amino salicylic acid	*Mycobacterium tuberculosis*
	Isonicontinic acid hydrazide (INH)	*Mycobacterium tuberculosis*
	Sulfonamides	*Escherichia coli* (urinary infection)
II. Cell wall inhibitors	Bacitracin	Gram-positive bacteria and *Neisseria*
	Cephalosporin	Gram-positive and gram-negative bacteria
	Cycloserine	*Mycobacterium tuberculosis*
	Penicillin	Gram-positive bacteria
	Vancomycin	Penicillin-resistant staphylococci
III. Plasma membrane inhibitors	Amphotericin B	Fungi
	Nystatin	Fungi
	Polymyxin B	*Pseudomonas*, fungi
	Chloramphenicol	*Salmonella*, rickettsias, chlamydias
IV. Inhibitors of protein synthesis	Erythromycin	Gram-positive bacteria and mycoplasmas
	Gentamicin	Gram-positive and gram-negative bacteria
	Kanamycin	*Escherichia coli, Proteus*
	Lincomycin	Gram-positive bacteria
	Neomycin	Gram-positive and gram-negative bacteria
	Streptomycin	Gram-positive and gram-negative bacteria
	Tetracyclines	Gram-positive and gram-negative bacteria, rickettsias, chlamydias
V. Inhibitors of nucleic acid synthesis or function	Cytarabine	Viruses
	Idoxuridine	Viruses
	Nalidixic acid	Gram-negative bacteria
	Rifamycin (used with INH)	*Mycobacterium tuberculosis*
	Vidarabine	Herpes simplex viruses

Table 9–1: Mode of Action and Preferential Use of Some Important Chemotherapeutic Agents

■   **PRACTICE 2**   Read the following excerpt and study the illustration that accompanies it.

The causal relationship between microorganisms and disease was first demonstrated in animals other than humans. In 1835, the Italian amateur microscopist Agostino Bassi showed that a certain pathogenic* fungus was responsible for a disease of silkworm larvae. Interestingly, the first demonstration of a nonfungal micro-organism as a disease agent also involved the silkworm. In 1865, Louis Pasteur produced evidence that a protozoan caused the disease of silkworm larvae known as pebrine. The first disease for which bacteria were definitely implicated was sheep anthrax. This relationship was shown by Robert Koch in 1876.

Despite the lack of conclusive evidence of the relationship between microorganisms and certain human diseases, microbiologists and physicians of the mid-nineteenth century began to assume more and more often that there was such a relationship. As a matter of fact, the Austrian physician Ignaz Semmelweis had shown conclusively in 1850, on the basis of clinical evidence, that childbed fever was a contagious disease. (We know now that it is caused by certain streptococci.) But because etiology (the study of the causes of disease) was so hard to pursue, especially under the primitive laboratory conditions of the time, rigorous guidelines for investigating disease-microorganism relationships were needed.

In 1884, largely because of his own difficult experience with the causative agent of tuberculosis, Robert Koch proposed a series of procedures that have come to be called *Koch's postulates*. (See also Figure 9–4.)

1. **The organism must be isolated from the tissues or discharges of a patient in every case of the disease.**
2. **The organism must be grown in *pure* culture and subcultured several times. The observable characteristics of the organism must remain constant.**
3. **This pure culture must be used to produce the disease *consistently* in experimental animals.**
4. **The organism must be reisolated from the tissues or discharges of these experimental animals and must be shown to be identical to the original isolate.**

---

*pathogenic: an agent that causes disease

Although these rules have been modified considerably over the years, especially with regard to viral* diseases, they were invaluable guidelines for Koch and his contemporaries and for those who followed them in the science of etiology. In fact, by 1900, largely due to Koch's postulates, the causative agents of most of the dreaded bacterial diseases—such as pneumococcal pneumonia, tetanus, and tuberculosis—had been identified.

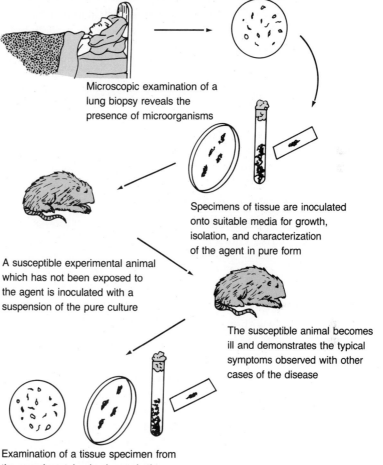

Microscopic examination of a lung biopsy reveals the presence of microorganisms

Specimens of tissue are inoculated onto suitable media for growth, isolation, and characterization of the agent in pure form

A susceptible experimental animal which has not been exposed to the agent is inoculated with a suspension of the pure culture

The susceptible animal becomes ill and demonstrates the typical symptoms observed with other cases of the disease

Examination of a tissue specimen from the experimental animal reveals the presence of an infectious agent. Laboratory characterization reveals that the organism isolated from the experimental animal is the same organism as isolated from the initial tissue biopsy

Figure 9–4: Drawing of Koch's Postulates

*viral: caused by viruses

Now make a block diagram that you think would effectively represent the four steps that have come to be called "Koch's postulates."

BECOME COMFORTABLE WITH SCIENTIFIC SYMBOLS IN TEXT

When reading scientific writing, be prepared for passages in which authors move from words to mathematical and scientific symbols. Conventional language is often not precise enough to describe adequately a chemical process or physical phenomenon. At times more refined and precise symbols are necessary, particularly if an explanation in words would be too lengthy and time-consuming.

Compare, for example, these two versions of the same chemical reaction:

Zinc added to hydrochloric acid produces zinc chloride
and hydrogen

or

$$Zn + 2HCl \rightarrow ZnCl_2 + H_2 \uparrow$$

For precision, writers of scientific textbooks use scientific symbols, so familiarize yourself with their meaning so that they do not intimidate you. In general, you should be ready to do the following:

1. Match words with symbols.
In the sciences, textbook authors are aware that you are not generally familiar with many of the shorthand symbols they employ. They, therefore, make it a point to tell you initially what word each symbol represents. This is certainly true of the following example in which the author introduces Newton's law of universal gravitation first in words and then in mathematical symbols. Notice how each symbol is carefully defined:

Every material particle in the universe attracts every other material particle with a force that is proportional to the product of the masses of the two particles, and inversely proportional to the square of the distance between their centers. The force is directed along a line joining their centers.

In mathematical form, the magnitude of the force is represented by

$$F_{gravity} = Gm_1m_2/r^2$$

From *Seven Ideas That Shook the World*, Nathan Spielberg and Bryon D. Anderson, © 1987. Reprinted by permission of John Wiley and Sons, Inc.

where $F_{gravity}$ is the magnitude of the force, m_1 is the mass of one of the objects, m_2 is the mass of the other object, r is the distance between the centers of the two objects, and G is a proportionality constant (which is needed just to use units already defined for mass, distance, and force).

Your job as a reader is to read these passages analytically, carefully matching words with scientific symbols. You must understand the meaning of each symbol, word, and concept to grasp the meaning of this compressed passage.

2. Write out all scientific formulas.

As you write out formulas, make sure you understand each term of each equation and pay attention to every sign or symbol.

3. Learn the standard symbols that represent key relationships or operations.

Some of the symbols commonly used to identify scientific operations or mathematical relationships are familiar to you. You will have little difficulty figuring out what $+$ and $-$ represent, but what about the arrows in the previous chemistry equation?

$$Zn + 2HCl \rightarrow ZnCl_2 + H_2 \uparrow$$

To understand the process represented by this equation, you must know that the horizontal arrow pointing right indicates that the elements on the left-hand side, zinc and hydrochloric acid, react to form the combination on the right-hand side, zinc chloride and hydrogen, while the vertical arrow shows that the hydrogen formed was a gas and passed into the atmosphere. Authors usually explain the meaning of such symbols the first time they appear in the text, but from then on, it's up to you to remember their meaning.

Authors in the sciences often assume a certain level of mathematical competence and will sometimes use, without explanation, symbols they think you know. For example, when explaining Newton's law of universal gravitation, the author defined all the letters in the formula. But he assumed that the reader was familiar enough with algebra to know that the raised number 2 is an exponent indicating how many times a variable or number is to be multiplied by itself:

$$b^2 = b \times b$$
$$b^3 = b \times b \times b$$

Albert Einstein writes out the equation for the density of the "Milky Way" on a blackboard at the Carnegie Institute in Pasedena, California.

When you find passages where mathematical symbols are used without explanation, learn what those symbols represent. You may have to review an introductory math (algebra or geometry) text where such terms are defined and explained, or you may have to refer to an introductory text in one of the basic sciences (chemistry, biology, physics).

4. Wherever possible, make abstractions concrete.

Matching words with mathematical symbols is an important first step. Whenever possible, go a step further and try to relate those symbols to what you already know about the world, developing your own examples, analogies, images, or patterns. Let's say, for example, that you were studying the following formula:

$$Fe + CuSO_4 \rightarrow FeSO_4 + Cu$$

It represents the chemical reaction called *replacement,* which takes place when iron combines with copper sulfate. Yes, the first step is to recognize that Fe represents iron and $CuSO_4$ stands for copper sulfate. But to understand what that formula really means, you might also evoke the analogy of a dance between copper and sulfate where copper is left in the cold after iron cuts in. In this respect, reading scientific symbols is no different from reading words: much of your understanding depends on your willingness to interact with those symbols, looking for links between what you already know about the world and what you are learning.

When you encounter scientific or mathematical formulas in your texts, study them carefully. Do not skip any; decipher them one by one. If your own analytical reading doesn't do the trick, ask your instructor or a well-prepared classmate for help. Chances are that these same formulas will reappear in later chapters, where you will be expected to know them. It's worthwhile to master scientific formulas when they are first introduced because at this point the author will provide the most detailed explanation of each symbol.

WORKING SPACE

READING ASSIGNMENT

In his book *Science: Good, Bad, and Bogus,* Martin Gardner evaluates the achievements of the Israeli magician Uri Geller and suggests that scientists who believe Geller can actually move objects with his mind may have been misled.

Magic and Paraphysics

Any magician will tell you that scientists are the easiest persons in the world to fool. It is not hard to understand why. In their laboratories the equipment is just what it seems. There are no hidden mirrors or secret compartments or concealed magnets. If an assistant puts chemical "A" in a beaker he doesn't (usually) surreptitiously* switch it for chemical "B." The thinking of a scientist is rational,† based on a lifetime of experience with a rational world. But the methods of magic are irrational and totally outside a scientist's experience.

The general public has never understood this. Most people assume that if a man has a brilliant mind he is qualified to detect fraud. This is untrue. Unless he has been thoroughly trained in the underground art of magic, and knows its peculiar principles, he is easier to deceive than a child.

---

*surreptitiously: secretly
†rational: believing in the power of reason

Some physicists also have not understood this. In the late nineteenth and early twentieth centuries, a number of prominent scientists (Oliver Lodge, William Crookes, John Rayleigh, Charles Richet, Alfred R. Wallace, and others) were firmly persuaded that mediums, aided by discarnate* "controls," could levitate† tables, materialize objects, and call up audible and even photographable spirits from the vasty deep. An Austrian astrophysicist, Johann Zöllner, wrote a book called *Transcendental Physics* about an American medium, Henry Slade, who specialized in producing insipid†† chalked messages from the dead on slates, and knots in closed loops of cord. . . . It was as impossible for anyone to convince Zöllner that so charming a man as Slade could be a magician as it was impossible for Houdini to persuade Conan Doyle that he (Houdini) did not perform his escapes by dematerializing his body.

And now the wretched story is happening all over again, with Uri Geller in the center of a cyclone of irrationalism that is churning over the Western world. Geller is a young, personable Israeli who began his spectacular career by performing what magicians call a "mental act" in Israeli night spots. An American parapsychologist, Andrija Puharich, discovered him, and introduced him to Edgar Mitchell, the astronaut who once walked the moon and who now runs his own organization devoted to investigating the paranormal. Mitchell financed Geller's trip to the United States and arranged for him to be tested at the Stanford Research Institute by Harold Puthoff and Russell Targ, two former laser physicists now engaged in full-time psychic research. After a series of poorly designed experiments with Geller, Puthoff and Targ published their favorable findings in *Nature.* Although Puthoff and Targ are personally convinced of Geller's ability to bend metal by PK *(psychokinesis)* and to perform even more remarkable miracles, their *Nature* report was limited to Geller's power of ESP (extrasensory perception). His most sensational feat was guessing correctly, eight times in a row, the number on a die that had been shaken in a metal file box by "one of the experimenters." It later turned out that Geller had been allowed to handle the box, and that many prior trial runs had been made. Because the experimenters always shook the box before Geller was permitted to touch it, Geller's handling seemed irrelevant, so it was not mentioned in the *Nature* report. This seemingly trivial detail gave Geller a splendid

---

*discarnate: without a physical body
†levitate: lift in the air
††insipid: silly

chance to obtain information by a technique known to conjurors.*
Had Puthoff and Targ been aware of this technique it would have
been easy to take steps to preclude† it. The fact that they did not
makes the dice experiment worthless.

---

*conjurors: magicians
†preclude: prevent

---

1. According to Gardner, scientists are readily fooled by the tricks of a magician. How does he support this claim?

2. What does Gardner mean when he says that Geller is in the "center of a cyclone of irrationalism that is churning all over the Western world"?

3. Why do you think Gardner wrote this article? What was his purpose?

WRITING ASSIGNMENT

According to Robert H. March, a physicist and author of *Physics for Poets,* "the worst possible attitude with which to approach the study of physics is awe." Respond to March's statement by explaining how a feeling of "awe" could affect a person's ability to learn not just physics but any other subject as well.

JOURNAL ASSIGNMENTS

1. Describe your attitude toward learning science.

2. What science courses have you taken? Did you think the texts were more difficult than those in nonscience courses?

CHECKING OUT

Check your understanding of Chapter 9 by writing answers to the following questions. You may work alone or with a friend, whichever you prefer.

1. What are some questions to keep in mind when reading discussions of scientific theories?

2. What are some pointers to keep in mind when you read scientific illustrations?

3. What is a process diagram?

4. Why do science writers use scientific formulas in place of words?

IN SUMMARY

Learning how to read science does not mean you have to abandon all of the strategies introduced in previous chapters. You do, however, have to expand upon them by learning the goals and methods of scientific investigation. You also have to analyze the illustrations—figures, tables, diagrams—in your science books as carefully as the written prose. Many passages will require a careful analytical reading, after you have completed both an inspectional and intensive reading. By combining an understanding of how to analyze classification passages with a knowledge of scientific symbols, you will find that your science textbooks are more accessible than ever before.

U N I T   3

Most of the courses you take in college will include some type of test or examination that will help determine your grade. But beyond deciding your grades, tests serve another important function. Preparing for and taking them give you a chance to integrate all the different parts of the course—the various readings, homework assignments, and lectures—into a coherent whole.

Because tests *are* such a central part of college life, Unit 3 offers a comprehensive discussion of tests and test-taking. Chapter 10 will show you how to schedule and organize your reviews so that you can avoid cramming for exams. It will also give you a step-by-step strategy for *synthesizing* or combining information from different sources. Chapter 11 will tell you how to proceed once you are actually in the classroom with your heart pounding and your pencil poised over the test booklet. You'll learn how to read and respond to test questions; and not least, you'll learn how to calm your nerves.

CHAPTER 10

PREPARING FOR EXAMS

Talking over the things which you have read with your companions on the first opportunity you have for it, is a most useful manner of repetition or review, in order to fix them upon the mind.

—Isaac Watts

OVERVIEW

As the quotation from Isaac Watts* suggests, the purpose of a review is to "fix" information firmly in your mind, integrating it into your own personal store of knowledge. To ensure that the integration of new and old information does indeed take place during your reviews, we offer six principles for exam preparation.

- Instead of cramming before exams, plan well ahead for reviews.
- Make synthesis sheets that combine information from different sources.
- Use stimulus cues.
- Anticipate test questions.
- Prewrite essay answers.
- For those occasions when you just have to cram, cram with a method.

---

* Watts was writing in the seventeenth century, thus the odd punctuation and syntax.

THE DRAWBACKS OF CRAMMING

FIRST STUDENT: I can't believe I'm still walking. I have been up for two days straight to prepare for this exam.

SECOND STUDENT: Only two days! I've been up for three days. I'm living on coffee to keep me awake.

THIRD STUDENT: Two days, three days. That's nothing. I haven't slept for a week.

At one time or another, most of us have boasted about cramming for exams—about sleepless nights and countless cups of coffee. Bragging about hours spent cramming is practically a freshman tradition, seeming proof of youthful endurance and confidence. But pleasurable as it can be to boast about cramming, we still caution you against it. Desperate to commit pages of text or notes to memory in a short amount of time, you are bound to memorize without any real understanding or learning taking place. If one of your goals is to become an educated and thoughtful human being, cramming will not help you reach that goal; it will give you little more than a parrot-like understanding of material you're supposed to be learning in-depth.

But there is a more subtle reason why you should avoid cramming: it can be a strategy for masking a fear of failure.

Because they are afraid of making their best effort and failing, some students cram and don't let themselves perform as well as they could. Then if they fail, they can always say: "I didn't really study. If I had, I would've passed the exam, but I tried to learn everything in one night. I didn't give it my best effort." The result is a vicious circle in which students do not do as well as they could because they cram, grow even more unsure of themselves as a result, and hide their anxiety by cramming for the next exam.

Once in a while, you may have to cram for an exam. Everyone does *once in a while*. But if you find that cramming is your sole strategy for taking tests, you had better think about why this is so. Was it really impossible to schedule time for reviews throughout the semester? Did you try? Or did you feel that it was safer to cram for the exam since it offered you a ready-made excuse for failure?

> If one of your goals is to become an educated and thoughtful human being, cramming will not help you reach that goal; it will give you at best only a parrot-like understanding of material you're supposed to be learning in-depth.

PLANNING FOR REVIEWS

Good reviews don't just happen. They have to be carefully planned. Although your methods of review will depend on the type of material you're studying, there are some general guidelines you should follow if you want to make sure your reviews produce the best results—a solid understanding of the material and a high grade on the exam.

1. Look at reviews in a positive light.

If you think of your reviews as a chore that must be gotten over with, that's what they'll be. But they don't have to be. Reviewing for exams gives you a chance to bring together and integrate all the individual parts of the course—the readings, lectures, handouts, and homework. Seeing how all these pieces fit together can be an invigorating experience as you start to feel you've truly mastered a large and complicated body of knowledge. If you think of reviews from this perspective, they will produce a sense of accomplishment rather than exhaustion.

2. Match the length of your reviews to the difficulty of the material.

If biology is difficult for you, give yourself a month to review, scheduling hour-long reviews twice or even three times a week. On the other hand, if introductory sociology seems to come easily, allot only a week for review, planning on just two or three sessions. The basic principle is simple: **the harder the course, the earlier you should start your reviews.**

3. Establish priorities.

Use your first review to collect all of your lecture and reading notes, to make a list of the chapters covered, and to gather together all handouts, homework assignments, and outside readings. Once you have collected everything assigned in the course, decide which information is particularly essential and which is not. Did your biology instructor spend two class sessions on Charles Darwin's contributions to science and fifteen minutes on Jean-Baptiste Lamarck's? If so, plan on spending a good portion of your time studying Darwin's ideas but allot considerably less time to the work of Lamarck.

At least three or four weeks before exams start, make up an **exam review schedule,** listing approximate times to review all the chapters and all the notes you need to cover for each course. Schedule time for reworking some math or chemistry problems from your homework or old tests. Every evening, review your exam schedule to see if it is working out or if it needs rethinking.

4. Develop an overview of the course.

Make **synthesis sheets** that unite all the diverse parts of the course—readings, homework, labs, and handouts. (For more on synthesis sheets, see the next section, pp. 251–254.) Think about how the course was organized. What points were emphasized? How were they introduced? How do they relate to one another?

5. Be flexible.

If you have to cover twelve chapters in American history, begin by planning on three two-hour reviews with four chapters per session. But if you find yourself falling behind, rethink your review schedule. Maybe you need four reviews with only three chapters per session. The point is to be flexible and pace yourself, so that you can comfortably cover everything of importance in time for the exam.

6. Employ a variety of learning strategies.

Your reviews will be more productive *and* more stimulating if you use a variety of learning strategies. In addition to working alone, plan on reviewing with friends so that you can discuss the material. Attend any review sessions your teachers hold. Don't just write notes, recite them. Read your notes into a tape recorder and then play them back, listening to your own words. Make drawings, diagrams, time lines, and flash cards. Visualize. The more you **find different ways to rework and review the material,** the better your understanding will be. Review Chapter 3 on learning and remembering.

7. Use the night before the exam for a final review.

The night before the exam is the perfect time to give extra attention to particularly difficult material, to go over answers to potential test questions, and just generally to review—one last time—everything you've studied. It's not, however, the time to tackle three chapters you've never looked at before. Tackling new material the night before the exam will usually make you feel anxious and unprepared. Those are *not* the kinds of feelings you want to have when you walk into the exam.

You should also use the last night to give yourself a pep talk. Tell yourself that you've studied hard and will do well. There's no reason why you shouldn't.

> Good review sessions don't just happen. They have to be carefully planned. Develop your exam review schedule well ahead of your exams.

Preparing is an important part of test-taking. This conductor must prepare for his test—the concert.

MAKING SYNTHESIS SHEETS

By the time midterms or finals roll around, you may have gathered and recorded information from a variety of sources: texts, lectures, outside readings, lab assignments, and so forth. But you don't want to be frantically shuffling through three or four different sets of notes the week before exams—a time-consuming and unproductive approach. Why reread lecture notes that restate your reading notes, or vice versa? Instead make a series of **synthesis sheets** that combine under one heading all the relevant information for the course.

Because they give you an overview of the course, synthesis sheets are useful devices for final reviews. With synthesis sheets you know exactly what has been covered and are less likely to leave anything out during your reviews. But even more important, **synthesizing forces you to think** about *how* all your sources of information—text, lectures, and outside readings—relate to one another. This is the kind of active learning that leads to in-depth remembering rather than rote memorization.

Synthesis sheets are not hard to make if you follow four basic steps:

1. Identify the primary source of information in the course.

Some instructors use their lectures to present the essential material in their discipline, relying on the textbook and outside readings to supplement their lectures. Others prefer to make the textbook the backbone of the course, using lectures and outside readings to flesh out what was said in the text. Your job is to identify the primary source of information within your particular course.

2. Make a list of major topics covered in the course. Underneath each one indicate all the subtopics discussed in any detail.

To make this list, look at your course syllabus, the headings in your lecture notes, and the table of contents in your textbook. The table of contents will identify the topics generally covered in a course in your particular subject, while the syllabus and the lecture headings will identify the ones actually covered in your course prior to the exam. Figure 10–1 shows the first jottings of a synthesis sheet for a course titled "Marriage and the Family":

MARRIAGE AND THE FAMILY

Mate Selection
    Age
    Race
    Religion
    Social Class
    Propinquity
    Basic Theories of Mate Selection

Husband and Wife Relationships
    Marital Adjustment
    Employed Wives
    The Effect of Children
    Sexual Adjustment and Maladjustment

Figure 10–1: Beginning a Synthesis Sheet: List of Major Topics

3. For each subtopic on your list, make a separate list of the key points covered. Using your text or lecture notes—whichever one is the major source of information—list each subtopic with its main points and supporting details. Abbreviate as much as possible, relying primarily on words and phrases rather than whole sentences. Be sure, too, to **give yourself plenty of space** for recording additional information from the sources that remain.

Figure 10–2 is a partially completed synthesis sheet dealing with theories of mate selection. At this point, the sample chapter on mate selection (pp. 173–181) is the sole source of information.

Basic Theories of Mate Selection

1. *Roles*
   Choose mate who agrees with our expectations about
   social and sexual roles.

2. *Values*
   Choose mate with similar values (ideals, customs, behavior patterns).

3. *Exchange*
   Look for mate to maximize our personal advantages.

4. *Complementary Needs*
   Choose person who has what we don't.

Figure 10–2: Partially Completed Synthesis Sheet

4. Look over your other sources of information and add whatever is useful or pertinent.

Once you develop your synthesis sheet using only one source of information, you have to decide what the other sources contribute. Do the text and the lecture notes repeat each other while outside readings provide new and contrasting points of view? If that's true, you may need to add to your list only the information from your outside readings. Or perhaps the instructor uses lecture notes and outside readings to provide research studies and statistics illustrating main points from your textbook. If so, you'll probably need to add some or all of those studies and statistics to your synthesis sheet.

Figure 10–3 is a synthesis sheet completed by student Ed Rosenthal. It contains information from three sources: (1) the textbook chapter on mate selection, (2) the reading on birth order (pp. 182–186), and (3) the lecture notes taken in class. For purposes of explanation, we have identified the source of each additional point or fact, but this is something you can omit on your own synthesis sheets (although you may want to identify the sources of your outside readings, making it clear who said what).

In the act of synthesizing, think about *how* all sources of information—text, lectures, handouts, homework, outside readings—relate to one another.

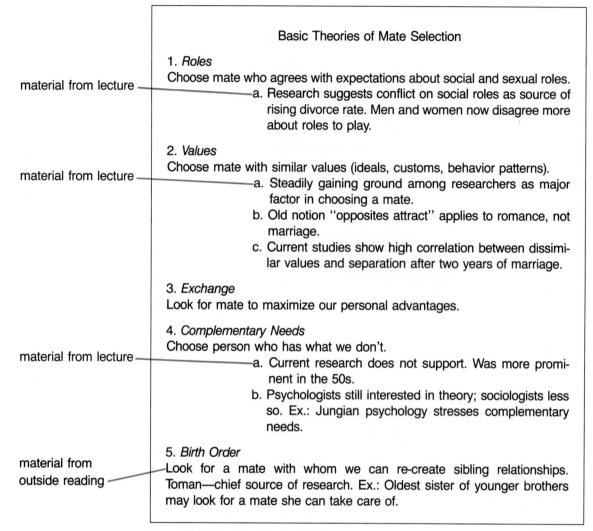

material from lecture

material from lecture

material from lecture

material from outside reading

Basic Theories of Mate Selection

1. *Roles*
Choose mate who agrees with expectations about social and sexual roles.
   a. Research suggests conflict on social roles as source of rising divorce rate. Men and women now disagree more about roles to play.

2. *Values*
Choose mate with similar values (ideals, customs, behavior patterns).
   a. Steadily gaining ground among researchers as major factor in choosing a mate.
   b. Old notion "opposites attract" applies to romance, not marriage.
   c. Current studies show high correlation between dissimilar values and separation after two years of marriage.

3. *Exchange*
Look for mate to maximize our personal advantages.

4. *Complementary Needs*
Choose person who has what we don't.
   a. Current research does not support. Was more prominent in the 50s.
   b. Psychologists still interested in theory; sociologists less so. Ex.: Jungian psychology stresses complementary needs.

5. *Birth Order*
Look for a mate with whom we can re-create sibling relationships. Toman—chief source of research. Ex.: Oldest sister of younger brothers may look for a mate she can take care of.

Figure 10–3: Completed Synthesis Sheet

■   PRACTICE 1   For each of your courses, identify the major source of information—reading assignments or lectures. In the third column, identify any additional sources of information like outside readings, labs, or tapes. When you complete the third column, ask yourself what the primary function of the additional sources is. Would you say they duplicate, elaborate, or challenge key points of the reading assignments or lectures?

Course	Major Source of Information	Additional Sources

USING STIMULUS CUES

As you become more familiar with the material on your synthesis sheets, you should reduce your original notes to a series of brief stimulus cues—single words or phrases that stimulate your mind into action. Given these cues, you should be able to search your memory and retrieve the information they represent. To illustrate, the following list shows you how the notes on page 254 have been reduced to a few brief stimulus cues, each one representing a far larger amount of information:

Theories of Mate Selection

1. Roles
2. Values
3. Exchange
4. Complementary Needs
5. Birth Order

Condensing your notes into stimulus cues serves two essential functions. First, because you have to search for the key words that can represent larger ideas, condensing forces you to think about and analyze the material you want to learn and remember. Second, stimulus cues can tell you if you are ready for an exam. When you can look at one word and respond with the supporting details or the paragraph it represents, make no mistake; you're ready.

■   PRACTICE 2   Here are some notes on Franz Gall, a man who claimed he could measure intelligence by feeling bumps on a person's head. Read the notes and then condense them into a few brief stimulus cues.

Original Notes

Phrenology

1. Franz Gall claimed that you could measure intelligence by feeling bumps on the head.

a. Different bumps represented different powers of mind.

b. Popular then, considered unscientific today. Scientists now know that size or shape of brain shows no relationship to intellect (Anatole France and Walt Whitman had very small brains).

c. Still, contained kernel of truth: there may be no one intelligence but a series of different ones, such as language ability, problem solving, visual acuity, musical aptitude, etc.

Stimulus Cues

_____

_____

_____

_____

_____

ANTICIPATING TEST QUESTIONS

My roommate is a master at anticipating what is going to be on the exam. Every time she takes a test, she predicts half of the questions. I don't know how she does it.

—Pam Ciarlone, student

Correctly anticipating exam questions is not some special talent possessed by only a few gifted individuals. Everyone can learn how to predict at least some of the questions on an exam. Perhaps more to the point, every student who takes an exam should **make the anticipation of test questions an essential part of reviewing.**

Study Old Exams and Quizzes

Increase your chances of correctly anticipating test questions by looking at previous exams and quizzes and analyzing the types of questions your instructor asked. Does your instructor favor essay or short-answer questions? Does he or she specialize in detailed questions that demand a close and careful reading of the text—including the minor exceptions? Does your instructor favor questions drawn from lectures as opposed to ones drawn from the textbook?

If you don't have a previous test, ask your instructor for an old one. Many instructors will be glad to give you one or tell you where they are on file. If tests are not available, you can still ask about the number and the kind (short-answer or essay) of test questions.

Many instructors will readily tell you about test format. They're just waiting to be asked. But if you don't show any interest, they will assume you know exactly what you're doing and do not need any help from them.

Listen for Clues in Your Lectures

Listen to the kinds of questions your instructor asks to stimulate class discussions. Those questions may closely resemble the ones that appear on exams. If a classmate asks a question and your instructor responds with a detailed answer, make a note of both the question and the answer.

Be attentive to the way your instructor begins a lecture. Many instructors open with transitional statements that point out significant connections between lectures and that suggest possible test questions:

> In the previous lecture we talked about how antibiotics were considered a triumph of science over nature. But in this lecture I want to talk about how that rosy picture has changed and outline for you some of the dangers now associated with their use.

Given this transitional statement, you might predict an essay question like the following:

> Contrast the current view of antibiotics with the way they were viewed when first used to fight dangerous diseases.

Use Your Textbook

Your textbook can also help you predict what might be on an exam, and certain kinds of textbook information are very popular with instructors. For example, highlighted definitions of specialized vocabulary like the one appearing on page 141 of Chapter 6 are a common source of questions:

> Homeostasis refers to
>   a. the absorption of energy by carbon dioxide and water.
>   b. the tendency of living things to maintain a constant internal
>   environment.
>   c. a rare blood disorder.

Look, too, for passages in which the author explains a *system of classification* by describing how one large group can be divided into smaller categories:

> A *typology* is a system for classifying people according to types. One of the first typologists was the Greek physician Hippocrates (460–377 B.C.), who focused upon the four fluids or "humors" of the body as they were assumed to be present in people at that time: black bile, yellow bile, blood, and phlegm. Persons with an excess of black bile were classified as *melancholic* and were presumed to be depressed and pessimistic. The *choleric*, possessing excess yellow bile, were considered quick-tempered and irritable. Persons with a predominance of blood were *sanguine*, as reflected in their cheerful, optimistic manner. The *phlegmatic*, possessing excess phlegm, were slow, impassive, and uninvolved with the world at large. While the theory has long since been discarded, the meanings of some of these terms persist.

Passages like the one above are often the basis of exam questions that ask you to explain a system of classification:

> According to the Greek physician Hippocrates, people could be classified according to four different categories or humors. Name and describe each category.

Pay attention as well to passages in which the author outlines a *process* or *sequence of steps:*

Every cell in our bodies contains a set of chromosomes almost
exactly like the chromosomes in every other body cell. That is
because each cell in the body is produced by cell division from one
original cell. Each time the cells divide, they produce a duplicate set
of chromosomes, one for each new cell.

The process is really very complex. The chromosomes produce their
"twins" before the cell divides. This reproduction has been called the
"dance of the chromosomes." The chromosomes line up, like soldiers
on parade. During the dance, or parade, a twin set of chromosomes
is produced. Then half the chromosomes move to each side of the
cell nucleus, and the cell divides in two. After the two daughter cells
have grown to full size, the chromosomes again do their dance, and
another cell division takes place. In this way, a complete set of chromosomes has been produced for each cell in our bodies. Each set is
exactly like those found in the original fertilized egg cell that produced the individual's body.

—Mark Lanfield, ed.,
GED *Book of Basic Science*

Explanations like the above frequently form the basis of test items that ask
you to describe the individual steps in some larger sequence or process:

Describe the individual steps in cell division.

Don't overlook either the way questions are posed or answered within a
text. Authors use this device to highlight key information. The following is
an example:

1. Can everyone be hypnotized? No. The susceptibility to hypnosis
varies rather widely from person to person. Some people resist and
cannot be hypnotized. Contrary to popular belief, you cannot be
hypnotized against your will. Other individuals are excellent subjects
for hypnosis, can readily be put into deep hypnotic states, and may
even be able to hypnotize themselves (Hilgard, 1975; 1978). What
seems to matter most is a willingness to cooperate with the hypno-
tist.

It would not be at all unusual to find this very same question—"Can everyone be hypnotized?"—on an exam. Only in this case, *you* would have to
provide the correct answer.

■   **PRACTICE 3**   After you read the following selections, imagine you are the teacher, and write out one or two questions you think would test students' knowledge of the material.

1   **The modern understanding of sleep began quite by accident in 1952, when a graduate student was assigned to observe the eyelids of sleeping volunteers to see whether any movement occurred. He observed that at certain times during the night the eyeballs of sleepers darted about furiously beneath the closed lids. (Eye movements are very easy to detect, even when the lids are closed; ask someone to perform these movements and see for yourself.) Such activity was totally unexpected, since sleep had long been thought to be a time of quiescence, not one in which the brain was actively generating eye movements that were often faster than could be produced by a waking person. Since then, much more has been learned about rapid eye movement (technically known as "REM") during certain stages of sleep. REM sleep is always accompanied by very distinctive brain-wave patterns, a marked increase in blood flow and in the temperature of the brain, irregular breathing, convulsive twisting of the face and fingertips, and the erection of the penis and clitoris. REM sleep is active sleep, even though the large muscles of the body are completely relaxed. The other kind of sleep is known as "NREM" (that is, non-REM). During this state, breathing is regular, body movement is generally absent, and brain activity is low. Perception shuts down because the senses are no longer gathering information and communicating it to the brain. NREM sleep is sometimes called "quiet sleep" but in one respect that is not so; snoring occurs during this state.**

        —Peter Farb, "The Levels of Sleep"

_____

_____

_____

_____

2   **Specific gravity is a number representing the ratio of the weight of a mineral to the weight of an equal volume of water. For example, if a mineral weighs three times as much as an equal volume of**

water, its specific gravity is 3. With a little practice, you can estimate the specific gravity of minerals by hefting them in your hand.
For example, if a mineral feels as heavy as the common rocks you
have handled, its specific gravity will probably be somewhere
between 2.5 and 3. Some metallic minerals have a specific gravity
of two or three times the average. Galena, which is an ore of lead,
has a specific gravity of roughly 7.5, while the specific gravity of
24-carat gold is approximately 20.

_____

_____

_____

_____

_____

From *Essentials of Geology,* Frederick K. Lutgens and Edward J. Tarbuck, Merrill,
1986. Reprinted by permission of the publisher.

3   Why does rock weather? Simply, weathering is the response of
       earth materials to a changing environment. For instance, after
       millions of years of uplift and erosion, the rocks overlying a large
       intrusive igneous body may be removed, exposing it at the sur-
       face. This mass of crystalline rock, which is formed in a high-
       temperature, high-pressure environment perhaps several
       kilometers below ground, is now subjected to a very different and
       comparatively hostile surface environment. In response, this rock
       mass will gradually change until it is once again in equilibrium, or
       balance, with its new environment. This transformation of rock is
       what we call weathering.

_____

_____

_____

_____

From *Essentials of Geology,* Frederick K. Lutgens and Edward J. Tarbuck, Merrill,
1986. Reprinted by permission of the publisher.

4   **The first step in the breakdown of glucose is called glycolysis (*glyco,* sugar; *lysis,* breakdown), a process that takes place in the cytoplasm. Glycolysis is the first step toward converting the energy within a glucose molecule to the usable energy of ATP.* As we will see, though, glycolysis alone doesn't produce very much ATP.**

　　In glycolysis, a 6-carbon glucose molecule is first destabilized by the addition of two phosphate ions in separate reactions. These ions come from two molecules of ATP, changing them to ADP. We see, then, that whereas glycolysis produces ATP, it also uses up two ATPs at the beginning of each sequence, "priming the pump" as it were. So, whereas four ATPs are produced in the process, the net gain is only two. In any case, the phosphorylated molecule quickly breaks down into two 3-carbon fragments. The two fragments are then repeatedly rearranged from one kind of molecule to another until, finally, two molecules of pyruvate (or pyruvic acid) are formed. Pyruvate is the end-product of glycolysis.

　　—Robert Wallace, *Biology*

_____

_____

_____

_____

PLANNING YOUR ESSAY ANSWERS

Some instructors may tell you beforehand that an exam will consist solely of short-answer objective questions that ask you to fill in the blanks. But if there is any chance that the exam will include essay questions, you should anticipate those questions before the exam day arrives.

　　You should also outline or diagram your answers on a series of large note cards that you can carry with you and flip through in your spare moments. Even if you don't accurately anticipate the actual essay question, you will

_____

*ATP: adenosine triphosphate, an energy source in certain metabolic reactions, often involving muscular activity

have so thoroughly thought about the material being covered in the exam, you'll have little trouble composing a new answer.

To anticipate essay questions and plan your answers successfully, you need to know about the types of questions instructors frequently ask. Here then are five common kinds of questions.

Comparing and Contrasting

Many instructors like to include questions that ask you to compare (cite similarities) or to contrast (cite differences between) two people, events, or objects:

> Although Ulysses S. Grant and Robert E. Lee were both great generals and superb strategists, they represented two very different American traditions. In your essay, explain some of the differences that separated the two men.

In anticipation of a question like this one, make a note card that itemizes specific similarities or differences as we have done:

Grant	*Lee*
grew up on the frontier	born in the South
democratic tradition	aristocratic tradition
a failure until the war	successful all his life
national consciousness	regional consciousness
progressive	conservative

Tracing a Sequence or Process

Be prepared for questions that ask you to trace or outline the steps, stages, or events making up some larger sequence or process.

> According to Piaget, human intelligence develops through a series of distinct stages. Write an essay that traces those stages.

There is no need to prepare for questions like this in paragraph form. Instead, make a rough diagram to help you visualize (1) the individual steps or events, (2) the order and time frame in which they occur, and (3) any key terms used to characterize the individual steps or events. (See Figure 10–4.)

In an essay question you may be asked to compare and contrast two people, events, or ideas.

How are the trees and the dunes similar? How are they different?

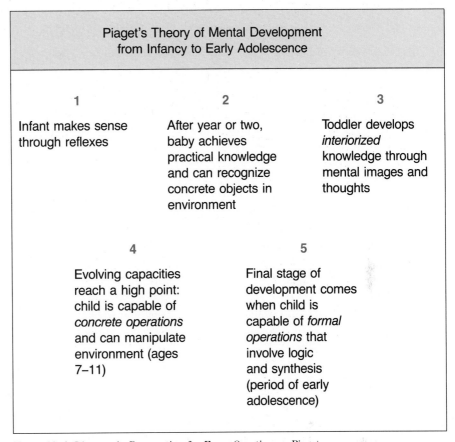

Figure 10–4: Diagram in Preparation for Essay Question on Piaget

Analyzing Cause and Effect

Instructors will often include questions that ask you to explain how one or more events (the cause) led to or produced another event or series of events (the effect):

Write a brief essay in which you explain how fear affects the human body.

If you anticipate this type of question, prepare yourself by drawing a diagram that illustrates the cause-and-effect relationship:

Cause	Effects on Body
Fear	Breaths are much deeper
	Heart beats faster
	Stomach and intestines stop contracting
	Saliva stops flowing
	Blood vessels shrink
	Pupils enlarge

Figure 10–5: Diagram in Preparation for Cause-and-Effect Essay

Characterizing or Describing

Some essay questions will ask you to characterize or describe events, people, or social change. The following is an example:

How would you characterize the mood of America immediately following our failure to win the Vietnam War?

If you think there is a chance your instructor might ask such a question, make a note card that lists key characteristics.

America after Vietnam

1. Initial rejection of returning veterans
2. Sense of profound shock and disbelief
3. Needed more than a decade to come to grips with Vietnam
4. Americans polarized about how to view the war
5. Veterans angry and resentful

Giving Opinions Backed by Reasons

Many essay questions will ask for your opinion. But the last thing the instructor wants in response is an *unsupported* opinion. Questions like the following ask you not only to take a stand but also to supply specific reasons for your position:

> During the last semester, we have discussed the controversy surrounding intelligence testing. What is your position on this issue? Do you believe that intelligence tests measure what they claim to?

If you think your instructor might ask this type of question, formulate, in advance, a clear statement of your opinion. You must also be able to cite several strong reasons in support of that opinion. Again, there is no need to write out the entire answer. A rough outline like the following will do:

Opinion: Existing tests do not accurately measure human intelligence.

Reasons: 1. Questions rely on middle-class language and experience.
2. Tests predict success in school but do not predict how successfully the mind works.
3. Current research supports idea of many different kinds of intelligence that have to be measured in different ways.

CRAMMING WITH A METHOD

In the opening pages of this chapter, we warned you against making cramming a consistent method of test preparation. Don't let the heading for this section fool you. Our initial advice still holds, but we know that cramming is sometimes an unfortunate necessity, particularly if you are just learning to manage your time efficiently. Initially at least, it is easy for time to get away from you, and you may end up facing an exam that you have not systematically prepared for throughout the semester.

For those infrequent times when you find it necessary to cram, we offer a six-step method that will give you a chance of success. Most important, it will help you avoid the most common kind of cramming behavior in which students desperately try to learn everything at one sitting, grow disheartened at the task, and give up before they have done themselves much good. Unfortunately, it's not uncommon for freshmen to make it all the way through a semester and then drop out during the week of final exams. They believe they are unprepared for their finals and have no idea how to deal with the enormous task that confronts them.

While we strongly oppose cramming as a general practice, we also don't want you to give up before you take your exam, convinced that your lack of preparation is a guarantee of failure. If cram you must, make sure you have a method.

A Six-Step Method for Cramming

1. Be highly selective about what you study.

Look over and list the most important topics that were covered in both your lectures and readings. Check the topics that received the most attention during lectures. Concentrate on these; they have the greatest chance of being covered in the exam. Yes, you do run the risk that the topics you ignore will be the subject of the exam, but you run an even greater risk if you try to study everything at once. Your mind will not absorb all that material in a brief amount of time.

2. Assess your strengths and weaknesses.

Now look at the topics you have checked. Are there any that you feel fairly confident about discussing—perhaps because you knew something about the topic before you took the class or because your personal interest in it made you pay special attention during the lectures? Plan on spending only one study session working your way through this material. Use most of your time to concentrate on the remaining topics, the ones you feel less sure of.

3. Determine your priorities.

If you have made the mistake of failing to prepare for *all* of your exams, don't, at the last minute, even consider trying to cram for all of them. Decide which of your exams are most important to you in terms of your long-term goals and allot them the most hours of preparation. And by all means speak to your counselor about strategies to tide you over.

4. Study in two-hour shifts, taking an hour break between them.

Marathon cramming without adequate breaks will confuse and exhaust you. Try instead to **schedule several two-hour sessions throughout the day.** Every two hours, make sure you take a long break in which you let yourself completely unwind. This is a good time to take a walk, play music, or jog around the campus. These activities will help you relax and dissipate tension. When you return to study, you will feel fresh and able to concentrate once more.

5. Use all of the review techniques described in this chapter.

In the previous pages, we introduced particular strategies for making the most of your review sessions. Don't abandon or ignore them when you cram. On the contrary, they are even more essential when you have to make the most of every minute. Don't forget to make synthesis sheets, develop stimulus cues, and anticipate test questions.

6. Know when to stop.

When you cram, **it's particularly important to monitor the quality of your concentration.** If you take a break for an hour and return feeling more exhausted than before, it's time to quit and go to sleep. Don't assume that every hour spent studying will have an equal return in information learned. When you are overtired, the quality of your concentration decreases, and you can be studying without really learning. Even worse, you can push yourself into a state of exhaustion right before the exam. This is the last thing you want to do since physical exhaustion all but guarantees mental confusion.

If, after cramming, you make it through your exams successfully, make a vow to begin exam reviews much earlier in the future.

WORKING SPACE

READING ASSIGNMENT

The following selection by Donna Britt offers some suggestions for surviving a difficult semester. As you read it, evaluate the suggestions, asking yourself which ones you think are of practical value. When you finish, check off the ones you think you might use or suggest to a friend who is in a panic at the thought of facing finals.

Salvaging a Bad Semester

During the second semester of her freshman year at Wayne State University in Detroit, Michigan, Jeanette Bryant, eighteen, fell in love and fell off her academic pedestal.

Bryant faced her moment of truth one night late in the semester, several weeks after she'd decided that partying with her boyfriend was more exciting than cracking the books.

While cramming for an exam, the former B-plus student realized that she'd spent more time listening for the phone to ring than reading the chapter. "For the first time, I looked at my test scores and realized that I was in trouble in several courses," Bryant remembers. "Then it hit me: I'd either have to quit school or quit him and study. It was an easy choice—I decided to study."

Almost every student experiences the panic-prompting realization of possible failure, but freshmen are more likely to find themselves in such a situation. Nearly 25 percent of all freshmen at four-year colleges drop out of school, according to the 1985–1986 College Board's Annual Survey of Colleges.

How can you tell whether you're on your way to becoming part of this statistic? "Too often, students do lousy on a couple of tests in a few classes and think they're failing," says Robert Kriegel, the author of *The C Zone: Peak Performance Under Pressure* (Ballantine, 1985). "Some even drop out of school." If you usually earn A's but are making C's, stop worrying. You're not failing, just underachieving.

But if you acknowledge during the last two or three weeks of a semester that you're going into a final examination after missing more than half the questions on the midterm, or that your semester attendance totals three weeks' worth of classes, or that you really did blow off the term project that's due next week, you *are* well on your way to flunking. You know who you are, and if you're not careful, a couple of bad grades can lead to academic catastrophe.

"Most students who drop out of college do so because they get intimidated when they see failure on their record," says Bert Ockerman, the assistant executive director of the American Association of Collegiate Registrars and Admissions Officers. "Often, students on the brink of failure are sure that they'll never raise their GPA, so they give up."

A bad first-year experience doesn't always mean that you should quit school, however. "If students can just make it through their sophomore year, they have an excellent chance of graduating," says Ockerman.

As corny as it sounds, you should adopt the credo of successful athletes: never give up. "No matter what the score or how far behind athletes are in a race," says Kriegel, "they give everything they've got. Sometimes the extra effort pays off."

It's also important to pinpoint exactly what's preventing you from doing well. For Bryant that meant having a serious discussion with her boyfriend. Together they agreed to limit telephone conversations and to adopt a new rule. If either of them scored below a C on an examination, the two would separate until their grades improved.

The plan worked—almost. Though Bryant received B's in three of her classes, she failed geology. "I was devastated and disappointed for letting myself get off the track that way," she says.

For others, the source of a late-semester grade crisis is less controllable. New York University law student Tanya Heidelberg was a sophomore in telecommunications at Syracuse University in New York when her grandmother suffered a stroke. A few weeks later, her grandmother died. Despite her grief, Heidelberg returned to school as if nothing happened, then watched her semester GPA fall to a 2.4. "It was painful to see someone so strong and feisty become helpless, and I didn't have a chance to grieve," she says now. "My grades really suffered."

Although many factors contribute to flunking out of school, including homesickness, lack of preparation, and enrolling in the wrong school, students most often blame their lack of funds. But Ockerman believes that's merely a cover-up. "Low grades are the real reason so many students don't make it back on campus," he says.

Counselor Peg Taylor, who is the assistant director of the University of Kentucky's counseling center, agrees. "In nearly 75 percent of the cases, students haven't allotted enough time for studying," she says. "They're too busy partying and working, or they procrastinate because they don't like a subject."

If you think nothing short of a miracle will see you through this semester with passing grades, don't panic. Try some of these last-ditch efforts to rescue yourself from a late-semester crisis.

• **Realize that you have a problem.** Accepting that something is amiss is the first step in solving any problem. "One day I figured out that I'd created a pattern," says University of Georgia senior Dalerick Cruver, who admits to having survived many bad semesters. "I wasn't putting forth the effort; therefore, I wasn't performing up to my abilities. Once I became dissatisfied with my lack of progress, I began to work my way out of the poor-performance pattern."

• **Determine which classes are worth rescuing.** If you can't remember the last time you attended mathematics or chemistry class—or any class in which the professor teaches information cumulatively—your chance of pulling a passing grade is slim, even with marathon cramming. However, you may be able to salvage courses that require reading and memorization, such as American history, child psychology, and English literature.

For courses that demand lots of reading, Taylor suggests that you create an information map, a spiderweb-type graph in which lesser ideas encircle the major theme of each chapter.

• **Reduce your class load.** Dropping an elective course gives you extra study hours to focus on the required classes. But be forewarned: Unloading a class late in the semester often results in automatic failure. Some colleges allow students to take an Incomplete and then make up the course the following semester. Check with the admissions office to learn your school's policy.

• **Obtain a copy of last semester's exam.** Some professors will give you a copy of an old exam if you'll just ask. If a professor refuses, ask a student who's already taken the course for a copy, advises Taylor. Note how the questions are asked. For tests that quiz you on memorized information, study flash cards complete with dates, names, and definitions. Concentrate on those concepts and terms highlighted in the exam. Chances are that similar ideas will appear on your examination.

• **Hire a tutor.** Seek help from a tutor if you've tried hard in a course but haven't grasped the fine points, advises Rebecca Jones, who tutors Spanish at Georgetown University in Washington, D.C. "A lot of times, students don't ask questions in class because they're afraid that their questions are silly," she says. "They feel more comfortable asking tutors."

But remember, even a terrific tutor can't help certain students. "If you haven't gone to class all year and really have no idea what's going on, hiring a tutor won't help," Jones warns. "A few hours of intensive tutoring won't replace an entire course."

To find a tutor, check with your professor or an administrator in the department that offers the class.

• **Consult a counselor.** Academic counselors can identify trouble areas and teach such study techniques as cramming. "Students should ask for help if they think they need it," advises Taylor. "Many students who bother to see me really *are* failing something, and I can usually help."

• **Make a deal with your professor.** Confiding genuine problems to your instructor can't hurt, according to Heidelberg, especially if you've already displayed a sincere interest in your class. Ask if you can turn in an extra-credit paper to make up for that failed midterm, or strike a similar deal. "Talking to a professor shows that you're concerned, and a concerned professor is more likely to give you hints about what's on the exam," says student Cruver.

When Jeff Rivers was flunking a required health-education class at Hampton University in Virginia, he dressed in a suit, visited the professor, and explained the trouble he'd had balancing college's social life with academics. After completing an extra-credit paper, Rivers passed the course. "The professor was probably astounded to see me in a tie and figured the class had to be worth something to me," he says.

• **If you survive this semester, don't wait until it's too late next term.** If you take stock of your grades two weeks before final exams, you're playing a dangerous game. Assess your progress at regular intervals, and don't leave your studies until the last minute.

• **Take a break.** If you're floundering in school because you're unmotivated or unsure whether you even want to attend college, consider leaving for a semester or two. "Dropping out can be positive if students use the time to get some good work experience or to think about what they really want to do." But don't blow off school forever, Taylor advises. "College is the best place to grow up."

If all last-ditch efforts fail to save your GPA, hang in there. Remember that *one* bad semester may tarnish your academic career, but it won't end it. "A few bad grades aren't the end of the world," says Heidelberg. "Chances are, if you learned where you went wrong, you won't make the same mistake next semester."

---

1. How can dropping out of school be a positive experience?

2. According to the article, "College is the best place to grow up." Do you agree? Why or why not?

3. If you had to say which of the suggestions for salvaging a semester was most crucial, which one would you choose?

WRITING ASSIGNMENT: "Why Do Freshmen Fail?"

According to the previous article, freshmen are the most likely students to panic and drop out of school. Using your own version of the question-and-answer format described on page 259 of this book, write a paragraph describing what you believe to be the one source of this problem.

JOURNAL ASSIGNMENTS

1. Write a brief description describing the kinds of tests your favorite (or least favorite) instructor likes to give. Here is one student's description:

   Professor Pellegrino's test questions are taken almost straight from her lectures, but you need to do the reading because that's where you get specific reasons or examples for the generalizations she puts on the board. She uses multiple choice for key terms but everything else is an essay question, and you lose points if you're not specific enough. If you keep up with the reading and pay close attention to the lectures, her exams aren't hard. But if you let yourself get behind, you are really in trouble because her exams cover a lot of information, and the essay questions don't let you guess. If you try to pad the answer, I think she gets mad and takes off even more points than if you didn't say anything. My roommate thinks so, too. She once gave him only five points out of thirty for a full-page essay answer. In the margin, she wrote: "There are a lot of words here, but very few of them answer the question asked."

2. What did Aldous Huxley, the author of *Brave New World,* mean when he said every person "who knows how to read has it in his power to magnify himself, to multiply the ways in which he exists"?

CHECKING OUT

Check your understanding of Chapter 10 by writing answers to the following questions. You can work alone or with a friend, whichever you prefer.

1. What is a major drawback of cramming?

2. What are stimulus cues?

3. Why are synthesis sheets so valuable?

4. In what ways can you anticipate test questions?

5. Name the five common categories of essay questions.

IN SUMMARY

Pleasurable as it can be to boast about long nights spent cramming, you'll do much better in college if you prepare for your exams *systematically*, giving yourself time for a series of spaced reviews. During those reviews, make synthesis sheets, anticipate test questions, and prewrite essay answers. In short, pull the material apart and put it back together in terms you understand. With this kind of preparation, you couldn't fail an exam if you wanted to.

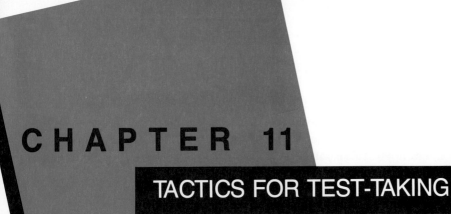

CHAPTER 11

TACTICS FOR TEST-TAKING

Much of our life hinges upon how we do our various tests. And the tests go on for as long as we live.

—Virginia Voeks

OVERVIEW

Michael is a bright, hard-working student who should have gotten a B on his exam. He got a C because he ignored two essential guidelines for taking tests: (1) look over the entire exam before writing, (2) check the finished exam for errors or omissions before handing it in. Doing either or both of these would have saved Michael needless frustration.

While it is true that the only way to pass an exam is to study, it's also true that many students who *are* prepared still lose points because they ignore test-taking tactics or strategies. They don't know that there are efficient and inefficient ways to begin, take, and complete their exams. To make sure that you are not one of these students, this chapter provides basic strategies for taking exams, both essay and objective.

- Know the seven basic pointers for taking any exam.
- Do an analytical reading of all essay questions.
- Learn how to write exams under the pressure of time.
- Take a step-by-step approach to answering objective questions.
- Learn how to manage exam anxiety.

SEVEN GENERAL TIPS FOR TAKING ANY EXAM

Test-taking tactics will shift according to the requirements of each exam. The way you answer an objective or short-answer test will be very different from the way you respond to essay questions. Still, some general tips or pointers apply to all kinds of exams. The following are among the most essential:

Tip 1. Look over the entire test as soon as you get it.

Study the kinds of questions asked and the number of points allotted for each question. See if the exam is divided into sections and **establish how much time is allotted and how much credit is given for each individual part.** With this preview, you can budget your time better, deciding which sections of the test will be the most difficult for you and will require the most time.

Tip 2. Read the directions carefully.

Anxious to complete their exams, many students don't read the directions carefully enough. Because they don't do what they were asked, they lose credit. When you take an exam, make sure *you* understand what you're being asked. **Do an analytical reading and mentally paraphrase the directions.** If, after paraphrasing, you have any questions, don't be embarrassed to ask your instructor whether you have correctly interpreted the question. It's possible for directions to be worded ambiguously and to be in need of further clarification. If you think you need it, ask for clarification.

The most common mistake of students is that they do not do what the directions ask for. If a direction says to answer only two of three parts, and you answer all three, you are hurting yourself by taking time away from other questions. So remember to **read all directions with maximum attention.**

Tip 3. Answer the easy questions first.

If there are any questions you consider easy, answer them first to make sure you get credit for them. Answering the questions that you are sure you know will build your confidence and make you feel ready to tackle the more difficult ones. Avoid beginning with a question that puzzles or confuses you. After wrangling with that question for several minutes, you may feel so frustrated that you will lose your test-taking momentum and confidence.

Tip 4. Give yourself time to proofread the entire exam.

Allot at least five minutes to proofread your finished exam. When you proofread, look for unanswered questions and rewrite any smudged or illegible

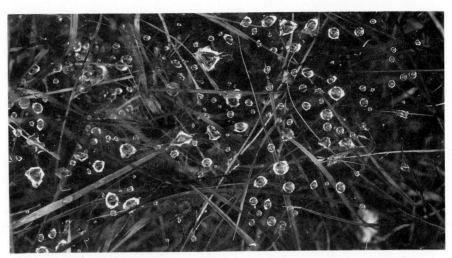

Just as a spider provides support to its web by spinning silk lines, support your answer to an essay question by providing details.

words. In general, those last five minutes are *not* the time to start frantically changing your original answers, *unless you are absolutely sure your first answer is wrong.* Last-minute changes made under pressure can detract from rather than improve your score.

Tip 5. Unless you are penalized for guessing, try to answer every question.

Although on some standardized tests you can lose points for guessing, this is not true for most of the exams you take in college. There's no harm, therefore, in answering every question even if you are not completely sure that your answer is correct. This advice holds particularly true for essay questions that have no one set answer. In most cases, it's better to put down something you think is reasonable than to write down nothing at all. At least you might get a few points for the question rather than losing all credit.

Tip 6. Allot the appropriate amount of time for each section of the exam.

At the beginning of the exam, you should allot a suitable amount of time for each portion of the exam, giving the most minutes to those sections offering the most points. While you work, keep an eye on your watch and notice when your self-imposed time limit is up. Too often, students get involved in completing one section of the exam and let so much time go by that they fail to complete the remaining portions. Don't let this happen to you.

Tip 7. Look for questions that help answer other questions.

As you work your way through the exam, be alert to questions that might help answer other questions. For example, one question might ask you to name two scientific thinkers who influenced the work of Charles Darwin, while another might ask you to explore the ways in which the evolutionary theory of Jean-Baptiste Lamarck affected Darwin's thinking. In this case, the second question gives you a partial answer to the first.

These seven tips for taking exams are no substitute for serious study. They can, however, ensure that the hours you spend reviewing produce the grades you deserve.

> **At the beginning of the exam, you should allot a suitable amount of time for each portion of the exam, giving the most minutes to those sections offering the most points.**

UNDERSTANDING ESSAY QUESTIONS

I found that reading the essay questions more carefully pays off. I do much better on exams now than I used to.
—Leon Spearman, student

The first step in answering essay questions is to know precisely what you're being asked. Obvious as that sounds, many students do not spend enough time analyzing essay questions. Nervous about finishing, they rush through the question, write a reply that does not respond to the question, and lose points on their exam. While this haste is understandable—who isn't nervous about finishing?—it's not productive.

Faced with an essay exam, your best option is to slow down. **Give yourself time to do an analytical reading of the question.** While you read, ask yourself questions that will help you understand what you are being asked to do.

1. What topic should you discuss in your essay?
2. What kind of thinking are you being asked to do? How should you develop your ideas? Are there any key words in the question that tell you how to proceed?
3. Are there any specific criteria you have to fulfill?
4. Does the question have multiple parts?

To show you how to apply these questions, we'll use this sample item from an essay exam:

Based on your reading, identify at least three methods television journalists use to make their news reports more exciting or interesting to the public. How would you evaluate the use of these techniques? In your opinion, do any or all of them lead to news distortion?

What is the topic you should discuss? In this case, it's the news-gathering methods of television journalists. That's the precise topic or subject to be addressed in your essay.

Once you have established the topic or topics to address, your next question is "How should I develop my ideas about this topic?" This is the time to **look for key words** that can tell you what information to include in your essay and how to organize it. Often the verb or verbs used in the question play a crucial role and tell you specifically what your essay should accomplish. The verb "identify," for example, tells you to name and describe the methods television journalists use in order to make their reports entertaining or exciting. (For a list of commonly used verbs and what they mean, see pages 282–283.)

Next, determine whether or not the question establishes any specific criteria for correctness. The essay question on television journalism states that a good answer must be "based on your reading." With this phrase, your instructor tells you to avoid including information that might be accurate but is not drawn from the text you've been studying. You won't get any points for information taken from other sources.

According to the sample question above, a good essay answer must also identify "at least three" news-gathering methods. Although you can certainly include more than three, you will lose credit if you include fewer than three. After you read an essay question, you should locate and **underline any words or phrases that identify the criteria your essay must meet** in order to be considered correct.

Note that our sample essay question, although not actually numbered, does have multiple parts. Part 1 asks you to identify three or more methods used to gather news. Part 2 then asks you to "evaluate" these methods. You have to *give your opinion* and *support* it by citing specific advantages or disadvantages. (Here again note that the verb provides significant information about how to structure the essay.)

Being prepared for an essay exam is obviously a crucial ingredient of doing well, but careful reading of the essay question is equally important. When you are confronted with an essay question, read it twice, carefully underlining all the key words and phrases until you fully understand what you are being asked to do. Then you are ready to write.

Key Verbs in Essay Questions

Argue for or against

Support a particular position or point of view, making it convincing through reasons, illustrations, statistics, or studies. Synonymous terms include *take a stand on* and *prove.*

> "Argue for or against President Truman's use of the atom bomb during World War II."

Compare and contrast

Compare means "point out similarities" while *contrast* means "show differences." If you are asked to compare and contrast two people, events, or objects, you should describe precisely how they are similar and different.

> "Compare and contrast the approach to civil rights taken by Martin Luther King, Jr. and Malcolm X."

Discuss

Explain some point or concept putting down everything you know about it.

> "Discuss the ways in which parents can detect signs of child abuse."

Demonstrate how

Give specific examples of how some generalization applies or functions.

> "Demonstrate how Einstein's theory of relativity affected the world of philosophy."

Describe the sequence or process

List in chronological order the individual steps, stages, or events that led to or comprised some event, process, or happening. Synonymous terms are *outline* and *trace.*

> "Describe the sequence of events that led to America's entry into World War I."

Explain why, how

Describe the causes of some event or happening. Analyze what factors contributed or produced the end result. Synonymous terms are *show how* and *trace the origins*.

> "Explain why Harriet Beecher Stowe's *Uncle Tom's Cabin* profoundly affected the status of women writers."

Describe the effects

Concentrate *not* on the causes of some event but on the results or aftereffects. Synonymous terms are *explain the consequences, describe the aftermath,* and *how did . . . affect?*

> "Describe the effects of long-term sleep deprivation."

Evaluate

When you evaluate some theory or contribution, you list its pros and cons, explaining positive and negative points. A synonymous term is *judge the effectiveness of.*

> "According to Daniel Goleman, self-deception plays a crucial role in both remembering and forgetting. How would you evaluate his claim?"

Illustrate

Provide some specific examples of a broad generalization.

> "Illustrate the way in which chemical pollutants have affected the environment."

Interpret

When you are asked to interpret a statement, you can respond in several ways. Although you can begin by paraphrasing the statement, you should also explain how it applies to specific examples and what it means to other experts in the field.

> "How would you interpret Freud's claim that dreams are the *royal road* to the unconscious?"

■ PRACTICE 1   Read each essay question at least twice. When you are finished, answer the questions that follow.

1. Explain why we cannot tell merely by looking in the sky that stars in a given constellation are at different distances, while in

a room we can easily tell that objects are at different distances from us. What is the difference between the two situations?
—Jay Pasachoff, *Contemporary Astronomy*

What topic are you being asked to discuss?

_____

What key words or phrases tell you how to proceed in your essay?

_____

_____

Does the question have multiple parts?

_____

What specific criteria should you apply to your answer?

_____

_____

2. **Although the Portuguese made contact with China and Japan in the sixteenth century, both countries were still able to isolate themselves from foreign influence until the late nineteenth century. What happened in the nineteenth century to change this situation? In your essay be sure to compare and contrast each country's reaction to Western invasion.**

What topic are you being asked to discuss?

_____

What key words or phrases tell you how to proceed in your essay?

_____

_____

Does the question have multiple parts?

_____

What specific criteria should you apply to your answer?

_____

_____

3. In the case of *Escobedo* v. *Illinois,* how did the Supreme Court's decision affect criminal procedure? What was the public's reaction to the court's decision?

What topic are you being asked to discuss?

_____

What key words or phrases tell you how to proceed in your essay?

_____

_____

Does the question have multiple parts?

_____

What specific criteria should you apply to your answer?

_____

_____

4. What is the "electoral college" and how does it affect the way we choose our presidents? Throughout the years the electoral college has been the subject of controversy. In your essay, explain the source of that controversy.

What topic are you being asked to discuss?

_____

What key words or phrases tell you how to proceed in your essay?

_____

_____

Does the question have multiple parts?

_____

What specific criteria should you apply to your answer?

_____

_____

GUIDELINES FOR ESSAY EXAMS

Many students don't know how to answer essay questions effectively. Some firmly believe that the only good answer is a long one, and they pad their responses with extraneous or irrelevant information. Unfortunately, these students don't realize that pointless padding can detract from or even disguise a good answer, making it appear as if they didn't really know how to answer the question.

To make sure that you _do_ know how to answer essay questions, here are nine essential guidelines for responding to essay questions. Apply them to your next essay exam, and you will write the kind of clear, detailed, and concise answers that instructors look for when they grade your exams.

1. Briefly list, outline, or map key points.

Unless you are pressed for time, begin writing by roughing out your answer on a separate sheet of paper, briefly jotting down the points you want to make. Figure 11–1 provides an illustration.

Question

What effect did the two Supreme Court cases, _Escobedo_ v. _Illinois_ and _Miranda_ v. _Arizona_, have on criminal procedure? What was the public reaction to the Court's decision? Did that reaction influence the ruling in any way?

Key Points

Case: Escobedo v. *Illinois,* 1964

   While questioning Escobedo, police didn't inform him of right to attorney. S.C. reversed murder conviction, 5–4 vote.

Effect: Suspects must be allowed access to counsel, or confession can't be used.

Case: Miranda v. *Arizona,* 1966

   Police didn't inform Miranda of his rights. His confession of kidnapping and rape not allowed as evidence. His conviction reversed by S.C.

Effect: After arrest but *before* being questioned, suspect must be read right to remain silent and right to lawyer.

Public Reaction: Some felt criminals treated better than victims. Members of legal community argued only coerced confessions should be banned.

Figure 11–1: Outline of Key Points

An outline like this will help you clarify your thoughts and organize your information in a clear sequential order. You can also use it to make sure that you haven't left out something important. Before you hand in your exam, compare your list with your finished essay to make sure that you haven't forgotten anything.

2. In the first sentence or paragraph, give a general answer to the question being asked.

Once you have your rough outline, you're ready to write the first sentence of your essay. In an essay written for an exam, that sentence should always be a general answer to the question asked:

   Television uses three methods to make news coverage exciting: staging, tape doctoring, and ambush interviewing.

If you have thirty or forty minutes to write your essay, you might use the entire first paragraph to introduce your answer in general terms. Then you could use the remaining paragraphs to provide more specific supporting details.

   In gathering news for television, journalists employ a variety of techniques designed primarily to make the news visually exciting and entertaining. Three of the most common are *staging, tape doctoring,* and *ambush interviewing.* "Staging" occurs when an event is not filmed live but reenacted. "Tape doctoring" is the practice of editing an interview to make it more controversial or shocking. "Ambush interviewing" is what journalists do when they approach a subject by surprise and ask him or her to comment on some current event without advance preparation.

In your composition classes, you may be encouraged to write detailed introductions that lay the groundwork for your main point or thesis statement. But this advice seldom applies to essay exams, where the instructors are reading with one key question in mind. Do you know the answer to the question they have asked? Your first sentence or paragraph should tell them that you do.

3. Don't skimp on supporting details.

Many students skimp on supporting details, leaving out the facts and figures that would make their point convincing. Sometimes they just don't have enough information at their disposal. But often students skimp on details because they don't understand the role instructors play when reading exams. They assume that instructors know the material; therefore why spell it out? Unfortunately, this line of reasoning completely misses the purpose of exams as well as the role instructors play when reading them.

Your professors give exams in order to discover how well you have absorbed the information introduced throughout the term. To test your knowledge, they read an exam as if they were relatively unfamiliar with their own subject matter. If you have really understood what you've been taught, you should be able to explain the material to them in detail almost as if you were the teacher and they were the students.

When you write your essay, don't expect your teachers to fill in the supporting details. That's your job, not theirs.

4. Use transitions to help your instructor follow your train of thought.

If you are citing three different examples of the way in which animals respond to territorial invasion, it's important that you help your reader sift and sort those examples by using transitions. These can be words like *first, second,* and *third.* Or they can take the form of sentences that explicitly link your thoughts:

In addition to the visual warnings previously described, animals also use a variety of gestures or cries; the following are some examples.

Transitional sentences are particularly important if your essay question has more than one part. They are an excellent way of telling your instructor that you have finished answering one portion of the original question and are moving on to another:

> Having described three methods that television journalists use to make the news more exciting, I will now illustrate how these methods can and do distort the actual events.

5. Use paragraphing to highlight shifts or changes in thought.
At all costs avoid long answers that go on for pages without a single indentation. Indent every time you take up a new main point in your outline. Indent, as well, each time you answer a different part of the same question. This will make it easier for your instructors to follow the development of your ideas.

6. Whenever possible, put your strongest ideas, explanations, examples, or reasons first.
The way in which you order information may be prescribed by the question you're asked:

> Name and describe the specific steps in the scientific method.

In this case, the order in which you present information is not up to you. There is an established sequence you have to follow.

Many exam questions, however, do allow you to decide how to order information:

> Explain the reasons why Americans abandoned their initially neutral position and decided to enter World War I.

After reading this question, you might know immediately that there were two basic reasons for America's decision to give up neutrality: (1) the discovery of the Zimmerman telegram* and (2) Germany's resumption of submarine warfare. However, you might be better informed about the effects of the Zimmerman telegram than about Germany's resumption of submarine warfare. If so, begin with your strongest answer, a detailed discussion of the Zimmerman telegram. When you are writing essays for exams, don't save your best answer for last. Start instead with your most persuasive point and show your instructor the depth of your knowledge.

---

*Zimmerman telegram: In a message to Mexico, the German foreign secretary proposed that Mexico side with Germany if war broke out.

7. Check your essay answer with the original question.

Before you hand in your exam, read the essay question again to check it against your answer. This is the time to make sure you have responded to every part of the question. Check also that you have fulfilled all specific criteria identified in the question. If your instructor asked for three examples, make sure your essay contains no less than three.

8. Proofread for illegible words and mechanical errors.

When writing under the pressure of time, many students forget about legibility. Faced with twenty to fifty exams to correct in a week or two, few instructors have the time to pore over your paper and decipher illegible words or mangled word order. If the answer to the question they ask is not legibly written, most instructors won't try to analyze your handwriting until they figure out your answer. Even if they wanted to, they just don't have the time.

Whenever you write an essay, make it easy for your instructor to read it. **Write on every other line of the test booklet,** a practice that makes even the most cramped handwriting more legible. In addition, **proofread your answers** before you hand in your exam, checking them carefully for missing or illegible words, run-on sentences, and unintended fragments (see Chapter 18 for more on sentence structure).

> Your professors give exams in order to discover how well you have absorbed the information introduced throughout the term. To test your knowledge, they read an exam as if they were relatively unfamiliar with their own subject matter. If you have really understood what you have been taught, you should be able to explain the material to them almost as if you were the teacher and they were the students.

■ PRACTICE 2   Here is one essay question and two responses. After you have read the question carefully, read each response; then decide which answer you think is better. In the blanks that follow, explain why you chose one answer over the other.

Question

What effect did the two Supreme Court cases, *Escobedo* v. *Illinois* and *Miranda* v. *Arizona,* have on criminal procedure? What was the public reaction to the Court's decision? Did that reaction influence later Supreme Court rulings in any way?

Answer 1

The *Escobedo* and *Miranda* cases profoundly influenced criminal procedure by rigidly restricting and controlling police behavior with accused criminals. In 1964 Danny Escobedo was questioned in regard to the murder of his brother-in-law. During the questioning, police repeatedly disregarded his requests for a lawyer. Nor did they inform him of his right to remain silent, and he incriminated himself through a confession. When Escobedo's appeal came before the Supreme Court, his conviction was reversed by a five to four vote. As a result, police were forced to inform every suspect of his or her right to counsel before questioning could take place.

That right was further extended by the *Miranda* v. *Arizona* case of 1966. In this case, Ernesto Miranda had confessed to kidnapping and rape after a two-hour interrogation session in which he was not informed of his right to remain silent or to have counsel. Once again the Supreme Court reversed the conviction, claiming that the confession was inadmissible evidence. As a result of this case, police had to be sure that each and every suspect had been "Mirandized." The suspect had to be explicitly told *before* questioning that he or she had the following rights: (1) the right to remain silent in order to avoid making incriminating statements, and (2) the right to an attorney. Furthermore any suspect who asked for an attorney could not be questioned until that attorney was present.

The public was angry at the Escobedo *decision, but it was the Miranda* decision that really drew public outrage. Many saw it as a legal loophole that would allow criminals to go free on a technicality. Several movies made in the early seventies, like Clint Eastwood's *Dirty Harry,* reflected the public's dislike of both the *Miranda* and *Escobedo* decisions, and audiences cheered when Eastwood flouted police procedure in pursuit of criminals.

Members of the legal community who were opposed to these decisions argued that only those confessions that had actually been coerced could be considered illegal. From this point of view, Miranda's and Escobedo's confessions could not be considered illegal; the two men had not been coerced. They simply had not been warned of their rights. To a large degree, legal objections to the Court decisions centered more on the interpretation of the cases themselves than on the way they affected police procedure.

Richard Nixon, aware of public feeling, promised in his 1968 presidential campaign to appoint justices who would overrule these two unpopular decisions. But despite Nixon's election and the resulting four conservative appointments to the Supreme Court, the Court did not overrule itself. In 1984, however, the Supreme Court did formulate an exception to the *Miranda* ruling, which says that if concern for public safety leaves no time to issue warnings, confessions can be used as evidence.

Answer 2

In old-time movies about the police, scenes concerning the third degree were very popular, and it was commonplace to see criminals being brutally beaten by police who wanted to extract a confession. Aware that criminal defendants could be subjected to abuse, the framers of the Bill of Rights formulated the Fifth Amendment, which says that no person "shall be compelled in any criminal case to be a witness against himself." Since that time, many people, both guilty and innocent, have "taken the Fifth" in response to questions.

Research shows that most people believe that suspects have to be protected against the possibility of police brutality. But when the *Escobedo* and *Miranda* decisions appeared to favor the rights of criminal defendants, people were outraged. Both men had con-

Pictured is Ernesto Miranda (right) and his attorney, John Flynn.

fessed to their crimes but were allowed to go free. It seemed as if the rights of the victims were being ignored while the criminal defendants were being treated with kid gloves. This is probably one reason for the success of films like *Dirty Harry,* where the detective hero simply ignored the rights of the criminals he pursued and used any means possible to bring them to justice.

Despite the public outcry against the *Escobedo* and *Miranda* decisions, the Court did not reverse itself. Even the conservative Supreme Court justices appointed by Richard Nixon have not reversed these decisions, although recent Supreme Court decisions have given the police more latitude in combating crime. These decisions are probably a reflection of the Court's current composition as well as a response to public interest in victims' rather than criminals' rights.

Which answer do you think is better, and why did you choose it?

_____

_____

_____

_____

_____

TAKING AND PASSING OBJECTIVE TESTS

Objective tests are designed to eliminate individual interpretation on the part of the scorer. Ideally each question on an objective test should have only one right answer. Even if corrected by several different people, objective tests should always produce the same score—something you can't count on in an essay exam where one instructor's criteria for completeness or correctness might be quite different from another's.

The objective tests you encounter in college will usually consist of three types of questions: (1) multiple choice, (2) true or false, and (3) matching. In the following pages, we give you pointers on how you should answer each type. Like your grade on essay exams, you can markedly improve your score on objective tests by knowing and applying some test-taking tactics.

Multiple Choice

Multiple-choice questions are currently the most popular type of question on objective tests. Consisting of two parts, multiple-choice questions often open with a partial statement or unanswered question called the *stem*. That stem is then followed by anywhere from three to five possible options, each of which could complete the statement or answer the question. Your job is to choose the correct one.

> The cells that compose muscles are traditionally divided into three groups:
> a. muscle cells, cardiac cells, and striated muscle cells.
> b. smooth muscle cells, cardiac muscle cells, and striated muscle cells.
> c. capillaries, venules, and arterioles.

To answer a question like this one, consider three basic pointers:

1. Read the stem separately with each option to hear how they sound together.
Multiple-choice questions rely on your ability to recognize the correct answer when you see it. Often combining the stem with the correct answer will create a sentence familiar from your text or lecture.

2. Cross out any obviously incorrect answers.
In the above answer, someone who had actually studied the composition of muscles would know immediately that answer "c" is wrong: capillaries, venules, and arterioles are blood vessels rather than muscles. Crossing out this answer as soon as you saw it would help you concentrate on the correct possibilities. It would also eliminate any chance of your knowing the correct answer but circling the incorrect one in a flustered moment.

3. Eliminate answers until you are left with one that seems most completely correct.
Multiple-choice tests frequently contain two answers that may seem equally correct. When this happens, you need to read each answer very slowly looking for any indication that one is only partially correct. If you look, for example, at the above multiple-choice item, you can see that choices "a" and "b" are quite similar. But think for a moment about the stem of the question: "The cells that compose muscles are traditionally divided into three groups." In this question, you are asked to identify three different types of muscle cells. But answer "a" ("muscle cells") simply restates wording in the stem ("cells that compose muscles"). This is a circular answer. It says that "muscle cells can be broken down into muscle cells." Since this

doesn't make any sense, your answer has to be "b," the only option that identifies three different categories or groups of muscle cells—smooth muscle cells, cardiac muscle cells, and striated muscle cells.

4. Be alert to the presence of words like "not," "except," "but," and "all but" in the stem; they will affect your answer.

If you read too quickly and overlook one of these vital words or phrases, you are bound to choose the incorrect answer.

> Identify the philosopher who did *not* make plant growth the subject
> of his investigations.
> a. Plato
> b. Aristotle
> c. Jan Baptista van Helmont

If you read the stem too quickly, you might think you are being asked to identify the philosopher who studied plant growth, and you would circle answer "b" or "c." Both Aristotle and van Helmont were interested in plants and their growth. But, actually, the question asks you to identify the philosopher who was *not* interested in this subject. There is only one answer, "a. Plato."

5. Look for answers that allow you to combine options.

Answers like "all of the above" and "both a and b" are quite often the correct ones, so consider them carefully if they appear on an exam. For example, in the following test item, "a," "b," and "c" offer answers that are all just partially correct. Only option "d" allows for a complete answer to the question posed in the stem:

> Freud's model of consciousness explores:
> a. the id.
> b. the ego.
> c. the superego.
> d. all of the above.

True-False Questions

True-false questions are often used to test your knowledge of specific names, dates, and definitions. Your instructor asks you to decide if a statement is true or false.

The second battle of Bull Run took place on July 21, 1861.   T or F

When answering questions like these, keep in mind the following:

1. Study the statement carefully, looking for words or phrases that might make a seemingly true answer false.

If you read our example too quickly, you might be ready to circle "T" for true. The *first* battle of Bull Run actually took place on July 21, 1861. The second one, however, occurred between August 27 and September 2 of 1862. When reading true-or-false statements, be alert to any words that could determine whether your answer should be true or false, particularly in two-part statements like this one:

> World War II's Battle of the Bulge was a terrible defeat for the Germans; repulsed by the Allies, they had to retreat to the Maginot Line.   T or F

The first half of this statement is true. The Battle of the Bulge did force the Germans to retreat. However, they retreated not to the Maginot Line but to the line of defense known as the Siegfried Line. In this case, the second half of the sentence makes the whole statement false.

2. Don't overinterpret true-or-false statements.

When reading true-or-false statements, some students are obsessed with the notion of the "trick question" and confuse themselves by creating elaborate interpretations of what is being said, as in this case:

> Alexander Hamilton wrote for and supported the pro-Federalist newspaper *Gazette of the United States*.   T or F

Most students would read this question and immediately circle "T." They would be correct. Hamilton did write for and generally support the *Gazette*. But a few students would agonize over the word *support*, wondering whether to interpret it as moral or financial support. They would worry that Hamilton might have supported some but not all of the paper's positions. In short they would overinterpret the language of the statement, assuming a level of complexity or trickiness that the question just doesn't have.

Generally your instructors will not expect you to split hairs over word meaning; they will expect you to apply the most commonly accepted meaning or context for a word. In answering true-or-false questions, choose the obvious answer and avoid the one that relies on a long and belabored interpretation of what a word might mean in every possible context.

3. When in doubt, choose "true."

If you have to guess, then it's a good idea to guess "true." Most teacher-made tests contain more "true" statements than false ones.

Matching Questions

Matching questions usually consist of two columns. The left column contains a list of names or terms; the right column a list of definitions, quotations, or descriptions. Your job is to pair or match items in one list with items in the other, as shown in the following example:

1. specific heat c

2. sublimation a
3. latent heat b

a. a process by which gas changes directly to a solid
b. heat energy stored in vapor
c. heat energy absorbed or released by a unit of water per degree of temperature change

To answer matching questions like the above *correctly,* follow these four basic guidelines.

1. Before you choose your answers, read both columns.

Don't rush to match items until you have read both columns and have a clear sense of the alternatives. Although one option may seem correct at first, you may find a better match when you reach the bottom of the column.

2. Use word analysis to help you choose the correct definition.

Sometimes the suffix or ending of a word can help you make the correct choice. Item "a," for example, uses the word *process* in its definition. That definition signals you to look over the list of terms for one that contains a suffix used in words describing a process. In this case, only one word contains such a suffix (-tion), the word *sublimation.* While a knowledge of suffixes and what they mean is no substitute for solid preparation, it can help you to zero in on the most likely choices.

3. Cross out options as you choose them.

Each time you match a pair of items, put a line through the definition, description, or quotation you have chosen. Eliminating the number of options to choose from will make it easier for you to focus on and analyze those that remain.

4. Pay attention to the directions for matching items.

For some reason, many students think that the correct way to take a matching test is to draw lines between the two columns, something like this:

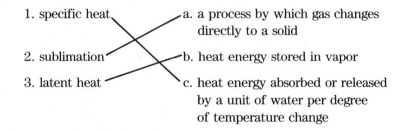

1. specific heat
2. sublimation
3. latent heat

a. a process by which gas changes directly to a solid
b. heat energy stored in vapor
c. heat energy absorbed or released by a unit of water per degree of temperature change

Yet few instructors favor a method so difficult to decipher. They will direct you, instead, to "write the letter of the correct definition next to the appropriate term." Or they will provide blanks for you to fill in the appropriate letter or number. **Whatever the directions, read them carefully.** In your haste to finish, don't just start drawing lines from one column to the other.

MANAGING EXAM ANXIETY

Although few, if any, students escape some form of preexam jitters, some students know how to manage their anxiety and make it work for them. Others are defeated by it. Overwhelmed by nervousness, they forget what they have studied and fail a test they should have passed. If you are one of these students, don't assume there's nothing to be done about the way you react to exams. You can do a great deal to help yourself gather your thoughts and calm down. The following pages offer some specific suggestions. Make use of them, and you will be surprised at how much better you feel about taking exams.

1. Know that some anxiety is good for you.

A little anxiety before an exam is good for you; it keeps you mentally active and alert. Don't panic, therefore, at the first signs of nervousness and assume that feeling anxious is bad. Instead, **manage your anxiety by telling yourself that you have studied, know the material, and will do well,** so there's no need to be unduly nervous.

2. Get to the exam early and take a few minutes to compose yourself.

Rushing into class at the last minute, grabbing your exam, and hunting for your pen or pencil is not going to calm your nerves. This kind of behavior will make you so flustered and nervous that you'll have a hard time concentrating. It's much more productive to get to the exam early and get every-thing ready—before the exams are distributed.

3. Use deep breathing to combat nervousness.

It's amazing but true that breathing deeply can reduce anxiety. If at any time during the exam, you feel so frazzled that you can't concentrate, take a few moments to inhale deeply, counting to five while you hold your breath. Then exhale slowly also counting to five. Do this three or four times, and you'll begin to feel calm.

4. Don't look at your classmates while taking your exam.

One way to double your anxiety quotient is to compare your progress with that of other students. Should the person next to you turn to page 2 while you are only halfway down page 1, you'll probably panic and assume that you are not going fast enough. In fact, your classmate may not have been able to answer most of the questions on page 1. **When you take an exam, work at your own speed.** Don't try to match anyone else's.

5. Think positively.

If you have prepared long and hard for your exam, tell yourself that you are bound to do well. Research has repeatedly shown that a positive attitude contributes to achievement. Students who think they are going to do well on exams usually do. Obviously a positive attitude *without* thorough test prepa-ration will not get you the grade you desire. But if you can combine solid preparation with a belief in your success, you'll increase your chances of getting a good grade.

6. Eat the right food before an exam.

Before an exam, don't gorge yourself on cokes and potato chips thinking they'll give you quick energy. High in carbohydrates, this kind of snack food has a negative effect on your mental alertness. Carbohydrates trigger the production of *serotonin*, a chemical in the brain that produces drowsiness, but drowsy is not how you want to feel when you sit down to take your exam.

To make sure you feel mentally alert before a test, eat a meal low in fat and high in proteins like cereal, chicken, or eggs. Unlike carbohydrates, proteins do not encourage drowsiness. They have exactly the opposite effect on brain chemistry, helping you feel awake and alert.

If you want to get a good night's sleep before an exam, try snacking on cookies and milk to encourage drowsiness. But when the time comes to take your exam, stay away from snacks and choose a meal that is high in protein and low in fat.

A little anxiety before an exam is good for you; it keeps you mentally active and alert.

WORKING SPACE

READING ASSIGNMENT

In the following article Anne McGrath addresses the problem of test anxiety. As you read it, underline those passages where the author identifies possible sources and cures for this common problem.

Mettle-Testing

They open doors—or close them—to prep school, college, professional school, the Army. They decide who qualifies for government jobs or who will advance in business. And they determine whether, after years of sweat and study, you are indeed ready to practice law or medicine or accounting or teaching or many other licensed professions.

"They," of course, are standardized tests. Millions of Americans each year have an anxiety attack as they pick up a No. 2 pencil and tackle them. But, like them or not, standardized tests are often considered the most important (or, at least, most objective) measures of achievement, potential, suitability or even sanity. There is no prospect of their disappearing any time soon.

In its most virulent* form, "test anxiety" paralyzes, guaranteeing an abysmal score. Even in mild cases it makes the test-taker's life miserable and louses up performance. Charles Spielberger, a clinical psychologist now studying test anxiety, estimates that 20 to 25 percent of college students suffer from it to some degree.

Among younger students, the problem is even worse. The University of Illinois' Kennedy Hill, an expert on test-taking fear in children, thinks as many as half of the 40 million students now in primary and secondary school are affected.

—————————

*virulent: poisonous

"An individual lacks confidence, so he anticipates failure and focuses on that," explains Bob Parrino, a counselor at the University of South Florida. "His heart rate increases, he feels sick, he starts breathing rapidly. Instead of concentrating on the task at hand—A plus B equals C—he's thinking, 'What am I doing in college? I can't pass this test. I'm the stupidest person in the class.' "

If you or your child experiences such disabling fear under exam pressure—fear that makes your scores wildly out of sync with ability—Parrino suggests professional help. Many college mental health centers routinely offer short group-discussion programs designed to help students recognize their anxiety and practice techniques to conquer it.

But, fortunately, this is one condition many people can cure themselves, assuming no physiological cause. Basically, there are two major triggers of test anxiety: a misguided attitude and lousy preparation. Here are a few tips on their control, culled from experts:

- Remember that failing one test, no matter how important, is never the end of the world. The more aware you are of your strengths and the more options you keep open—in the way of backup schools, say, or in acceptable variations on a chosen career—the less threatening the test becomes.

- Squelch immediately any doubts about your ability. Nobody—yourself included—can do a perfect job.

  Parents, unfortunately, often reinforce a child's fear of tests by setting a standard of excellence and expressing bitter disappointment when it isn't met. So what if Junior can't make your alma mater?* "Expose your child early to activities at which he can succeed," says Spielberger. "Give him a sense of identity based on who he is rather than how well he performs."

- Finally, remember that entrance exam scores are rarely considered alone. A strong academic history, leadership ability, positive recommendations and a well-executed interview will go a long way toward offsetting mediocre scores. Harvard, for example, no longer requires business school applicants to take the much-dreaded Graduate Management Admission Test (GMAT).

No matter how healthy your attitude, however, adequate preparation for a test is a must. And that means boning up not only on the subject matter but also on the particulars of the test you will be taking.

---

*alma mater: college

Read everything you can about the test. Know how many items you'll face and how much time can safely be spent on each. Know if you'll be penalized for guessing (as on the Scholastic Aptitude Test and the GMAT) or if any old answer is better than none. Practice on sample tests until the skills most such tests measure—ability to analyze, interpret, predict, compare and to recognize main and supporting ideas—are sharp.

"Get down inside those test items," advises Thelma Spencer of the Educational Testing Service. "Compare your answers with the key and understand why they're wrong."

What about expensive coaching courses? College prep courses like the ones Stanley Kaplan offers, at around $400, can indeed boost test scores. Kaplan says his pre-SAT program (some 44 hours of classroom review of fundamental math and verbal principles and test-taking strategies, plus an optional 350 hours of practice testing) can raise students' scores an average of 150 points. The ETS more conservatively estimates that drilling for the SAT, if it does any good, would add no more than 60 points to a first score. If nothing else, a prep course can alleviate the willies.

---

1. According to the article, what does test anxiety stem from? Do you agree with the author's assessment of the origin?

2. What can a person do to combat test anxiety?

3. What does it mean to "get down inside those test items"?

4. Do you have any additional suggestions for combating test anxiety?

WRITING ASSIGNMENT: "Eliminating Exam Jitters"

It's been suggested—but not proven—that injecting a little humor into test questions could help relieve students' anxiety and improve their performance. Do you have any similar suggestions? Write a paper in which you explain what you think instructors could do to ease student nervousness at exams.

JOURNAL ASSIGNMENTS

1. What other kinds of situations besides tests make you anxious? Are there any similarities between these situations and test-taking ones?

2. According to Ralph Waldo Emerson, "Books are the best things, well used, abused among the worst." What do you think he meant by the phrase "well used"? by the word "abused"?

3. Evaluate your exam preparation. Are you preparing in advance, or are you cramming? If you're doing the latter, ask yourself why you haven't scheduled time for reviews. What's keeping you from doing it?

CHECKING OUT

Check your understanding of Chapter 11 by writing answers to the following questions. You can work alone or with another student, whichever you prefer.

1. What's the very first thing you should do after receiving your exam?

2. What do many students fail to do when they take an essay exam?

3. What questions should you ask yourself in order to understand what you are being asked to do on an essay exam?

4. Why are verbs in essay questions important?

5. When you write an essay for an exam, what should the first sentence or paragraph do?

6. What are some of the ways you can help your instructor follow your train of thought?

7. Name two ways to combat test anxiety.

8. Is test anxiety all bad?

IN SUMMARY

Tactics for test-taking are no substitute for solid preparation. But they can help you avoid the kind of pointless mistakes that result in a lower grade. Why lose five points because you forgot to look at page 5 and didn't answer the last question? Why agonize over how quickly your neighbor is finishing when, in fact, your neighbor isn't answering half the questions? Now that you have at your disposal a repertoire of test-taking strategies, make sure you use them to get the high grades you deserve.

U N I T 4

BECOMING A CRITICAL THINKER

What is critical thinking? Essentially it is **learning to think for yourself** and to develop your own independent opinions, backed by sound reasons and support. It is learning to drop the role of a passive student and to assume the role of a self-reliant thinker and researcher.

As a child, everyone is necessarily told what to do and how to think by parents, teachers, experts, and authorities of all kinds. But sooner or later each of us must learn to think independently and to take responsibility for what we say and do.

Critical thinking, therefore, enters into important decisions in your daily life and also affects your growth and progress in school and work. In everyday life it means learning to make sound decisions on many small matters that collectively affect your life in a major way. In school it is learning to be excited by questions for which you yourself have to search for the answers.

In this unit on critical thinking, we move to the whole notion of **evaluation—how to evaluate your own ideas and the ideas of other writers.** Thus in Chapter 12, we discuss how to evaluate your own practical and personal decision making. In Chapter 13, we give methods for analyzing and evaluating the viewpoint of a single author; and in Chapter 14, we show you how to evaluate the viewpoints of several authors to form your own synthesis, that is, your own creative work.

C H A P T E R   12

THE STRATEGIES OF A CRITICAL THINKER

The having of wonderful ideas is the essence of intellectual development.

**—Eleanor Duckworth,
Harvard School of Education**

OVERVIEW

What do you do when you have a hard choice to make? Should you go to College A or College B? Should you go to the library to catch up, or go hear your best friend's new band? Should you clean up the mess after a party or hope that someone else will? Everyone faces choices—large and small.

The term *critical thinking* describes the deliberate thinking that helps you decide what you should believe or how you should act. It helps you examine a problem or issue from many angles and reach the best possible decision. It helps you learn to think creatively and to find pleasure in ideas.

In every chapter of this text, we have made one basic assumption: we have assumed that you will think hard and carefully—that is, *think critically*—about a given study skill and how to apply that skill. For example, in Chapter 2, on time management, we have given you useful strategies that will provide results for most students. But only *you* can think about how best to apply this advice to yourself, day after day, and how to allocate your time to study most effectively. You have to learn to think hard about your choices and to make the right choices most of the time.

Critical thinking is by no means restricted to academic matters or to study skills: it encourages us to *examine* responsibly all the important issues and choices that we face in our lives and to deal with them productively. It means we have thought through the reasons for our actions and judgments and do not act impulsively or emotionally.

In Chapters 13 and 14, we will apply critical-thinking skills to specific issues of reading and writing, including evaluating and synthesizing texts. But in the present chapter, we want to consider how critical thinking is applicable, and at times crucial, to many aspects of our everyday lives. And the same basic critical-thinking process you learn to apply to your personal decisions carries over to your academic work. Most important, it applies to complicated moral choices that all of us face throughout our lives.

In this chapter we encourage you to use the following strategies:

- Apply basic critical-thinking strategies to everyday decision making.
- Become familiar with the characteristics of a critical thinker.
- Be aware of the kinds of thinking operations most commonly used for gathering and analyzing information.
- Be open to new ideas, and be willing to rethink or modify your opinions.
- Make moral choices by examining the kind of person you want to be, by foreseeing the effects your decisions will have on others, and by deciding if you can live with your choices.

CRITICAL THINKING IN PRACTICAL DECISIONS

At certain points in our lives, each of us faces some serious decision in which it is not clear what we should do. Take senior Sarah Boone's case. She has to decide between Job A (as a word processor) and Job B (as an assistant reporter for a local paper).

Job A pays considerably better but sounds like more routine work and has little future potential. Job B pays less well now but offers more opportunities to learn about the newspaper business, and the work offers more challenges. This is Sarah's first full-time job after college; she remains a bit undecided about her long-range goals but is leaning toward getting a master's degree in special education.

Faced with this kind of decision, Sarah should sit down in a comfortable spot and weigh all the choices *and* their possible consequences. One way to do this is to list in separate columns all the possible benefits or advantages and all the possible costs or disadvantages. In other words she should make a list of every pro and con she can think of. Then she should rank them in order of importance to her (see Figure 12–1).

In making a decision, she should especially consider what is the worst thing that can happen to her in either situation. The worst thing in this particular decision is not too serious: she can leave either job if it turns out disappointing and quickly look for another one. But in other situations, the worst outcome might be something she does not want to risk.

If people do not take the time to make these carefully thought-out decisions, they may instead make a spur-of-the-moment or an emotional decision that is not in their best interest—and one that they may live to regret.

Upon jotting down all the benefits and costs (both financial and psychological) of each choice, Sarah saw that she was deciding between a job with more salary immediately (enough to save for tuition) and one with more opportunities in the future (but a smaller salary now). Making this decision forced Sarah to focus on her important long-range goals. She realized that, most of all, she wanted a master's degree and that in her case journalism would be a detour. Therefore she accepted the job with the larger salary to save for tuition.

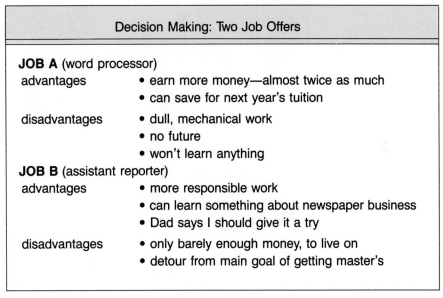

Figure 12–1: Weighing the Pros and Cons

An Olympic Athlete's Critical Thinking

In her autobiography *Creating an Olympic Champion,* gymnast Mary Lou Retton describes her critical-thinking process in preparing for the Olympics.

First, she knew she had to perform very well in several major tournaments the year before the Olympics to qualify for the American team. To give herself the best chance to win in these preliminary events, she knew she had to do well during her demanding daily workouts in the gym. Sizing up her skillful competitors—the best gymnasts in the world—she understood she would have to analyze and perfect every detail of the four skills required of a female gymnast, including the vault, her specialty.

To do well in the grueling daily workouts with her coaches, Mary Lou realized that she had to get to bed early for many months, which meant she had to give up almost all of her social life. Since winning the Olympics was her personal goal, the sacrifice of her social life was worth it to her. But she had thought through her decision by using critical-thinking skills. She knew her goal; she knew the consequences of not maintaining her peak form. She made her decision.

Mary Lou Retton chose to forgo much of her social life to pursue her Olympic dream. Personal decisions require a basic critical-thinking process.

The Decision-Making Process

In a certain sense, most personal decisions require a basic critical-thinking process. It is helpful to write down your ideas and see them in front of you—instead of having them float around in your mind:

Making a Careful Decision

If you are trying to make an intelligent decision of any sort, it helps to go through these steps:

1. Gather all possible facts and information: Study, read about, or research the problem. Ask many questions of yourself and others.
2. Write out a tentative statement of your problem: What is the decision you have to make? What are your realistic choices?
3. List the advantages and the disadvantages of each choice and rank the issues in tentative order of importance to you.
4. Think of the long-range consequences to yourself and to others. Always think of future consequences.
5. Ask yourself if your expectations are realistic or too high.
6. Think hard—think critically—about your choices, discarding any that have clear weaknesses. After weighing your choices, make plans to take action.

	Advantages	Disadvantages
Choice A	1. _____ 2. _____ 3. _____ 4. _____	1. _____ 2. _____ 3. _____ 4. _____
Choice B	1. _____ 2. _____ 3. _____ 4. _____	1. _____ 2. _____ 3. _____ 4. _____

Figure 12–2: Decision-Making Checklist

- Determine what you hope to achieve as a result of the decision.
- Gather information deliberately (read up on the issue and ask friends, family, and knowledgeable people), making no hasty decisions.
- List all the realistic possibilities for each choice:
  1. Consider all known benefits and all advantages.
  2. Consider all disadvantages, costs, problems.
  3. Foresee the worst that can happen to you and decide if you could live with it.
- Evaluate each choice by estimating its short-range and long-range consequences.
- Consider if you are overestimating or exaggerating.
- Rank each factor in order of its importance to you; work out your priorities.
- Make a choice.

In everyday life, we constantly face situations in which we have to make decisions—even decisions between two good things. Some are small—whether to go away for a weekend vacation or to earn overtime by working all weekend. And some are larger and more difficult—whether to accept a scholarship to a graduate program in business or to accept a very good job offer that might not come up again. In each instance we have a choice to make, and these choices, day by day, determine whether we take some control over our lives or not.

We can choose to work and build toward some larger goals and thereby make the future more predictable. Or we can drift along, not making too many plans, and wait to see what happens to us. Many adults have some regrets that they did not take more advantage of their opportunities when they were younger and freer of responsibilities. Make sure to take advantage of any opportunities to achieve more of your potential. Don't sit back; make things happen for yourself. Do some critical thinking about your life.

■   PRACTICE 1   Make a list of your possible choices, with advantages and disadvantages, for one of the following decisions.

1. **You have misjudged your time, and your paper is due. You simply did not allow yourself enough time to finish. Should you (a) pass in a paper hastily written and try to do better on other grades, (b) speak to your instructor and ask for more time, or**

    (c) not speak to your instructor, improve your paper, pass it in late, and hope for the best? What are the advantages of each choice? What are the disadvantages? What would you do and why?

2. You are about to graduate and have to make an important decision: should you continue in school to get a graduate degree (and borrow money for tuition) or look for a job right after graduating (and save up money for tuition)? What are some of the considerations you should weigh?

3. In 1936, King Edward VIII of England gave up his throne in order to marry a divorced American woman, someone he had decided he loved too much to live without. According to English law and tradition, Edward was forced to abdicate when he insisted on marrying a divorced woman. Find some information in the library on King Edward's life before and after his marriage to Wallis Simpson. Then imagine you are King Edward, deciding whether to marry Wallis Simpson or not. Weigh all the advantages and disadvantages. Do you think that King Edward VIII made a wise decision?

4. Imagine a difficult practical decision you have to make: A friend invites you and your group of friends to his summer camp on a lake for the weekend. Everyone else is finished with exams, but you have a last important and hard exam coming up the day you get back. How would you come to a decision?

CHARACTERISTICS OF A CRITICAL THINKER

As children, all of us are told what to do and what to think. That is fortunate, because if not, we would be in danger of being burnt by matches, being hit by a car, or getting into other serious trouble. But at some point, as we mature and gain experience, we must take over responsibility for ourselves. We must then make our own decisions about what to do and how to think in order to become self-reliant adults.

As students, year after year, we are given the opinions of many experts, authorities, teachers, writers, scholars, and scientists. And quite naturally we agree that they know quite a bit more than we do. But at some point, we must gain confidence in our own abilities to think, and we must begin to question thoughtfully the opinions of these authorities and experts.

We eventually begin to realize that these well-respected thinkers often disagree, respectfully, among themselves. And in time we must learn to identify which experts we agree with and which we do not. In fact, it is just at these points of disagreement and conflict that new discoveries are often made by creative people; they see that the current explanation does not quite fit, and they find a better one.

To become a critical thinker, set a high priority on forming your own independent viewpoint—and not simply adopting secondhand your friends' (or anyone else's) viewpoints. To learn to think independently, consider these guidelines:

- **Avoid making inaccurate generalizations,** such as:

  "Women are overemotional, and men have no emotions."
  "Everyone from New York City is rude and aggressive."

  Whenever you make such sweeping statements, ask yourself to be more precise: Do you really mean everyone, or only a few people you have come across? How accurate are your estimates? Have you any accurate research or statistics? Are you exaggerating?

- **Avoid oversimplifying complex problems.**
  Some problems by their nature are complex, and there are no simple black-and-white or correct and incorrect answers. When there are no clear-cut answers, learn to live with some uncertainty or ambiguity. For example, the problem of whether to keep alive a young accident victim—someone who is in a coma, with no brain function—by using hospital machinery is a question for which no one has simple answers.

- **Accept that diversity of opinions exists** and that your opinion is not the only or, necessarily, the best solution. Work hard to understand another person's viewpoint—and the experiences that helped form that person's viewpoint. Examine the *ideology,* or firm set of beliefs, of those with clear positions, such as liberals who favor social change and conservatives who know that change has risks as well as benefits, as well as feminists, behaviorists, environmentalists, minorities, and so forth.

- **Remain open to new or stronger ideas.** Be willing to rethink an opinion if someone you know or some writer offers good reasons for modifying your beliefs.

- **Withhold judgment until you are sure.** Gather as much evidence as you need, and wait to take a position until the evidence persuades you. Was Darwin right or wrong in his scientific theories of evolution? Find out and decide about the controversy for yourself. What are the arguments? What are the counter-arguments?

- **Evaluate for yourself the opinions of authorities** and why they hold them: family tradition, past experience, faith in a text, religious teachings. What do *you* personally think about the death penalty, about abortion? What are your arguments for or against? How do such legal or moral conflicts develop?

- **Ask questions for clarification** when addressing someone who holds an opposing view:

    > Do you have a good example of this?
    > Explain what you mean by the words . . .
    > How do you define the term _____?
    > Let me restate your position to see if I have it right.
    > What are the advantages of X as opposed to Y?
    > What is the source (book or article) of your information?
    > Where can I learn more about this?
    > What is your objection to point X?

- **Avoid conventional or stereotyped thinking;** be willing to side with an unpopular view if you believe in it. Resist peer pressure; do not just go along with the crowd. Know yourself.

- **Gradually form a consistent value system of your own**—what you personally believe in and why.

Remember that critical thinking and questioning lead to creative insights. Critical thinking involves becoming responsible for your own ideas and for your own actions. It encourages you to true intellectual growth.

> It is just at these points of disagreement and conflict that new discoveries are often made by creative people. They see that the current explanation does not fit, and they find a better one.

■   PRACTICE 2   Of the characteristics of a critical thinker listed above, which do you feel describe you now and which do not?

■   PRACTICE 3   Which of the following statements are inaccurate generalizations or oversimplifications? Give a reason to support each answer.

Example: All men watch football on TV.
Answer: Inaccurate generalization. Not *all* men watch football on TV.

1. **The days of great movies are over; there will never be another Alfred Hitchcock or Humphrey Bogart.**

_____

2. **Surrounded by ugly billboards, Americans have no interest in making their surroundings beautiful.**

_____

3. **Lady Bird Johnson formed a committee to beautify America and to encourage the planting of wildflowers along superhighways.**

_____

4. **Every signer of the Constitution was a white male.**

_____

5. **Europeans believe that American educators should discipline their students more and not let them have so much freedom.**

_____

6. **No woman writer has made an impact on the literary world.**

_____

7. **Although B. F. Skinner's ideas are considered manipulative by some, his theory of positive reinforcement—a reward for a good job—seems to work.**

_____

8. No one understands what happened in Vietnam.

_____

9. Canadians think Americans are unimaginative.

_____

10. Everything has gotten worse in the last ten years.

_____

SOME METHODS FOR GATHERING AND ANALYZING INFORMATION

The thinking strategies we have introduced to describe personal decision making carry over directly to academic and creative work. In most academic problems, you first want to collect information—enough relevant material so that you feel you have a good picture of the situation and its background. Then you want to make some sense and order out of the raw material you've collected. Finally you want to reach conclusions that your research has convinced you are reasonable.

To study any problem or issue, a student or researcher has to decide how to gather information that is relevant, fairly complete, and convenient to find. Educational specialists have made studies of the different kinds of mental operations that are commonly used to find and make order of raw data.

In Figure 12–3, we provide a list of some of the mental operations that specialists have identified. The list is arranged by the thought processes used (1) for collecting information, (2) for examining or analyzing it, and (3) for evaluating or acting on it—the three steps most useful in problem solving and decision making. Can you think of any additional thought processes that should be added to this list?

Making Observations

Rather than surveying the many mental operations in Figure 12–3, all frequently used in academic disciplines, we will look into one of the most essential operations of critical thinking in or out of school—**learning from observation.** Say you have a tentative guess or a *hypothesis* (a possible

Mental Operations

Ways to Gather Information
Review what is written on the subject (see Chapter 16)
Design a project or plan a study
Make careful, direct observations
Collect data
Take measurements in experiments
Imagine or invent (for creative projects)

_____

_____

Ways to Analyze Information or Data
Make order out of unorganized material by using any of the following methods:
Compare items (for what is like, unlike)
Summarize large quantities of detailed or raw material
Classify items into orderly units; divide a whole into many parts
Hypothesize, that is, form a tentative explanation of the unknowns
Interpret data by explaining what it means
Analyze by looking for underlying assumptions
Synthesize by combining the information into a new whole (see Chapter 14)
Make analogies or create metaphors to explain the data
Make a mathematical model

_____

_____

Ways to Evaluate or to Take Action
Draw reasonable conclusions from an analysis
Make appropriate decisions
Plan to apply findings to new situations
Criticize constructively
Make thoughtful ethical or value judgments
Write a report or give a presentation

_____

_____

Figure 12–3 Mental Operations: Various Ways of Thinking

explanation of some unknown) that you want to study. How can you readily gather data to prove or disprove your idea? One convenient way, particularly for students, is to make direct or *controlled observations* and to take detailed notes on your observations. To make controlled observations means to make sure the process of carrying out the experiment does not change the result.

One high school student, for example, observed that teachers treated her differently when she wore her hair in a radical cut than when she wore it in a more conservative style. She decided to make a study of teachers' perceptions of their students and to investigate whether they favored students who appeared less radical. She won a Westinghouse Science prize for this sharp observation—one that she followed up with a written research report.

Observations can be carried out close to home; they usually require little special equipment or money. They often require time and patience. You might conveniently observe insect or animal behavior, for example, by studying closely the population of a beehive, an anthill, or a bird's nest. Or to study government regulations of the TV industry, you might observe how many commercials appear on TV in an hour and how much time is left for programming. Or you might use yourself as a subject, and observe yourself studying, for example, your energy levels at various times of the day. To emphasize the importance of making careful observations, a text on psychology states: "observation is the source of all psychological knowledge."

Another convenient way that you as a student can collect data is to con-

Photographers capture interesting and out-of-the-ordinary views with the use of a camera. Your writing is another means to express fresh and insightful observations.

duct *interviews* or *surveys*. To study student attitudes about school, you might ask an appropriate sample of students what they like most about their school, what they like least, and what they'd like to see changed. Or to study the leisure habits of students at your school, you might distribute a *questionnaire*, asking how many times in the past month the student went to a movie, a restaurant, a bar, a rock concert, or whatever.

Another means to gather information is to administer a test: you might ask a group of students to answer test questions on cultural topics in order to find out how many students have knowledge of major cultural figures like Picasso or Rembrandt.

Yet another way to gather information is to search for local *artifacts*, for example, to study tombstones of early settlers to find out the average life span of early Americans. Or you might go to nearby museums to study American Indian arts or costumes or to historic houses to learn more about the earliest settlers in your area. Even such items as old high school or college yearbooks can yield information on the social history of earlier generations.

After collecting raw data, students and researchers must choose a method of analyzing their data and raw information (see Figure 12–3). Basically they try to shape their raw information into manageable groups, and they try to determine what their data means. Scientists Watson and Crick, after studying the X rays of DNA crystals and the research of other biochemists, were able to work out the spiral structure of DNA—and also to win a Nobel Prize for their insight.

■ PRACTICE 4

1. Stand at a checkout counter and carefully *observe* what people buy in a food market. Take systematic notes about their food purchases. Are they buying junk food? Vegetables? Candy? Frozen foods? Diet foods? How many of the people in your study appeared to pay some attention to nutrition and health? How much can you tell about a shopper's diet from your observations?

2. Make some observations on the type of clothing worn in your school: (a) make a simple list of what each male who passes is wearing (sports jacket, sweater, T-shirt, tie and jacket, and so forth) and what each female is wearing (pants, skirt, sweater, dress, coat, and so forth); (b) after you observe about thirty people, decide which styles are most common in your location and whether the people you've observed are conformists or individualists.

The Different Frameworks of Academic Subjects

Each academic discipline has its own methods of asking and answering questions. For each of your courses, make sure you understand how the discipline goes about its tasks of organizing and classifying well-established information, of looking for new information, and of conducting new studies on unknown questions.

In many cases, your instructor will set up the framework and explain the methods by which a particular discipline tries to answer questions. If the instructor does not give this framework in an introductory course (or if you take a course in which it is assumed you know the framework), you can and should work it out for yourself.

First, study what the discipline is basically trying to find out and how it collects or organizes its information and analyzes it. For example, botanists and anthropologists both do field work, but botanists gather and classify plants whereas social anthropologists observe and compare the customs and beliefs of tribes and isolated cultures. Second, determine the high priorities: what are the most important questions presently being studied in a discipline? Third, learn in which areas new research is being done, that is, ask yourself how sociologists—or zoologists or musicologists—carry out their research.

Very different ways of learning and thinking are practiced by different disciplines. It is important that you find out the way a given discipline goes about its work and that you understand the materials, issues, and methods of each subject that you are studying.

Each academic discipline has its own method of asking and answering questions.

PRACTICE 5

1. Examine any two courses you are presently enrolled in and see if you can outline the basic framework of the discipline: How does it gather data? How does it work with the data? And how does it come to its conclusions? Which of these questions take highest priority in the discipline and where are the new discoveries taking place?

2. Take a subject that is entirely new to you, one in which you have never taken a course. Determine the basic issues or framework of the discipline by asking questions of students who have taken courses in it and by looking at the table of contents and preface of their textbooks. What questions

should you ask these students to gather an overview of the discipline?

TAKING MORAL POSITIONS

By carefully questioning the viewpoints of others (authorities, scholars, friends) and by forming your own independent opinions, you will become a critical, self-reliant thinker. You will develop your own views on an issue by determining whether the thinking behind someone else's opinion is sound or not. You will not go along with the crowd if you believe something seriously wrong is being done.

In seventeenth-century Massachusetts, women were burned at the stake after being accused of being witches by other residents in the town of Salem. A judge at the trial later publicly admitted to the error of his verdict. In the 1950s Senator Joseph McCarthy accused people of being "reds" or American Communists based on flimsy evidence. Later McCarthy was accused of conducting a "witch hunt." It is always to the advantage of fanatic leaders to have passive followers who do not think for themselves and who simply go along with whatever a leader tells them to do.

The most vital form of critical thinking, therefore, is for you to think through and develop your own moral viewpoint. Do you, for example, believe it is your responsibility to help others, or do you believe you are only responsible for yourself? Say you were in a boat accident; your motor boat overturned, and you needed help. Would you want other people boating in the area to decide your problem was none of their business, or would you want them to drop their own business and come to your rescue? Should people only be interested in their own concerns and feel no moral responsibility for others?

If you examine your own position on moral issues, you will become more alert to the type of person you now are and the type of person you want to be in the future. Would you help someone in a situation like the boat accident? Some people want to aid anyone in trouble, without question, because that is the kind of person they are and want to be—thoughtful of others and giving of themselves. Others, more motivated by practical common sense, would go to the aid of those in the water because they themselves, in similar circumstances, would want help. Other people, a minority, would ignore the people in trouble in the water, letting someone else go to their rescue. What type of person are you?

In examining your own moral choices, you must determine if you can live with your own decision. And you should also consider what the long-term consequences may be for you and for others. When U.S. Senator

Joseph Biden, as a law student, copied several paragraphs, word for word, from a legal article into one of his own papers (without footnoting them as another writer's words), perhaps he did not realize how serious plagiarism is. Perhaps he thought he would not get caught at it. When he decided to *plagiarize*, to use someone else's words as if they were his own, he made a moral decision that he was willing to live with. In his case, the bad decision was discovered immediately: as a penalty he had to repeat the course as well as repeat all the assignments for the course, and he did not graduate with his class.

Biden probably thought he had put the incident behind him; but when he had an opportunity to run for president in 1987, reporters began to accuse him of using other politicians' phrases in his speeches, and then someone remembered that old problem of plagiarism in law school. Biden himself felt that his campaign could not survive these questions of his poor moral judgment, and he withdrew as a candidate.

Critical thinking applies to every kind of moral issue, from stealing a library book to stealing someone's ideas in that book. No one is free from making moral choices. The Greek thinker Socrates said the unexamined life is not worth living, and critical thinking provides the tool for determining our choices and examining our lives.

WORKING SPACE

READING ASSIGNMENT

The following selection is by journalist Martin Gansberg. Read the article and write down all the reasons you can think of to explain why no one acted to help.

Thirty-eight Who Saw Murder Didn't Call the Police

For more than half an hour thirty-eight respectable, law-abiding citizens in Queens watched a killer stalk and stab a woman in three separate attacks in Kew Gardens.

Twice their chatter and the sudden glow of their bedroom lights interrupted him and frightened him off. Each time he returned, sought her out, and stabbed her again. Not one person telephoned the police during the assault; one witness called after the woman was dead.

That was two weeks ago today.

Still shocked is Assistant Chief Inspector Frederick M. Lussen, in charge of the borough's detectives and a veteran of twenty-five years of homicide investigations. He can give a matter-of-fact recitation on many murders. But the Kew Gardens slaying baffles him— not because it is a murder, but because the "good people" failed to call the police.

"As we have reconstructed the crime," he said, "the assailant had three chances to kill this woman during a 35-minute period. He returned twice to complete the job. If we had been called when he first attacked, the woman might not be dead now."

This is what the police say happened beginning at 3:20 A.M. in the staid, middle-class, tree-lined Austin Street area:

Twenty-eight-year-old Catherine Genovese, who was called Kitty by almost everyone in the neighborhood, was returning home from her job as manager of a bar in Hollis. She parked her red Fiat in a lot adjacent to the Kew Gardens Long Island Railroad Station, facing Mowbray Place. Like many residents of the neighborhood, she had parked there day after day since her arrival from Connecticut a year ago, although the railroad frowns on the practice.

She turned off the lights of her car, locked the door, and started to walk the one hundred feet to the entrance of her apartment at 82–70 Austin Street, which is in a Tudor building, with stores in the first floor and apartments on the second.

The entrance to the apartment is in the rear of the building because the front is rented to retail stores. At night the quiet neighborhood is shrouded in the slumbering darkness that marks most residential areas.

Miss Genovese noticed a man at the far end of the lot, near a seven-story apartment house at 82–40 Austin Street. She halted. Then, nervously, she headed up Austin Street toward Lefferts Boulevard, where there is a call box to the 102nd Police Precinct in nearby Richmond Hill.

She got as far as a street light in front of a bookstore before the man grabbed her. She screamed. Lights went on in the 10-story apartment house at 82–67 Austin Street, which faces the bookstore. Windows slid open and voices punctuated the early-morning stillness.

Miss Genovese screamed: "Oh, my God, he stabbed me! Please help me! Please help me!"

From one of the upper windows in the apartment house, a man

called down: "Let that girl alone!"

The assailant looked up at him, shrugged, and walked down Austin Street toward a white sedan parked a short distance away. Miss Genovese struggled to her feet.

Lights went out. The killer returned to Miss Genovese, now trying to make her way around the side of the building by the parking lot to get to her apartment. The assailant stabbed her again.

"I'm dying!" she shrieked. "I'm dying!"

Windows were opened again, and lights went on in many apartments. The assailant got into his car and drove away. Miss Genovese staggered to her feet. A city bus, O–10, the Lefferts Boulevard line to Kennedy International Airport, passed. It was 3:35 A.M.

The assailant returned. By then, Miss Genovese had crawled to the back of the building, where the freshly painted brown doors to the apartment house held out hope for safety. The killer tried the first door; she wasn't there. At the second door, 82–62 Austin Street, he saw her slumped on the floor at the foot of the stairs. He stabbed her a third time—fatally.

It was 3:50 by the time the police received their first call, from a man who was a neighbor of Miss Genovese. In two minutes they were at the scene. The neighbor, a seventy-year-old woman, and another woman were the only persons on the street. Nobody else came forward.

The man explained that he had called the police after much deliberation. He had phoned a friend in Nassau County for advice and then he had crossed the roof of the building to the apartment of the elderly woman to get her to make the call.

"I didn't want to get involved," he sheepishly told the police.

Six days later, the police arrested Winston Moseley, a twenty-nine-year-old business-machine operator, and charged him with homicide. Moseley had no previous record. He is married, has two children and owns a home at 133–19 Sutter Avenue, South Ozone Park, Queens. On Wednesday, a court committed him to Kings County Hospital for psychiatric observation.

When questioned by the police, Moseley also said he had slain Mrs. Annie May Johnson, twenty-four, of 146–12 133d Avenue, Jamaica, on Feb. 29 and Barbara Kralik, fifteen, of 174–17 140th Avenue, Springfield Gardens, last July. In the Kralik case, the police are holding Alvin L. Mitchell, who is said to have confessed that slaying.

The police stressed how simple it would have been to have gotten in touch with them. "A phone call," said one of the detectives, "would have done it." The police may be reached by dialing "O" for operator or Spring 7–3100.

Today witnesses from the neighborhood, which is made up of one-family homes in the $35,000 to $60,000 range with the exception of the two apartment houses near the railroad station, find it difficult to explain why they didn't call the police.

A housewife, knowingly if quite casually, said, "We thought it was a lovers' quarrel." A husband and wife both said, "Frankly, we were afraid." They seemed aware of the fact that events might have been different. A distraught woman, wiping her hands in her apron, said, "I didn't want my husband to get involved."

One couple, now willing to talk about that night, said they heard the first screams. The husband looked thoughtfully at the bookstore where the killer first grabbed Miss Genovese.

"We went to the window to see what was happening," he said, "but the light from our bedroom made it difficult to see the street." The wife, still apprehensive,* added: "I put out the light and we were able to see better."

Asked why they hadn't called the police, she shrugged and replied: "I don't know."

A man peeked out from a slight opening in the doorway to his apartment and rattled off an account of the killer's second attack. Why hadn't he called the police at the time? "I was tired," he said without emotion. "I went back to bed."

It was 4:25 A.M. when the ambulance arrived to take the body of Miss Genovese. It drove off. "Then," a solemn police detective said, "the people came out."

---

*apprehensive: fearful about the future

---

1. Why do you think no one called for help? What do people mean when they say, "I didn't want to get involved"?

2. How do you think you would react in a situation like this?

3. Do you know of any similar situations, or do you think this one was highly unusual?

WRITING ASSIGNMENT: "Are We All That Bad?"

In the sixteenth century, Machiavelli wrote a theoretical work on how a state should be governed. He believed that anyone holding political power was justified in using deceit.

Write a short paper applying critical-thinking skills to agree or disagree with the following statement by him, looking for generalizations and oversimplifications: "Whoever desires to establish a state and give it laws must start with the assumption that all men are bad and ever ready to display their vicious nature whenever they find occasion to do so."

JOURNAL ASSIGNMENTS

1. A Polish-Jewish doctor, Marek Edelman, who lived through the brutal Nazi period of World War II and the later Russian takeover of Poland, said recently that he didn't think it mattered what country you were from or what politics you believed in. His simple morality was to help the person who was at the bottom of the pile and who was being beaten up by bigger, tougher groups. "Never mind who is being beaten," he said, "I believe you have always to take his side." Do you agree or disagree with this moral principle? Do you have a moral principle of your own?

2. Discuss this question in your journal: Is it better to suffer an injustice than to inflict some injustice on another person?

CHECKING OUT

Check your understanding of Chapter 12 by writing answers to the following questions. You can work alone or with a classmate, whichever you prefer.

1. When making a major decision, why is it important to use critical-thinking strategies?

2. Why should you evaluate the long-term benefits and the costs of each of your choices? Why is it useful to consider the worst possible outcome?

3. What are the basic steps to follow for making a reasonable decision?

4. What are the characteristics of a critical thinker?

5. In attempting to solve any problem, why is it essential to collect as much relevant information as possible? What are some ways to collect it?

6. How does critical thinking encourage and lead to creative thinking?

7. When making moral decisions, why is it important to think for yourself and not follow the crowd blindly?

IN SUMMARY

Students who think critically about the issues they are studying remember the ideas longer than students who simply memorize facts or who are satisfied with surface knowledge. You will make an issue more meaningful for yourself if you find out how the separate facts are related in a broader context and what you personally think about a given subject.

Critical thinking is helpful in making productive decisions that occur in your daily life. The critical-thinking process carries over to academic issues: it requires that you gather all relevant information and then analyze the information in a thorough and thoughtful manner. In essence, critical-thinking strategies help you avoid making hasty or oversimplified judgments about an issue. You should remain open-minded, and be willing to rethink your opinion based on the information you uncover.

Students who think for themselves take nothing at face value and do not accept an opinion merely because some friend supports it. Critical thinking requires that you examine the strengths and weaknesses of any argument, that you stay flexible, and that you do not look for simplistic right-or-wrong answers. Critical thinking helps you understand that many issues have no single answer and that many thoughtful people disagree over an issue.

As its most important goal, critical thinking requires that you think hard about moral issues. You must decide how you want to act in relation to others and whether you can live with your own moral decisions. Thinking through the long-range consequences of any action will help you make a more responsible choice.

C H A P T E R 13

CRITICAL READING:
EVALUATING AN AUTHOR'S VIEWPOINT

IRIS: When I read this particular book, I get into amazing arguments with the author.

LISA: You mean it? What for? I always go along with whatever it says on the page.

IRIS: It gets me more involved if I can figure out some weaknesses in the ideas.

LISA: I just let the writer tell me what I should think.

IRIS: Try looking for any statements that don't ring true. I don't let a writer get away with anything.

OVERVIEW

In this chapter we will discuss how you, as a reader, should examine and evaluate an author's opinions, neither accepting nor rejecting ideas quickly. Then we will show you how to find legitimate grounds for agreeing or disagreeing with an author's views. Your willingness to question an author's opinions lies at the heart of critical reading and distinguishes an active from a passive reader.

By the very process of trying to decide whether to accept or reject an author's opinions, you begin to develop your own viewpoint. You engage the author in a two-way communication in which you become an active participant. You become caught up in the ideas under discussion.

Passive students make the mistake of accepting everything on the printed page as written by an authority and therefore not open to question. But active students always probe the statements and opinions they read, asking themselves whether they agree or disagree with the writer's views—and for what reasons. If they own the book, they make notes in the margins—one place they can be more honest than polite.

Teachers look for students who do more than merely repeat the information in the text without thinking about it deeply. They want students who apply what they have learned to new contexts. What sets apart skillful students from average students is this very ability to think critically—to think for themselves—when they are reading.

By challenging an author's viewpoint, you can help yourself in several ways. You can offer your own independent views in class discussions. Your disputes with an author's opinions will often provide you with excellent topics for writing assignments or essay exams. And by thinking critically, you are learning to **push yourself to new levels of awareness** that lead to creative work. You are not just repeating what scholars have told you; rather you are learning to question as scholars themselves must question in order to make their new discoveries.

The topics included in this chapter will give you the basic tools for critical reading and creative thinking:

- Develop a questioning attitude.
- Look for other possible sides to an issue.
- Distinguish objective fact from subjective opinion.
- Learn to evaluate an author's opinions or viewpoint.
- Learn to detect bias or a one-sided argument.
- Learn to detect your own biases.

DEVELOPING A QUESTIONING ATTITUDE

Advertising has already taught most of us to adopt a questioning attitude about what we view on television commercials. We take it for granted that a product is probably not as good as the manufacturer claims, that the detergent does not take out every stain instantly without scrubbing—or at least not as quickly as the TV commercial shows. And you know you will never become a star tennis player just by wearing a certain kind of sneaker. The sneaker may, however, turn out to be a well-made brand that will improve the comfort of your tennis game. In any case, sensible people question the information they receive from advertisers and do not simply assume it is accurate.

In a similar way, skillful students do not simply assume that everything they read is accurate or up-to-date—or even the complete picture. Instead they question what they read by asking themselves probing questions like these:

- Does this information sound reasonable to me?
- In my personal experience, does it sound true or not?
- Can I think of any other examples like it?
- Does it apply in every case?
- How does the writer know this information?
- Does the writer give me any sources for checking this information?
- Is this a recent or an out-of-date study?

You should always ask yourself these or similar questions as you read. And read with an openness to new ideas—almost as if you are on a search for good ideas to improve your life. Be willing to listen to the writer's opinions as well as to the reasons used to back up these opinions.

If you heartily agree with the author because the information makes sense to you and matches your own past experiences, consider jotting it down in your journal as something to remember. For example, one student was attracted to this sentence in her reading:

I, however, can help, provided that I think not of going out to make the world a better place, but only of going *in* to make the world a better place.
—Richard Mitchell

Our student wrote in her journal: "This author means I can help make the world a better place by making myself a more thinking, better person. And there's something to it because I often get discouraged about how little difference anyone makes. But Mitchell shows me how to have a small effect."

If you heartily disagree with an author, you may want to bring the point up during a class discussion or probe it further as a paper topic. Be demanding of all writers; challenge any writer whose opinions you believe are questionable or wrong.

Asking questions as you read is not a mere academic skill-building exercise. When you raise such questions and answer them as well as you can, you make the ideas far more meaningful for yourself by evaluating them according to your own experiences. You begin to sort out your own values and to understand yourself better by pinning down what you think and why.

Say you come across this statement in your reading: "It has long been known that people periodically need new challenges at work if they are to remain highly motivated.'' You should routinely ask yourself a series of probing questions about such a statement:

- Do you think the statement is generally correct?
- Do you personally agree or disagree with the statement?
- Does your personal experience lead you to think it is a good explanation of human behavior?
- Where does the author claim this information comes from?

When the author states, ''it has long been known,'' the vagueness of this claim should make you a bit uneasy. Writers should give you more specific sources of their information if they expect you to accept their views.

By asking yourself such leading questions, you probe the author's view as well as your own view of the issue. One characteristic of creative people is that they tend to question from many angles what other people simply accept.

In many cases in the past, you may have depended on the judgment of others—teachers, family members, friends—to form your opinions. But we urge you to become less accepting and more assertive and demanding as you read your assignments. Confront the writer with your questions and disagreements. Ask where the information came from. Ask for some solid proof. You don't have to take anyone's word on faith; you want to know their sources of information.

Take on the writer in a lively, ongoing debate.

> **One characteristic of creative people is that they tend to question from many angles what other people simply accept.**

■   PRACTICE 1   Read the following statements carefully. Develop some questions you should ask yourself to probe these statements—both about the statement and about your personal response to the statement. Then give answers to the questions you have posed.

Example: ''A cathedral, a wave of a storm, a dancer's leap never turn out to be as high as we had hoped.'' (Marcel Proust)

Answer: "Is what the writer says true, and do I agree? Yes, our hopes are always much too high. We expect too much and then are disappointed."

1. Parental loss of control is quite common. All eighty parents in an interview study of two-parent families reported hitting, and 90 percent reported yelling. Forty-three percent of the families reported loss of control, which was defined as treating the child with a greater degree of physical or verbal aggression than the parent found acceptable. However, no child is going to be damaged for life by an occasional parental temper tantrum, particularly if the parent briefly apologizes and offers to explain later.

   —Marilyn Heins, M.D.;
   Anne Seiden, M.D.

2. According to a 1972 statistical analysis by Sidney Verba, a political scientist of Harvard University, about 22 percent of the American population is completely inactive politically: they do not vote, do not work in political organizations, and do not even talk about politics very much.

3. A particularly dangerous form of yelling is the prolonged loud temper tantrum when a large adult hovers over a small terrified child. Parents can easily underestimate how terrifying an experience this can be for a child, and how long the effects can last. Some parents feel relieved—"at least I didn't hit"—but doctors have seen adult patients in psychotherapy who still suffer from that memory of terror years ago. The child, recognizing that the parent is out of control, cannot know what to expect next. In many cases they actually fear that the parent is going to kill them, or develop the belief that they are so bad that they ought to be killed.

   —Marilyn Heins, M.D.; Anne Seiden, M.D.

4. Political scientists divide voters into those who are self-regarding and those who are other-regarding. The *self-regarding* voters are most influenced by their own economic situation, and vote based on what they think will help them most in their personal lives. The *other-regarding* voters worry more about the welfare of the nation as a whole, and vote for what they think will benefit the prosperity of the whole nation.

IDENTIFYING OTHER SIDES OF AN ISSUE

One way to help yourself think critically is to look for the other possible side or sides of an issue. Search for any opposing opinions that might be used to counter an author's statement. For example, some author might argue that the main purpose of a writing course is for students to learn to express their personal viewpoints and that correct grammar and the mechanics of spelling and punctuation are of secondary importance.

To argue against this statement, you might say that such students might be judged unfairly at some later point because of their weaknesses in spelling and punctuation. In fact, these obvious errors might prevent someone from even reading through a job applicant's letter to discover his or her personal qualifications. You might also argue that such weaknesses are not readily overlooked in the business world and that therefore these basics should be given some emphasis in a writing course.

Sometimes you will be able to identify more than two sides of an issue. Even if, for example, an author supports the viewpoint of the farmer who favors heavy use of pesticides to control insects and crop damage, you also want to keep in mind the environmentalists' views on the harmful effects of pesticides on wildlife. In support of environmentalists who favor a limited use of pesticides, you may recall once reading how the overuse of pesticides in California has bred a ''superbug'' that now resists every kind of insecticide farmers throw at it.

Seeing things from different angles will help you to form a knowledgeable opinion.

You may also consider yet another viewpoint, the average citizen—neither a farmer nor a concerned environmentalist—who is affected by the problem of runoff from pesticides getting into lakes and rivers and affecting the drinking water.

You do not have to resolve these complex questions as you read, but you should at least raise them. Remember that you want to avoid simplistic, black-and-white thinking; and recognize that **several viewpoints often coexist,** each view held by various experts and each view having some merit.

If you investigate all the sides of an issue, you will come to a deeper, more complete understanding of the problems involved. To identify the opposing views of an issue as you read, call on all your previous knowledge, reading, memories, and experiences about it. Use all these resources to help you find support for *your* own opinion.

> If you investigate all the sides of an issue, you will come to a deeper, more complete understanding of the problems involved.

■ **PRACTICE 2**   In the following sentences, give the other side or sides of the issue. Then give several reasons that someone could use to support or defend this opposite viewpoint. Finally give your own opinion of the issue and the reasons for your viewpoint.

1. **Bringing up children is a woman's work.**

2. **Abused children should be taken from their parents and brought up by others.**

3. **It's a waste of time trying to rehabilitate juvenile criminals.**

4. **Every child should go to a school of equal quality; therefore, parents should be able to choose which school they want their child to attend, no matter what neighborhood or town they live in.**

5. **It is easy to define pornography.**

6. **The American Indian was well-off living safely apart on reservations and was always well treated and protected by the government in the past.**

7. **Billboards should not be abolished. They make the landscape more interesting when you are driving.**

8. **Instead of worrying about birth control and overpopulation, we should concentrate on raising more food to feed everyone.**

9. **Varsity college football players should be given special treatment and be allowed more time to pass their courses. After all, they have to spend a lot of time at football practice.**

10. **Student newspapers should be supervised by teachers who should decide what material is appropriate and censor the paper accordingly. Students have only a limited right to free speech because they at times lack judgment.**

OBJECTIVE FACTS OR SUBJECTIVE OPINIONS?

To develop critical-reading skills, a reader first has to learn to distinguish between objective fact and subjective opinion. At times writers present personal opinions that sound very much like neutral facts, and in such cases, the reader must be very careful to make distinctions.

What is an **objective fact?** A fact is something that we can count on as being reliable and accurate. It is a piece of information that can be verified by research—by checking in an encyclopedia or in a reference book in the library, or by making personal observations, such as in a laboratory experiment.

Here we have two sentences providing facts—two events that occurred in the same year:

Abraham Lincoln was assassinated on April 14, 1865, by John Wilkes Booth—just five days after the Civil War ended at Appomattox on April 9.

William Butler Yeats, the Irish poet, was born in 1865.

These two events of 1865, a birth and a death, are facts: both were verified in *The Timetables of History* by Bernard Grun—a collection of historical facts from 5000 B.C. to the present. Anywhere else you look up these same facts, you will find the same information, and reasonable people will accept this kind of information without question. The dates of medical breakthroughs (an artificial heart was first used in 1963), of inventions (the Xerox machine was invented in 1946), and of achievements (the first humans stepped on the moon in 1969) are all facts.

A fact is usually expressed in *concrete* language, that is, by words that refer to physical objects, measurements, time, distance, or weight. We know more facts about recent events than we do about earlier historical periods from which surviving records are lost or scarce. For example, scholars would give a good deal to know more facts about the life of William Shakespeare, about whom much remains unknown.

Of all the disciplines, the sciences attempt to keep their knowledge as objective as possible by eliminating any subjective factors. The principles of science are based on experiments and observations that, whenever they are repeated, will produce exactly the same results. Only in the frontier areas where answers do not yet exist—such as what explains the pull of gravity—do scientists differ in their interpretation of the data.

In contrast to a fact, a **subjective opinion** is a statement of a personal judgment or evaluation. It is based on relative values that cannot be verified either by objective experiments or observations. The writer, however, can support his or her opinion by providing the specific facts, evidence, assumptions, and reasons for holding such an opinion.

Opinions generally can be detected by the language the writer chooses, such as (1) comparisons (*"more* efficient than," *"less* disciplined," "the *best* administrator in years"), (2) adjectives ("insightful," "incompetent," "powerful"), and (3) evaluations ("this cautious approach," "a dictatorial manager with inflexible ideas," "questionable research"). Look for clues in the language to see whether a writer is presenting you with opinions or facts.

What would you consider the following statement—fact or opinion?

> Abraham Lincoln was a shrewd and practical leader who spoke out against slavery cautiously, knowing that to force the issue would anger the Southern states even more.

Here we see a writer expressing an opinion of Lincoln. The writer evaluates Lincoln's political skill ("shrewd") and makes an assumption about Lincoln's motives (that he did not want to take on the issue of slavery directly).

Another writer might study the same events of Lincoln's career and come to another, less favorable opinion:

> Despite the myths, Lincoln was a hesitant, even weak, moral leader who was willing to drag his feet on the great issue of freeing the slaves even to the very end of the Civil War.

Even when these opinions are stated quite firmly, the reader has to realize that these are not objective facts but the writer's own **interpretation** or reading of the facts. And the opinions of the writer often slip in without any special announcement or fanfare. It is always up to the reader to distinguish between neutral facts and the author's personal opinions and evaluations. Facts are generally agreed upon by everyone; opinions are usually more subject to heated dispute.

Even when scholars attempt to summarize Lincoln's own words from original documents or letters, they will often have different opinions about his exact meaning. As his thinking evolved, Lincoln himself wrote various comments on his attitude toward slavery, and so the issue remains a complex question for historians. To analyze these differences of opinion among scholars, you will need to use critical-thinking skills. It is up to you to form your own opinion of Lincoln. Was he a shrewd and practical president, or was he a weak moral leader?

> **It is always up to the reader to distinguish between neutral facts and the author's personal opinions and evaluations.**

■ **PRACTICE 3**   In the following exercise, decide if you think the information is probably factual information or a personal opinion, and give a reason to support your answer.

> **Example: The poet Emily Dickinson wrote the line, ''Split the lark and you'll find the music.''**
> **Answer: Fact—can be checked in a book of Dickinson's poems in index of first lines.**

1. **Franklin Delano Roosevelt was the first and only president to be elected to four terms.**

2. **Men are five to ten times as likely as women to commit most kinds of crimes.**

3. **Many journalists felt that Gerald Ford's quick pardon of Richard Nixon soon after Ford became president was badly timed and made Ford look as guilty as Nixon.**

4. **No one should be allowed to smoke now that doctors have shown extremely strong evidence that smoking causes cancer.**

5. **President Harry Truman did not even know that the atomic bomb was being developed when he suddenly became president after Roosevelt's death, and then he had to decide whether to use it or not.**

6. Emily Dickinson was certainly a great American poet and some devoted fans say she is one of the greatest of all poets, man or woman.

7. Joe DiMaggio still holds the record for getting a hit in the most consecutive games (56 straight games) of the regular baseball season (1941).

8. A few American birds and insects are washed ashore every spring on the coasts of Ireland and England, carried across the Atlantic by winter storms.

9. Some people say that the dinosaurs had small brains and were too dumb to survive, but they lasted roughly 100 million years, whereas man has only lasted one million years.

10. In 1859 an English gentleman introduced a few rabbits into his estate in Australia, and by 1950 the whole of Australia was overrun by rabbits, stripping bare all vegetation.

EVALUATING AN AUTHOR'S VIEWPOINT

When you analyze any piece of writing, you should look into how well the author has interpreted the various facts and conflicting opinions surrounding an issue. You want, that is, to examine and **evaluate an author's viewpoint or position on the issue.** How, for example, do we evaluate the viewpoint of a historian who thinks Lincoln dragged his feet and didn't make bold moves? Is he right or wrong? This is not a simple matter. It again involves asking yourself a series of questions:

Ask Questions about Sources

Ask yourself where the writer's facts came from and what sources (books, magazines, journals) the author has quoted. Can you verify the sources through footnotes or endnotes? Or does the author assume that you don't need to know where the information comes from? If the author does not give you the sources of the information, consider why he or she does not.

Ask Questions about the Quality of Support

Does the writer back up his or her opinions with **support,** that is, with facts, reasons, evidence, or examples, which taken together lead you to understand the author's viewpoint? Does the author discuss the possible opposing views or assume there isn't any opposition? Are the facts, as given, consistent? Are the opinions reasonable?

Ask Questions about Documents

Does the writer refer to original or **primary documents,** that is, letters, writings of witnesses, authentic papers in Lincoln's handwriting? Or does the writer use **secondary sources,** that is, works of other or later writers commenting on the original documents?

Ask Questions about Credentials

What do you know about the author's background? Has he or she written anything else on the subject? Is the author considered an expert in the field? Is the writer on the faculty of a major university or in an important position in the government, such as the head of the Internal Revenue Service (IRS), that gives authority to his or her views on taxes?

Ask Questions about Language

Is the language neutral and reasonable ("he's undoubtedly made some regrettable errors") or is it emotional and exaggerated ("he's the most pig-headed dolt who's ever been elected")? Is the writer appealing to reason and fairness (using legal or moral principles) or to prejudices and passions (calling names, using insults, using vague and imprecise language)?

Ask Questions about Bias

Does the author attempt to be objective? Or does the author appear openly *biased* or one-sided in favor of a certain group or position? Does the writer openly represent and defend a political cause—for or against gun control, for or against abortion? Or does the author try to disguise a bias? If the writer is employed by a company, be skeptical, or at least cautious, about any writing about the company's products or interests. And be sure to look at what the opposing side has written about the issue.

Ask Questions about the Author's Purpose in Writing

Does the author want to *inform* you—that is, does the writer want to present evidence for opposing sides of an issue and let you come to your own conclusions?

Or does the author try to *persuade* you? In other words, does he or she give you both sides but persuade you to favor one side? Or does the author only give you a one-sided view of the issue?

Ask Questions about Dates

Is the study up-to-date? Is it the most recent study available? What is the date of its publication? When was the research carried out? Is the author aware of the most recent research?

Can you find a more up-to-date study? Since many fields are changing very rapidly, you want to be sure to have the most recent publications whenever possible.

As you study texts by various authors, it is finally up to you to evaluate a writer's use of facts and opinions. Is the author fair, straightforward, convincing? After all your questioning, do you generally agree with his or her conclusions? Do you think the approach is objective—with the opposing viewpoints presented fairly?

And it is up to you to determine the credentials and the possible biases of the author. If Professor Alice Bush has studied prison conditions in the United States for twenty years, has written a respected text on the nature of crime, and teaches criminology at a well-known university, her opinions deserve careful attention. If, on the other hand, an author has written several books on taxes but has only recently turned to the study of prisons, this person's viewpoint has less authority than Professor Bush's.

How trustworthy is the writer? Is he or she openly employed by a lobby or cause, such as the Gun Owners of America (in favor of private citizens' owning handguns), or an industry, such as the tobacco or oil industry? If so, you want to look very closely at the writer's viewpoint for any signs of bias.

If the writer is not openly employed by a political group or cause, you should still look closely to **see if the author consistently takes a one-sided position.** For example, when writing about the women's movement, Phyllis Schlafly, who is known to support traditional values, will predictably and strongly oppose feminist positions. Gloria Steinem, who is known for her support of equal rights for women, will consistently support feminist positions. You as a reader have to be vigilant in detecting biases—both those that are openly stated and those you have to read between the lines.

■ PRACTICE 4   If you come across the following information about an author, what would you think of his or her credentials? Put a check in the space that you think describes the author's qualifications.

1. **Stephen Jay Gould teaches biology, geology, and the history of science at Harvard University. He frequently writes a column for** *Natural History Magazine* **and has written many collections of essays, including** *Ever Since Darwin.*

   As a writer on Darwin's theories, he is
   Very qualified _____   Qualified _____   Not well qualified _____
   Not enough information given to decide _____

2. **Judy Syfers is the author of a very popular essay titled ''I Want a Wife,'' which originally appeared in** *Ms.* **magazine in 1971 and**

has been republished many times. Syfers writes about herself: "I am not a 'writer' but really am a disenfranchised (and fired) housewife, now secretary. I have published other articles in various types of publications (one on abortion, one on union organizing, for instance) and have edited . . . a newsletter for school paraprofessionals in San Francisco."

As a writer on American unions, she is
Very qualified _____ Qualified _____ Not well qualified _____
Not enough information given to decide _____

3. Gail Levin is an art historian and photographer who from 1976 to 1984 was curator of the Edward Hopper collection at the Whitney Museum of American Art in New York City. Among her publications are *Edward Hopper: Complete Prints* and *Edward Hopper: The Art and Artist.*

For information on the paintings of Edward Hopper, she is
Very qualified _____ Qualified _____ Not well qualified _____
Not enough information given to decide _____

4. Iris Lee is a graduate student in anthropology at the University of Arizona. She is now writing a master's thesis on the Pima Indians of Arizona. The present article on the Pima culture is her first published work.

As a source on the Indian cultures of the Southwest, she is
Very qualified _____ Qualified _____ Not well qualified _____
Not enough information given to decide _____

5. Leon Edel is a biographer who has specialized in the life and works of the American novelist Henry James. Edel's five-volume definitive biography of James was completed in 1972.

As a writer on the short stories of Henry James, he is
Very qualified _____ Qualified _____ Not well qualified _____
Not enough information given to decide _____

Examining Your Own Biases

In addition to checking out the biases of other writers, you should check out your own possible biases. Sometimes we are unaware of some of our own prejudices, and adopt some of the negative attitudes within our culture without even examining them. Do you have any personal negative feelings towards any group, considering everyone in the group as just alike rather than as unique individuals? Make sure that you want to hold such opinions and that you are not just maintaining someone else's old prejudices.

WORKING SPACE

READING ASSIGNMENT

After reading the following article written by Mark Nelson, an editor for *Chevron World,* a quarterly publication sent by the Chevron Corporation to its stockholders, make a rough outline of the opinions held by both sides. Then answer the questions that follow.

One of America's Last Oil Frontiers

On the surface, it's difficult to see why an arctic desert tucked into the northeastern corner of Alaska would attract much interest. This vast, treeless tundra is frozen to a depth of 2,000 feet year round. The sun disappears for two of the nine months of the winter, and the wind drives temperatures to 100 degrees below zero (Fahrenheit).

It's not what's on the surface, however, that's attracting attention. It's what might be trapped beneath this desolate expanse that is turning it into a national battleground of sorts.

The oil industry believes this area is the last onshore frontier in the United States holding exceptionally high promise for the discovery of a major oil field.

Environmentalists, on the other hand, want to preserve what they feel is one of the last untouched areas along the U.S. arctic coastline. They contend that much of the rest of the coastline has been disturbed because of oil discoveries, most notably the Prudhoe Bay Field, the nation's largest.

The land in question is a 1.5-million-acre area known as the Coastal Plain of the Arctic National Wildlife Refuge. Within the entire 19-million-acre Refuge, which is about the size of South Carolina, only 210 Inupiat Eskimos hunt and fish from the village of Kaktovik, a former whaling and fur-trading outpost on the Beaufort Sea.

Little else here stirs during the long teeth-chattering winters. During the brief summers though, the ice melts, and lakes dot the usually bleak landscape. Streams spring to life and feed sedge tussock—a kind of swamp grass. The Eskimos share this transformed landscape

What will happen to one of the last untouched areas along the arctic coastline of the U.S.?

with such wildlife as the porcupine caribou, various waterfowl, some sheep and moose, and an occasional grizzly or polar bear.

Despite its isolation, the Coastal Plain has become a cause célèbre* in the latest, and perhaps fiercest, rivalry between the petroleum industry and some environmental groups. Congress, following the lead of an Interior Department recommendation, probably will decide sometime this year whether or not to open up the Coastal Plain for oil and gas exploration.

"It's unfortunate this is an environmental conflict at all," says Thomas Cook, who, as Chevron U.S.A.'s Exploration Representative for Alaska, has widely debated the issue. "It means this probably will become an emotional issue, and it's one that should be judged solely on the facts."

"It's inconceivable to me that this has even become an issue," adds Bill Crain, Chevron U.S.A.'s Senior Vice President for Exploration, Land and Production. "This is truly the last major onshore frontier in the U.S. with all the earmarks for significant discoveries."

"Overall," Crain says, "our exploration room is running out in the U.S. Many of the industry's recent exploratory efforts have been disappointing. These include wells in many deep water areas of the Gulf of Mexico, offshore along the East Coast, in the Bering Sea and the Gulf of Alaska, and the Mukluk dry hole in Alaska. And all this is

*cause célèbre: an issue arousing heated public debate

happening at a time when we're becoming dangerously dependent on imported oil. The only issue here is one of national security."

Environmentalists don't see it that way. "You could safely say that preserving the entire Arctic National Wildlife Refuge, which means closing the Coastal Plain to future oil development, is the environmentalist's No. 1 priority now," says Mike Matz, Associate Field Representative in Alaska for the Sierra Club. "We see it as the last chance we have to preserve a section of the arctic coastline in the U.S."

The Refuge was established in 1960, but the present controversy stems from 1980, when Congress passed the Alaska National Interest Lands Conservation Act. This legislation expanded the boundaries and set aside about 92 percent of the area, making it off-limits to oil development.

Further, Congress instructed the Interior Department to study whether the small area of the Coastal Plain should be opened up for oil and gas development or managed as a wilderness area. That study is due early this year.

Another influential group, the Arctic Slope Regional Corporation (ASRC), an Inupiat Eskimo-owned corporation, also has studied the issue. Last fall, ASRC wholeheartedly endorsed oil exploration in the Coastal Plain, exhorting Congress not to designate the area as a wilderness preserve.

ASRC represents the economic interests of native Alaskans in all eight villages along the North Slope and owns the subsurface mineral rights to 92,000 acres of land belonging to the Kaktovik Inupiat Corporation (KIC). It is in this area, which includes the village of Kaktovik, that Chevron and partners hold an exclusive land position. Chevron is operator and holds a 50 percent interest in the partnership, which also includes British Petroleum (25 percent) and the Standard Oil Company (25 percent).

After years of developing rapport and trust with ASRC and Kaktovik villagers, Chevron obtained permission in 1980 to explore KIC lands. Although these lands are private, they lie within the Coastal Plain and, consequently, further oil development is subject to Congressional approval.

The Coastal Plain is located less than 100 miles east of the Prudhoe Bay and Kuparuk River fields, which together produce 20 percent of the nation's oil. It also lies within the same geologic province. A 1980 U.S. Geologic Survey report estimates that the Coastal Plain could contain as much as 17 billion barrels of oil and 34 trillion cubic feet of gas in place—potentially placing it in the same class as Prudhoe Bay. . . .

Matz of the Sierra Club doesn't dispute the petroleum potential of the region, but he questions whether the energy needs of the country outweigh potential environmental hazards.

"I don't have a response to whether oil development is really in the national interest," Matz says. "Basically though, the need for energy isn't an argument that should wash. We should be developing new technologies and using less energy by practicing more conservation measures."

According to Matz, environmental groups—such as the Sierra Club, Wilderness Club, Northern Alaska Environmental Center and Trustees for Alaska—have three basic concerns.

First, they're concerned about the habitat of the porcupine caribou. It's estimated that about 200,000 of these migratory animals, which get their name from the Porcupine River, roam the Coastal Plain. However, Matz acknowledges that caribou herds to the west have tripled since oil development began at Prudhoe Bay and elsewhere along the North Slope.

Second, Matz suspects some Eskimos might be worried that their centuries-old hunting and fishing cultures will change with oil development. "We don't want to tell natives what they need," Matz says, "but to let them know that life-style changes could occur."

Chevron's Cook points out that the villages and the regional native corporations have supported oil development along the North Slope. "Oil operations have not altered the life styles or cultures of Eskimos who choose to continue their customs," he says.

The third concern of environmental groups is to protect the aesthetic qualities of the virgin wilderness. "The Coastal Plain is one sweeping continuum, and the only part of the entire 1,100 miles of the arctic coastline where we've had some token effort to preserve a natural state," Matz says.

Crain points out that oil operations within the Coastal Plain would occupy only a small fraction of the land. "Millions of acres have been set aside for parks and wildlife protection in the arctic," he says. "Our interests are focused on a relatively small area."

Cook emphasizes that the oil industry shares the environmental groups' goal of protecting the environment. After 40 years of engineering experience in the arctic, which has led to numerous technological advances and safeguards, the oil industry has learned to exist in harmony with the environment.

1. What are the views of the oil industry?

2. What are the views of the environmentalists?

3. Do you know what the author's viewpoint is? Is there any other group whose opinion should be part of the debate?

4. Do you think the author is trustworthy? Why? Would you expect this publication to be one-sided? Do you consider the writer fair-minded or biased?

5. Who makes this comment: "This probably will become an emotional issue, and it's one that should be judged solely on the facts." What is your reaction?

6. What do you think should be done? How can this problem be solved?

WRITING ASSIGNMENT: "Who Puts More Effort into Their Jobs?"

In a short paper of one or two pages, agree or disagree with Lester Thurow's viewpoint, raising any questions you think are appropriate and looking for other sides of the issue.

Men are programmed to provide for their families economically while women are programmed to take care of their families emotionally and physically. As a result men put more effort into their jobs than women. The net result is a difference in work intensity that leads to that 40 percent gap in earnings. But there is no discrimination against women—only the biological facts of life.

—Lester Thurow

JOURNAL ASSIGNMENT

Do you think it is possible for anyone to be purely objective in his or her thinking, or do you think everyone has a certain viewpoint depending on his or her individual background? Do you believe that everyone has a certain amount of bias?

CHECKING OUT

Check your understanding of Chapter 13 by writing out answers to the following questions. You can work alone or with a classmate, whichever you prefer.

1. Why is it a good strategy for the reader to agree or disagree with a writer's opinions and to challenge any of the writer's statements that seem questionable? How does this help the reader?

2. After considering a writer's opinions, give some reasons why the reader should play the devil's advocate and search for the opposite sides of the argument.

3. What are some ways in which you can distinguish between fact and opinion? How should a writer back up or support his or her opinions?

4. What are appropriate questions to ask about an author's credentials?

5. Why is an author who gives the sources of his or her material more useful to a reader?

6. What is a biased viewpoint and how can you detect it? Why is it important to know if a writer represents some special group or interest?

IN SUMMARY

To become a critical reader, we encourage you to raise questions as you read, to agree or disagree with the writer continually, and to examine your own point of view by reflecting on the author's views. Use your own past experiences and knowledge of the world to help you evaluate an author's viewpoint. When reading, compare your own opinions and personal experiences to those of the author.

A skilled reader acts as a devil's advocate and brings up all opposing views. By looking at all sides of an issue, the reader can get closer to the heart of the matter. We have given you a checklist of questions (p. 342–343) to raise when you want to evaluate an author's credentials. Examine, in particular, the sources of an author's information and decide whether or not the author presents a one-sided or biased viewpoint. And check the dates of the author's research; in general you want to be familiar with the most recent studies on an issue.

To analyze an author's viewpoint, distinguish between objective facts and subjective opinion. You can often determine by a writer's use of language whether he or she is attempting to be impartial and neutral, or subjective and opinionated.

In this chapter, we have discussed how to use critical-thinking skills when evaluating a single writer's viewpoint. In the next chapter, we will discuss how to use these same skills when evaluating the conflicting views of several authors as they discuss the same issue.

CHAPTER 14

CREATIVE THINKING: DEVELOPING A SYNTHESIS

The competent reasoner proceeds by *challenging and altering* his or her own premises while thinking through a problem, that is, by accumulating then abandoning assumptions.

—V. A. Howard, J. H. Barton

OVERVIEW

In Chapter 13, we discussed how you—or any reader—should go about evaluating the opinions and viewpoint of an individual author. In this chapter we will discuss how you can thoughtfully evaluate the conflicting viewpoints of several authors and **develop a viewpoint of your own.**

Depending on whether you agree or not with each author's evidence and opinions, you will learn how to select whichever ideas you think are the key issues in order to develop your own *synthesis*. And the material will be transformed by your own new connections and insights into an original and fresh form.

We will also discuss the idea of *interpretation*—how to interpret other writers' evidence and language so that you can evaluate them fairly and constructively. The challenge and pleasure of doing serious reading and research on a topic is that you yourself can become something of an expert in the area you are investigating. And you can use your critical-thinking skills to create a new work, one that represents your own responses and your own views.

The key notions we introduce here will help you think critically and creatively; you will learn to:

- Identify conflicting opinions.
- Interpret evidence and language.
- Evaluate authors' different viewpoints.
- Create your own synthesis.

EXPLORING CONFLICTING OPINIONS

In this chapter we will follow the progress of a student, Karen Fry, as she uses critical-thinking skills to prepare a short paper that she will read aloud in class and then pass in for 20 percent of her grade. For a course on American film, Karen will research a paper in which she will evaluate and synthesize several writers' views of Marilyn Monroe.

Her specific assignment is to explore whether the Hollywood system helped Marilyn Monroe become a superstar creation or whether Hollywood ruthlessly manipulated and exploited her. Monroe committed suicide at age thirty-six when she was still at the height of her popularity as a film actress and one of the most famous Hollywood stars of all time.

Karen's first task was to explore the issue that she was going to analyze by familiarizing herself with Marilyn Monroe's film career and the Hollywood system. Looking up Monroe in the library card catalog, she took out three books that sounded useful, one by Gloria Steinem, a leading feminist; one by Norman Mailer, a well-known novelist; and one by an English journalist, Anthony Summers.* Her teacher also called her attention to an article by the respected critic Diane Trilling that had appeared in the *New York Times*. Karen was soon caught up in exploring the topic and looking for answers to her questions. Did the Hollywood studios exploit Marilyn and eventually destroy her? Or did Hollywood allow Marilyn to use her talents to the fullest and to make the most of herself?

Karen discovered that Marilyn Monroe had experienced a particularly stressful childhood. When Marilyn was only seven, her mother suffered a serious mental breakdown and could no longer care for her daughter. After the breakdown, Marilyn's mother spent the rest of her life—except for short intervals—in an institution. Marilyn's father had disappeared before she was born and had virtually no influence on her life.

Consequently a guardian, a friend of Marilyn's mother, placed her carelessly in one foster home after another, and at one point deposited her without any warning—screaming in protest—in the Los Angeles orphanage. Finally, her guardian, planning to move to another state, arranged for

---

*For information on how to do library research, see Chapter 16.

Marilyn to marry as soon as she turned sixteen—as an alternative to another foster home or the orphanage. As Marilyn later explained, "Again, it was the case of no one wanting me."

From that grim beginning, Marilyn went on to become first a model, then a hopeful starlet, and finally one of Hollywood's most celebrated and successful stars—her films shown around the world. Since she had signed a long-term contract when she was an unknown, she continued to be paid a modest amount under the terms of the old contract, even after she had become a major star. So she personally earned relatively little compared to what she earned for the Hollywood studio. But she explained to reporters that she was less interested in large sums of money than in being recognized as "a great actress."

Eventually Hollywood came around and agreed to give her a contract for what she was worth. And eventually some film critics agreed that she had taken what were unpromising parts and made them into great comic roles; they saw that she was much more than a typical Hollywood product.

Marilyn remained at the peak of her popularity for about ten years, taking her acting very seriously and hiring leading coaches to help her reach her goal of becoming a great actress, not merely a pretty face. But at the age of thirty-six she was fired from her final movie, and two months later she either accidentally took too many sleeping pills or deliberately committed suicide. Because she died so young, many writers ever since have wanted to understand what happened to Monroe. Since everyone believed she had achieved the American dream of rising from poverty to the heights of success, writers like Gloria Steinem and Norman Mailer have been drawn to explore what went wrong with her dream.

Studying the books on her topic with growing interest, Karen remained open-minded about the issue she was studying, listening to opinions on all sides and changing her mind several times about what she thought. When she came upon conflicting facts and opinions about Monroe, she tried to sort these out. She slowly laid the groundwork for her later discoveries. In Practice 1 are some of the conflicting opinions Karen came upon in her explorations.

■   PRACTICE 1   Read the following pairs of conflicting opinions. Then decide which opinion supports the Hollywood system and which one blames Hollywood for exploiting Marilyn. Mark each opinion either "for Hollywood" or "against Hollywood."

   1. a. Although Hollywood forced Marilyn to play the same kinds of roles, a policy called typecasting, her films were highly profitable, and the studio thought it made sense to maintain the successful formula.

    b. Hollywood limited Marilyn's roles to playing dumb blondes in light comedies, didn't take her acting seriously, and stunted her growth as an actress.

2. a. Marilyn was often hours late for work—or didn't show up at all. She was unprofessional, forgetting her lines, demanding endless retakes, and annoying the other actors. It was inexcusable behavior.

    b. Marilyn's lateness was due to serious psychological problems, probably stemming from her unstable childhood. Her behavior was self-destructive but beyond her control.

3. a. Firing Marilyn pushed her into a depression and probably into suicide. The studio bosses should have thought of a less extreme and humiliating tactic.

    b. On her final film, the costs were mounting, and she rarely appeared for work. Firing her was a sensible move from the studio's viewpoint. It charged her with ''willful violation'' of the contract.

4. a. Film-making is a business and must be run like a business. She ignored all the basics of a profit-making industry.

    b. Marilyn thought of herself as an actress—even as an artist. She wanted to get the character she was playing just right and worked very hard at perfecting her acting skills. Hollywood never understood her ambition to grow and improve

5. a. Hollywood made her a great film star and gave her life all its meaning and purpose. Without Hollywood, who would have heard of Marilyn Monroe?

    b. Hollywood exploited her ruthlessly and destroyed her by its callousness—its lack of understanding of an obvious problem.

INTERPRETING EVIDENCE AND LANGUAGE

A single fact by itself is usually not as significant as a cluster of related facts. Coming upon a cluster of facts as you read, you can interpret the meaning of one fact in relation to another. The challenge becomes how to interpret a group of facts in a way that makes the most sense to you—and eventually to your reader or listener. **To interpret means "to explain the meaning of,"** and to interpret the facts and evidence surrounding an issue, it is necessary to think critically.

By **evidence** we mean the facts, the data, and the detailed explanations that writers use to back their opinions. Good writers use evidence to convince the reader that their opinions are reasonable.

Collecting Facts and Evidence

As Karen begins to establish for herself the facts about Marilyn Monroe's childhood, she has to determine:

- how accurate and reliable the facts are
- how complete the facts are (what information is missing or unknown)
- what evidence is in dispute
- how reliable the witnesses are

Certain facts can be easily *verified* or checked for accuracy. It is a fact that Marilyn lived in the Los Angeles Orphans' Home for almost two years. Official government records report her as a full-time resident there; years later after she had become a well-known star, the superintendent answered questions about her stay in the orphanage. Most reasonable people would accept such evidence as fact, particularly the official government records.

Other facts about Marilyn's childhood are far less certain. It is not clear, for instance, exactly how many foster homes she lived in. Karen found that the number mentioned by various writers varied from six to twelve foster homes. Karen can reasonably conclude that Marilyn stayed in a number of foster homes, although the exact number is unknown.

And some key facts probably can never be verified: the identity of her father is not known. He did not wish to marry Marilyn's mother and left her even before Marilyn was born. Nor can what happened the night she died be stated with certainty. Such questions remain open questions; a researcher can only speculate about them, that is, make intelligent guesses—and clearly identify them as guesses.

Examining Witnesses

What about using Marilyn Monroe herself as a witness? How trustworthy are her reports of her childhood? Here Karen has to make her own judgments about Marilyn's reliability. Karen has read in several places about Marilyn's tendency to invent tales and fables about herself, particularly about her childhood. Most of the books on Marilyn agree that she would alter facts, exaggerate a point, even lie a bit. Some writers suggest that she wanted to make what happened to her sound even worse than it was—to make it unmistakable that she was mistreated in her childhood and deserved some sympathy.

Karen tried to evaluate the reliability of Monroe's statements: Was Marilyn put in a dozen foster homes as she claimed? Was she sexually molested by a boarder in one of them? Karen decided that some variations in Marilyn's stories can be explained because anyone's memory of past events can be hazy.

On the other hand, Marilyn may have deliberately altered the facts either to improve a story or because the truth was too painful for her to face, such as the time she told reporters her mother was dead instead of saying she was in a mental institution. Karen decided that Marilyn was not too reliable in regard to specific facts but that Marilyn's various stories gave some insight into her lasting painful feelings about her stressful childhood.

In general, participants or eyewitnesses who have nothing to hide or defend are probably more reliable than those who must defend their actions or behavior. For example, those who saw Marilyn in the hours just before she died may want to defend what they did—or not mention what they should have done.

When several witnesses describe an event or behavior in the same way, the researcher usually feels more confident about their explanation than if only one witness mentions it. Researchers, in general, look for several reliable witnesses who agree on an explanation that sounds reasonable and consistent.

Interpreting: Looking for the Larger Meaning

To interpret the larger meaning of a group of related facts dealing with Marilyn's life, Karen asks herself:

- What do these facts and this evidence add up to, taken as a whole?
- Do they explain something, such as earlier events explaining later behavior?
- What evidence is most important; what is least?
- Do the facts and the evidence lead to some larger or more general point?
- Can these pieces of information be connected in a new way?

For example, Karen learns from her reading that Marilyn suffered from acute insomnia and that doctors often prescribed sleeping pills to help with her problem. Many friends and witnesses agree that she became gradually addicted to sleeping pills. Her problems with insomnia and sleeping pills worsened over the last few years of her life, and her doctors and psychiatrists could not help her drug dependency.

Karen next looks for a *pattern of events* that would reasonably explain Marilyn's problems with insomnia and drugs. She looks carefully at the evidence and decides that Marilyn's deep childhood insecurities and fears of being unwanted contributed to her obsessive worries and insomnia as an adult.

In turn, her inability to sleep led to her taking more and more sleeping pills, which in time grew into a drug dependency. Her drug dependency contributed heavily to her lateness to work and caused her many absences from the movie set. Karen thinks she sees a clear chain or pattern of events emerging in Marilyn's life.

One of Marilyn's lasting fears had to do with growing old and no longer being able to play the role of an attractive young woman. Several witnesses mention that she coated her face with a thick layer of Vaseline—even when still very young—to prevent wrinkles. How does Karen interpret the comments of friends or witnesses on Marilyn's behavior or character? If only one eyewitness makes a statement about Marilyn's behavior, Karen correctly feels unsure about how to interpret the statement. But if several eyewitnesses mention the very same trait—like her worry about aging—Karen begins to recognize *patterns of behavior.* And she will use these emerging patterns to form her interpretation.

Once she has become deeply immersed in the material, Karen finds it helpful to explain to a willing friend all that she has discovered about Marilyn Monroe and Hollywood, recalling all the major facts and opinions she had read. And by reviewing and sifting the material as she tries to explain it to her friend, Karen clarifies her own interpretation.

For instance, as she repeats the facts about Marilyn's childhood, she suddenly recognizes a clear pattern: Marilyn never had a single caretaker, a secure home, or any stability as a child. During her childhood, Marilyn felt she was worth very little to anyone, and that worthless feeling stayed with her throughout her life, no matter how much she was later heaped with money, fame, admiration, or love.

After immersing yourself in your reading, explain the material you have researched to a friend. Trying to explain exactly what you have learned to someone else will help you clarify your own interpretation.

■   **PRACTICE 2**   Read the following generally accepted facts about Marilyn Monroe's childhood. Then answer the questions that follow.

1. **When Marilyn was seven, her mother was confined to a mental institution and was unable to take care of her ever again.**

2. **During her childhood, Marilyn was shifted from one foster family to another, living with at least six different families.**

3. **One foster family made her ride around all day in a car for an entire summer delivering bottles of furniture polish.**

4. **Without telling Marilyn where they were going, her guardian drove her to an orphanage. When Marilyn realized what was happening, she screamed that she wasn't an orphan because her mother was still living, and she begged not to be placed in an orphanage. Marilyn stayed in the institution for about two years.**

5. **Monroe was probably molested sexually in one of her foster homes.**

6. **Her guardian was moving out of state, and rather than put Marilyn back in the orphanage or in another foster home, she arranged for her to marry as soon as she turned sixteen.**

7. **Marilyn had no one person who cared about her deeply as a child. Her guardian could not or would not personally care for her and made poor choices for her care.**

8. **Marilyn's father left her mother before Marilyn was born.**

Taking these facts as a whole, how do you interpret them? (1) What was Marilyn's childhood like? Was it like yours or harder than yours? Was it harder than that of most people you know? (2) Do you think what happens to someone as a child affects that person as an adult? (3) What do you know, in general, about adults who have had difficult childhoods? What do you know about abused children? (4) Do you think psychologists exaggerate the importance of a stable childhood and the need for a parent or caretaker that loves and looks out for the child? (5) Why do you think Marilyn might have had little self-esteem as an adult?

Looking Hard at Language

In addition to interpreting facts and evidence, Karen has to look long and hard at the language—the precise words—chosen by writers to describe Monroe and her world. Karen is looking for the kind of emotional language that could reveal an author's bias. Although the writers she is studying generally use the kind of objective or neutral language that allows readers to form their own interpretations, Karen discovers that Norman Mailer chooses the kind of emotional, loaded language that she has learned to be wary of.

For example, if a writer describes Marilyn Monroe as an "actress," this is a neutral word that no one feels strongly about, one way or another. But if a writer describes her as a "sexpot" or "dumb blonde," the **connotations** of this language, that is, the associations aroused by it, are emotional. Some readers find such language tasteless or offensive because it belittles women and treats them as stereotypes rather than individuals.

As Karen reads Norman Mailer's biography of Marilyn, she notes that his choice of language suggests some mild contempt for Marilyn's intelligence. He describes her as a "dumb and dizzy blonde" and "uneducated," and speaks of her as having a mind that was a "basket case." (The other writers, Karen finds, do not agree with Mailer's opinion that Marilyn was "dumb"; in fact, they consider her clearly intelligent and eager to learn.) Karen decides that the language used by her other sources is far more neutral and objective than Mailer's.

Like Karen, a critical reader learns to recognize writers who use loaded or opinionated language that arouses strong reactions in their readers and those who use neutral language in an effort to be objective and open-minded.

■   PRACTICE 3   In the following sentences, underline those words that you personally feel have emotional connotations. (If you don't know the precise meaning or *denotation* of a word, check it in your dictionary.) Then think of a word or phrase that would be more neutral.

1. **The lawyer's obsession with details can be traced back to an early case he lost. He griped about backbiting in the legal profession.**

2. **Because he was a perfectionist and had no sense of humor, his workers considered him a prig.**

3. **She appeared to be helpful and honest in her dealings with us, but under the polished surface she was a smart operator.**

4. **Johnson fumed to his aide, "What does that simpleton think I sent him out there for?"**

5. The film director was strong, imaginative, hardworking, but nevertheless an oddball; and despite our sensible advice, he would not cut his seven-hour film.

6. The producer, penny pincher that he was, made millions of dollars for the backers.

7. Even if James was domineering, opinionated, and at times hysterical, he achieved results.

8. I didn't think he made a good impression: he was nervous and restless, and his clothing looked sleazy and disreputable.

9. T. E. Lawrence was courageous but sometimes too daring, and probably a maniac to go into such hostile territory.

10. She was manipulative and in my opinion a smug egotist; she never thought of anyone but herself.

EVALUATING WRITERS' OPINIONS

As she continued her research, Karen began to determine the viewpoint of each writer she was reading. She informed herself about their credentials and backgrounds and came to realize their opinions and biases.

Gloria Steinem, as Karen knew, is a respected leader of the feminist movement and was for many years an editor of the influential magazine *Ms.* Steinem consistently speaks out for the rights of women and on women's issues. In her book, Steinem mentions how Marilyn Monroe was not helped by the insights of the women's movement, which became a popular movement shortly after her death. She points out how neither Marilyn nor Marilyn's mother was helped by a society that was indifferent to the real economic problems of a single woman trying both to work full-time and raise a child (with no child care of any sort available).

Steinem's viewpoint is clearly feminist, but Karen felt that Steinem admitted her bias and that her opinions about Marilyn's problems were reasonable and supported by current psychiatric thinking. In *Marilyn*, Steinem argues that Marilyn's underlying problems were psychological, stemming directly from the repeated rejections of her childhood and the lack of any single person to give her total and unquestioning love: "Emotional security, continuity, a sense of being loved unconditionally—all those turn out to be as important in a child's development as all but the most basic food and shelter."

Karen noted that Steinem backs her opinion with several scientific studies by psychiatrists, describing children who suffer from emotional neglect. For Steinem, it was clear that the damage done to Marilyn Monroe as a child was almost impossible to repair. Marilyn worried about her acting skills and the appearance of her face and body in an obsessive way.

Another of Karen's sources, the writer and critic Diane Trilling, agreed with Steinem's view, but added that another equally important factor was Marilyn's family background of mental illness. Trilling mentioned several of Marilyn's close relatives who had died insane, including her mother's father, brother, and grandmother.

Most interesting to Karen, Diane Trilling strongly felt that Hollywood had established Marilyn as a great star and had given her life all its meaning, and therefore it was unfair to blame Hollywood for exploiting her. Trilling blamed instead the unlucky fate of a family history of insanity.

Novelist Norman Mailer was so intrigued by Marilyn's personality that he wrote two books about her. Mailer pointed out in his book *Marilyn* that he himself did not do much original research but used earlier studies to interpret her life. With his evident bias against Marilyn's intelligence ("she cannot concentrate long enough to clarify her thoughts"), Mailer's opinions, Karen felt, were highly subjective and personal. In time she began to mistrust his interpretation.

Compared to Mailer, the journalist Anthony Summers took an opposite approach: he did intensive fact-finding research, interviewing witnesses and recording the opinions of everyone who knew her. But Summers, Karen felt, presented evidence rather than interpreted his research: he largely left the interpretation of his evidence up to his readers.

In *Goddess*, Summers gives arguments on both sides of Karen's issue. He gives the Hollywood viewpoint by quoting the producer who fired Marilyn from her final film. The producer said: "The star system has got way out of hand. We've let the inmates run the asylum and they've practically destroyed it." And Summers also gives support for those taking Marilyn's side against Hollywood: "It was said she died in a state of depression following professional disgrace."

At this point Karen has studied, read, and thought enough about the issue to feel confident that she understands it thoroughly. Her final task is to form her *own* viewpoint about the question she is trying to answer.

■   PRACTICE 4   The following selections discuss Marilyn Monroe as a young actress. In evaluating these passages, decide which ones basically share the same viewpoint and which ones do not. After reading them all, what would you conclude about Marilyn's interest in learning? Was it genuine or not?

1. "Her search for knowledge was to become a lifelong preoccupation, one many would mock as pretentious posturing. It was not. Marilyn devoured Thomas Wolfe, James Joyce, poetry (mostly romantic), biographies, and history books.

"Abraham Lincoln became Marilyn's special hero. (She would later strike up a friendship with Lincoln's biographer, Carl Sandberg.) Lincoln's portrait would follow her from home to home till the end of her life, and his Gettysburg Address usually hung nearby." —Anthony Summers

2. "I knew how third-rate I was. I could actually feel my lack of talent, as if it were cheap clothes I was wearing inside. But, my God, how I wanted to learn! To change, to improve! I didn't want anything else. Not men, not money, not love, but the ability to act." —Marilyn Monroe

While Marilyn Monroe's reputation was as a blond bombshell, she was also an intellectual who was very interested in fine literature and in the poetry of Carl Sandburg, in particular.

3. "Volumes of Shelley, Whitman, Keats, and Rilke accompanied her on movie sets where she played the classic dumb blonde. So did novels by Thomas Wolfe and James Joyce, and books on history and mysticism. Often the contrast was too much for observers. Jack Paar was sure Marilyn was putting on an 'act' when she read Proust. . . .

"Marilyn might not read a book straight through, but she dipped into a book until she connected with a passage, or until she had a sense of the sincerity of the author. As her third husband, Arthur Miller, has testified, she had an odd ability to absorb the essence of a writer's message." —Gloria Steinem

4. "Uneducated (that familiar woe of a beautiful blonde) she was also cultureless." —Norman Mailer

5. "During this workless period, Marilyn plunged into the acquisition of 'culture.' In school, which she had quit when she was fifteen, her work habits had been generally graded as only 'acceptable'; but she had been rated 'good' in English classes. Now, seeking to broaden her mind—partly to help her career, partly because she was thirsty for information—she began to build up a considerable library." —Anthony Summers

DEVELOPING A SYNTHESIS

Building a *synthesis* based on other writers' facts and opinions requires that Karen select the most useful and significant ideas from her reading about Marilyn and put them together in a new combination. She then comes to her own new conclusion, which she in turn must explain and support for her readers.

At this point in her research, Karen has established facts and evidence, has evaluated the opinions of other writers, and has reached the final task of forming her own viewpoint. Reviewing all the issues, she must come to her own conclusions and develop her own synthesis. In her synthesis, Karen will combine all the key ideas and opinions—both her own and other writers'—into a new whole. She must *support* her synthesis by selecting appropriate reasons, facts, opinions, and evidence to explain her thinking. She must credit her sources for any and all ideas that were not her own, not only her direct quotations but also her paraphrases.*

---

*See Chapter 16 for information on taking notes on sources; Chapter 18 for information on citing sources.

To develop her synthesis, Karen uses more than her specific reading on Monroe's life. She also calls upon her own personal experiences and past reading to support her opinions. She uses her own personal knowledge of psychology. (She refers to a study on the lasting effects of a traumatic childhood that she remembered from a previous psychology course.) She uses her knowledge of the women's movement: she knows that single women in the 1950s with young children and low-paying jobs were unable to survive economically. She uses her knowledge of the film industry of that period: she knows that Hollywood producers controlled many film stars by signing them to long-term contracts, by forcing them to take limiting roles, and by running their personal lives.

By the end of her life, all the writers agreed that Marilyn was taking many kinds of drugs and that she had difficulty getting herself under control to appear each day at the studio for work. Finally the studio executives fired her without warning and shut down the filming. Karen thought the firing was an important issue to concentrate on.

She asked herself a series of questions and tried to give herself the answers, working toward her own conclusions. "Do I believe Hollywood helped or hurt Marilyn—or some of both? Hollywood certainly hurt her by firing her. Why did the studio fire her? For not showing up and for chronic lateness. But more important, why was she always late? Either she was deliberately being uncooperative, or she had deep psychological problems. Both Steinem and Trilling agree she had problems, and in my opinion they are right. Marilyn had a double dose of bad luck: first she had inherited a tendency to insanity, and then she was badly mistreated as a child."

Karen then asked herself questions on Hollywood's role: "Were the producers smart to fire her? Perhaps from a business point of view; her delays cost money. But why were the producers totally uninformed about her fragile psychological state? Why didn't they understand her behavior was a symptom of much going wrong inside her?

"And even if they knew nothing about psychology, the producers were definitely callous in their treatment of her, embarrassing her so publicly—the news splashed on newspapers across the country. They could have done it more privately, in a more civilized fashion out of respect for her."

So Karen agreed with Diane Trilling that Hollywood had enabled Marilyn to become a great film star, but she did not agree with her that Hollywood should be free of blame. The studio executives certainly had some responsibility for triggering the final depression. Weighing and rethinking all the ideas she had read, Karen came to her own conclusion: by firing her the studio had fed into her worst secret fears. As Marilyn had put it, "again, it was the case of no one wanting me."

Now that Karen had questioned herself and answered her own questions, she felt ready to complete her short report. She summed up her viewpoint at the end of her paper: "Hollywood helped Marilyn get what most people would think of as everything. For a while, she was famous, rich, and admired, but all this couldn't make up for earlier hardships, and gradually all of it drifted away from her."

WORKING SPACE

READING ASSIGNMENT

Imagine you found the following two articles in the library when you were doing research on animal rights. They express different viewpoints on how animals should be used in medical research.

Take notes on your reading, establishing what view each side holds and why. Then compare and evaluate the evidence and opinions on both sides, and decide which side you agree with.

The first article is by reporter Dianne Dumanoski who is writing for the general audience of a daily newspaper. She describes the efforts of Jane Goodall to protect chimps from harmful treatment when they are used for medical research.

The second article is by Professor Carl Cohen, who presents the case for using animals in medical research. His article appeared in a scholarly journal written for an audience of doctors.

Bettering the Chimps' Lot

Jane Goodall, who gained fame through National Geographic articles, TV specials, and her books about the wild chimpanzees of Tanzania, has resolved to put her celebrity and scientific clout behind the fight to improve the care of captive chimps, especially those used for biomedical research.

Her stand is turning a long-simmering conflict within the scientific community over the care of laboratory chimpanzees into a public battle, with biomedical/pharmaceutical researchers in one camp and those who study the animals themselves increasingly in the other.

Goodall . . . said in a recent telephone interview from Tanzania that she had tried quietly, without success, to push leaders in the biomedical community into improving the situation of captive chimpanzees. She now plans to take the issue to the public.

"I wish there were a way of avoiding it," she said, referring to the confrontation with medical researchers. Goodall said she had "talked to the top people," who responded that they "don't have the money" to make the changes she seeks.

Through lectures, media appearances, and her network of personal contacts, she said, she plans to do all she can to call attention to captive chimpanzees kept in conditions she considers unacceptable.

"People have said, 'Why are you suddenly launching into it?' I've just finished a book [*Chimpanzees of Gombe: Patterns of Behavior*] that took seven years, and this coincided with the Immuno case in Vienna and the SEMA case in the U.S.," Goodall said, referring to two recent controversies concerning the treatment of chimpanzees in laboratories.

Immuno AG, a multinational drug company, has been criticized by conservationists and animal welfare advocates for importing chimpanzees from Africa and for its care of the animals it has in captivity. SEMA Inc., a Rockville, Maryland, laboratory that contracts with the National Institutes of Health to care for animals used by NIH staff researchers, was raided last year by animal rights activists who made a videotape of the condition of primates kept there and stole four young chimpanzees and records.

Goodall's decision to go public, some observers say, could have a significant impact. Andrew Rowan, who follows the issue from the Tufts Veterinary School of Medicine's Center for Animals, says that because of her "immense credibility,"* Goodall's influence could be "tremendous."

Others question her motives and those of a committee of scientists with whom she is aligned. Among her critics is Dr. Frederick King, who heads the Yerkes Regional Primate Research Center in Atlanta. King said he suspects Goodall's real goal "is to eliminate biomedical research on apes."

Last November Goodall and about thirty scientists who do non-invasive [†] studies of the animals formed The Committee for the Conservation and Care of Chimpanzees. It plans to promote the survival of chimps in the wild and to improve the lot of those in captivity, especially chimps in "biomedical-pharmaceutical laboratories where individuals are routinely stressed and mistreated while serving the medical needs of mankind."

---

*credibility: trustworthiness
†non-invasive: means without cutting

King, in a recent interview, said he is "afraid what lies behind this is not simply a desire to see conditions bettered in laboratories." When Goodall visited Yerkes several months ago, King acknowledged, he told her the center lacks money to make major changes. But, he said, there are long-range plans "to remodel the great ape wing, so we can make the habitat for chimps better." Yerkes also agreed to allow one of Goodall's associates to visit the center and suggest what might be done to improve the environment for chimps in the near term.

"The battle is not against the use of chimpanzees right now," Goodall asserts. "It's to get humane conditions for the chimps that are being used."

Goodall, in the interview, listed two minimum requirements for "chimps being used in the service of humanity" in laboratories: no solitary confinement and significantly bigger cages. "The minimum-sized cage now legal in the United States is, in my opinion, way below what it should be," she said. "They should keep chimps at least in compatible pairs. They should not ever be isolated."

"What she is opposed to," King responded, "is keeping animals in cages. If you want to study diseases, you must have periods of time when they are kept in isolation."

Late last month, Goodall fired an opening shot with an affidavit condemning conditions at SEMA Inc.'s Rockville laboratory, which were publicized by an underground animal rights group calling itself True Friends. In early December, the group secretly made a video-tape, removed records, and kidnapped four young chimpanzees slated for research. The tape shows chimpanzees rocking back and forth in isolation chambers the size of a shower stall.

"My impression, from viewing the film," Goodall said, "is that they have become insane as a result of these conditions."

In attacking SEMA, Goodall is indirectly taking on the National Institutes of Health, which is the largest source of funding for biomedical research in the nation. Although SEMA is a private company, it receives $1.5 million a year in federal funds to maintain animals used by NIH staff researchers. Beyond saying that it is investigating, NIH has declined to comment on the charges against SEMA.

Dr. John Landon, SEMA's president, defended conditions at the lab, asserting that it is "a superb facility."

But Goodall insists that the conditions are "totally unacceptable. It is my professional opinion that these apes are not housed adequately and that the care they receive seldom complies with the minimal legal and scientific requirements. The stark, barren conditions are highly psychologically damaging to the apes, and inevitably cause profound stress leading to despair."

One researcher who works closely with chimpanzees, veterinarian James Mahoney of New York University's Laboratory for Experimental Medicine and Surgery in Primates, says he does not find Goodall's minimum demands "unreasonable." But it may be difficult, he said, to make major physical changes within existing buildings housing research animals. "Obviously, the larger the caging, the fewer the animals that can be maintained in one room, so it gets very expensive," he said. . . .

Mahoney said he himself wrestles with ethical questions regarding the use and care of animals in laboratories. "I'm in a difficult position. I do believe in biomedical research using animals, but I have difficulty feeling good about it," he said. "Because of pressure from the animal rights groups, there is increasing awareness among the biomedical community that the way animals have been kept in the past and are kept in the present isn't adequate in the psychological and physical aspects. I don't think most people cared about things like that before." . . .

Over the past 25 years, Goodall said, she has received a great deal from the chimpanzees she has studied. Now it is time "I should make a return to chimps for what I've received."

Researchers often use chimpanzees such as the one shown in the photo for medical research.

The Case for the Use of Animals in Medical Research

Every advance in medicine—every new drug, new operation, new therapy of any kind—must sooner or later be tried on a living being for the first time. That trial, controlled or uncontrolled, will be an experiment. The subject of that experiment, if it is not an animal, will be a human being. Prohibiting the use of live animals in biomedical research, therefore, or sharply restricting it, must result either in the blockage of much valuable research or in the replacement of animal subjects with human subjects. These are the consequences—unacceptable to most reasonable persons—of not using animals in research.

Reduction

Should we not at least reduce the use of animals in biomedical research? No, we should increase it, to avoid when feasible the use of humans as experimental subjects. Medical investigations putting human subjects at some risk are numerous and greatly varied: The risks run in such experiments are usually unavoidable, and (thanks to earlier experiments on animals) most such risks are minimal or moderate. But some experimental risks are substantial.

When an experimental protocol* that entails substantial risk to humans comes before an institutional review board, what response is appropriate? The investigation, we may suppose, is promising and deserves support, so long as its human subjects are protected against unnecessary dangers. May not the investigators be fairly asked, Have you done all that you can to eliminate risk to humans by the extensive testing of that drug, that procedure, or that device on animals? To achieve maximal safety for humans we are right to require thorough experimentation on animal subjects before humans are involved.

Opportunities to increase human safety in this way are commonly missed: trials in which risks may be shifted from humans to animals are often not devised, sometimes not even considered. Why? For the investigator, the use of animals as subjects is often more expensive, in money and time, than the use of human subjects. Access to suitable human subjects is often quick and convenient, whereas access to appropriate animal subjects may be awkward, costly, and burdened with red tape. Physician-investigators have often had more experience working with human beings and know precisely where the needed pool of subjects is to be found and how they may be enlisted.

---

*protocol: a plan, or the steps of an experiment

Animals, and the procedures for their use, are often less familiar to these investigators. Moreover, the use of animals in place of humans is now more likely to be the target of zealous protests from without. The upshot is that humans are sometimes subjected to risks that animals could have borne, and should have borne, in their place. To maximize the protection of human subjects, I conclude, the wide and imaginative use of live animal subjects should be encouraged rather than discouraged. This enlargement in the use of animals is our obligation.

Consistency

Finally, inconsistency between the profession* and the practice of many who oppose research using animals deserves comment. . . .

One cannot coherently object to the killing of animals in biomedical investigations while continuing to eat them. Anesthetics and thoughtful animal husbandry render the level of actual animal distress in the laboratory generally lower than that in the abattoir.† So long as death and discomfort do not substantially differ in the two contexts, the consistent objector must not only refrain from all eating of animals but also protest as vehemently against others eating them as against others experimenting on them. No less vigorously must the critic object to the wearing of animal hides in coats and shoes, to employment in any industrial enterprise that uses animal parts, and to any commercial development that will cause death or distress to animals.

Killing animals to meet human needs for food, clothing, and shelter is judged entirely reasonable by most persons. The ubiquity†† of these uses and the virtual universality of moral support for them confront the opponent of research using animals with an inescapable difficulty. How can the many common uses of animals be judged morally worthy, while their use in scientific investigation is judged unworthy?

The number of animals used in research is but the tiniest fraction of the total used to satisfy assorted human appetites. That these appetites, often satisfiable in other ways, morally justify the far larger consumption of animals, whereas the quest for improved human health and understanding cannot justify the far smaller, is wholly implausible. . . .A given sheep is surely not more justifiably used to put lamb chops on the supermarket counter than to serve in testing a new contraceptive or a new prosthetic device. The needless

---

*profession: claim, declaration
† abattoir: slaughterhouse
†† ubiquity: existense everywhere

killing of animals is wrong; if the common killing of them for our food or convenience is right, the less common but more humane uses of animals in the service of medical science are certainly not less right. . . .

---

1. In the article "Bettering the Chimps' Lot," does Jane Goodall claim that animals should *not* be used for medical research?

2. Briefly summarize Goodall's positions.

3. In the article "The Case for the Use of Animals in Medical Research," how does the author support his claim that animals must be used for medical research?

WRITING ASSIGNMENT "Animal Rights and Wrongs"

Here is an additional opinion on the subject of animal rights by Peter Singer, an Australian who teaches philosophy. He is considered the founder of the "animal rights" movement, which dates from 1973 when Singer published "Animal Liberation," a part of which is reprinted here. Using the earlier readings as well (pp. 369–375), write a paper in which you develop your own viewpoint on this subject, giving at least two reasons to support your position. Be sure to discuss the other writers' conflicting opinions.

Animal Liberation

Man may always have killed other species for food, but he has never exploited them so ruthlessly as he does today. Farming has succumbed* to business methods, the objective being to get the highest possible ratio of output (meat, eggs, milk) to input (fodder, labor costs, etc.). Ruth Harrison's essay "On Factory Farming" gives an

---

*succumbed: given in

account of some aspects of modern methods, and of the unsuccessful British campaign for effective controls, . . . Among the proposals, which the government refused to implement on the grounds that they were too idealistic, were: *"Any animal should at least have room to turn around freely."*

Factory farm animals need liberation in the most literal sense. Veal calves are kept in stalls five feet by two feet. They are usually slaughtered when about four months old, and have been too big to turn in their stalls for at least a month. Intensive beef herds, kept in stalls only proportionately larger for much longer periods, account for a growing percentage of beef production. Sows are often similarly confined when pregnant, which, because of artificial methods of increasing fertility, can be most of the time. Animals confined in this way do not waste food by exercising, nor do they develop unpalatable muscle.

"A dry bedded area should be provided for all stock." Intensively kept animals usually have to stand and sleep on slatted floors without straw, because this makes cleaning easier.

"Palatable roughage must be readily available to all calves after one week of age." In order to produce the pale veal housewives are said to prefer, calves are fed on an all-liquid diet until slaughter, even though they are long past the age at which they would normally eat grass. They develop a craving for roughage, evidenced by attempts to gnaw wood from their stalls. (For the same reason, their diet is deficient in iron.)

"Battery cages for poultry should be large enough for a bird to be able to stretch one wing at a time." Under current British practice, a cage for four or five laying hens has a floor area of twenty inches by eighteen inches, scarcely larger than a double page of the *New York Review of Books*. In this space, on a sloping wire floor (sloping so the eggs roll down, wire so the dung drops through) the birds live for a year or eighteen months while artificial lighting and temperature conditions combine with drugs in their food to squeeze the maximum number of eggs out of them. Table birds are also sometimes kept in cages. More often they are reared in sheds, no less crowded. Under these conditions all the birds' natural activities are frustrated, and they develop "vices" such as pecking each other to death. To prevent this, beaks are often cut off, and the sheds kept dark.

How many of those who support factory farming by buying its produce know anything about the way it is produced? How many have heard something about it, but are reluctant to check up for fear

that it will make them uncomfortable? To non-speciesists,* the typical
consumer's mixture of ignorance, reluctance to find out the truth,
and vague belief that nothing really bad could be allowed seems anal-
ogous† to the attitudes of "decent Germans" to the death camps.

JOURNAL ASSIGNMENTS

1. Respond to this statement by animal rights activist Tom Regan: "It's not
   better cages we work for, but empty cages. We want every animal out."
2. What do you think are the arguments for and against being a *speciesist,*
   someone who believes humans should use other species for their own benefit?

CHECKING OUT

Check your understanding of Chapter 14 by writing out answers to the following
questions. You may work alone or with a friend, whichever you prefer.

1. Why should you explore several writers' conflicting opinions fully before
   making up your own mind on any issue?

2. What is an interpretation, and how does a writer use evidence and opinions to form his or her own interpretation?

3. What kinds of evidence are most reliable? Why should you acknowledge
   that some of your evidence is not conclusive or cannot be verified? Why
   are facts the most conclusive evidence?

---

*speciesist: one who believes humans should use other species for their benefit
†analogous: comparable to

4. Why is it useful to look for underlying patterns, such as patterns of behavior, revealed in the evidence of witnesses?

5. How can you check the reliability of witnesses?

6. How does a writer form a new synthesis based on the interpretations of several other writers?

IN SUMMARY

Using critical-thinking skills to develop a synthesis is a major part of writing a research paper (see Chapter 18). Your task is to weigh other writers' viewpoints, select all the important facts and evidence, and form your own opinion of the issue or situation. To do so, you would follow a procedure like the one Karen followed. You would

- explore the issue thoroughly by reading and research
- identify conflicting opinions surrounding the issue
- evaluate other writers' opinions
- establish key facts and evidence
- interpret the larger meaning of these facts and evidence, that is, what they all add up to as a whole
- develop your own synthesis, based on your own opinions and supported by your best evidence

Ask yourself key questions—for example, about the causes of problems (why did Marilyn Monroe have acute insomnia?) or about relationships (between insomnia, lateness, and drugs). Look for patterns (do witnesses agree that she was afraid of aging?). Using your answers to your own questions, make connections between the pieces of evidence and form your own opinion (fame is not enough when self-esteem is so badly damaged).

In this chapter, we have focused on the *critical thinking* needed to develop a synthesis—the major goal of a research paper. If you need help with the writing and the library skills required for a research paper, turn to Unit 5, "Writing Papers."

U N I T   5

WRITING PAPERS

Just as reading is a form of learning, writing is another powerful means for exploring a subject and coming to understand it thoroughly. By searching for ideas, by organizing those ideas, and by drafting and shaping them into written form, you wrestle with a subject at length and begin to see its larger meanings and deeper implications.

We want to give you some basic tools for tackling all forms of writing so that you will take a constructive and efficient approach to any writing task. We want you to think of writing as a skill every student—including you—can improve and even master over time. Writing skills will help you in your college career and may prove invaluable later in the work world. (Those employees who can write reports clearly explaining what they have accomplished on each of their projects are often highly useful to their employers.) Writing skills can also help you personally by allowing you to get to know yourself better over time as you record your opinions and reactions in your writing journal.

In Chapter 15, we discuss the recent research on how writers actually produce their writing, introducing many ideas that you can apply to your own writing. In Chapter 16, we discuss how to find ideas in the library and how to do library research. In Chapter 17, we introduce prewriting—that is, all the specific tasks that lead up to writing a first draft with efficiency. In Chapter 18, we show you how to draft and revise a paper, and then turn specifically to writing the research paper.

CHAPTER 15

HOW A WRITER WORKS

You're finding out what to say as well as how to say it, and that takes time.
—Philip Larkin

OVERVIEW

We want you to think of a writing assignment as an opportunity and a challenge, not as something to avoid or even dread. We will show you a step-by-step approach to writing assignments that will improve your performance. Even more, we want you to begin to enjoy writing—and even to think of yourself as a writer.

Beginning writers often have misconceptions about writing a paper. Some think that it should be done in a burst of inspiration, all in one sitting. The reality is that writing is done by trial and error. It is done by a slow process of discovering what you want to say and how you want to say it. And whenever possible, it should take place over several sessions, allowing you time to rethink your work after being away from it.

Many students find writing—one of the important ways students learn to think—too challenging and therefore put off tackling papers until the last possible minute when they do not have the time to develop their ideas fully or to revise their drafts over a few days or weeks. These same students find answering essay questions on exams difficult—the part of the exam that they find the hardest and often do most poorly on.

We want you to learn how to improve your writing, but more than that, we want you to master the process because writing will empower you: you will be able to communicate your views to others—to your teacher, your employer, your newspaper, your representatives in government—and thereby make your voice heard.

In this chapter, we give you some useful insights on how writers work; you will learn to

- Familiarize yourself with the overall writing process.
- Tackle each step in the right sequence.
- Concentrate hard and then allow ideas to incubate.
- Search for a topic that you believe in.
- Set specific goals for improving your own writing.
- Read many kinds of writers and writing.
- Find a writing model to guide your writing.
- Decide between using a formal or informal tone.

UNDERSTANDING THE WRITING PROCESS

In recent years many researchers have studied how writers—both student and professional—actually go about producing a finished piece of writing. They have found many clues about how writers think, how they handle the overall process, and how they cope with the uncertainties. You will probably find the results of this research, as explained here, helpful whenever you face a writing assignment.

First, it is useful to think of writing a paper as a process in which you start with uncertainty about what you want to write and gradually move toward certainty. You slowly move toward a finished paper in which you have discovered what you wanted to write. It is this **process of discovery** that makes writing a satisfying experience: you often discover something that you were not previously aware of by the very act of searching hard for words to express exactly what you mean.

The process consists of roughly four phases, and you should limit yourself to specific tasks at each phase, although you may also have to repeat certain tasks more than once:

1. The **prewriting** phase* in which you
   —search for your best ideas by using a discovery technique
   —then evaluate your ideas, discarding the weakest
   —search for a focused topic that interests you

---

*See Chapter 17 for a full discussion of prewriting.

—look for a tentative main idea or *thesis statement*

—begin to organize your best ideas into a rough or scratch outline

2. The **drafting** stage* in which you

—write out a complete first draft of the final paper

—revise or refine your thesis statement

—tighten your outline

—think in terms of constructing unified paragraphs

3. The two-step **revising** stage in which you

—first, concentrate on the larger issues of reworking the overall ideas and the organization of the ideas thoroughly, until you are satisfied

—second, check each sentence closely for correct sentence structure, grammar, punctuation, and spelling

4. The final **proofreading** stage in which you

—type (or neatly write) a final draft

—proofread word for word and correct spelling, punctuation, and any typos in the final draft

Through all these stages, be sure to incorporate any new ideas—as they come to you—that will strengthen your paper. In this way you will take advantage of the emerging insights that occur to you in the process of thinking and writing about the subject. This is what we mean by discovery: you will find out more clearly just what you want to say as you continue to work out the paper. Take advantage of these stronger new ideas even when it means backtracking or reworking sections.

Even experienced writers change their minds as they move through the writing process—after they have begun to focus sharply on their ideas—and they may come to a wholly new conclusion. Writing will force you to think sharply on a subject, and often you may find yourself revising your thinking.

Once you have completed a first draft, you may find that you now understand much more clearly what you want to say, and in some cases you may decide to scrap your first draft and start again. But you have learned a great deal from your first discarded draft, and so it is by no means wasted effort.

> You often discover something that you were not previously aware of by the very act of searching for words to express exactly what you mean.

*See Chapter 18 for a full discussion of drafting, revising, and proofreading.

E. B. White, noted for his flawless prose style, struggled with the rough drafts of his essays.

■   PRACTICE 1   Compare nature writer Annie Dillard's description of her writing process with the process we have outlined above. What are the similarities? What does she suggest about outlining, about a main idea or a thesis statement, about revising?

> It doesn't hurt much to babble in a first draft, so long as you have the sense to cut out irrelevancies* later. If you are used to analyzing texts, you will be able to formulate a clear statement of what your draft turned out to be about. Then you make a list of what you've already written, paragraph by paragraph, and see what doesn't fit and cut it out. (All this requires is nerves of steel and lots of coffee.) Most of the time you'll have to add to the begin-

---

*irrelevancies: unrelated material

ning, ensuring that it gives a fair idea of what the point might be, or at least what is about to happen. (Suspense is for mystery writers. The most inept writing has an inadvertent* element of suspense: the reader constantly asks himself, where on earth is this going?) Usually I end up throwing away the beginning: the first part of a poem, the first few pages of an essay, the first scene of a story, even the first few chapters of a book. It's not holy writ. The paragraphs and sentences are tesserae—tiles for a mosaic. Just because you have a bunch of tiles in your lap doesn't mean your mosaic will be better if you use them all.

BEGINNING THE PROCESS: TACKLE EACH STEP IN THE RIGHT SEQUENCE

At the beginning of any writing assignment, everyone feels some mild anxiety, some doubts. Will I finish in time? Will I find anything to say? How can I fill three to five pages if I have nothing to say?

These are common worries that even professionals feel because every writing task requires the writer to start back at the beginning, going through all the phases of the process and hoping to finish with a good paper of the right length in the time allowed. The only way to defeat those nagging doubts is to take positive action and calm them by *beginning*—by starting the first exploratory steps of the process.

What are the first things you should think about? As soon as you hear about a paper, start to play around with possible topics and possible ideas—even at odd moments when, say, you're taking a shower. Search for strong ideas and for a topic that you care about early—while you have time available to do these tasks justice. (We will give you many specific suggestions for discovering ideas and topics in Chapter 17.)

As soon as you know when the paper is due, by all means make a rough

---

*inadvertent: unintended

schedule, allowing about equal time for each major phase of the writing process (prewriting, drafting, revising, proofreading). And build in some extra time at the end of the schedule in case you hit unexpected snags. Remember to use the divide-and-conquer approach described in Chapter 2 where you learned how to break a large task into a series of smaller subtasks—so that you are not overwhelmed by the whole project at once.

Plan to deal with one—and only one—step at a time. This is crucial. For example, when you are first looking for ideas, you want to put down every idea you can possibly think of on your scratch pad. And you also want to dismiss from your mind any thoughts about how to evaluate or how to organize these ideas because evaluating and organizing are *separate and later steps* (see brainstorming p. 439). And it is far simpler and more effective to concentrate on each step in turn.

As you go through the writing process for an assignment, use our model as a rough and flexible guide. The most important thing about the model is the general direction you should follow: always confront larger issues before you worry about smaller refinements. Do not try to be a perfectionist in the early stages when you are roughing out your paper. It is time-consuming to perfect a first sentence or paragraph that you may later decide is not exactly what you want to say. Keep in mind that your first steps must be rough and approximate and that you will reach a smoother and more polished version as you continue.

The writing process we have outlined encourages you to follow the basic steps in an efficient and productive order. Stopping to check a grammar rule in a sentence that eventually will be cut is obviously inefficient. In fact, all rules of grammar, punctuation, and usage should be put out of your mind until a late stage of revision. At that point you should check whether you have used troublesome words correctly and punctuated clearly (such as the usual problems everyone has with ''effect'' or ''affect'' or with apostrophes). Toward the end of the writing process you can—and should—check the spelling of any word you are doubtful about.

LET IDEAS INCUBATE

After you have concentrated hard on any major phase of the writing process, it always helps to put your papers aside and **allow your ideas to incubate.** Studies have shown that the unconscious mind works over the ideas that your conscious mind has stored away. This incubation period allows your thinking to clarify so that when you return to your ideas and reread them in a few hours—or even better in a few days—you see more clearly just how to handle them. This fresh reading is considered indispensable by experienced writers.

Creative people deliberately take advantage of this phenomenon by intensively studying a problem and then putting it aside to incubate while they turn to other matters. When they return to the problem, they find they have many fresh new insights and can solve what they did not know how to solve before. Especially after completing the first rough draft, try this incubation technique. Build it into your schedule.

As you reread your first draft, you may suddenly see new relationships, think of new evidence, or come up with new and better examples that support your main point (or thesis) more convincingly. For example, you may want to establish that it is a myth that Emily Dickinson never wanted to get her works published. After letting your ideas incubate, you think of some persuasive evidence: until she was thirty-two, Emily Dickinson did try very hard to get her poems published; she contacted two editors repeatedly, sending them many of her poems. It was only after neither editor encouraged her that she gave up trying to publish for good.

Incubation is especially helpful in enabling you to switch roles and become a more objective *reader* of your draft. After being away from your paper, you will be able to tell if you have provided your actual reader with enough information to follow your ideas easily. Will your reader be able to figure out what you as the writer intended, or do you need to clear up some possible confusion? You can then revise your draft, keeping the reader's needs in mind.

We have all had the experience as readers of not understanding what a writer was trying to explain. As a writer you want to foresee your reader's possible problems in making sense of your prose. According to one estimate by Strunk and White, authors of a highly popular book on writing, *The Elements of Style,* "readers are in trouble about half the time."

If you find yourself bogged down writing one particular section, let it incubate while you continue with other tasks. Many writers make the mistake of getting bogged down rewriting certain problem sections and running out of time (and steam) for developing the overall piece. Force yourself to move around any roadblock and come back to it later. And when you do come back, chances are that you will see a clever way to handle the problem passage.

Incubation is helpful in enabling you to switch roles from writer to reader and allows you to become a more objective reader of your draft.

■   PRACTICE 2   Find several old pieces of your writing from other classes or use old entries from your learning journal, introduced in Chapter 1. Reread them. Do you understand what you meant? Can you find a way of making the unclear parts clearer? What do you like about these samples of your writing? What would you like to improve?

FINDING A TOPIC THAT YOU CARE ABOUT

Your paper will only be as good as the quality and freshness of the ideas you incorporate into it. You may write correct sentences entirely free of grammar and punctuation problems, but if your ideas are too bland or too familiar, and if you have nothing to offer of your own views, no one will read your paper with much interest or enjoyment.

How can you tell if your ideas are of interest to anyone else? In general, **assume that if the ideas you have found interest and excite you, they will interest and excite your reader.** Your reader will sense your involvement and be carried along by it.

But this search for strong ideas and a specific topic takes some doing, and producing a good paper usually takes a determined effort, even for experienced, gifted writers. Noted for his flawless prose style, E. B. White produced essays that sound as if the sharp, witty ideas came to him without too much struggle. But the truth was, as he wrote his editor, that such writing did not come to him easily, and each piece required an intense, lengthy, all-out effort on his part—so much so that he resigned from writing his regular magazine column several times. He achieved the effect of an easy flow of words only in the final version, where all the earlier struggles and indecision go undetected by the reader.

Even when you are assigned a specific topic, you should look for a perspective that you personally care about. Generally, as you probe your own thinking on the assigned topic and get more into it, you will find some slice of it that you can handle with genuine interest. You will be able to put some of yourself into what you write. What is truly needed is that you care about what you are saying. There is no substitute for your honest involvement with the topic.

If you are unsure about a possible topic, explore its possibilities without committing yourself. If you are thinking about a paper on the future use of nuclear power, ask yourself what you personally think about it. For example, how close to population centers do *you* think nuclear plants should be located? How close to your home would you like a nuclear power plant? What are the dangers of a radiation leak, of a meltdown? Should you look into how to conserve energy in order to build fewer nuclear power plants?

Should you discuss nuclear accidents like Chernobyl?

Consider carefully which aspects of the topic interests you the most and also which aspect will enable you to find supporting facts and evidence conveniently. You might, for example, see how much you can find out about Chernobyl in the library. If material is available and if you decide this is an important issue for you to know more about, you can choose it for your paper.

Do's and Don'ts

Don't tell yourself you're not a born writer. Decide you can write and will improve with practice.

Don't think you will improve your writing unless you practice.

Don't think writing is done in a burst of inspiration; it is a trial-and-error process, with much backtracking and many dead ends.

Don't bog down on the introduction; try writing it at the end when you know better what you're introducing.

Don't obsess over grammar, sentence structure, word meaning.

Don't repeat a mistake in paper after paper. Conquer it.

Do read widely—sports pages, novels, poems—to study how all kinds of writers write.

Do let ideas incubate. Put a draft aside and go back to it later for a fresh reading.

Do find a topic that interests, even excites you—one that you want to learn about or want to tell your reader about.

Do switch roles and become the *reader* of your writing.

Do identify writers that you admire and use their work as models for your own writing.

Do take the steps of the writing process in the right sequence, concentrating on larger issues first.

If you have only a weak interest in a topic—or if you have no topic at all—look through your lecture notes for other possible ideas; do library research (see Chapter 16); ask your instructor for suggested readings. Look for a controversy that is unresolved; look for a popular belief or myth that is debatable.

Spend a reasonable amount of time looking for a strong topic; if you are still stuck, then you must make an effort to like the topic you settle for. It is only when you know nothing about a subject that you feel detached from it and uninterested. Once you get more deeply into a topic, you often will feel your interest building.

> Everyone has strong interests and passions. Good writers turn their deepest interests into good writing topics.

■ PRACTICE 3   Compile a list of topics, general or specific, that you care about most—things that interest you personally; things in the world that you would like to see changed; or problems at home, school, or work that you would like to do something about.

SETTING PERSONAL GOALS FOR IMPROVING YOUR WRITING

Although your teachers will gladly give you many profitable words of advice, in the last analysis you will have much of the responsibility for teaching yourself how to write better. We would like to suggest five useful devices for helping you improve your writing skills. These suggestions will allow you to work on your writing skills in association with your other courses.

1. Find a model for your writing.
Look for a well-known writer whose work you find clear, direct, persuasive, skillful—or some other quality you admire. Professional writers often mention that they discovered a writer, when they first started out, whose work they admired and used as a model for their own writing. The English poet Philip Larkin pointed to Irish poet William Butler Yeats as the first writer he consciously tried to use as a model, and later he began to admire the more rugged verse of Thomas Hardy. Look in your texts or reading anthologies for what you consider clear and effective writing. Study the essays of Joan Didion, E. B. White, John McPhee, Russell Baker; ask your instructor for other essayists whose works you might use as models.

After you read a paragraph that you think is well written, try to analyze it in two stages: first, read it for its ideas, and then read it again carefully sentence by sentence to analyze how the writer constructs the sentences and links them together.

In the following paragraph, the author has a very simple goal. He wants to tell you about the place where he was born, Arequipa, and about the strange fits that periodically strike its inhabitants. Read the paragraph and then read our analysis of the second stage—the author's choice of sentences.

> Arequipa, the city where I was born, is in an Andean village in the south of Peru. It is famous for its clerical and rebellious spirit, its jurists, its volcanoes, the clarity of its sky, the fine flavor of its shrimp, its regionalism. It is known as well for *la nevada* (the snow-fall), a kind of transitory* madness that suddenly turns the mildest of Arequipans into a belligerent† and obnoxious person. No one is surprised, no one is angry; everyone knows that soon the victim of *la nevada* will be his usual benign†† and affable self again.
> —Mario Vargas Llosa, "A Passion for Peru"

The beginning sentence tells very simply where the author was born. One phrase, set off by commas ("the city where I was born"), interrupts the otherwise straightforward first sentence. Sentence 2 becomes a long list: "It is famous for its . . . " But notice how carefully the writer has chosen the specific and unusual examples in his list: rebellious spirit, volcanoes, sky, shrimp, and local ways.

Then notice how he links sentence 3 to the one before it by the simple phrase "as well" when he says "It is known as well for . . . " At this point the author gives his best example: he describes in his last two sentences how a sudden craziness affects most people of the city, but they return to their ordinary kind and harmless selves in short order.

Now, of course, this writer is a great writer, but he uses very simple means. And if you are committed to improving your writing, you will consciously note some of his writing devices, and put them into your own bag of writing tricks.

If you do this sort of rough analysis of passages, in time you will have a wide variety of choices available to express your ideas.

2. Practice your writing.
Just like learning any other skill, you will learn to write by practicing writing—daily if possible. If you avoid the task, you probably will never make much progress. But if you write at least one paragraph every day, either as part of a course assignment or as a journal entry, you will gradually learn how to control words and sentences and make them mean what you want them to mean.

The first step is to begin, and as usual, we suggest you begin with a small

---

*transitory: temporary
†belligerent: hostile
††benign: gentle

Just as a dancer attains her goals through hours of practice, your goals as a writer can be achieved through practicing your writing skills.

task: start by writing individual paragraphs until you are comfortable and confident that you can handle a paragraph. If you have no immediate subject for your journal, write about one thing that happened to you yesterday.

The paragraph is the key building block of all forms of writing. A paragraph should begin with a sentence either giving the main idea of the paragraph (called the *topic sentence*) or making a transition between two paragraphs. The paragraph itself should generally discuss one and only one subject—the one you mentioned in the topic sentence. A shift to a new paragraph gives the reader a cue that you are taking up a whole new topic. Professional writers, you will notice, often construct paragraphs with more freedom, but they are able to maintain control. Beginning writers should, as a rule, start with a topic sentence and provide support for it in the rest of the paragraph.

3. Identify your own weaknesses as a writer and work on them.
Most students have more problems with one part of the writing process than with another. Some students have trouble with finding "good" ideas, that is, ideas that satisfy them; other students like their ideas but have problems with casting those ideas into sentences; some students have few problems until the final revising stage where they are shaky about punctuation and spelling. Students with several weaknesses should start with their most seri-

ous mistakes or with the mistakes they make most often and tackle them one by one.

You will probably notice some patterns emerging from the written comments of your teachers. If you see a consistent pattern—one particular area where you run into trouble—speak to your teacher about ways to attack the problem head-on. You may be surprised at how some direct attention to the problem will help.

For instance, you may know your weakness is sentence structure. You are not always sure of what is a complete sentence and what is only a fragment. Many English handbooks will help you identify the three characteristics of a sentence: it has a subject, a verb, and expresses a complete thought. "Bob empties," for example, has a subject and a verb, but it is clearly not a complete thought. Bob empties what?

Now consider "Bob empties the candy dish." Here we have a complete sentence because all three conditions of a sentence are satisfied. (Work exercises on sentence structure until you are absolutely sure you know what a sentence is. If you do so, you will also learn to avoid making two other common sentence errors—comma splices and run-on sentences.)

Say you still have trouble identifying a complete sentence because you cannot always identify the verb within a sentence. Again consult grammar books to help you identify verb forms, and be sure to work the exercises. There is nothing that needs to remain a mystery to you. Ask your teacher where to locate workbooks and additional exercises. Focus your efforts on your own particular problems.

Or say you personally have trouble inventing interesting sentences: your sentences all sound too simple and too similar. Consult texts on sentence combining and sentence style, such as *Style* by Joseph Williams. These books will give you various patterns for constructing sentences in optional ways. Like most writers, you may often be looking for a sentence that will connect your new idea to the previous sentence. If you are familiar with various sentence-combining options, you will be able to pick your best option and make clear connections between your ideas.

4. Read, read, read.

Nothing will help you with your writing as much as reading widely. Detective books, magazines, novels, poetry—any and all forms of written language can help you. Good writers spend much time reading other writers looking for ways to improve their craft. You can best learn how to put sentences and paragraphs together from studying the works of writers who have mastered the skill. If some writer uses an unfamiliar word that catches your attention, try to use it yourself. (Be sure you understand its meaning and correct usage; if you have any doubts, ask a teacher if you are using it correctly.)

5. Establish a set of goals for improving your writing.

For your first goal, say you decide to concentrate on writing simply and clearly. This is not too different from explaining your ideas to a friend in a conversation. One difference is that you cannot backtrack: "I meant to tell you that . . . " won't work in writing; on paper you can only go forward. You have to explain in a clear order what you have in mind.

Just as you are able to explain what you mean to a friend in a conversation, you can teach yourself to write what you mean on paper. You will use the very same language, but you will use it more deliberately, selecting your words with more care.

■   PRACTICE 4   Write a paragraph on how you get up in the morning or how you go to bed at night. Describe the routine or ritual you follow. List the events in roughly the order you do them (in chronological order).

After letting it incubate, read your paragraph again pretending you are the reader and have never read it before. Make sure your eventual reader can clearly visualize the process. Rework the paragraph until you are satisfied with it.

■   PRACTICE 5   Write a paragraph modeling it on the paragraph by Mario Vargas Llosa on page 393. Discuss the place where you were born, some of the characteristics of the people in it, and one particular example that is very special about the place.

A FORMAL OR INFORMAL PAPER: CHOOSING A VOICE AND A TONE

As you read and analyze various types of writing, notice variations in style among writers. Some use a minimal amount of simple language to do the job; others revel in more complex and elaborate language. Style is an area where you can decide what is appropriate and what kind of language you need for the writing task at hand.

We use the word *style* here to mean all the gradations from formal academic writing to informal personal writing. You can usually distinguish easily between the two extremes. **Academic writing** often uses more complicated sentence construction and at times a vocabulary found only in written prose. **Personal writing** is much more informal, uses simpler sentences, and allows expressions used mainly in spoken conversation.

Here is an example of the more formal style:

In developing nations, participation by local farmers in irrigation projects has increased crop productivity.

The writer attempts to be deliberately impersonal, neutral, and objective. This style is traditionally used in most academic writing.

On the opposite side of the spectrum is the informal and conversational style, fine for personal essays and letters, but inappropriate for professional or scientific writing. If someone were planning to submit the following example to a serious scientific journal, it should be rewritten to achieve a more formal and less casual style.

> To do this really terrible project, the lab technicians had to search for blood samples in this huge freezer, a pretty painful way of spending the afternoon, and most of them could last for only a few minutes.

In this example, the writer has used the informal phrases ''really terrible'' and ''pretty painful.'' In informal writing the writer can inject personal opinions and reactions, but someone writing a formal report would try to eliminate such phrases. (These phrases are also vague in meaning instead of being precise. A careful writer should choose more exact language.) This sentence might be rewritten:

> To complete this difficult project, the lab technicians searched for blood samples in a large freezer, but finding the freezing temperatures painful after only a few minutes, most of them were forced to take frequent breaks.

In formal writing, avoid any current or slang expressions, such as ''I was blown away by what he said.'' On the other hand, you do not want to use inflated language, picking words that make your readers think you are trying to impress them with your knowledge. As you read various types of writing, you will notice great variations in style among writers. Try to find a writing style that reflects you and your own inner voice. It is wise to be neither too flip nor too formal.

As a writer you can also choose whether to write in the **first person** (using *I, me, we, us*):

> I performed an experiment that showed . . .

or in the **third person** (using *she, he, it, they, the study*):

> This study showed . . .

In the past, all scientific papers were written only in the third person (and ''I'' was never used). Recently more writers have begun to use ''I'' as a pronoun in serious writing than previously—a sign that more informality is gradually coming into the language.

As a rule of thumb, for personal essays (in which you describe your own ideas and reactions), the first person is usually appropriate. However, in research reports and other formal papers, keep yourself in the background and write in the third person. In certain assignments, your teacher may want you to write in the third person, using expressions like "The experiment revealed that the oxygen was removed." If in doubt, clarify the matter with your instructor.

Similar guidelines apply to *tone*. Avoid being sarcastic or ironic in your papers—or humorous in a serious piece. Avoid as well being too emotional or dramatic. Generally a calm neutral tone is the one you should adopt unless you know your teacher wants something special or different.

Avoid whenever possible common clichés like "too hot to handle" or "better late than never." Before you resort to a cliché, see if you can discover some more inventive language.

■ PRACTICE 6   In the following sentences, decide if you would classify the style as *informal* or *formal* and give reasons. Underline the expressions that are informal.

1. He wasn't being careful and dropped the contents of the beaker all over the place, and needless to say, made a sort of large mess and an explosion that brought the fire department. That's the truth.

2. Nixon must have really been feeling the heat, especially when some guy found the tape that caught Nixon saying things that he admitted "were at variance with the truth" or some such ridiculous expression.

3. Nixon won election to his second term with a commanding victory, but the man's character and his lack of self-confidence had involved him in some questionable and illegal election activities that culminated in his resignation from the presidency.

4. So the man had his good points and his bad points, to put it in simple black-and-white terms. Just think what Nixon did in China; foreign policy was his bag. But basically, when all is said and done, the man was a loser.

5. In geological terms, human beings have been in residence on this earth for a relatively short term.

WORKING SPACE

READING ASSIGNMENT

Find passages of three different writers whose work you admire. First, read to understand their ideas, and then reread to analyze their sentence and paragraph construction. For example, do they use short simple sentences or long complex ones? What punctuation do they use? What word choices do you think are most effective? Do you like one writer better than the others? Is there anything they do that you might want to adapt for your own writing?

WRITING ASSIGNMENT: "Writer's Questionnaire"

Identify and discuss which of the following statements describe your problems as a writer:

1. My problem is with finding ideas; I can't think of anything I want to write about.

   _____

   _____

   _____

2. I have plenty of ideas. I am brimming with things I want to say. But when it comes to putting my ideas into words, sentences, or paragraphs, I can't do it. Many sentences don't quite say what I want to say and they don't satisfy me.

   _____

   _____

   _____

3. My biggest problem is with the basics of spelling and punctuation. Sometimes I don't know whether I've written a correct sentence or not. All the comments on my papers mention these basics. My ideas are lost in the shuffle.

_____

_____

_____

4. My problem is time. I never leave enough time to do the writing project. I can never get concerned until the pressure is on, and then I have no time to do it right.

_____

_____

_____

5. My problem is I feel very uncomfortable when I have to write. It isn't something I do very naturally. It's a strain.

_____

_____

_____

6. My sentences sound too simple, like a beginner; I hate to read my own papers.

_____

_____

_____

7. I think some people have more ability at writing than others. I have a friend who can dash off a decent essay quickly. To write even a bad essay takes me hours and hours.

_____

_____

_____

8. I'm a perfectionist. I write one sentence, erase it, rewrite it, and never get the first paragraph right.

_____

_____

_____

Drawing by W. Steig; © 1987.
The New Yorker Magazine, Inc.

JOURNAL ASSIGNMENTS

1. To practice your writing, either write a description of the cartoon on p. 401, explaining what you think it means, who is in it, and whether you like it or not, or ask several people what they think it means and write about their reactions.

2. Write a response in your journal to the following passage by the writer William Stafford. What does he mean when he says "Writing is one of the great, free human activities"? What are some other "great, free human activities?"

    Writing is one of the great, free human activities. There is scope for individuality, and elation, and discovery, in writing. For the person who follows with trust and forgiveness what occurs to him, the world remains always ready and deep, an inexhaustible environment.

CHECKING OUT

Check your understanding of Chapter 15 by writing out answers to the following questions. You may work alone or with a classmate, whichever you prefer.

1. Briefly describe the four phases of the writing process and the tasks that should be completed by the end of each.

2. Why is it efficient to take the steps of the writing process in order?

3. Explain why writing is more trial and error than a burst of inspiration.

4. What can you learn about writing from analyzing the works of other writers?

5. What is informal writing and when is it appropriate?

6. Why is it useful to target your own writing problems?

IN SUMMARY

You can learn to improve your writing if you practice regularly, preferably by writing a small amount each day and by asking your teachers for help with any part of the writing process you don't understand. As we suggested in Chapter 1, keeping a journal—on your studying strategies, on your social activities, on reactions to your reading—encourages this writing habit. At first try to write only one paragraph a day. You will soon begin to feel comfortable when you face a blank page, confident that you can explain your ideas clearly to a reader.

If you familiarize yourself with the sequence of the writing process—prewriting, drafting, revising, and proofing—and with the tasks you should concentrate on in each phase, you will learn an efficient method for tackling any writing task. You can then concentrate on larger issues, like finding your strongest ideas, and postpone polishing and fussing over smaller matters until later in the process. We do not mean that spelling and punctuation errors are not important; we mean that they should be taken up at the right time.

In addition to practicing writing daily, you should read widely—all kinds of papers, magazines, books—and pick several writers who you think write with imagination and skill. Take one of these writers as a model for your own writing and study how he or she puts sentences and paragraphs together. Experienced writers have learned to write in large part by studying how other writers write.

We continue our discussion of writing in Chapter 17, on prewriting and discovering ideas, and in Chapter 18, on drafting and revising. In the next chapter (Chapter 16), we take up how to use the library for researching ideas for your writing.

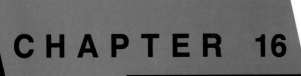

CHAPTER 16

USING THE LIBRARY

The library is a school and the librarian is in the highest sense a teacher, and a reader is a workman among his tools.

—Melville Dewey

OVERVIEW

If you are asked to write an *informal personal essay,* you can make use of your own experiences, memories, and knowledge of the world. If, however, you are asked to write a *formal research paper,* dealing with what is currently known about a specific subject, you need to look for broader sources of information. You must begin to explore what scholars and experts in the field have written on this specific area.

The rich sources of a library will give you great quantities of new information about a given topic and will help you expand your own ideas and opinions about it. To locate useful sources of information—books, journals, newspapers, microforms—you have to become familiar with your college library.

In reality, most students find that their first research paper prods them into becoming familiar with the library. In this chapter, we will show you how to use the resources of the library to gather material for a research paper:

- Find out what sources are available in your library.
- Plan a strategy for doing library research.

- Carry out research in card catalogs, by computer search, or with hardbound indexes.
- Write bibliography cards to keep track of sources.
- Take appropriate notes on note cards (or photocopy your sources).

For any subject that you want to delve into more deeply, the library is at your disposal.

FAMILIARIZE YOURSELF WITH THE LIBRARY

The library obviously gives a reader access to many more ideas than the relatively limited knowledge already stored in one person's mind. It can provide ideas on every conceivable subject, including in-depth, detailed studies for the specialist and broad overviews of a topic for the non-specialist or the general reader.

Libraries keep their collections as up-to-date as possible and purchase new texts, journals, and *microforms* (miniaturized print) that will be useful to their specific readers. Many libraries are also connected by computer to a network of other libraries for *interlibrary* loans, providing their readers access to many additional publications.

On a study break, wander around the library and familiarize yourself with its floor plan and its resources. With the ongoing revolution in library services, it probably contains media, microforms, and computer equipment that you are not aware of; it also contains many additional holdings not in plain view—backstage in what are called ''the stacks,'' where rarer and little-used publications are kept.

On your exploratory tour, find out where the library keeps its main collections—the actual books and magazines as well as the card catalogs, computers, and hardbound indexes that will help you locate these books and magazines. While a casual tour will give you a start, many libraries schedule frequent training sessions on the services available. Such an orientation is invaluable; it will save you time in the long run.

Most of all, learn to **call on reference librarians for assistance;** their primary job is to help readers find the information they are looking for. Particularly with the new technology and the various computer searches, a librarian can often save you time by pointing out the right software or terminal, by showing you how to operate the microform equipment, or by helping you find the key words to research your topic. They have expert knowledge that they are happy to pass on.

By its very nature, research can be very time-consuming: you can come to frustrating dead ends, such as discovering the key book you need is missing.

So it is wise to save time whenever possible by asking librarians for advice. They might be able to rescue you by calling other libraries or by recalling a book out on loan.

> The primary job of reference librarians is to help readers find the information they are looking for.

LEARN THE TECHNIQUES OF A RESEARCHER

Before you begin a research paper, it is helpful to get some simple equipment that will make the task easier. Buy note cards (or small pads of paper) for several purposes:

1. You will need some note cards to keep track of all the authors and titles of the books and articles you find on your subject as you do your research. These cards will eventually be used to compile your **bibliography** or list of works used in your research. Use small-size index cards (3 x 5 inches) for listing the authors and titles of the works you discover. These are known as your **bibliographic cards.** (See pp. 409–410 for the specific information you should record on each card.)

2. Get yourself some **larger note cards for taking notes** as you read the various books and articles on your topic. Some students prefer the lined cards (4 x 6) for notes; other students prefer the larger unlined cards (5 x 7) to take longer notes. (Some people use small blocks of unlined paper because they are less bulky than cards.) Use what works for you.

Resist the temptation to fill each card with writing. **Put only one piece of information on a card** so that you can sort and organize the cards into groups later. By taking individual notes on small cards (rather than running them together on large notebook sheets), you can shuffle the cards around easily and organize them by subject; with this method you can later outline and write a draft very efficiently.

Some people like to use colored cards to distinguish various subtopics; you might, for example, use blue cards for taking notes on writers who favor restoring prayers in public schools and yellow cards for those opposed to prayers. Whatever system you use, make it convenient and not too complicated.

Hold your two piles of cards (the bibliography cards and the notes on your reading) together with elastics. Some students like to buy an accordion-like folder for their notes so that they can file different topics in separate compartments.

3. In the upper-right corner of a card, **always identify the source from which you have taken a note** by the author's last name—and by one word of the title if you are using two works by the same author. (Some people put a number on each of their bibliographic cards and then identify each note card from that source by giving it the same number.)

4. After you take your notes, **give each note card a short heading** or title in the left corner that will remind you of what information is on the card and thereby help in your ongoing sorting and sifting of material.

5. As you collect and read your sources over a few weeks, it is definitely a good habit to **keep reading and sorting the cards by headings** and to keep related ideas together by clips or elastics. Sorting and resorting will help you clarify the direction of your research. Your note cards will help you read and organize as an ongoing orderly process.

> **Put only one piece of information on a card so that you can sort and organize the cards into groups later.**

PRACTICE 1   List the main benefits of using note cards. List the problems with other methods, such as relying on memory or keeping ongoing notes in a notebook.

BUILDING YOUR WORKING BIBLIOGRAPHY

Let's assume you have a tentative and fairly focused subject, a subject that you're interested in learning more about. (If you need some help with finding and narrowing a subject, see pages 437–439.) To begin to gather library sources on your tentative subject, you need to **act like a detective and follow leads.** Here are some ways to begin:

- Ask your instructor for a few key authors or titles that can get you started.

- Speak to a person knowledgeable on the subject—anyone who knows the subject well—for some leads.

- Speak to a librarian, describing your subject and asking advice on a good search strategy—whether to search by computer, by traditional card catalog, by the major hardbound indexes of journals—or by all of them. Be sure to have some specific questions for the librarian.

- Start by looking for a few books to start you off, searching in the card catalog or by a computer search, looking under **author** (if you know names), **title,** or **subject.** (See page 415 for how a student started her research by looking up "utopia" under subject in a computer search.)
- Check *Readers' Guide to Periodical Literature,* which indexes articles in about 180 well-known magazines (by year). It is also useful to search in it for subjects, listed alphabetically, such as "adoption."
- Check the hardbound indexes to scholarly journals in various academic fields (as described on pages 418–420). Every academic field has a major index that the librarian can guide you to.
- In every source you locate on your subject, search its footnotes or bibliography for other related books or articles.
- Use an encyclopedia, like the *Encyclopaedia Britannica,* for an overview of your subject and for bibliography.
- Use reading lists or "suggested readings" supplied by your instructor for the course.

We suggest that you **search in stages.** As you begin to learn more about your topic, you will have a clearer understanding of which sources are worthwhile. And it is probably more efficient to do a thorough search after you have completed some preliminary reading. For a start, find a few reasonably helpful sources and begin to read about your topic. Although this means several library trips, it is probably a time-saving device in the long run.

PREPARING YOUR BIBLIOGRAPHY CARDS

To keep track of your sources, you will need to **write a bibliographic card for each source** that you plan to read. Remember to

- Record only one source per card.
- Be sure to distinguish between books and articles and take down the correct information for each (usually found on the copyright or title page).
- Even if you photocopy an article, make a bibliography card because the interior pages of the article will not have the full information you need later for your own bibliography list (called the "Works Cited" page).

- Always take cards to the library to help you keep track of your sources.
- Always jot down a call number in case you need the book again.

Record the following information for books:
1. author's *full* name (or authors if there are two or three; if four or more authors, list only the first author and add "and others" or "et al.")
2. complete title, *underlined*
3. city of publication (add the state if the city is not well known—such as "Englewood Cliffs, N.J.")
4. publisher (usually the short form of the name—Knopf rather than Alfred A. Knopf, or Princeton UP for Princeton University Press)
5. year published

Record the following information for popular magazines and scholarly journals:
1. author's full name (as for books)
2. full title of article; use *quotation marks*
3. name of journal or magazine, *underlined*
4. volume number plus issue number (or month or season if no issue number is given)
5. year published
6. complete pages on which the article is found: 14–19

Note: You do not need city or publisher for articles; you do need volume and issue numbers.

Record the following information for newspaper articles:
1. author's full name
2. full title of article; use *quotation marks*
3. name of newspaper, *underlined*
4. full date (day, month, year)
5. page or pages on which the article is found

See Figure 16–1 for some sample bibliographic cards a student wrote out to record the correct bibliographical information on a book, a scholarly journal, a popular magazine, and a newspaper.

For any miscellaneous publications that you use in your research, collect information—particularly the date and the place published—that a reader would need in order to locate the source.

See pages 475–480 for instructions on how to cite your sources in your paper. There we describe the Modern Language Association (MLA) parenthetical style of documentation, which calls for brief references in the text and full information about sources on your Works Cited page.

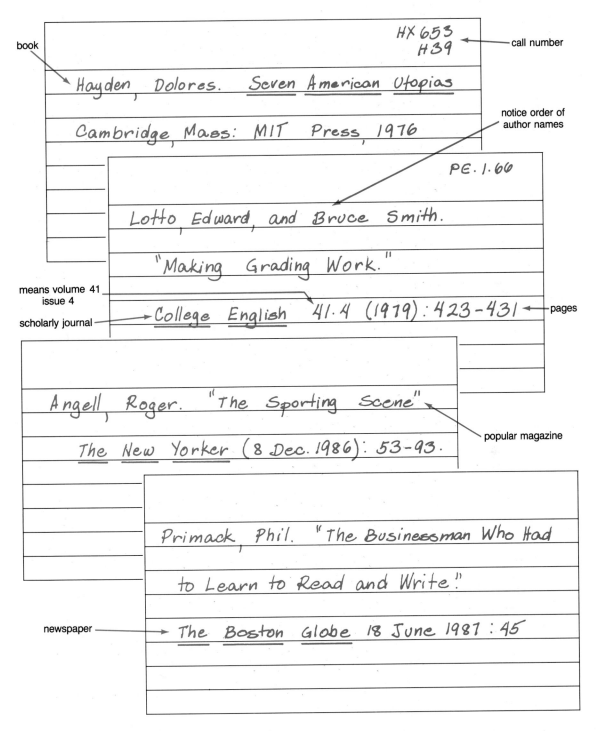

book

call number

HX 653
H 39

Hayden, Dolores.   Seven American Utopias

Cambridge, Mass: MIT Press, 1976

notice order of
author names

PE. 1·66

Lotto, Edward, and Bruce Smith.

"Making Grading Work."

means volume 41
issue 4

scholarly journal

College English   41·4 (1979): 423-431

pages

Angell, Roger.   "The Sporting Scene"

The New Yorker (8 Dec. 1986): 53-93.

popular magazine

Primack, Phil.   "The Businessman Who Had

to Learn to Read and Write."

newspaper

The Boston Globe 18 June 1987 : 45

Figure 16-1 Bibliographic Cards to Track Sources

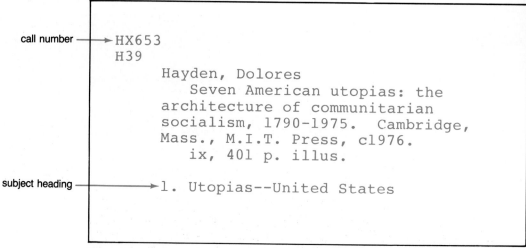

call number → HX653
H39
     Hayden, Dolores
       Seven American utopias: the
architecture of communitarian
socialism, 1790-1975. Cambridge,
Mass., M.I.T. Press, c1976.
      ix, 401 p. illus.

subject heading → 1. Utopias--United States

Figure 16–1 continued: Compare the bibliographic card (p. 411 top) to this card from the card catalog.

SEARCHING FOR USEFUL BOOKS

To help readers locate them, books are now often classified into twenty groups or subjects under the Library of Congress system, as follows:

A   General works
B   Philosophy, psychology, religion
C–D History, general, foreign
E–F American history
G   Geography, anthropology, sports
H   Social science
J   Political science
K   Law
L   Education
M   Music
N   Fine arts
P   Language and literature
Q   Science
R   Medicine
S   Agriculture
T   Technology, engineering
U   Military science
V   Naval science
Z   Bibliography and library science

Think of how difficult it would be to collect scattered materials on any

How does a cornet differ from other brass instruments? To learn more about cornets, you would look under the listing *cornet* in the reference materials at the library.

subject without a library collecting and cataloging the information systematically year by year. These Library of Congress initials are often used as the **call number** or identification number, both on the book spine and in the card or computer catalog.

Finding a Book: The Card Catalog

Until very recently, every college library has maintained a **card catalog** with every single book in its collection listed several times on printed cards. Some libraries now have replaced their catalogs entirely by computers, whereas others still maintain and update their card catalogs. In the traditional catalogs, the cards are kept in chests containing many small drawers, with alphabetized titles on the outside to identify the range of the cards within.

For its card catalog, the library usually makes from four to six (or more) cards for *each* book. One card is listed under the **author;** one is listed under the **title;** and the rest are listed under **subject headings** (that is, the three or four main subjects that the book discusses). The subject headings can be useful in your research if you are searching for additional or related sources; they are generally listed at the bottom of both author and title cards.

See Figure 16–2 for some typical cards from a card catalog. Always **copy the complete call number** so that you can locate the book precisely on the shelf.

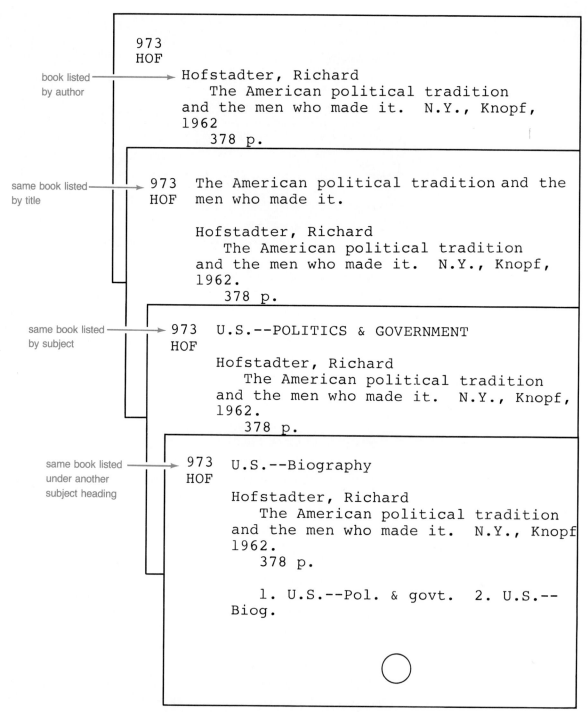

Figure 16–2: Sample Cards from a Card Catalog

Finding a Book: The Computer Catalog

More and more libraries are closing their card catalogs and moving to on-line computer catalogs. These terminals are convenient, fast, and usually easy to operate; they also provide important information on the book's status—whether it is presently "in the library" and available for you or not.

By using the computer catalog, student Margaret Murano hoped to find some useful books through a "subject" search since she did not know the names of any specific authors or titles. When the computer gave her the option of asking for an author, title, or subject, she pressed the subject button. The screen instructed her to "start at the beginning of the subject and enter as many words of the subject as you know."

Margaret typed in "utopia America," since she was looking for books on such utopian communities as the Shakers. The computer responded with a list of worldwide utopian communities, and Margaret spotted what she wanted on the screen, "Utopias—U.S.," and called for it. The computer immediately produced a title that looked very promising to her as a starting point, giving her information on several utopian communities in addition to the Shakers. This is the screen the computer produced:

Author	Hayden, Dolores	All Subject Search
Title	Seven American Utopias	
Imprint	Cambridge, Mass.: MIT Press, 1976	
Status	in library	
Includes	index, bibliography	
Call no.	HX653.H39	

On the next screen the computer produced subject headings, including "millennialism," another term for the movement describing such communities. So Margaret was in luck: she saw on the screen that her book was in the library and that it had a bibliography to lead her to other books; and the computer had given her another key word so that she could continue her research.

Feeling she was making progress, Margaret continued her search immediately, asking for yet another subject, "Shakers." The subject search is most useful when the researcher has a strong interest in a specific subject but no specific books in mind; it is always faster, when possible, to search for specific author names and titles.

Some systems will give computer printouts of any screen indicated by the user; Margaret's, however, did not, and she copied all the information she needed on *Seven American Utopias* onto a small bibliography card.

Research can be frustrating if you finally locate a promising book in the catalog—only to find that it is checked out. The computer gives the librarian precise information on the book's whereabouts—where it is and when it is due back. A computer can also tell the librarian what other university libraries own the book and whether it is available for an interlibrary loan. Since books may not be immediately available, allow yourself time in your schedule for such delays.

Useful Research Techniques

It is easy to spend too much time on unproductive research; use your time carefully to maximize results:

1. Be alert for leads and clues to other sources.
Let one book help you find others: check its bibliography and footnotes for other related texts. If you locate one book on the shelf as you are researching, look around in the same area for other books that might be useful to you. Because libraries shelve related subjects together, you might stumble upon other good leads. Many a researcher has found good books by happy accidents.

2. Read selectively.
Look in the index for the key concepts on your subject and for the pages where they appear. Go directly to those pages. Forget the old habit of reading from cover to cover: check the table of contents for the chapters that cover what you want; quickly check the index to see if key words like *Shakers* or *utopia* are listed; use exploratory reading techniques and skim until you come to material that will help you; then read more carefully. **Research requires selective reading;** you must **hone in on what is important to your topic** and read alertly—at all times asking yourself, "How vital is this information to my paper?"

3. Reread key books at the end of your research.
Sometimes it is helpful to return to a book toward the end of your research and reread it. At a later stage, after you have gained more insights on the topic, you may understand more clearly the author's perspective.

4. Review frequently what you have already discovered—to guide your further research.

Always take a time-out to get perspective on your research; read over the notes you have taken and see if you have found something truly surprising, or some point you want to study further, or some controversy you want to investigate. Do not continue to take notes aimlessly: stop to **check your progress**—to see what you have found and where you are headed.

5. Mull over your research at odd moments.

Mulling over your material in any form—in your journal or even in your head—is a good idea as you begin to work with and connect your ideas and put them into new relationships. Use spare moments to review what you have found out so far.

In doing research, you must learn enough about your topic so that you can write confidently about it and explain what you have discovered. You have to become fired up by it; you have to make it *your* own subject.

> Do not continue to take notes aimlessly: stop to check your progress—to see what you have found and where you are headed.

■ PRACTICE 2   What are your experiences with searching for books? Do you feel comfortable searching for books in a catalog or do you find it confusing?

■ PRACTICE 3   Use either the card catalog or the computer catalog to look up (1) two authors, (2) two titles, and (3) two subjects; copy on note cards the information given to you on the computer screen or the printed card. Ask the librarian to explain any terms you do not understand. If you do not have a favorite author or subject, look up sources on a well-known subject such as Martin Luther King, Jr. or the civil rights movement.

SEARCHING FOR ARTICLES: MAGAZINES AND JOURNALS

We have seen how books can be found by using either a card catalog or an electronic computer. Similarly, journal articles can be found either in traditional **hardbound indexes** (large volumes listing, year by year, all the articles published in a large field such as business or engineering) or by a computer search of various data bases. These data bases are likewise developed to help you locate useful articles in specific disciplines, but they have some limitations of coverage (see pp. 420–422).

Traditionally, to find articles on their chosen topic, students have used hardbound indexes to the various journals in a given discipline. These multi-volume indexes, each index occupying several long shelves, usually require some time and effort to use since they are bound in many individual volumes year by year.

If you were looking up, say, "adoption" in *Readers' Guide to Periodical Literature,* you would have to look in many volumes, one for each year—a time-consuming task if you were interested in the last twenty years. (In a library context, the word *periodical* refers to magazines and journals.) Figure 16–3 illustrates a page from *Readers' Guide.*

Many libraries now supplement the traditional printed indexes of journal articles with computer searches. If your library has several types of computer searches, learn what each search offers. Many libraries have short training programs to explain the more specialized searches. You may have to spend a few hours at your own terminal learning the system even after the training.

Using Hardbound Indexes to Find Articles

Every academic subject has one or more indexes that cover the field you are interested in. Ask the reference librarian for the indexes that cover your research topic. The indexes are usually located in the reference section, and they can be helpful for preliminary browsing when you are looking for key words or subject headings. Here are a few titles to show you the range of the available hardbound indexes:

Name of Index	Coverage
Readers' Guide to Periodical Literature	Covers articles from 180 journals of general interest (such as *Newsweek, Scientific American, New Yorker, Wilderness*)
Humanities Index *Art Index* *Music Index* *Philosopher's Index*	Cover the humanities (literature, fine arts, and philosophy)
Education Index *ERIC**	Cover education

*Educational Resources Information Center

AUGUST 1988   5

ADJUSTMENT (PSYCHOLOGY)—cont.
Coping with change [adolescents] J. P. Comer. il *Parents*
63:189 Ap '88
The new you (and your old life). J. G. Fitzpatrick. il
Parents 63:87-90 Ap '88
ADLER, JERRY
What if your worst nightmare came true? A father's
tale. il *Esquire* 109:147-50 Je '88
ADLER LECTURESHIP
APS establishes Adler Lectureship. por *Physics Today*
41:114+ Je '88
ADLON, PERCY
                        about
Bagdad Cafe [film] Reviews
Gentlemen's Quarterly il 58:83+ My '88. K. Turan
Percy Adlon [interview] il por *American Film* 13:11-14
My '88
ADMINISTRATIVE   EFFICIENCY   *See*   Efficiency,
Administrative
ADMINISTRATIVE REMEDIES
See also
Ombudsman
ADMIRALS
See also
La Rocque, Gene Robert
ADMISSION TO COLLEGE *See* Colleges and univer-
sities—Admission
ADOLESCENCE
See also
Black youth
High school students
Peer groups
Problem children
Puberty
Young men
Young women
Youth
As they grow/11 through 13. J. P. Comer. See issues
of Parents
As they grow/14 through 18. D. Elkind. See issues of
Parents beginning January 1987
Fathering an adolescent boy [cover story] W. J. O'Malley.
il *America* 158:575-9 Je 4 '88
Relating. A. Wood. See issues of Seventeen
Teenage tumult: when feelings get you down [teenage
girls] P. S. Rix. il *Teen* 32:28+ Je '88
ADOLESCENT DRINKING *See* Alcohol and youth
ADOLESCENT LITERATURE *See* Young adults' literature
ADOLESCENT RUNAWAYS *See* Runaways
ADOPTION AND ADOPTED CHILDREN
Adopting and fostering children with AIDS: policies in
progress. P. Tourse and L. Gundersen. bibl f il *Children
Today* 17:15-19 My/Je '88
Adoption update. L. Weber. il *Good Housekeeping* 206:225
My '88
Babies with AIDS. L. Gilman. il *American Health* 7:88
My '88
The battle over Baby K. [Navajo Indians resist adoption
of child by non-Indians] R. Lacayo. il *Time* 131:64
My 2 '88
When it comes to adoption, it's a wide, wide world.
S. Woolley. il *Business Week* p164-5 Je 20 '88
When they first dated, these two Kansans felt a strong
attraction to each other; now they know why [C.
McClellan and R. Sloan discover they are half-brother
and half-sister] G. Pick. il pors *People Weekly* 29:81-2
Je 13 '88
ADP RIBOSYLTRANSFERASES *See* Transferases
ADRENAL GLANDS
                    Transplantation
Brain graft puzzles [behavioral changes after implanting
adrenal gland tissue into brains of Parkinson's disease
patients] R. Lewin. *Science* 240:879 My 13 '88
Cloud over Parkinson's therapy [adrenal gland transplants]
R. Lewin. il *Science* 240:390-2 Ap 22 '88
Experimental cell grafts for Huntington's [grafting of
adrenal tissue into the brain] *Science News* 133:268
Ap 23 '88
Six who dared: the Parkinson's pioneers. P. Michelmore.
il *Reader's Digest* 132:75-84 Je '88
ADRIAN, JANE *See* Leach, Penelope
ADRIENNE (NEW YORK, N.Y.: RESTAURANT) *See*
New York (N.Y.)—Restaurants, nightclubs, bars, etc.
ADRS *See* American depositary receipts
ADS *See* Advertising
ADULT-CHILD RELATIONSHIP *See* Child-adult relation-
ship
ADULT CHILDREN AND PARENTS *See* Parent-child
relationship

ADULT EDUCATION
See also
Labor—Education
Literacy education
University extension
The graying of the campus. C. Leslie. il *Newsweek* 111:56
Je 6 '88
ADULT RESPIRATORY DISTRESS SYNDROME
Preventing fire fatalities [research by William A. Pryor]
il *USA Today (Periodical)* 116:13-14 Ap '88
ADULTERY
Can a marriage survive infidelity? [views of Fumiko
Hosokawa] il *USA Today (Periodical)* 116:8-9 Mr '88
Good news for a fallen leader [recommissioning of G.
MacDonald to public ministry] P. Hoffman. il por
Christianity Today 32:65 Je 17 '88
"I fell in love with another man". D. Kent. il *Redbook*
171:36+ My '88
ADULTERY IN MOTION PICTURES
Fatal attraction: single girl, double standard. B. G. Har-
rison. *Mademoiselle* 94:197 My '88
ADULTS AND CHILDREN *See* Child-adult relationship
ADVANCED COMPATIBLE TELEVISION
Picture perfect. W. J. Hawkins. il *Popular Science*
232:64-6+ Je '88
ADVANCED SOFTWARE INC.
Succeeding technologies [L. Korn and C. Queen] E. Dyson.
il *Forbes* 141 Ann Directory:122 Ap 25 '88
ADVENT
See also
Second Advent
ADVENTURE [television program] See Television program
reviews—Single works
ADVENTURE AND ADVENTURERS
See also
Voyages
Voyages around the world
Tough guys—a breed apart. D. G. Brown. por *U.S. News
& World Report* 104:7 My 23 '88
Women adventure guides. J. Mills. il *Women's Sports
& Fitness* 10:47-51 Ap '88
ADVENTURE STORIES
See also
Detective and mystery stories
Anecdotes, facetiae, satire, etc.
Porter McKay, Justice Machine: secrets of a male fantasy
writer. R. Hacker and J. Kaufman. il *The New York
Times Book Review* 93:27 Ap 17 '88
ADVERSARY SYSTEM (LAW)
The real crisis in the courts [cover story] F. D. Strier.
il por *The Humanist* 48:5-9+ Mr/Ap '88
ADVERTISEMENTS *See* Advertising
ADVERTISING
See also
Airlines—Advertising
Alberta—Advertising
Automobile industry—Advertising
Books—Advertising
Bottled water industry—Advertising
Buy American campaign
Cigarette industry—Advertising
Cosmetics industry—Advertising
Liquor industry—Advertising
Meat industry—Advertising
Motion picture industry—Advertising
Music in advertising
National socialism in advertising
Perfume industry—Advertising
Physicians—Advertising
Premiums
Rug and carpet industry—Advertising
Sauces—Advertising
Sex discrimination in advertising
Sex in advertising
Shopping carts in advertising
Telephone companies—Advertising
Television advertising
Television industry—Advertising
Women in advertising
The allure of ad hoc ads. A. Miller. il *Newsweek* 111:51
My 2 '88
On Madison Avenue. B. Kanner. See issues of New
York
Selling it. See issues of Consumer Reports
                    Prize contests
See Prize contests
                    Terminology
The Bloopie Awards. W. Safire. il *The New York Times
Magazine* p26+ My 1 '88

Figure 16–3: A Page from *Readers' Guide to Periodical Literature*

> *Engineering Index*
> *Applied Science and Technology*
> *Biological and Agricultural*
>   *Index*   } Cover sciences and social sciences
> *Social Sciences Index*
> *Psychological Abstracts*
> *General Science Index*

A librarian wisely said it's not important to know the name of any particular index, but it is important to know that an index on every major field exists and *to ask* for the one you need.

Searching by Computer for Magazines and Journals

Discuss with your librarian which journals and magazines are available on which computer systems. Usually popular magazines and scholarly journals are on separate systems. What kind of articles are you looking for—recent scholarly research or more general magazines like *Newsweek* and the *New Yorker?* Ask the librarian which is the correct terminal.

Before you begin a search, jot down key words on your subject; the more you have a focused subject, the easier it will be to find key terms (descriptors) to feed the computer.

On the other hand, you may work toward focusing your subject with computer prompts. One student called up "adoption" on the system and was dismayed to find five thousand documents. This first groping, however, produced for her a "see also" list of other subjects—such as adoptees, biological parents—that helped her.

Later she tried "adoption—secrecy" with no luck, but eventually she hit upon the phrase "sealed adoption records"—and that was the magic descriptor, producing exactly what she wanted.

If necessary, ask the librarian for assistance in conducting a computer search for articles; your librarian is accustomed to thinking in terms of a key word or *descriptor* and, even more important, of several overlapping descriptors that will bring you closer to your specific topic. An appropriate thesaurus is usually on hand that can help you find synonyms in a specific subject area.

Computer Search Strategy

Keep in mind the following points to make your computer search more

AN   ACCESSION NUMBER: 15298. 871.
AU   AUTHOR/S: Churchman-D.
TI   TITLE: The debate over open adoption.
SO   SOURCE: Public Welfare, 44(2): 11-14, 1986.
HC   HARDCOPY: 23(1), 1987, No. 71.
DE   DESCRIPTOR/S: Adoption: open, debate over.
CC   CLASSIFICATION CODE: FAMILY-AND-CHILD-WELFARE (CC2035).
PT   PUBLICATION TYPE: JOURNAL (J).
AB   ABSTRACT: Several vocal, grass-roots adoption rights organizations have sprung up in the last 15 years to protest the closed-records system, which prevents birth parents and adoptees from ever meeting once the adoption papers are signed. Agencies and social workers are discovering that methods they thought were compassionate and humane are perceived as cold and coercive. Today, the birth mother not only sees her child but is usually given profiles of the prospective adoptive parents, often including autobiographies. It is also common for many local agencies to ask the birth mothers what sort of people they would like to have as parents for their children. Yet "radical" birth parents want to meet with, get to know, and, in some cases, cooperate in raising the child with the adoptive parents. Exchanging identifying information is not a popular option with many adoptive parents, who feel threatened by the possibility of the birth parents revising their decision to relinquish the child. Local agencies, which emphasize that the adoption decision needs to be the birth mothers' alone, offer extensive counseling services, groups for birth mothers, and outside speakers. (This issue of Public Welfare features three additional articles about adoption.)

HIT ENTER FOR NEXT SCREEN OR TYPE Q TO QUIT PRINTING

AN   ACCESSION NUMBER: 4214. 853.
AU   AUTHOR/S: *Zeilinger-R.
TI   TITLE: The need vs. the right to know.
SO   SOURCE: Public Welfare, 37(3): 44-47, 1979.
AD   ADDRESS: *Children's Bureau, New Orleans, LA.
HC   HARDCOPY: 16(3), 1980, No. 1193.
DE   DESCRIPTOR/S: Adoption: adult adoptees' right to open records.
CC   CLASSIFICATION CODE: SOCIAL-POLICY-AND-ACTION (CC3000).
PT   PUBLICATION TYPE: JOURNAL (J).
AB   ABSTRACT: Sealed Adoption Record Statutes should not be changed because a very small minority claim they have a right to open records. Their need may be acknowledged but this does not constitute a right. It is the responsibility of an adoption agency to safeguard all, insofar as this is within its power, the rights and interests of biological parents and extended families, adoptive parents, the adopted child, and the agency. The concept that adoption agencies should assist in the search is illegal and unethical. It would divert scarce resources from issues of greater priority. Adult adoptees may apply to the court in all states to open the record if unsatisfied with the nonidentifying medical or genetic information which agencies supply. (Author abstract, edited.)

Figure 16-4: Computer Printout on Sealed Adoption Records

efficient:

- Notice *the years covered by the system;* if the data base only goes back to 1984, the coverage may be too limited.
- Learn the *specific strengths of the data base;* you may be searching in a system that covers more journals in business than in other areas.
- Learn whether the data base covers scholarly or more popular journals: if you are looking for a popular article by Margaret Mead in *Redbook,* make sure the magazine is in the system.
- Find out which data base on the system is best for your topic; perhaps Social Work Abstracts (SWAB) is better than Sociological Abstracts (SOCA) for a paper on ''adoption.''

Our student finally came up with six articles on ''sealed adoption records'' and was delighted with the results. She was able to obtain a computer printout of the abstracts (short summaries) of the articles so that she could evaluate each. Figure 16–4 shows part of her printout.

Where to Start: Books, Articles, or Newspapers?

In general, recent articles will give you the most up-to-date research on a given topic; but often the scope of an article is limited, and the reader does not get a full picture of the subject. A book, much wider in coverage, usually presents a more detailed view of the entire subject. You may want to use some combination of both: books for the background information and the broad perspective; magazines for events that are relatively recent or fast-changing. As a rule of thumb, start with books for historical events, like the nineteenth-century Shaker settlements, and with magazines for more recent issues, like the ongoing discussions about AIDS.

If some key event occurred on a specific date, consider starting with newspapers—for background on what else took place at the time. And by all means, read several papers for different interpretations. If you are studying reasons for the United States' hesitation in entering World War II, read newspaper accounts of the time, particularly the days just before and after the bombing of Pearl Harbor in December 1941. (Check the *New York Times Index* as well as the indexes of other major papers, such as the *Chicago Tribune* and the *Washington Post*).

Whenever possible, try to locate several authors with opposing perspectives on your issue; such writers will give you a clash of views to resolve. Often authors mention in their books or articles other writers or scholars with whom they disagree.

For topics like the framing of the Constitution that have a complex past history and many, many sources covering them, find a few of what are considered the classic books on the subject. Then, if possible, look for recent authors who have questioned the thinking of earlier scholars. (See Chapter 14 for developing a synthesis from library sources.)

WHAT NOTES TO TAKE ON NOTE CARDS

The most difficult task, particularly at the start of research, is deciding what information to record on your note cards. Invariably you—like everyone else—will take notes on what you don't need and will *not* take down what would have been a perfect quote. (If you are determined, sometimes you can relocate the book with that quote.)

Try to resist taking notes until you get a good grasp of your subject. Rather than taking notes, force yourself to read a little faster than a comfortable pace and get an overview of your topic. As you grow more familiar with your material and develop a working thesis statement, you will be able to take notes more productively (see Chapter 17 for ways to narrow your topic and develop a thesis statement). Remember: keep reviewing your notes as you read and research so that you know what else you need to find.

What form should a note take? You have three options: direct quote, paraphrase, and summary.

Direct Quotation

Use a direct quote when the author's words are especially witty, controversial, to the point, or well phrased. For example, Oscar Wilde's words should be quoted exactly: ''The only way to get rid of temptation is to yield to it.'' If you reworded it (Oscar Wilde notes that if you give into temptation, it usually goes away), the sentence loses its bite.

Put quotation marks at the beginning and end of the quote on your note card to remind yourself to transfer the quotation marks to your paper. When using a quotation in your paper, be sure to lead into it smoothly, so that it sounds natural in context. Study how good professional writers introduce quotations, and ask your teacher for some pointers.

Paraphrase

If, on the other hand, the author's language is ordinary or lifeless, factual or statistical, you may want to paraphrase it. In a paraphrase, you restate the author's meaning—but in your own words. (In a pinch you may use no more than two of the author's exact words in a row.) Reproduce the author's exact sense but express it in your own and different words. Just as in the case of a direct quote, *you must cite the source of the idea* (see pages 475–480 on how to cite a direct quote and a paraphrase).

Summary

Your third option is to summarize a long passage on a note card, boiling it down to essentials: "The author gives seven arguments for opposing the Equal Rights Amendment—none of them new: among them, whether women can be drafted into the army, whether we can manage single-sex bathrooms, and why we need the ERA if other laws cover it already."

You might want to photocopy this author's long seven-point argument in case you need it later, and put the note card with your summary in your pile of note cards to have available when you are planning the paper.*

To prevent your own later confusion, label all photocopies immediately with the author's name at the top. You might also want to use a highlighting pen on the photocopy to mark the key phrases that you have summarized. Figure 16–5 illustrates three types of notes: direct quotation, paraphrase, and summary.

Should You Take Notes on Photocopies?

Should you make note cards on all the pages you photocopy? Should you bother to copy direct quotes and write out paraphrases? We think you should because, as you do so, you absorb and rethink the arguments of a specific author. Just as you take notes on your texts as a learning device, we think you should write paraphrases and record quotes on note cards, even if you have a photocopy close by. By doing so, you engage with the material and evaluate its usefulness.

---

*Be sure that you are aware of current copyright laws before photocopying *any* copyrighted materials.

subconscious + writing   Hemingway   p. 13

Quotation ——————→ "It was in that room too that I learned not
to think about anything that I was writing
from the time I stopped writing until
I started again the next day that way
my subconscious would be working on it..."

subconscious + writing   Hemingway   p. 13

Hemingway tried not to think about anything
he wrote from the time he quit writing until   ←—— Paraphrase
he started the next day so his subconscious
could help him.

stone tools perfected   Ascent   p. 80

For about a million years, early humans
(Homo sapiens) seemed to be making no
progress but actually technology of stone tools
Summary ——————→ and hand axes was developing and early
man was evolving.

Figure 16-5 Note Cards of a Quotation, Paraphrase, and Summary

Make Note Cards on Your Own Ideas

As you read, you often may get useful ideas and responses of your own that you want to remember. Put these ideas on note cards, labeled clearly so that you know they are your own original ideas.

Final Cautions on Taking Notes

When you paraphrase, take pains not to distort the author's intention. And be sure not to steal an idea from an author by not acknowledging where you found the idea. This stealing of ideas is called *plagiarism* and is to be avoided scrupulously. **You must give a reference for every idea that you take from your library sources** (see Chapter 18 for how to cite ideas taken from sources).

The key to searching for sources is to do it efficiently, in a way that leads you to some good results in a reasonable amount of time. If you have invested many hours and have come up with only a few sources, you may be researching a topic where material is simply not readily available from the usual books and journals. In most cases, it is advisable to change your topic to one for which you can find more material.

> The key to searching for sources is to do it efficiently, in a way that leads to some good results in a reasonable amount of time.

■ PRACTICE 4   (1) Find two passages that are suitable for quoting and make note cards. (2) Find two passages that are suitable for paraphrasing and make note cards. (3) Find two passages that are suitable for a summary and make note cards. Choose passages from a book or article you have read with interest.

WORKING SPACE

READING ASSIGNMENT

Read the following essay by Russell Baker. How does he feel about the new technology? How do you feel? Would you prefer to study and do research at a computer in your room rather than go to a library? What would be gained and what would be lost?

Terminal Education

Ever since reading about Clarkson College's plan to replace its library with a computer, I have been worrying about what college students will do in the spring. I mean, you can't just haul a computer out on the campus and plunk it down under a budding elm and lie there with the thing on your chest while watching the birds at work, can you?

You can do that with a book, and it is one of the better things about going to college. With a computer, though, you've got to have a video terminal, which is basically a television set that rolls little, green, arthritic-looking letters and numbers across a dark screen.

It's not much fun reading a television screen, since, for one thing, the print has a terribly tortured look, as if it had spent four months in a Savak* cellar, and since, for another, you always expect it to be interrupted by a commercial. Which is neither here nor there, of course, since this kind of reading is not supposed to convey pleasure, but information.

The difficulty is that you can't take your television screen out under the elm tree and plug it into the computer—the information bank or the information center or the information conveyor, or whatever they choose to call it—since (1) television screens are expensive and fragile and no college president in his right mind is going to let students expose them to ants, dew and tree sap, and since (2) colleges aren't going to shortchange the football team to pay for installing electrical outlets in the tree trunks.

What this means for college students of the future—and Clarkson's electronic library is the library of the future, make no mistake—what it means is that students are going to be spending their springs sitting alone in stale air staring at television screens.

Give them a six-pack of beer or a glass of bourbon, you might say, and you have the ideal training program for American adult home life, which, one supposes, they will still be expected to undertake once they leave college stuffed with information. All I can say is: What does this have to do with education?

The answer comes from Dr. Walter Grattidge, director of Clarkson's

---

*Savak: Iranian secret police under the Shah

new Educational Resources Center—Clarkson's term, not mine. "Education," he told a New York Times reporter, "is basically an information-transfer process." At the risk of sounding somewhat snappish, I say, "Fie, Dr. Grattidge! Fie!"

"Information-transfer process" indeed. Education is not like a decal, to be slipped off a piece of stiff paper and pasted on the back of the skull. The point of education is to waken innocent minds to a suspicion of information.

An educated person is one who has learned that information almost always turns out to be at best incomplete and very often false, misleading, fictitious, mendacious*—just dead wrong. Ask any seasoned cop or newspaper reporter. Ask anybody who has ever been the defendant in a misdemeanor trial or the subject of a story in a newspaper.

Well, let's grant that Dr. Grattidge's opinion about being "basically an information-transfer process" is only 80 percent baloney. If you're going to learn the importance of mistrusting information, somebody first has to give you some information, and college is a place where people try to do this, if only so the professors can find out how gullible you are.

Knowing that, they can then begin to try to teach you to ask a few questions before buying the Brooklyn Bridge or the newest theory about the wherefore of the universe. I'm talking about the good professors now, not the ones who spend all their time compiling fresh information to be transferred to the book-buying public. Even the good professors, however, rarely have enough time to teach the whole student body the art of doubting, which leads to the astonishing act of thinking.

This is why so much of whatever educating happens at college happens in places like the grass under the elm where somebody has gone to read a book, just because it seems like a nicer place to read than the library, and has become distracted by the shape of the clouds, or an ant on the elbow, or an impulse to say to the guy or the girl crossing the quadrangle, "Let's chuck the books for a while and get a beer."

If the time is autumn, and the campus has an apple tree, who knows? Maybe somebody half asleep in an informational-transference volume will look up, see an apple fall and revolutionize science.† Not much chance of that happening if you're sitting in a room staring at

*mendacious: lying, untrue
†reference is to Sir Isaac Newton and the theory of gravity

a TV screen plugged into the Educational Resources Center, is there?

In there you are just terribly alone, blotting up information from a machine which, while very, very smart in some ways, has never had an original thought in its life. And no trees grow, and no apples fall.

---

1. According to Russell Baker, what is the real goal or purpose of education?

2. Why is he so opposed to Dr. Grattidge's claim that education is basically an information-transfer process?

3. What is Baker's definition of an educated person? What is yours?

4. How does the art of doubting lead to the art of thinking?

WRITING ASSIGNMENT: ''Searching for Sources''

To familiarize yourself with the library services, pick a lively topic and see how many books and articles you can find on it in an hour. Search for sources on the Salem witchcraft trials, the California gold rush, Watergate, the space program, or a topic from another course you are taking. Use the card catalog or the computer catalog for books; use hardbound indexes or a computer search for articles. Write bibliographical note cards for ten sources, following the examples on pp. 410–411. If possible, try to find at least one journal article and one newspaper article.

JOURNAL ASSIGNMENT

Take your journal to the library and write several paragraphs describing one of the following: (1) any activities that take place in front of you in your library reading room, (2) some of the students and their various postures and expressions while studying, (3) the kinds of computer and microform equipment your library has (and any problems you had using it). In your description, try your hand at imitating Russell Baker's comic touch.

CHECKING OUT

Check your understanding of Chapter 16 by writing answers to the following questions. You may work alone or with a friend, whichever you prefer.

1. Explain the differences between bibliographical cards and note cards.

2. Explain what information you need to cite on a book and what information you need to cite on a scholarly journal or a popular magazine. What are the major differences?

3. What is the purpose of adding a short title or a heading to each note card describing what is on it?

4. What is a "subject" card in a card catalog? Can you search for a book by subject on a computer?

5. What is a hardbound index to a discipline? How are the volumes organized? Where are they usually located?

6. What are descriptors and how do they help you locate an article?

7. Why is it important to keep reading, titling, and sorting your note cards as you continue to do research?

8. How do you decide whether to quote, paraphrase, or summarize when writing a note card?

IN SUMMARY

A library offers a wealth of resources that you can use to full advantage if you familiarize yourself with how your library organizes its collections. To search for sources, learn how to find books in a card catalog or a computer catalog, or both, and how to find articles in periodical indexes (bound by year, usually kept in the reference department) or by a computer search. To find and learn to use the various forms of miniaturized print or microforms, you must inform yourself about the various systems in your particular library.

Above all, ask the reference librarian for help. He or she can answer questions on the options for carrying out a search as well as on effective methods for searching by finding key words for the computer.

As a researcher, make bibliographic cards for all your sources (to incorporate later in your Works Cited page) and take note cards on any information you think contributes to your understanding of the subject. Take notes in the form of direct quotation, paraphrase, or summary; we recommend taking notes even on pages for which you have photocopies. And whenever you use ideas or information that you have learned from your sources, you must cite the work (see pp. 475–480).

In this chapter, we have covered only the initial phase of doing research: locating library sources and taking notes. For more on developing the ideas that you have discovered into a synthesis, review Chapter 14. For more on identifying your strongest ideas and other prewriting strategies, see Chapter 17. For more on drafting, revising, and documenting a research paper, see Chapter 18.

CHAPTER 17

PREWRITING:
DISCOVERING IDEAS FOR WRITING

Writing . . . is only incidentally a way of telling others what you think. Its first use is for the making of what you think, for the discovery of understanding.

—Richard Mitchell

OVERVIEW

This chapter covers *prewriting,* or all the tasks writers should carry out before actually writing a first draft. For this prewriting phase, we emphasize discovery techniques (to help you learn ways to pry good ideas out of your mind) and planning strategies (to help you prepare for the writing of a first draft). If you tackle this prewriting phase with commitment, you will find that the actual writing of the first draft will be much more focused and satisfying because you have both your ideas and organization well thought out.

By the end of the prewriting phase, you want to accomplish three things: you want to find (1) a tentative main idea (or *thesis statement*) that satisfies you, (2) many strong ideas to back up or support that main idea, and (3) a good scratch outline to guide you in writing a first draft.

As we said in Chapter 15 (How a Writer Works), writing is done by trial and error—by breaking new ground into the wilderness, not by following a marked trail. Some backtracking, indecision, and confusion are to be expected especially in the earlier phases of the writing process. Many students, however, enjoy the tasks of prewriting, finding them creative and pleasurable—and not that demanding.

The strategies covered in this chapter will help you plan your writing in an enjoyable and efficient manner:

- Narrow your topic by funneling or focusing it.
- Learn to brainstorm and then cluster.
- As an alternative to brainstorming, try focused freewriting.
- Use probing questions along with brainstorming.
- Learn additional discovery techniques: formulate a problem statement or challenge conventional opinions.
- Shape your tentative thesis statement.
- Prepare a working or scratch outline.

After following the sequence we describe, you will be prepared to write a first draft with confidence.

SELECTING YOUR BEST IDEAS: TAPPING YOUR INNER RESOURCES

All readers want to read stimulating ideas, ideas that make them think: "Good point!" or "Nice idea" or "That never occurred to me before." The writer's task therefore is to *select* ideas that the reader will find stimulating and striking. Among all the possible ideas you may consider when planning a paper, you want to select those ideas that will capture your reader's attention. And to do so, you will have to imagine or predict your reader's reaction to your ideas.

You may well ask, How do I guess my reader's response? In the early planning stage, you will have to select those ideas that *you* feel are your best, strongest ideas. Later you can think of ways to convince your reader that your ideas are worth reading. In other words, *first interest yourself* as the writer—by discovering ideas you want to discuss. Then think of how to interest your reader in those ideas.

You may personally be concerned about how many homeless pets—13.5 million—have to be put to death each year, or you may be more interested in discussing how to care for the homeless in your city. In either case you need to discover powerful examples and strong support to explain your ideas to your reader.

Many beginning writers worry needlessly about having no good ideas, nothing to say. You have many more ideas than you are aware of—if you can learn to tap them. Each of you has had **personal experiences** that your friends and your teachers have not had. You have **memories** of many events that occurred earlier in your life, and these events have meaning. You have your own **observations** about your family, about schools, about what works and what doesn't work in your community and your country. You have much to explain to your readers about how *you* view the world.

Learn to use all these resources—your own experiences, memories, conversations, reactions, and thoughts. Even make use of the meaningful experiences that have happened to your friends and family. Good writers draw on their past experiences to make their ideas more vivid and immediate to their readers. **You have a lot to write about—all that you have learned about the world up to now.**

> First interest yourself as the writer—discovering ideas you want to discuss. Then think of how to interest your reader in those ideas.

PRACTICE 1   Of the following three questions, pick one that interests you most. Then describe what sources you would use—your memories, observations, past experiences of school, or your journal (or any other sources)—to find ideas for a paper.

1. **Is watching television how I learn a lot about the world or how I waste a lot of time?**
2. **Should students who repeatedly make trouble in the classroom be removed to special classes or be allowed to stay with their own class?**
3. **When raising children, should parents firmly discipline their children, trying to teach them good guidelines, or should they be freer and more permissive, letting their children learn things for themselves?**

PLANNING AN ESSAY: FOLLOW THE ASSIGNMENT

As preliminaries, allow yourself enough time and, as soon as you know the due date, **schedule specific times for completing each phase of the writing process** (prewriting, drafting, revising, proofreading). Allow roughly the same amount of time for each phase.

Check that you have the requirements absolutely clear for your writing assignment. Be clear about the specific topic: are you to use a topic assigned by the teacher or one of your own choice? Does the assignment have specific directions, with a key word, such as *synthesize, analyze,* or *interpret?* Pin down the meaning of the key word.

And very important, find out the required length so that you can preplan and estimate how many pages or how many paragraphs you will need. Even experienced writers find it difficult to come out at precisely the desired length—neither too long nor too short. So keep the length roughly in mind, but plan to adjust—cut or add—after the first draft.

The length of the paper will also influence what topic you decide to handle: you can obviously take on a more ambitious topic if the paper can be ten pages; however, you will be wise to limit your topic sharply if you are allowed only five hundred words (roughly two typed pages).

Make sure you understand where you are supposed to get your information. Academic essays range from the more subjective and personal (primarily dealing with your own responses to the world) to the more objective (emphasizing the ideas of others). If you are asked to write a *personal essay,* you can rely on pulling ideas from your own mind—based on what you care about deeply. If, however, you are asked to write a *research paper,* you will have to gather your information and ideas from library books and journal articles dealing with the topic.

In some cases, you may be asked to write a paper that combines these two types and calls for some limited research as well as some personal responses. In any case, find out what sources of information you are expected to use. All such academic essays are called **expository essays** because they require the writer to explain, to inform, and to instruct. Dealing with issues in the real world, they have as their primary purpose to **get to the core of an issue**—to explore it fully.

In every kind of expository essay—even in a research paper based heavily on the ideas of other writers—you need to express your own ideas and viewpoints; it is never adequate to string together the ideas of others without explaining your own responses and reactions to those ideas.

■   PRACTICE 2   Think about and then answer these four questions.

1. **When you are a reader (that is, the audience for another writer), what do you look for—good ideas, clear writing, organization, word choice? What do you dislike most as a reader when studying someone else's writing? Is the meaning unclear? Are the sentences too complicated? Are the ideas too abstract?**

_____

_____

2. What do you think your instructors are looking for in your writing—strong ideas, clear writing, correct use of grammar, spelling, and punctuation? Anything else?

_____

_____

3. How does writing about an issue help the writer get to an understanding of the core of an issue? Do you agree that writing is a tool for learning—a way for the writer to learn?

_____

_____

4. Are you able to read your own writing objectively, as if you are reading it for the first time? Can you switch back and forth from the writer of your paper to the reader?

_____

_____

NARROWING YOUR TOPIC: THE FUNNEL

Because your paper has to be done by a certain date and has to be a specific length, don't try to tackle a topic that is too sweeping, such as "Drug Use in the United States." This topic covers so much ground that you'd never manage to cover all aspects of the subject—growth of drug use, kinds of drugs, sources of drugs, effects of addiction, and so forth—except very superficially. Choose instead a small segment or bite of the whole issue—one that you can handle successfully.

How do you "narrow" a topic? You whittle or funnel it down to a workable size. You may be able to hone in on a narrow topic quickly, or you may

Dig into your topic until you discover one specific area that interests you. By narrowing your focus you will discover new ideas.

come across one while doing library research, or you may have to wait until you have tried a discovery technique like brainstorming (p. 439). One student, James Simpson, wanted to write about drugs, either drug rehabilitation or drug availability, because one of his friends was fighting a drug problem. Having much he felt like saying, James was able to narrow his topic early in the writing process:

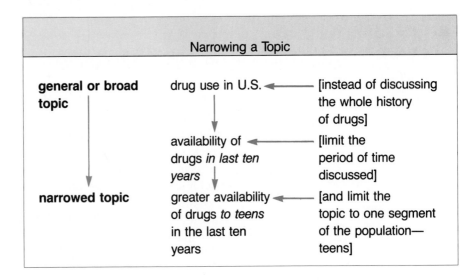

Narrowing a Topic		
general or broad topic	drug use in U.S. ←	[instead of discussing the whole history of drugs]
	availability of drugs *in last ten years* ←	[limit the period of time discussed]
narrowed topic	greater availability of drugs *to teens* in the last ten years ←	[and limit the topic to one segment of the population—teens]

In narrowing a topic, you always move from a broad and general topic, such as "protecting wildlife" or "adoption" to a more restricted subject. If you attempted to write on "Adoption Practices in America," you would need to write a whole book to cover the major issues: adoptive parents, biological parents, adopted children, adoptees as adults, medical records, psychiatric issues, legal issues, and so forth. Each one of these subtopics can be narrowed much further. Student Meene Bose successfully narrowed her topic on adoption to a discussion of adoption files and privacy (see pp. 481–486). Other examples of narrowing topics are shown in Figure 17–1.

As in all prewriting strategies, think of your narrowed topic as *tentative*, as something you will reconsider after you brainstorm and after you try to state your main point or thesis.

General Guidelines for Narrowing a Topic

1. How can I divide this broad topic into more restricted subtopics?

2. Can I limit a subtopic further by time (discuss the sixties versus the eighties, limit it to the late nineteenth century)?

3. Can I limit it by geography (local, state, national)?

4. Can I limit it by sex, age group, or ethnic group?

5. Which of these aspects most interests me?

6. Which aspects are most controversial?

7. Has there been a recent dramatic change affecting the topic (discuss before and after the crisis)?

■   PRACTICE 3   Narrow three of the following general topics: illness, education, entertainment, sports, personal relationships, technology, music. For example, you might limit the years covered, the population discussed, the places to be included, and so forth.

BRAINSTORMING AND CLUSTERING

To discover rich ideas for your writing, we recommend one or several brainstorming sessions. Brainstorming is a direct, effective, and fast method of searching for ideas, and one of the most efficient means for extracting material stored in your memory. Brainstorm alone or with friends. (At times you

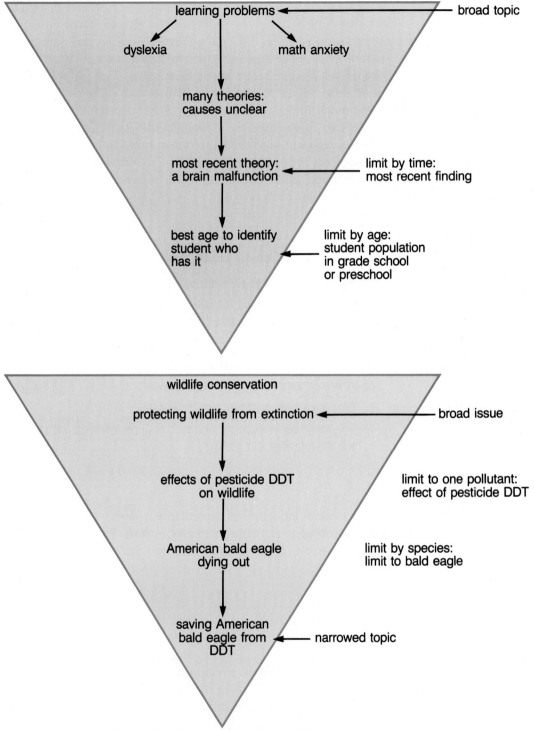

Figure 17-1: Examples of Narrowing a Topic

may want to ask yourself probing questions while you brainstorm, like those on page 445.)

Since you are only exploring possibilities, feel free and easy about starting this low-pressure but important task. You are in an experimental stage so try everything; be daring and see if you can come up with some ideas that interest you. You are not yet committed to any of your ideas.

Brainstorm briefly but with maximum concentration. Take a clipboard or a pad of paper and jot down *every* idea on a topic that occurs to you. **Do not stop to evaluate your ideas. Do not organize them. Simply list your ideas in any order,** just as they occur to you. (Be sure to jot down enough so that later you'll know what you meant.) Let the list grow messy; connect things by arrows, underline a good point, or put several stars on a great idea.

After you jot down each idea, press yourself: "What else do I know about this? Does it suggest anything else to me? What do I really believe about this?" Your mind works by associating ideas freely, that is, one idea triggers another.

Don't start to worry, midway, about how you will use these ideas or whether any of them have value. You are on an **idea search.** Spend about ten or fifteen minutes—or longer, if you are still making progress. Jot down anything and everything that might pertain to the topic, without considering whether or not you can use it. Keep going until you are unable to add anything more.

Next, read through and *evaluate* your ideas carefully, circling the best ones and crossing out those that are weak. Then **cluster related ideas into groups,** connecting related ideas by drawing arrows or by using numbers to identify those in the same cluster. At this point recopy your list, putting the clustered ideas together, and **label each cluster with a heading** or title.

For example, freshman Jay Thomas was brainstorming on the general topic of whether capital punishment should be abolished. He produced an unorganized list that looked like this:

- capital punishment is a final step—no way to correct error if wrong person executed

- humans make errors, and so do juries—it's very possible to execute innocent person

- how about family of victims—what is fair to them? I read about two little kids whose mother was murdered, what about them?—the husband says he's lonely

- there's parole and rehabilitation for criminal but victim is out of luck

- means of putting people to death—gas chambers, electric chairs, injections—painful?

rulings of Supreme Court in library)

- should a criminal be considered mentally ill?
- this is a grim subject; do I really want to write on it?
- how about preventing crime—identifying criminal tendencies early
- who are people in death row who face cap punishment—any patterns?
- victim is silent—rights of victim should be remembered

Labeling Clusters

Once Jay had finished his initial brainstorming, he went back to see if he could push any of the ideas further (What else do I know about rehabilitation?) or to see if he could come up with any stronger examples.

Next, he selected his strongest ideas, crossing out weaker ones. Then he clustered the ideas that belonged together by looking for similarities, patterns, and connections. After giving each cluster a heading, he recopied the list:

victims—rights of

- what are rights of surviving family, friends?
- rights of victim supposed to be protected by state, jury, court

victim—losses of

- in time, everyone forgets losses of victim
- victim loses rest of life, family—everything

criminal—if we abolish death penalty

- improve rehabilitation, rethink parole
- assume criminal is mentally ill
- prevents any chance of innocent person being put to death
- more productive than to have both victim and criminal lost to society

criminal—if we maintain death penalty

- might deter other criminals from killing victims
- gets rid of very dangerous people
- in cases of terrible crime, might be suitable

After this first brainstorming, Jay discovered that he wanted to narrow his topic and focus sharply on the victim. He decided to limit himself to two clusters—the rights and losses of the victim. After some thinking, he came up with the following tentative thesis statement:

> "Although we hear much about the rights of the criminal in cases of capital punishment, we should also consider the rights and the losses of the victim and the victim's family."

The great benefit of brainstorming is its efficiency: you can see at a glance the ideas you have already come up with. You can easily compare and evaluate them. You can move them around into various clusters. If you come up with nothing worthwhile, you have not lost too much time and can brainstorm again on another topic.

In fact Jay, although he had what he thought might work as a thesis statement, abandoned this topic and began to brainstorm on another one. Even though he found he did not want to write on capital punishment, he was making some progress—by eliminating a possibility.

■ PRACTICE 4   Brainstorm and then cluster ideas on one of the following topics:

1. **Insecticides—are they more harmful to people than to bugs?**
2. **Politicians—how much can people believe them?**
3. **Is an individualist at risk in a conformist society?**
4. **Peer pressure—is it useful or harmful?**
5. **Discipline—what does it accomplish?**
6. **Graffiti—is it art or destruction?**
7. **Is there such a thing as an ideal friend?**
8. **Cooperation or competition—which is more productive?**
9. **Who should provide food and housing for the poor?**
10. **Prayers in the public schools—what are the pros and cons?**

FOCUSED FREEWRITING

You have already practiced freewriting in your journal assignments. Some writers use freewriting as their preferred method of discovering ideas. In this strategy, as in brainstorming, you count on **free associations** to jostle you from one idea to another—and eventually to lead you to one or more ideas that catch your attention. In explaining how she found the idea for one of her well-known essays, Annie Dillard said she came up with the workable idea while freewriting in her journal but only "after pages of self-indulgent drivel."

Remember that when you freewrite, you keep on writing nonstop for ten or fifteen minutes. Don't bother about writing good sentences, checking spelling, or worrying over word choice. Concentrate instead on getting down your ideas.

Some writers, when freewriting, do not allow themselves to stop writing—no matter whether they stick to their topic or not—for at least ten minutes. A student produced this example:

> "I'm stuck now, I'm good and stuck, have zip to say and I'm also hungry but I have to keep on writing about my topic—of peer pressure in the schools. Yes, there is peer pressure to like what everyone likes; it's hard to want to go off to study . . ."

This writer eventually did get himself back on the topic after some initial "drivel."

Other writers recommend **focused freewriting, or sticking to the single topic you plan to write about.** For example, James Simpson did some focused freewriting on drugs and teenagers:

> I know from my best friend's experience that rehabilitation for drug users is not easy. It is a struggle. It is often unsuccessful. The parents suffer as much as anyone. The success rate—of someone giving up drugs for good—is a very small group of those who start a program, any program.
>
> An addiction is hard to break. Teenagers on drugs say they feel inferior, unsuccessful, and unpopular, and so they turn to drugs for a temporary escape. But they often end up in a permanent trap. Earlier generations had these same problems growing up, but they did not go on drugs. For a simple reason. What accounts for the difference is the increasing availability of drugs in the last ten or so years. Our society tolerated the drugs in our neighborhoods and, so far, makes only unsuccessful efforts to get rid of the supply. Maybe the huge profits, perhaps organized crime, possibly police involvement, and public indifference—who knows?—are responsible for ruining the lives of many teenagers. They are young and inexperienced. They don't grasp the full consequences. But the adults of this society should fight more to save them.

James then went through his freewriting to **underline and highlight the strong ideas** that he wanted to use. After much trial and error, James developed a working thesis statement:

"Public indifference toward drug addiction allows drug dealers to continue to supply teenagers. The adults in our society are responsible for allowing drugs in the schools and the neighborhoods."

Freewriting helps you free up the ideas stored in your own mind. By exploring ideas in an unpressured way, you are often able to stretch each idea further into new and unexpected territory.

The disadvantage of freewriting is that you may have to search out a few valuable points from a stream of material that is essentially useless. Sometimes you may be able to brainstorm more productively *after* you have had a freewriting session.

Discovery Questions to Ask Yourself
When Brainstorming or Freewriting

1. Can I briefly *define, describe,* or *identify* my *specific topic?* (For example, if you plan to discuss human rights, you should write a brief description of what you think human rights are.)

2. What does my topic apply to? Who is helped, or hurt, by it? Who favors it? Who opposes it? (For example, if a baby food manufacturer labels as apple juice what is only sugar and water, who is harmed?)

3. What is my topic like or unlike? Can I compare it to anything that will clarify my meaning? (To what, for example, can you compare a polluted lake?)

4. What about the *time* framework? Should I discuss the *present, past,* and *future* of my topic, or should I discuss an important decade, century, or year? (For example, what happened to attitudes toward women in the workforce since my grandmother's day?)

5. Are there any important individuals who made a change or difference? (Did Mao Tse-tung help or hurt China?)

6. What is the most unusual or significant thing about this topic? Is this a national issue? A local issue?

7. What about the origin or source of my topic? (If you are discussing nuclear power, you can date the origin of nuclear power to the testing done on atomic weapons during World War II.)

8. Are there any popular but debatable myths about the topic?

9. What about results, effects, and purposes? (For example, what are the long-range effects of drug rehabilitation programs?)

10. What are the alternatives? Future prospects?

CHALLENGING CONVENTIONAL OPINIONS

Another technique for stirring up your ideas is to challenge traditional, conventional opinions. First, jot down a conventional opinion, and then think of an unconventional position that challenges it.

Doctors, for example, are traditionally considered as useful and productive members of society. Such a statement would not make much of an impression on a reader. So a student might point out ways in which some doctors have failed to live up to their respected position in society.

Student Jill Woolsom began with a tentative thesis statement that challenged traditional thinking: "In recent years doctors have lost the faith of their patients." Then she began to brainstorm, coming up with some good points to support her thesis:

- doctors do not have the same respect from their patients they had in the past
- they work in teams and cover for one another; a patient might see her own doctor but more often sees a new doctor who is covering that shift
- some patients think doctors overcharge for short visits
- many HMOs (health maintenance organizations) have taken the place of the old family doctor; HMOs are cheaper and a staff doctor is always available
- it is hard to locate a private doctor on weekends or holidays
- when hospitals in California were shut due to a strike, the death rate went down
- most insurance plans insist that patients get a second opinion before surgery; many unneeded operations were performed in the past
- many operations have been botched—sponges left in incision

From this list, Jill decided she had enough material to support her thesis challenging a conventional opinion and to make her readers read with more than usual interest.

You may even want to challenge an opinion of the U.S. Supreme Court. A controversial question brought before the Supreme Court concerned whether or not school principals should have the right to examine students' private lockers. The Supreme Court recently gave principals this right. If you feel this decision is an invasion of personal privacy, you might want to research this Court ruling and write a paper explaining your view of it.

■ PRACTICE 5   Read each of the following traditional views and then write a tentative thesis statement that contradicts or challenges it.

1. **Exercise is good for you.**
2. **You should only take science courses if you are good at them.**
3. **People know instinctively how to be good parents.**
4. **Art and music are expensive frills in public schools.**
5. **Grammar is dull and has no applications.**
6. **A good friend should take your side in an argument—no matter what you say.**

TURNING A PROBLEM STATEMENT INTO A THESIS STATEMENT

If you are having a lengthy struggle focusing on a main idea, it sometimes helps to write out a **problem statement** in which you set down some controversy or conflict. Once you have clearly described the problem, you can think about which one of the following five perspectives you want to take. For example, you may set down this problem: "Public schools are not doing the job for many students." Then you can work out whether you want to

1. Identify the source of the problem:
"Teachers are not paid adequately compared to what they can earn in business. Many fine teachers have left the profession, and the schools suffer."

2. Identify a possible solution to the problem:
"Private citizens must let local officials and school boards know that they support larger salaries for teachers."

3. Prove that a problem exists:
"Basic skills in reading and writing have dropped, and the schools have come under attack for producing students who lack these skills."

4. Show that a misconception exists:
"Many people think teachers will put up with low pay because they love to teach. The truth is many teachers feel exploited and no longer want to teach for too little money."

5. Show a problem as well as a solution:
"Many pet owners are not aware that 17 million homeless pets were turned over to animal shelters last year and 13.5 million of these had to be destroyed. Pet owners should neuter their pets to stop the suffering caused by animal overpopulation."

■ PRACTICE 6   Each of the following *problem statements* describes a controversy or problem. Turn the problem statements into working thesis statements, using one of the five perspectives we have just explained.

1. *Problem:* **Some elderly people have no surviving friends or family nearby and suffer from acute loneliness.**

   Thesis statement: _____

   _____

2. *Problem:* **If abused as a child, a parent tends to treat his or her own children cruelly.**

   Thesis statement: _____

   _____

3. *Problem:* **Some people train for careers in fields that are suddenly filled with a glut of qualified people.**

   Thesis statement: _____

   _____

4. *Problem:* **When people are very ill with diseases such as AIDS, they are eager to try experimental drugs; however, the Federal Drug Administration (FDA) needs time to test these drugs to make sure they are safe.**

   Thesis statement: _____

   _____

5. *Problem:* **Government and business computer files contain all sorts of private information about every citizen. It is impossible to know who has access to this information.**

   Thesis statement: _____

   _____

ORGANIZING YOUR IDEAS

Let us now assume that you have a tentative main idea and some supporting ideas grouped in clusters. Next, you want to make a scratch or rough outline before you begin your first draft. How do you decide on a good, workable organization?

1. Find an organization by arranging the clusters from brainstorming.

Many writers study the headings of the clusters developed in brainstorming and quickly spot a logical order of presenting the clusters. They choose an order they think will be clear to their readers because it makes a clear framework for their ideas. For example, the writer may notice that the clusters can be easily grouped into an obvious time sequence of past, present, and future (chronological order).

When writing a comparison, writers often have some choice about the kind of sequence to use. For example, they may state all their points about Charlie Chaplin and follow with all their points about Woody Allen. Or they may decide to compare one of Chaplin's qualities with one of Allen's, and then another of Chaplin's with another of Allen's, and so forth. Let the clusters suggest clues about an initial framework, but be prepared to revise it as you draft and think of an even better scheme.

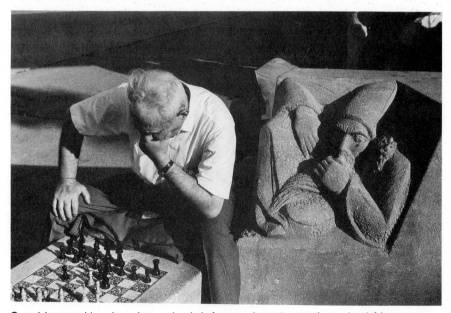

Organizing your ideas in a clear and orderly framework can be creative and satisfying.

2. Find an organization from the wording of the thesis statement.

Sometimes you may find a clue for organizing your working outline from your tentative thesis statement. Say your working thesis is "Public morality shows signs of declining, and some of the causes for that decline are now so widely accepted in society that they will be hard to eliminate." You want to give various causes for the decline and have produced a list of examples while brainstorming:

- more pornographic publications than ever
- availability of X-rated videotapes
- increases in child abuse
- blatantly suggestive rock music lyrics
- popularity of dial-a-porn

A simple scratch outline might be all you need as a guide to discussing these examples, one by one. Some writers put their strongest point first to "hook" the reader; others save their best point for last—just before the conclusion.

3. Find an organization by comparing several possible outlines.

If you are writing a longer essay, one with some research involved, you might first play around with several outline options and then choose the one you think will work best. As the writer, your goal in choosing an organization is to have the reader grasp your sequence of ideas clearly and quickly. The outline does not need to be too detailed—just list the main headings you plan to take up in some reasonable order—unless you prefer working from a detailed plan.

4. Find an organization while you are drafting.

Some writers postpone developing their outline until they are in the process of drafting. Their method is to complete a paragraph and then jot down a few words to describe it on their outline. However, this trial-and-error method sometimes can be inefficient.

5. Find the organization that suits your ideas and information best.

Choose an organization that you can explain or justify to your reader. Ask yourself, Will a reader be able to reconstruct my outline easily? For example, if you decide to discuss some possible reasons why poet Emily Dickinson became a recluse, you might consider this order:

1. chronology

- her early sociable years before she became a recluse
- the crisis in her early thirties

- her later reclusive years

2. comparison

- advantages she enjoyed as a recluse
- disadvantages of being a recluse

Your reader will be able to follow your ideas in this clear and orderly framework. Like brainstorming, finding a good organization can be creative and satisfying, especially the moment when you think of a brilliant way to outline your paper.

In Chapter 18 we discuss the steps that follow prewriting and describe drafting, revising, and proofreading.

WORKING SPACE

READING ASSIGNMENT

Read the following essay by Annie Dillard explaining how she wrote one of her best-known essays on a moth. Notice how she remembers an old journal and uses it as a source of ideas for the famous "moth" essay, written several years after the journal entry. What would you say were other sources of her ideas— memory, past experiences, reading, observations?

How I Wrote the Moth Essay—and Why

It was November 1975. I was living alone, as described, on an island in Puget Sound, near the Canadian border. I was thirty years old. I thought about myself a lot (for someone thirty years old), because I couldn't figure out what I was doing there. What was my life about? Why was I living alone, when I am gregarious?* Would I ever meet someone, or should I reconcile myself to all this solitude? I disliked celibacy;† I dreaded childlessness. I couldn't even think of anything to write. I was examining every event for possible meaning.

I was then in full flight from success, from the recent fuss over a

---

*gregarious: liking people
†celibacy: unmarried state

book of prose I'd published the previous year called *Pilgrim at Tin-
ker Creek*. There were offers from editors, publishers, and Hollywood
and network producers. They tempted me with world travel, film
and TV work, big bucks. I was there to turn from literary and commercial success and to rededicate myself to art and to God. That's
how I justified my loneliness to myself. It was a feeble justification
and I knew it, because you certainly don't need to live alone either
to write or to pray. Actually, I was there because I had picked the
place from an atlas, and I was alone because I hadn't yet met my
husband.

My reading and teaching fed my thoughts. I was reading Simone
Weil, *First and Last Notebooks*. Simone Weil was a twentieth-century
French intellectual, born Jewish, who wrote some of the most interesting Christian theology I've ever read. She was brilliant, but a little
nuts; her doctrines were harsh. "Literally," she wrote, "it is purity or
death." This sort of fanaticism* attracted and appalled me. Weil had
deliberately starved herself to death to call attention to the plight of
French workers. I was taking extensive notes on Weil.

In the classroom I was teaching poetry writing, exhorting† myself
(in the guise of exhorting my students), and convincing myself by my
own rhetoric:†† commit yourself to a useless art! In art alone is
meaning! In sacrifice alone is meaning! These, then, were issues for
me at that time: dedication, purity, sacrifice.

Early that November morning I noticed the hollow insects on the
bathroom floor. I got down on my hands and knees to examine them
and recognized some as empty moth bodies. I recognized them, of
course, only because I'd seen an empty moth body already—two
years before, when I'd camped alone and had watched a flying moth
get stuck in a candle burn.

Walking back to my desk, where I had been answering letters, I
realized that the burning moth was a dandy visual focus for all my
recent thoughts about an empty, dedicated life. Perhaps I'd try to
write a short narrative about it.

I went to my pile of journals, hoping I'd taken some nice, specific
notes about the moth in the candle. What I found disappointed me at
first: that night I'd written a long description of owl sounds, and only
an annoyed aside about bugs flying into the candle. But the next
night, after pages of self-indulgent drivel, I'd written a fuller description, a description of the moth which got stuck in candle wax.

---

*fanaticism: obsessive devotion to a cause
†exhorting: urging
††rhetoric: use of language

The journal entry had some details I could use (bristleworms on the ground, burnt moth's wings sticking to pans), some phrases (her body acted as a wick, the candle had two flames, the moth burned until I blew it out), and especially, some verbs (hiss, recoil, stick, spatter, jerked, crackled).

Even in the journals, the moth was female. (From childhood reading I'd learned to distinguish moths by sex.) And, there in the journal, was a crucial detail: on that camping trip, I'd been reading about Rimbaud. Arthur Rimbaud—the French symbolist poet, a romantic, hotheaded figure who attracted me enormously when I was sixteen—had been young and self-destructive. When *he* was sixteen, he ran away from home to Paris, led a dissolute* life, shot his male lover (the poet Verlaine), drank absinthe which damaged his brain, deranged† his senses with drunkenness and sleeplessness, and wrote mad vivid poetry which altered the course of Western literature. When he was in his twenties, he turned his back to the Western world and vanished into Abyssinia as a gunrunner.

With my old journal beside me, I took up my current journal and scribbled and doodled my way through an account of my present life and the remembered moth. It went extraordinarily well; it was not typical. It seemed very much "given"—given, I think, because I'd asked, because I'd been looking so hard and so long for connections, meanings. The connections were all there, and seemed solid enough: I saw a moth burnt and on fire; I was reading Rimbaud hoping to rededicate myself to writing (this one bald statement of motive was unavoidable); I live alone. So the writer is like the moth, and like a religious contemplative:†† emptying himself so he can be a channel for his work. Of course you can reinforce connections with language: the bathroom moths are like a jumble of buttresses for cathedral domes; the female moth is like an immolating§ monk, like a hollow saint, a flame-faced virgin gone to God; Rimbaud burnt out his brains with poetry while night pooled wetly at my feet.

I liked the piece enough to rewrite it. I took out a couple of paragraphs—one about why I didn't have a dog, another that ran on about the bathroom spider. This is the kind of absurdity you fall into when you write about anything, let alone about yourself. You're so pleased and grateful to be writing at all, especially at the beginning,

---

*dissolute: loose, unrestrained
†deranged: made insane
††contemplative: member of religious order devoted to meditation
§immolating: burning

that you babble. Often you don't know where the work is going, so you can't tell what's irrelevant.

It doesn't hurt much to babble in a first draft, so long as you have the sense to cut out irrelevancies later. If you are used to analyzing texts, you will be able to formulate a clear statement of what your draft turned out to be about. Then you make a list of what you've already written, paragraph by paragraph, and see what doesn't fit and cut it out. (All this requires is nerves of steel and lots of coffee.) Most of the time you'll have to add to the beginning, ensuring that it gives a fair idea of what the point might be, or at least what is about to happen. (Suspense is for mystery writers. The most inept writing has an inadvertent* element of suspense: the reader constantly asks himself, where on earth is this going?) Usually I end up throwing away the beginning: the first part of a poem, the first few pages of an essay, the first scene of a story, even the first few chapters of a book. It's not holy writ. The paragraphs and sentences are tesserae—tiles for a mosaic. Just because you have a bunch of tiles in your lap doesn't mean your mosaic will be better if you use them all. In this atypical case, however, there were very few extraneous passages. The focus was tight, probably because I'd been so single-minded before I wrote it.

I added stuff, too, to strengthen and clarify the point. I added some speculation about the burning moth: had she mated and laid her eggs, had she done her work? Near the end I added a passage about writing class: which of you want to give your lives and become writers?

Ultimately I sent it to *Harper's* magazine, which published it.

---

1. What were some of the events that triggered Dillard's essay?

2. What is the connection between the moth and the young poet Rimbaud?

---

inadvertent: not intended

3. Why, according to Dillard's account, did the writing of the essay go "extraordinarily well"?

4. How would you interpret this statement: "The writer is like the moth, and like a religious contemplative: emptying himself so he can be a channel for his work"?

WRITING ASSIGNMENT: "Stirring Up Ideas"

Freewrite or brainstorm on one of these statements:

1. Modern relationships are more difficult than old-fashioned marriages because no one knows the rules.
2. Success and happiness are within you.
3. Members of Congress only think of getting reelected, not of what is best for the people. Whoever contributes to their campaigns for reelection has influence on them.
4. Perhaps marriages arranged by parents were not such a crazy idea. Parents would look for stability and long-term benefits for their children.

JOURNAL ASSIGNMENT

Comment on this statement by Joan Didion: "I write entirely to find out what I'm thinking, what I'm looking at, what I see and what it means."

CHECKING OUT

Check your understanding of Chapter 17 by writing answers to the following questions. You may work alone or with a classmate, whichever you prefer.

1. What is clustering, and why does it follow a brainstorming session?

2. What are the pros and cons of focused freewriting?

3. Why should you give your clusters a title or a heading, and how can you use these headings for outlining?

4. What is a thesis statement? What is a problem statement, and describe some of the ways you can convert it into a thesis statement?

5. Why does a writer want to ''narrow the subject,'' and how does he or she do this?

6. What are some of the inner resources any writer can use to generate ideas? What are some ways the writer can stimulate a reader's interest?

IN SUMMARY

When planning any kind of paper, you can use several effective prewriting strategies to discover your best ideas. To probe your past experiences, earlier memories, and previous knowledge, try brainstorming or focused freewriting.

Both of these strategies can help you search your mind for possible ideas, as well as connections and patterns among ideas, by means of free association (the mind reminded of one idea by another). These strategies will help you identify your most creative and insightful ideas. While using either technique, you may also want to ask yourself probing "discovery" questions to help the search process.

After you brainstorm or freewrite, evaluate and then cluster your ideas, giving each cluster a descriptive heading. Try to rough out a thesis statement at this point. If you have trouble formulating a thesis statement, try writing out a problem statement and then converting it into a thesis statement—by identifying the source of the problem, suggesting a solution, or showing that a misconception exists. Or try questioning conventional opinions in order to arouse more than usual interest in your reader.

Idea searches can be very stimulating and satisfying, with little pressure and a great deal of freedom. They will help you generate your very best ideas as the raw material for a first draft. After you have clustered your related ideas, you can usually develop a short working outline either from your clusters or from your thesis statement. The purpose of the rough outline is to help you organize your writing as well as to help the reader understand your framework. In Chapter 18, we continue describing the writing process from first rough draft to the final polished draft.

CHAPTER 18

DRAFTING AND REVISING PAPERS

The writer must learn to read critically but constructively, to cut what is bad, to reveal what is good. . . . Making something right is immensely satisfying.

—Donald Murray

OVERVIEW

Some writers jump in and draft without much preplanning (they are actually freewriting). But you probably will save yourself time if you follow the prewriting strategies we provided in Chapter 17. These strategies will bring you to the point where you are well prepared to produce a first draft. In the present chapter, we will guide you through a step-by-step process for completing your paper—from first to final draft. And if you are writing a research paper, we will show you when and how to cite your sources. Taking up after our discussion of prewriting, we cover the following:

- When writing your rough first draft, concentrate on your ideas, explaining them simply and clearly to you reader.

- After an incubation period, read your draft to the end, marking weak and unclear sections.

- Plan a two-stage revision strategy based on doing the most essential tasks first.

- Rethink the larger issues: Is your main thesis sharp and clear? Is your outline strong? Are your supporting ideas convincing?

- Use our editing checklist as a guide for editing your papers.

• Recopy and proofread the final draft, rereading every word.

• For a research paper, cite the sources you have used; insert parenthetical references and prepare a Works Cited page.

WRITING YOUR FIRST DRAFT

Let us say that all your prewriting tasks are accomplished: you have a working thesis statement that interests you ("The almost constant violence on national TV indicates that Americans still have a fondness for settling disputes by aggressive, frontier behavior."); you have produced a rough working outline; and you have generated some strong support for your thesis by freewriting and clustering.

For writing out your important first draft, set aside a few quiet hours when you feel fresh and alert, and when you know you can work undisturbed. To produce a good paper, you need to think hard and concentrate through the whole drafting process. Now you have to deal with inventing sentences, one after another, to express your ideas. And you have to think of how to organize and connect your ideas so the reader can follow your train of thought. Even experienced writers find drafting—inventing and then connecting sentences—a challenge. Remember not to try to polish anything. Just get your ideas down roughly, simply, and boldly.

We recommend these simple guidelines for drafting:

1. Whether you use a pencil and lined paper, a typewriter, or a computer, **always double-space** to allow for later changes.

2. Be sure to **write out a complete first draft** before you start any revising. Push to the end. In this way, you can monitor the overall shape of your paper:

   — You will avoid spending too long polishing the start and running out of time for writing a good ending.

   — You can control the overall organization (shortening long or repetitive sections, expanding on ideas that are too sketchy to be clear).

   — You can see roughly how long your paper is. (Estimate roughly 250 to 300 words per typed page; if at all possible, plan to type rather than handwrite your final paper for the sake of your reader—and your grade.)

3. Generally, **to begin, set down your working thesis statement** in one or several sentences, but don't fuss over its precise wording. It might very

well change by the time you have completed your draft. And do not spend too much time on the introduction; wait until you have completed the draft and know more about what it should say.

4. **Concentrate on presenting your ideas forcefully.** Convince your reader your ideas are worth reading. Focus on how to introduce each new major point (or new cluster) from your brainstorming and how to express the supporting details convincingly to prove your point. Frame sentences that hold your reader's attention—sentences that are varied in length and impact. Don't forget an occasional short and emphatic statement, such as "Kennedy was now in deep trouble." In short, focus all your energy on conveying your ideas to your reader.

5. **Keep checking your outline** to present your ideas in a clear order. If you see, as you write, that your outline is not the best way to frame your ideas, make a midcourse correction. Call a time-out and rework your rough outline. Some writers like to draft and outline simultaneously.

   If you *have* steered away from the outline while drafting, go back and make a very simple outline of your major points—what each paragraph is now about. As you write and think further, you will often discover many other things you want to add or change. Make these changes, but be sure to stay in control by updating your scratch outline.

6. **Write in a simple and straightforward manner, as if explaining your ideas to a mature adult.** Try to sound like yourself. If you think your sentences are getting too complicated, break them into shorter units. (Sometimes it helps to experiment with problem sentences on a separate sheet of paper.) If you feel your sentences are too short and simple, try combining some (ask your teacher for specific help on sentence combining).

7. **Connect your ideas.** Show your reader in some way how each sentence connects to the one before it. For example, if you write, in three sentences: "Some students . . . Other students . . . Yet other students . . .," your reader can follow your train of thought—a clear sequence of three different types of students. Similarly, connect every paragraph to the next one by some transitional word or phrase that leads the reader to your next major topic.

8. **Think in terms of constructing paragraphs.** Each paragraph should take up a major new idea—usually a new cluster from your brainstorming. If you are a beginning writer, use a *topic sentence* when you begin a new paragraph (later you can experiment with other devices). A topic sentence is to a paragraph what a thesis statement is to the whole essay (see Figure 18–1).

The *thesis statement* explains the main idea of the whole essay. The *topic sentence* heads each new paragraph and gives the main idea of each paragraph. The topic sentence is usually more general than the detailed sentences in the rest of the paragraph.

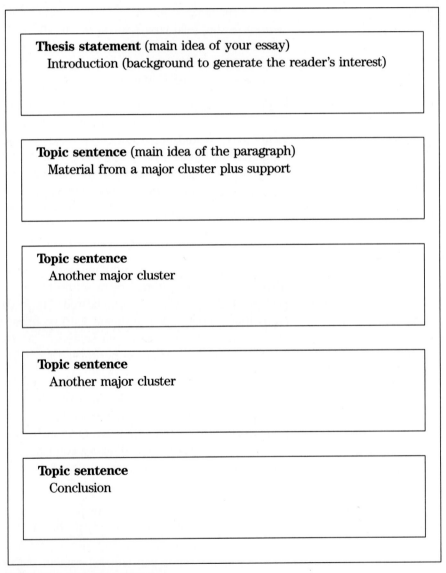

Thesis statement (main idea of your essay)
   Introduction (background to generate the reader's interest)

Topic sentence (main idea of the paragraph)
   Material from a major cluster plus support

Topic sentence
   Another major cluster

Topic sentence
   Another major cluster

Topic sentence
   Conclusion

Figure 18–1: Basic Essay Structure

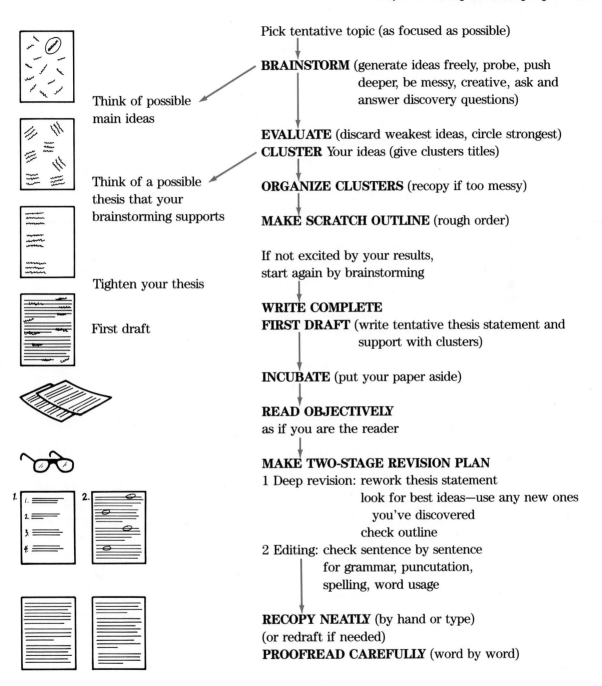

Pick tentative topic (as focused as possible)

BRAINSTORM (generate ideas freely, probe, push
deeper, be messy, creative, ask and
answer discovery questions)

Think of possible
main ideas

EVALUATE (discard weakest ideas, circle strongest)
CLUSTER Your ideas (give clusters titles)

Think of a possible
thesis that your
brainstorming supports

ORGANIZE CLUSTERS (recopy if too messy)

MAKE SCRATCH OUTLINE (rough order)

If not excited by your results,
start again by brainstorming

Tighten your thesis

WRITE COMPLETE
FIRST DRAFT (write tentative thesis statement and
support with clusters)

First draft

INCUBATE (put your paper aside)

READ OBJECTIVELY
as if you are the reader

MAKE TWO-STAGE REVISION PLAN
1 Deep revision: rework thesis statement
look for best ideas—use any new ones
you've discovered
check outline
2 Editing: check sentence by sentence
for grammar, puncutation,
spelling, word usage

RECOPY NEATLY (by hand or type)
(or redraft if needed)
PROOFREAD CAREFULLY (word by word)

Figure 18–2: Step-by-Step Writing—An Efficient Method

9. **Keep thinking of your reader.** Are you giving him or her the best examples to support your thesis? Are you making each idea clear to someone who only has your written words to go by—and doesn't know what else you may have in mind?

10. **Use your discoveries.** If you suddenly see something in a new way or get a new insight, take the trouble to work it into your first draft, even if you have to rework some of what you have already done. Chances are it will improve your paper considerably.

■ PRACTICE 1   Find a short magazine article you think is well organized. Jot down a short title or a heading for each paragraph. Can you reconstruct the writer's outline? How does the writer connect one paragraph to the next? Did you follow this writer's ideas easily or not?

■ PRACTICE 2   Brainstorm on this topic: "The almost constant violence on TV programs—is it harmful to young viewers or is it simply entertainment?" After putting your ideas in clusters, write out several rough outlines in which you organize the material in several sequences. Pick the order you think would work best in a paper.

VIGOROUS REVISING: FOCUS ON THE LARGER ISSUES

Before revising, be sure to set aside your first draft—rough but complete—for a period of incubation. When you read it again later—with a fresh eye—try to **imagine that you know nothing about the subject of your paper.** Forget what's in your head: the words and the sentences on the page are all you know about the paper. Do the words tell you all that you need to know?

Read the paper through to the end before you plan your revision strategy. Switching roles and acting as your reader, ask yourself these questions:

• Have I been told everything I need to know to understand the point of the paper? Should any basic information be added to the opening, such as any dates, names, places, the title and author of any book mentioned, more background, and so forth? (If in doubt, it is best to add brief background information—even if your intended reader will know it.)

• **What are the strongest, most convincing ideas presented here?** (You will want to **build on these.**)

• **What are the weakest ideas?** (Mark or circle these paragraphs or sentences to be revised first.) And don't be afraid to cut or completely rewrite weak passages.

- Can I think of any stronger supporting examples to make my thesis statement clearer to a reader?
- Is the thesis statement worded as precisely as possible? Can I say it better?
- Is the sequence of the ideas effective, or is there a better way of outlining the information?
- What is the overall impact on me as the reader? Good first draft or not?
- Does this draft need heavy or light revision?

Now plan a revision strategy. **Work first and hardest on the places you identified as the weakest.** Decide upon your other revision priorities, using your time and effort where it will help you most.

You might also want to ask a friend to read your draft and give you some feedback by pointing out to you what is clear and what is muddled, what are strong and weak points, and which sections should be reworked.

Checklist for Revising—Establish Your Priorities

After they complete the first draft, good writers are both vigorous and fearless when they revise. They concentrate primarily on three main goals:

Keep your paper "on track." Check for repetition and rework confusing passages.

1. **Are the ideas, both my thesis and its support, the best I can produce?** Have I discovered any new insights, while writing the draft, that I should add to the paper? (Write long inserts on a new page if you have no room in the margin.)

2. **Is the organization as good as it can be?** (Would paragraph 3 be clearer to my reader if it were paragraph 2, for example? If you have access to a computer, you can quickly rearrange paragraphs to try out alternatives. Otherwise you can cut and paste.)

3. **Are the connections from one sentence to the next clear?** Have I made explicit **transitions** so the reader knows why I am adding each sentence and each paragraph? Does every paragraph help to develop and explain my overall thesis?

Also check for the following:

- **Repetitions:** Cut any points you belabor. (Once is usually enough.)
- **Mysteries:** Rework any passages that may confuse the reader. (If in doubt, ask a friend to read the section.)
- **Rambling:** Have you stayed on track, or have you rambled? (Cut out any digressions.)
- **Tone:** Avoid being either too flip and informal or too pompous. (Find a middle, neutral tone.)

In the first revision stage, concentrate exclusively on the overall shaping of your ideas. Check out all the more minor problems in the *second* stage of revision, called *editing,* discussed below. If, however, you have too many of these minor editing problems, they may become major and hurt your grade.

> In the first revision stage, concentrate exclusively on the overall shaping of your ideas.

PRACTICE 3   Using the topic that you brainstormed in Practice 2, write a first draft of at least two typed pages (500 words). Then in the margins or on a separate sheet, propose what kind of major revisions you would make to improve the draft.

EDITING

When you are satisfied with the overall ideas and organization, turn your attention to errors at the sentence level. Following our checklist below, look first of all for problems in sentence structure, and then check punctuation, spelling, and word usage (use the dictionary). If you typically have problems with these matters, ask your teacher for help or refer to English handbooks and workbooks, or both. Ask a friend to point out any errors you may have missed.

Writers usually make the same types of errors in all their papers. Keep track of the types of errors you make in your papers, and try to eliminate the problems one by one by getting a clear understanding of what you are doing wrong. None of these problems by itself is very difficult. It is mainly a matter of being alert, spotting your typical errors, and fixing them before you submit the paper.

Any writing that appears in books and magazines is checked by a professional editor before it is published. What does an editor look for? An editor is looking for a variety of errors that writers, even professional writers, commonly make. You must be your own editor, and be alert to the trouble spots.

Basic Checklist for Editing Papers

☐ **Check Sentences**

- **Check for complete and correct sentences.** Are all your sentences complete thoughts, with a subject and verb? Does each sentence begin with a capital letter and end with a clearly visible period (or question mark)? Do you have any unintentional sentence fragments?

- **Do the main subject and main verb make sense together?** Drop out all the intervening words and check that the main subject and main verb make logical sense together. Take, for example,

  "Nixon, because he believed the president had special privileges, led to his own downfall."

  Cross out all the interrupting words and read the main subject and main verb together to see if they make sense together:

  "Nixon . . . led to his own downfall."

  In this sentence, the verb *contributed* probably would be clearer than *led*.

- **Check that subjects and verbs agree in number.** A singular subject requires a singular verb and a plural subject requires a plural verb.

Problems occur when interrupting words come between the subject and verb. To check subject-verb agreement, drop out the in-between words so that you can read the main subject and verb together:

"The cause of the street fights were drugs." (incorrect)

If you drop out the phrase "of the street fights," you can see that the sentence should read: "The cause . . . *was*." Both subject and verb are now singular.

- **Do not join sentences with commas** (known as a comma splice). Here we have several sentences incorrectly joined by commas:

   "Nixon did not handle his crisis well, he called in his advisers, who were divided about what to do, the situation grew out of control, he lost the presidency."

This problem sentence should be reworded. A writer has many optional ways to cure this comma splice; learn about them in texts on sentence combining and sentence styling. Here is one cure:

   "Nixon did not handle his crisis well. He called in his advisers, who were divided about what to do. With Nixon continuing to be indecisive, the situation grew out of control. He lost the presidency."

If you do not recognize this problem of comma splices in your own writing, discuss it with your teacher.

☐ Check Apostrophes

- **Any noun that shows possession should have an apostrophe.**

   my sister's coat (before final *s* in singular nouns)
   my brothers' farm (after final *s* in plural nouns)
   children's coats (before *s* if plural noun does not end in *s*)

- **Omit the apostrophe with these pronouns: yours, ours, his, hers, theirs.**

   The farm belonged to their uncle, but now it is *theirs*. (no apostrophe)
   She did not know it was *ours*. (no apostrophe)

- **Always use an apostrophe to make contractions.**

I'm	= I am	we're	= we are
you're	= you are	they're	= they are
he's, she's	= he is, she is	don't	= do not

- **Watch for problems with "it's" and "its."**
KEY: *It's* always stands for *it is.* If you can substitute *it is* in your sentence, use an apostrophe:

    "The bags are packed and it's time to leave." (Here you can substitute *it is* time to leave.)

But the next sentence makes no sense if you substitute *it is* right before the word *vacation,* so use *its:*

    "The school has *its* vacation starting in June." (correct)

- **Watch for problems with "their," "they're," and "there."**
Their shows ownership and is always followed directly by a noun:

    "Their car was stolen."

They're always stands for "they are":

    "They're ready to go." (If you can substitute *they are,* use *they're.)*

There's always stands for "there is":

    There's trouble at home."

There can also refer to a place:

    "She found him there in the shed."

- **Check for similar problems with "we're," "were," "where."**
Be sure you know what each of these means.

☐ Check Comparisons

- **Always check comparisons after "than" and "as":**

"She is stronger and tougher than he."

To see if the comparison is correct, finish the comparison by adding the verb:

"She is stronger than he [is]." (correct)
"We are as strong as they [are]." (correct)
"He is as strong as me." (incorrect; it should be "He is as strong as I [am].")

☐ Check Modifiers

* **Check introductory verb forms ending in -ed or -ing.**
  Introductory verb forms ending in -ed or -ing must refer to the subject:

  Running his fastest, my dog didn't catch the squirrel.

  Stopped by the police for speeding, I was nervous.

In the next case, the "I" is incorrectly hanging out of the drawer:

"Dangling out of my drawer, I put on my sock." (incorrect)

Verb forms ending in -ed or -ing can also correctly refer to the word directly before them:

"I put on my sock dangling out of the drawer." (correct)
"I saw a small deer running through the woods." (correct)

☐ Check Parallel Construction

* **Put a list of three or more items in parallel construction.**
  If you have a series of any three items, try to use parallel construction so that the reader can grasp the relationship quickly.

  "She ran a mile, swam ten laps, and played tennis." (three verbs)

  "I looked under the bed, in the closet, and through all my drawers." (three phrases)

  "Carrying the tray, balancing the coffee pot, and holding the cake, I tripped and dropped it all." (three phrases)

☐ Check Pronouns

- **Any pronoun you use must refer clearly to a noun** and be either singular or plural depending on that noun.

  "Each student ate their snacks." (incorrect)
  "Each student ate her snack." (correct)

- **Put pronouns that follow prepositions in the objective case:**
  Learn to recognize the fifteen or so common prepositions (such as *against, between, with, to, for, among*).
  Learn to recognize the objective case *(me, him, her, us, them).*

  "Between you and me, we can solve this grammar problem."
  (correct)
  "Annabel described her African trip to you and I." (incorrect)

☐ Check Spelling

- **Check the spelling of any word you are not sure about in the dictionary.**

PROOFREADING

Even if you are very tired, **proofreading is an important step.** If you let sloppy errors slip by, your teacher will get the wrong impression. After you have prepared your final draft, read it once again, looking for careless mistakes—missing periods, misspellings, words copied incorrectly, words left out in recopying. Make any final corrections neatly by hand: **a neat correction is far better than a mistake.**

Basic Checklist for Punctuation

- **Make sure each sentence ends in a visible period.**
- **Check for commas after dates:**

  "He came home on March 4, 1963, and returned to Europe by June." (Notice the commas around the year.)

- **Check for commas after place names:**

"He set out for Portland, Oregon, but only made it as far as Detroit, Michigan." (Notice the commas around the state.)

- **Commas are often used to separate items in a series:**

  "He added ketchup, mustard, and onions."

- **Commas are used between two independent clauses** joined by *and* or *but:*

  "The research provided unexpected new data, and the scientists were encouraged by their results."

- **Commas are often used after long opening clauses:**

  "After we both found out we were accepted to law school, we celebrated for a week."

- **Semicolons can be used to join several short related sentences:**

  "I heard brakes squeal; I saw a car heading into us; I knew we were in trouble; I shut my eyes and waited."

- **Colons very effectively tell the reader to read on quickly** and find out more:

  "Doctor Borg announced her diagnosis: the patient's disease was not fatal."

- **Dashes and parentheses can both be used for parenthetical comments,** that is, material that is not vital to the sense but adds some interest:

  "Emily Dickinson—one of America's most original writers—used a dash in preference to all other marks of punctuation."

WRITING THE RESEARCH PAPER

A research paper requires you to combine many skills, most of which we have already covered—long-term schedules, library research, critical reading and thinking, writing, notetaking on sources, and proofreading. You will need to plan in order to allow yourself enough time to do each job.

If you research correctly, you will become well informed—even an expert—on the area you are investigating. The research paper, far from being an impersonal survey of sources, should be based on your reactions and responses to the ideas and opinions of other writers, both those you agree and disagree with. You must show in your paper that you are truly knowledgeable about this material—and have some worthwhile ideas of your own about your topic.

Since this paper will probably be one of your major writing efforts, check your instructions carefully and speak to your teacher at intervals to be sure you are carrying out the assignment correctly. A research paper is one of the most demanding tasks you will survive in your college career. But one of your most satisfying experiences while in college will be finishing a research paper, especially when you have given it an all-out effort.

In Chapter 14, we discussed how to synthesize the ideas of several authors, and we strongly recommend you reread the chapter in preparation for writing a research paper. In Chapter 16, we suggested strategies for finding ideas and sources for your paper through library research.

As a brief review of our earlier chapters, the prewriting steps for a research paper follow.

Basic Checklist for Writing a Research Paper

- Make a long-term schedule giving yourself partial completion dates (see p. 37).
- Select a working subject.
- Collect your own bibliography of sources (a list of books and journals on your subject.) (See Chapter 16.)
- Read your sources, taking careful notes or photocopying important pages; continue to research and read.
- Sort, reread, and revise headings on your note cards often; see if you have collected enough information; see what else is needed to fill the gaps. (See Chapter 16.)
- Think about your research and sources in spare moments, comparing writers' different viewpoints. Describe what you've found thus far to a friend to clarify your own thinking. (See Chapter 14.)
- Narrow your subject, looking for a focused topic that interests you.
- Put your note cards in a tentative order by headings.

- Brainstorm to find out how you respond to the ideas and the interpretations found in your sources. (See Chapter 17.)
- Write out your tentative thesis statement.
- Jot down a rough outline. (See Chapter 17.)

If you do these prewriting steps thoroughly, you will be well prepared to write your first draft. As you write, follow the key steps for drafting given on pages 460–464. Then add the parenthetical references, giving all your sources, as explained in the following sections. Finally, follow the checklists for revising, editing, and proofreading given in the present chapter.

See the model of a good student research paper in the Reading Assignment at the end of this chapter.

Which Sources Should Be Cited?

To avoid plagiarizing or using anyone else's ideas, you need to *cite* (that is, give your source for) any idea that you use in your paper that came from your research. A rule of thumb is to ask yourself if you knew the information before you read about it in a source. If you did not, it is probably safer to give the source where you found the information or idea.

Any statistic, any data, any detailed information that you have discovered in your research—whether in a book, a magazine, a scholarly journal, a newspaper, a company's annual report, a personal interview, or wherever— must be cited. In this way, your reader knows where your information came from and, if interested, can verify it or look in that same publication for additional information. With practice, you will soon recognize when a source should be cited.

In general, **it is not necessary to cite common knowledge or well-known ideas,** such as

> "Thomas Jefferson of Virginia succeeded John Adams to become the third president of the United States."

But you *do* need to cite the source (and the page number) if you quote, word for word, historian Richard Hofstadter's remarks on Thomas Jefferson as a slaveholder:

> "During most of his mature life Thomas Jefferson owned about 10,000 acres and from one to two hundred slaves. The leisure that made possible his great writings on human liberty was supported by the labors of three generations of slaves."

Even if you decide to *paraphrase* Hofstadter's statement, you also must inform the reader of your source:

> Ironically, Jefferson found the leisure to write about human liberty
> by making use of the labors of as many as two hundred slaves.

Whether you decide to quote directly or to paraphrase Hofstadter's sentences about Jefferson, you must let the reader know the author's name and the page that you are quoting in the text itself; then in the "Works Cited" page, you must provide the title of the work and the rest of the publication information, as explained in the following pages.

In quoting or paraphrasing Hofstadter, you can choose either to mention the author's name directly in the text (Hofstadter notes ironically that Jefferson found the leisure to write . . .") or you can put the author's last name in parentheses right after the reference.

> Jefferson found the leisure to write about human liberty by employ-
> ing as many as two hundred slaves **(Hofstadter 23).**

Always place the page number in parentheses, either with the author or by itself (if you've already referred to the author in the text):

> Hofstadter notes ironically that Jefferson found the leisure to write
> by making use of the labors of about two hundred slaves **(23).**

Using this in-text information, the reader can then look up Hofstadter on your Works Cited page and find out the title of the book, *The American Political Tradition,* the publisher (Knopf), and the year published (1948). We explain in detail how to use the parenthetical or in-text style for citing sources in the next two sections.

In addition to citing all direct quotations, you must remember to cite all your paraphrases and summaries of other writers' ideas. As you take notes on note cards, jot down whether your note is a direct quotation (use quotation marks), a paraphrase, or a summary. Later, when you use the information on the card to draft your paper, you will know exactly whether your note is a direct quote or otherwise.

Documentation

Different academic disciplines follow different styles of citing sources. (Be sure to find out what style each of your teachers wants you to follow.) We will illustrate the style favored by the Modern Language Association (MLA) in their *Handbook for Writers of Research Papers*. In this style, the writer uses **parenthetical references,** so-called because the briefest possible reference to the source is enclosed in parentheses directly after the sentence (or phrase) in which the author's idea is mentioned. The writer then cites the complete source (author, title, all publication information) at the end of the paper on the Works Cited page.

The simplest way you can credit or cite a source is to **incorporate the author and title directly into your writing.** Then you will only have to **put the page number in parentheses** directly after the sentence (but before the final period). Here is an example of a reference to a book and its author that is cited directly in the text; notice how only the page number is given in parentheses:

> In her autobiography *Blackberry Winter,* Margaret Mead describes how her teacher Franz Boas wanted her to study adolescence on her first field trip to Samoa whereas she preferred to study cultural change (139).

If, however, you do not include the author and title (or the author alone) in your sentence, you would put the author's last name in parentheses followed by the page number:

> In the early days of field work, young anthropologists were guided in their choice of subject by the research interests of their teachers (Mead 139).

In either case, the full bibliographical information on Margaret Mead's book would be given on the Works Cited page at the end of the paper.*

If you are using two or more books by the same author, say two books by Margaret Mead, add a short form of the title in the parentheses:

> (Mead, *Blackberry,* 139).

Likewise, in using ideas from magazines, journals or newspapers, you can either mention the author's name in the text just before you use his or her idea, or you can place it in a parentheses just after the reference, whichever you prefer. Here is an example of a paraphrase—from an article by Margaret

---

*The book would appear thus on the Works Cited page:
Mead, Margaret. *Blackberry Winter.* New York: Morrow, 1972.

Margaret Mead with a native mother and child in the Admirante Islands.

Mead in the magazine *Redbook*—showing the two choices:

> Previously, an adopted child received a new name and a new birth certificate, and in Margaret Mead's view was considered "reborn" to her adoptive parents (100).

> Previously, an adopted child received a new name and birth certificate, and was virtually considered "reborn" to her adoptive parents (Mead 100).

Note, however, that magazines, journals, and newspapers are treated differently from books on the Works Cited page.*

---

*Mead's article would appear thus on the Works Cited page:
Mead, Margaret. "In the Best Interests of the Child." *Redbook* 151 (Oct. 1978) 100 + .
(The 151 refers to the volume in which the magazine has been bound. The plus sign means that the article skips to later pages.)

If you are referring to the whole book or work rather than to any one section of it, give the author's last name in your sentence:

Turnbull carefully documents the disintegration of tribal culture.

You would also list Colin Turnbull's book, *The Mountain People,* on the Works Cited page.

If you use a long direct quote, like the following from Mead's *Blackberry Winter,* indent it and set it off as a block, omit quotation marks, and put the parentheses outside the final period:

> We laughed at the idea that a woman could be an old maid at the age of twenty-five, and we rejoiced at the new medical care that made it possible for a woman to have a child at forty. (117)

In sum, when using the MLA style, include in parentheses the author's last name when the name is *not* included in your text: (Hofstadter 76). But if you do use the author's name in your text, put in parentheses only the page from which you have taken your information: (76).

PREPARING THE "WORKS CITED" PAGE

In preparing documentation, you want to be careful to distinguish between books and magazines. We previously described how you should distinguish between books and magazines (or journals) on your bibliographic cards (pp. 409–411). On your Works Cited page at the end of your research paper, you will treat books and journals differently.

To cite a book, follow this model:

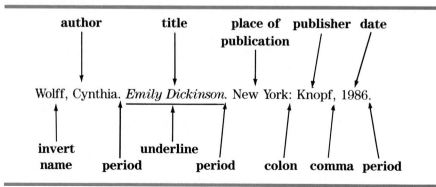

| author | title | place of publication | publisher | date |

Wolff, Cynthia. *Emily Dickinson.* New York: Knopf, 1986.

invert name — period — underline — period — colon — comma — period

For variations on author's name:

One author:	Mead, Margaret (note inverted order of name)
Two or three authors:	Strunk, William, and E. B. White (only first name inverted)
Four or more authors:	Montgomery, John, et al. (add "et al." or "and others")
An editor only:	Edel, Leon, ed. *The Letters of Henry James*

To cite an academic journal, follow this model:

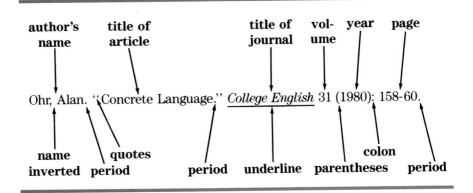

If the journal does not page consecutively through several issues, add volume plus issue number:

Kentucky Review 2.2 (means volume 2, issue number 2)

To cite a popular magazine published monthly, follow this model:

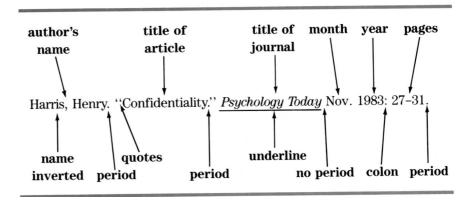

If the article is from a popular magazine published weekly, add the day it was published:

Time 3 June 1987:15-17. (abbreviate longer months: Nov.)

To cite a newspaper article, follow this model:

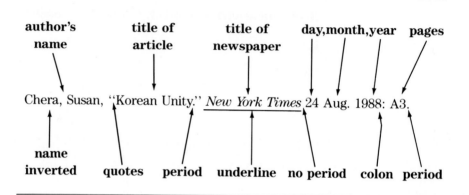

author's name   title of article   title of newspaper   day,month,year   pages

Chera, Susan, "Korean Unity." *New York Times* 24 Aug. 1988: A3.

name inverted   quotes   period   underline   no period   colon   period

WORKING SPACE

READING ASSIGNMENT

Read the following research paper written by student Meenekshi Bose. What points do you agree with and why? What objections might you raise? With three viewpoints involved in questions of adoption, how do you think issues can be resolved for the benefit of all?

Meenekshi Bose
Professor Flemming
Study Skills 101
9 April 1988

Adoption Files and Privacy

In 1971, adoptee Florence Fisher finally completed a twenty-year search for her natural parents. She then set up an organization titled "Adoptees' Liberty Movement Association" to help others locate their natural parents, and to persuade states to change their laws on closed files (Kupersmith 27). Unfortunately, the majority of the states still favor closed files (Hitchings 85), supposedly to prevent all parties from being hurt. However, many people today argue that adoptees must see the files to complete their identities, and that they should be allowed to choose whether or not they want to meet their natural parents.

In the past, adoptive parents kept the adoption a private family secret, and often tried to ignore it altogether. Previously, an adopted child received a new name and birth certificate, and was virtually considered "reborn" to her adoptive parents (Mead 100). Agencies advised parents not to tell the child she was adopted, and often matched children to parents who resembled them so that outsiders could not guess the truth (Soria 24). Only adoption officials had access to the files revealing the child's true name and information on the birth parents, who lost all claim to the child (Soria 86). Fortunately, today people realize that keeping adoptions secret could emotionally harm the child if she finds out, because the secrecy implies that it is something bad (Soria 26). In addition, many adoptees argue that being considered a natural child of their adoptive parents is fantasy, not fact, and that they have a right to know their heritage (Budgen 42). Thus, today many people agree that adoptive parents can no longer pretend the adoption never occurred, but must face the reality that the child has natural parents.

Often adoptive parents do not face reality because they consider searching for her natural parents to be a breach of faith by the child. To many adoptive parents, questions about the circumstances of the child's birth imply either that they did not take adequate care of the child, or that the child no longer loves them (Soria 28). They consider themselves her true parents because they reared, fed, and cared for her, and resent the child for wanting more than they can give (Kupersmith 3). However, many psychologists today argue that searching for one's natural parents doesn't mean that the adoptive parents have failed in their duty (Hitchings 85). Hitchings notes that adoptees search for their parents for emotional reasons or a "deep-felt need" (85). In fact, many adoptees wish to find their biological parents to achieve personal peace, and find out what really happened, not to form relationships with them at all (Kupersmith 30). Surprisingly, a recent study of over four hundred couples conducted by Nassau Community College professors in New York showed that two-thirds of the adoptive parents supported open files (Soria 86). Perhaps they realize that curiosity is natural, and that it will be healthier for the child if they aid her in her search, instead of forcing her to keep secrets from them (Soria 28). Most adoptees looking for their biological parents do love their adoptive parents, but simply need to know their past.

Some people argue that closed files protect the child from learning about an embarrassing past as well as from meeting inadequate parents. They feel that adoption files should be closed to prevent the child from embarrassment if she is illegitimate (Kupersmith 32). Sandra Soria responds, though, by saying the adoptee had no control over the circumstances of her birth, so she should not feel guilty about being "born out of wedlock" (28). Kupersmith further states that today illegitimate children are not as ostracized as before so this is an invalid reason for keeping files closed (320). Other adoption officials, however, believe that closed files protect the biological parents from memories of an unpleasant past and the child from emotional pain if her natural parents refuse to see her (Soria 86). Margaret Mead remarks that often the natural mother either gives up the child of her own free will, or loses the child because the state deems her an "unfit mother" for reasons including drug problems, mental illness, or simply that the mother is not taking proper care of the child (188). In contrast, Soria states that many parents give up the child for reasons which prove they "had the child's best interests at heart" (28), such as poor financial status or lack of education (28). She firmly believes that biological parents have a right to find out what happened to the child (86). Therefore, adoption officials can no longer use the outdated issue of illegitimacy or the unfair term "inadequate mother" as reasons for keeping closed files.

Adoption officials say that even closed files are accessible for "good cause," and Kupersmith believes that when "needs for

medical or psychiatric histories" arise, either side will be
granted permission to see the files (29). Nevertheless, in 1981,
Newsweek magazine covered a story on James Grant George, an adoptee
suffering from myelocytic leukemia, or cancer of the bone marrow.
He required a bone marrow transplant from a blood relative for
survival. Unfortunately, the courts did not feel the circumstances
justified opening the files to reveal who his natural parents were
(Williams and Foote 60). However, in this case the courts lack good
reasons for why the files should remained closed. No physical
contact must ever be made between the parent and child in giving
the bone marrow, so the adoptive parents need not worry about the
child's reaction to meeting his natural mother. Likewise, the
transplant should not disrupt the biological mother's private life,
because the hospital will not reveal her name or past to anyone.
Thus, parents and courts who still favor closed files in pressing
circumstances such as these are indirectly committing murder.

Although adoptees must sometimes open files for medical
reasons, more commonly they do so to achieve personal peace and
complete their identities. Soria says that some adoptees can never
relax or be happy until primary sources answer their questions,
which may range from medical histories to why the parent gave up
the child (28). In addition, she believes that adoptees searching
for their biological parents are also searching for roots and
identities (26). Several factors constitute one's identity,
including physical features from one's natural parents, the way one
lives, whom she lives with, and her role models (Soria 26).
However, because adoptees do not know their past, many feel that

they either lack or have incomplete identities (Soria 26). For
example, Soria quotes one girl who states, "Sometimes I get the
feeling that my identity was given to me by my adoptive parents,
and that nothing was really mine in the first place" (26). For the
adoptees' curiosity to be satisfied and for their identities to be
complete, they must be able to see the files and find their real
parents. As Mead says, a reunion between biological parents and
their child not only answers the mother's questions about what
actually happened to her child, but also reassures that child and
gives her an identity. She becomes more secure about herself and
her fears of the past cease (188).

Whether or not the adoptees have questions pertaining to their
past, they should have the right to choose if they want to meet
their biological parents. Most adoptees agree with Kupersmith that
minors should not see adoption records because the emotional
pressure and worry may be too much to handle (29). However, she
also agrees with the Adoptees' Liberty Movement Association that
"the truth of his origin is the birthright of every man" (27).
Kupersmith also argues that it is an adoptee's constitutional right
to see the files and learn her heritage, and not allowing her to do
so deprives her of "human dignity" (32). Similarly, Budgen states
that adoptees want to find their natural parents to "find out where
(they) came from, and to have a past" (43). Not allowing them to do
so forces adoptees to accept their adoptive parents when they never
agreed to give up their real parents (42). Mead compares the
adoptee liberation movement to immigrants who become American
citizens; they know their past, but choose to be Americans with the

American past instead. In both cases, the person should have the "freedom to choose" what she wants (100C).

Adoptees should have the right to choose whether or not they want to see their adoption records. Though some adoptees may not question the circumstances of their birth, those who do have a right to find out their past, roots, and medical heritage. Although very few states, including Alabama and Kansas, presently allow open files, other states should soon follow suit. Nobody should be forced to live feeling incomplete and insecure.

WORKS CITED

Budgen, M. "Right to Rediscover Roots." Maclean's, 93 (4 August 1980), 42-43.

Hitchings, B. "Adopted Children and Their Search for Roots." Business Week, (6 February 1978), pp. 85-86.

Kupersmith, N. "Fight to Open Up Adoption Records." Reader's Digest, 112 (June 1978), 27-30+.

Mead, M. "In the Best Interests of the Child." Redbook, 151 (October 1978), 100+.

Soria, Sandra. "Adoption: Searching for Answers About the Past." Teen, 28 (March 1984), 24+.

Williams, D.A., and Donna Foote, "I Do Not Feel He Is My Son." Newsweek, 98 (10 August 1981), 60.

WRITING ASSIGNMENT: "The Adopted Child"

Write a short research paper on (a) the rights of the adoptive parents, or (b) the rights of the adopted child, or (c) the role of the biological mother—with your perspective clearly presented in the thesis statement.

JOURNAL ASSIGNMENT

What do you think a research paper should accomplish? Use any of the following views to trigger your ideas.

1. The research paper should be a writer's interpretation of an issue and not merely an information-gathering exercise.
2. It should allow the student to develop a thesis, collect a bibliography, gather supporting evidence, compare and organize the evidence, and convince the reader.
3. It should help the student learn scholarly methods and good research practices.
4. It should encourage the student to think critically.
5. Obviously it is a trial run and is usually based on secondary research, that is, research based on the original research of others. Professional research requires much more digging, more expertise, and more original findings.
6. It is a good way of gaining in-depth knowledge—in much more detail than is usually the case—of a particular topic.
7. It allows the student to work independently and to understand how professional researchers strive for accuracy and verify their information by citing its sources.

CHECKING OUT

Check your understanding of Chapter 18 by writing answers to the following questions. You may work alone or with a classmate, whichever you prefer.

1. What major issues should you concentrate on when producing a complete, if rough, first draft?

2. Why is it important to see the whole first draft before you begin revising?

3. Explain the difference between revising and editing.

4. What are the three key tasks of a good revision strategy and why should they be done first?

5. How do you decide what information from your sources to cite?

6. What is plagiarism and how do you avoid it?

7. Why are editing tasks done sentence by sentence?

8. What are the differences between citing books and citing magazines or journals?

9. What is a ''Works Cited'' page?

IN SUMMARY

After completing your prewriting tasks, find a high-energy time to write out a rough but complete first draft. When you are satisfied with it, put it aside to incubate. Then, after reading your draft through with a fresh mind, plan a two-stage revision strategy. Initially concentrate on larger issues: improving your ideas and organization, connecting your ideas with sharper transitions, and locating the weakest sections for careful attention. Cut any repetition, but expand on ideas that are not fully explained. Later, in the editing stage, review the editing checklist on pp. 467–471 and check your draft, line by line, for mechanical and grammatical errors.

If you are working on a research paper, you must cite your sources by adding parenthetical references in the text and full references on your Works Cited page. If you are unsure what sources to cite, remember that you need to give a reference note for any information you have quoted, paraphrased, or summarized. Only commonly known facts and information need no reference. In writing a research paper, avoid simply stringing together ideas of other writers; you yourself must actively evaluate your sources and create your own new interpretation.

When all the revisions are completed, make a final neat draft and proofread it slowly, reading it aloud looking at every word to see if it is spelled correctly. Make any needed changes neatly and breathe a sigh of relief: you're finished and deserve a well-earned reward.

ACKNOWLEDGMENTS

Literary

Copyright © 1981 by Houghton Mifflin Company. Reprinted by permission from *The American Heritage Dictionary of the English Language.* (P. 147.)

Copyright © 1987 by Houghton Mifflin Company. Reprinted by permission from *The American Heritage Illustrated Encyclopedic Dictionary.* (Pp. 150–151.)

American Public Health Association, computer printout. Reprinted by permission. (P. 421.)

"What is Intelligence, Anyway?" by Isaac Asimov. Reprinted by permission of the author. (Pp. 112–113.)

"Terminal Education" by Russell Baker in the *New York Times,* November 9, 1980. Copyright © 1980, The New York Times Company. Reprinted by permission. (Pp. 427–429.)

Meenekshi Bose, "Adoption Files and Privacy." Reprinted by permission of the author. (Pp. 481–486.)

"Salvaging a Bad Semester" by Donna Britt in *Campus Voice,* Winter, 1986. Reprinted by permission of Whittle Communications, Knoxville, Tennessee. (Pp. 269–273.)

Buffaloe, Neil D. and Dale V. Ferguson. *Microbiology,* Second Edition. Copyright © 1981 by Houghton Mifflin Company. Used with permission. (Pp. 233, 234–235.)

Cohen, Carl, "The Case for the Use of Animals in Medical Research" *New England Journal of Medicine,* Vol. 315, p. 869, 1986. Reprinted with permission. (Pp. 373–375.)

Dahl, Robert A. *Democracy in the United States: Promise and Performance,* Fourth Edition. Copyright © 1981 by Houghton Mifflin Company. Used with permission. (Pp. 204–205.)

DeFleur, Melvin L., and Everette F. Dennis. *Understanding Mass Communications,* Second Edition. Copyright © 1985. Used with permission. (P. 109.)

Diane Dumanowski, "Goodall Going Public to Better Chimps," in *The Boston Globe,* reprinted courtesy of *The Boston Globe.* (Pp. 369–372).

Dillard, Anne, "How I Wrote the Moth Essay—and Why" Reprinted by permission of Blanche C. Gregory, Inc. (Pp. 386–387, 451–454).

From *Humankind* by Peter Farb. Copyright © 1978 by Peter Farb. Reprinted by permission of Houghton Mifflin Company.

"Thirty-Eight Who Saw Murder Didn't Call the Police" by Martin Gansberg in the *New York Times,* March 17, 1964. Copyright © 1964 by the New York Times Company. Reprinted by permission. (Pp. 325–328.)

"Magic and Paraphysics" by Martin Gardner in *Technology Review,* June 1976. Reprinted with permission from *Technology Review* copyright 1976. (P. 239–241.)

From *Psychology: An Introduction,* by Josh R. Gerow. Copyright © 1986 by Scott, Foresman and Company. (Pp. 59, 61–62, 140, 259.)

Edward T. Hall, *The Silent Language.* Bantam, Doubleday, Dell Publishing Group, Inc. Reprinted with permission. (P. 64.)

Fred R. Harris, *America's Democracy: The Ideal and the Reality.* Copyright © 1986 by Scott, Foresman and Company. (Pp. 190–191.)

From *Thinking Through Writing* by Susan Horton. Reprinted by permission of Johns Hopkins University Press. (P. 25.)

From *The Universe Within: A New Science Explores the Human Mind,* copyright 1982 by Morton Hunt. Reprinted by permission of Simon and Schuster, Inc. (Pp. 72–75.)

From *Biology: Evolution and Adaptation* by Mahlon G. Kelley and John C. McGrath. Reprinted by permission of Mahlon G. Kelley. (P. 231.)

Pp 228–247 from *The Family, Society, and the Individual* 5th ed, by William M. Kephart. Copyright © 1961, 1966 by William M. Kephart. Copyright © 1972, 1977, 1981 by Houghton Mifflin Company. Reprinted by permission of Harper and Row. (Pp. 170–171, 173–181, 194–196.)

Excerpt from *Pet Sematary* by Stephen King. Copyright © 1983 by Stephen King. Reprinted by permission of Doubleday, a division of Bantam, Doubleday, Dell Publishing Group, Inc. (Pp. 107–108.)

"For Mr. Johnson, The Elements of Style" by Sheila Klass in *The New York Times,* September 22, 1984. Copyright 1984 by the New York Times Company. Reprinted by permission. (Pp. 152–155.)

Mark Lanfield, ed. *GED Book of Basic Science,* copyright © 1972, Cambridge Adult Education/Prentice-Hall, Inc. Englewood Cliffs, NJ. (P. 259.)

Reprinted by permission of Faber and Faber Ltd from *The Whitsun Weddings* by Philip Larkin. © Philip Larkin 1964. (P. 119).

"A Passion for Peru" by Mario Vargas Llosa in *The New York Times,* November 20, 1983. Copyright 1983, The New York Times Company. Reprinted by permission. (P. 393).

"Mettle-Testing" by Anne McGrath. Reprinted by permission of *Forbes* magazine, November 4, 1985. © Forbes Inc., 1985. (Pp. 300–302).

Pp 105–107, 131–135 from *The Psychology of Being Human* by Elton McNeil. Reprinted by permission of Harper & Row. (Pp. 182–186, 208–209, 214–216.)

From *Basic Psychology* by Norman L. Munn, L. Dodge Fernald, and Peter S. Fernald, reprinted by permission of Springfield College, Springfield, Massachusetts. (P. 258.)

"One of America's Last Oil Frontiers" by Mark Nelson in *Chevron World,* Winter, 1987. Reprinted by permission of Chevron Corporation. (Pp. 347–350.)

From *The Random House Dictionary of the English Language,* Second Edition. Copyright © 1987 by Random House, Inc. Reprinted by permission of the publisher. (Pp. 147, 151.)

Specified page from the *Readers' Guide to Periodical Literature.* H. W. Wilson and Company. Reprinted by permission of the publisher. (P. 419.)

Excerpt from *How the World Works* by Boyce Rensberger, pages 180–181. Copyright © 1986 by Boyce Rensberger. By permission of William Morrow and Company, Inc. (Pp. 222–223.)

From "Open Admissions and the Inward 'I' " by Peter J. Rondinone in *Change* magazine, volume 9, number 5, May, 1977. Reprinted with permission of the Helen Dwight Reid Educational Foundation. Published by Heldref Publications, 4000 Albemarle Street, N.W., Washington, D.C. 20016. Copyright © 1977. (Pp. 17–23.)

From *1000 Most Important Words* by Norman Schur. Reprinted by permission of Ballantine, Del Rey, Fawcett, a division of Random House, Inc. (P. 143.)

From "Animal Liberation" by Peter Singer in *The New York Review of Books,* April 5, 1973. Reprinted by permission of the author. (Pp. 375–377.)

Maria Sofranski. "Compassion." Reprinted by permission of the author. (P. 156.)

From *Marilyn: Norma Jeane* by Gloria Steinem © 1986 by Henry Holt and Company, Inc. Reprinted by permission. (Pp. 364, 365, 367.) Canadian Rights by permission of Sterling North Agency.

"Polarization, Social Facilitation, and Listening," from the book *Speech* by Robert C. Jeffrey and Owen Peterson. Copyright © 1971, 1975 by Robert C. Jeffrey and Owen Peterson. Reprinted by permission of Harper & Row and Western Speech. (Pp. 94–96.)

Reprinted with permission of Macmillan Publishing Company from *Goddess: The Secret Lives of Marilyn Monroe.* Copyright © 1985 by Anthony Summers. (Pp. 365, 366, 367.)

Scott, Foresman Advanced Dictionary by E. L. Thorndike/Clarence L. Barnhart. Copyright © 1988 by Scott, Foresman and Company. (P. 148.)

"Why Women Are Paid Less Than Men" by Lester C. Thurow, in *The New York Times,* March 8, 1981. Copyright © 1981 by The New York Times Company. Reprinted by permission. (P. 352.)

From *Biology: The World of Life* 4th edition, by Robert A. Wallace Copyright © 1987 by Scott, Foresman and Company. Reprinted by permission (Pp. 63, 105-106, 141-142, 196-198, 199-200, 262.)

Weisberg, Joseph S., *Meteorology: The Earth and Its Weather,* Copyright © 1981 by Houghton Mifflin Company. Used with permission. (Pp. 68, 110, 139.)

From *The Autobiography of Malcolm X* by Malcolm X, with the assistance of Alex Haley. Copyright © 1964 by Alex Haley and Malcolm X. Copyright 1965 by Alex Haley and Betty Shabazz. Reprinted by permission of Random House, Inc. (Pp. 7-8.)

Illustrations and Photography

Unless otherwise acknowledged, all photos are the property of Scott, Foresman and Company.

6: Eve Arnold/Magnum Photos
11: Ethan Hoffman/Archive Pictures Inc.
40: UPI/Bettmann Newsphotos
43: Michael O'Brien/Archive Pictures Inc.
56: ANIMALS ANIMALS/Oxford Scientific Films
67: Photo Fest
88: Christopher Arneseu, Wildlife Photobank
114: Cornell Capa/Magnum Photos
118: Erich Hartmann/Magnum Photos
128T: Ethan Hoffman/Archive Pictures Inc.
128B: ANIMALS ANIMALS/E. R. Degginer
138: Ernst Haas/Magnum Photos
161: Stephen G. Williams/Black Star
171: Sybil Shelton/Peter Arnold, Inc.
192: Rene Burri/Magnum Photos
209: Woolaroc Museum, Bartlesville, Oklahoma
221: Walter Hodges/Aperature Photobank
238: Wide World
251: Dennis Stock/Magnum Photos
264T: C. C. Hodges/Earth Scenes
264B: Anthony Bannister/Earth Scenes
279: Erich Hartmann/Magnum Photos
292: UPI/Bettmann Newsphotos
312: Focus On Sports
321: Elliot Erwitt/Magnum Photos
338: Elliot Erwitt/Magnum Photos
348: Art Wolfe, Wildlife Photobank
366: Elliot Erwitt/Magnum Photos
372: Wardene Weisser/Bruce Coleman Inc.
386: Copyrighted by Jill Krementz
394: Inge Morath/Magnum Photos
413: Guy Le Querrec/Magnum Photos
438: Rene Burri/Magnum Photos
449: Roger Malloch/Magnum Photos
465: Burk Uzzle/Archive Pitures Inc.
477: UPI/Bettmann Newsphotos

APPENDIX: ANALYZING SENTENCE ELEMENTS

You may find it easier to divide sentences into meaningful chunks if you think in terms of the two essential sentence elements, subject and predicate. The subject is the person, place, object, or event which performs or receives the action described by the verb. The predicate includes the verb and any word or words needed to complete that verb.

1. The Iroquois /   have many religious rituals.
      S   P
2. The Germans / bombarded the submarine.
      S   P
3. The publishing company / needed to publish a best seller.
              S   P
4. Students and faculty / must compromise and reach a decision.
              S   P

Once you can identify the subject and predicate, look for modifiers that provide additional information about *time, place, characteristics, conditions,* or *causes.*

1. The Iroquois, who are a very religious people, have many sacred rituals.
                              M
2. Without warning, the Germans bombarded the submarine on all sides.
          M   M
3. Because it was close to bankruptcy, the publishing company needed to
                    M
   publish a best seller.
4. If the school is to survive this crisis, students and faculty must compromise
                    M
   and reach a decision that will satisfy both parties.
                              M

If a writer uses a semicolon (;) or linking words like *and, but, or, nor, for,* and *yet,* to combine two separate ideas, you will need to identify two subjects, two predicates and any accompanying modifiers.

1. Americans / did not want to enter the war, but Pearl Harbor /
      S   P   S
changed their minds.
          P

2. The decision / was not in the interests of workers; it /
      S   P   S
was in the interests of management.
                P

3. The French government / could accept the movement for
         S   P
political autonomy; it /   could spend the next ten years at war.
       S   S   P

Practice

Read the following sentences. Then underline and mark the subject or subjects (S), the complete predicate (P), and any accompanying modifiers (M).

1. Because the land was rich in artifacts, the anthropologist hoped to make a spectacular discovery.
2. Fifty years ago the Chinese rejected all foreign influence, but recently they have begun to seek out foreign investment.
3. Due to a lack of funds, research on the language of chimpanzees has ceased.
4. Central America, an area which for years has been in political turmoil, shows no sign of becoming peaceful in the near future.
5. The right to vote is a privilege that many people in other countries do not have, yet Americans do not always take advantage of that privilege.

INDEX